Lecture Notes in Computer Science 4986

Commenced Publication in 1973
Founding and Former Series Editors:
Gerhard Goos, Juris Hartmanis, and Jan van Leeuwen

Editorial Board

Matthew Robshaw   Olivier Billet (Eds.)

New
Stream Cipher
Designs

The eSTREAM Finalists

 Springer

Volume Editors

Matthew Robshaw
Olivier Billet
Orange Labs
38–40 rue du Général Leclerc, 92794 Issy-les-Moulineaux CEDEX 9, France
E-mail: {matt.robshaw, olivier.billet}@orange-ftgroup.com

Library of Congress Control Number: 2008927529

CR Subject Classification (1998): E.3, F.2.1-2, G.2.1, D.4.6, K.6.5, C.2

LNCS Sublibrary: SL 4 – Security and Cryptology

ISSN	0302-9743
ISBN-10	3-540-68350-X Springer Berlin Heidelberg New York
ISBN-13	978-3-540-68350-6 Springer Berlin Heidelberg New York

Springer is a part of Springer Science+Business Media

springer.com

© Springer-Verlag Berlin Heidelberg 2008
Printed in Germany

Typesetting: Camera-ready by author, data conversion by Scientific Publishing Services, Chennai, India
Printed on acid-free paper   SPIN: 12273416   06/3180   5 4 3 2 1 0

Preface

The question "Stream ciphers: dead or alive?" was posed by Adi Shamir. Intended to provoke debate, the question could not have been better, or more starkly, put. However, it was not Shamir's intention to suggest that stream ciphers themselves were obsolete; rather he was questioning whether stream ciphers of a *dedicated design* were relevant now that the AES is pervasively deployed and can be used as a perfectly acceptable stream cipher.

To explore this question the *eSTREAM Project* was launched in 2004, part of the EU-sponsored ECRYPT Framework VI Network of Excellence. The goal of the project was to encourage academia and industry to consider the "dead stream cipher" and to explore what could be achieved with a dedicated design. Now, after several years of hard work, the project has come to a close and the 16 ciphers in the final phase of eSTREAM are the subject of this book.

The designers of all the finalist ciphers are to be congratulated. Regardless of whether a particular algorithm appears in the final portfolio, in reaching the third phase of eSTREAM all the algorithms constitute a significant milestone in the development of stream ciphers.

However, in addition to thanking all designers, implementers, and cryptanalysts who participated in eSTREAM, this is a fitting place to offer thanks to some specific individuals.

The international and collaborative nature of the project was only possible with a good supporting infrastructure and many thanks are due to Joe Lano who got eSTREAM off to such a good start. His role was passed to Hongjun Wu and then to Orr Dunkelman, who both kept things moving seamlessly. Many experts dedicated their time by serving on the eSTREAM internal evaluation committee. Together they have helped the project navigate its way through some very difficult and sensitive decisions:

Steve Babbage	Vodafone, UK
Christophe De Cannière	K.U.Leuven, Belgium and ENS, France
Anne Canteaut	INRIA, France
Carlos Cid	Royal Holloway, UK
Henri Gilbert	Orange Labs, France
Thomas Johansson	University of Lund, Sweden
Joe Lano	K.U.Leuven, Belgium
Christof Paar	University of Bochum, Germany
Matthew Parker	University of Bergen, Norway
Bart Preneel	K.U.Leuven, Belgium
Vincent Rijmen	K.U.Leuven, Belgium and T.U. Graz, Austria
Hongjun Wu	K.U.Leuven, Belgium

The eSTREAM project depended on events and workshops so that ideas could be presented and debated. These were, without exception, highly successful and for their help as General or Program Chairs, or in chairing discussions, special thanks are extended to Steve Babbage, Christophe De Cannière, Anne Canteaut, Orr Dunkelman, Thomas Johansson, Lars Knudsen, Joe Lano, Kerstin Lemke-Rust, and Bart Preneel. Throughout, the administrational support extended by K.U.Leuven was outstanding and special thanks are due to Péla Noë.

Finally, the most important contributors to eSTREAM have been all the cipher designers, the implementers, and the analysts. We are very grateful for all the work that went into preparing a submission and to all those who crypt-analyzed, implemented, and commented on the candidates. While some will be disappointed that their algorithm was not advanced from the earlier stages of eSTREAM or that it is not included in the final portfolio, we would like to acknowledge all the contributions made to eSTREAM and to thank all submitters for collectively advancing the field of stream ciphers by a very significant margin.

April 2008   M.J.B. Robshaw

This work has been supported by the European Commission through the IST Programme under Contract IST-2002-507932 ECRYPT. The information in this document is provided as is, and no guarantee or warranty is given or implied that the information is fit for any particular purpose. The user thereof uses the information at its sole risk and liability.

Table of Contents

The eSTREAM Project

Matthew Robshaw

Orange Labs
38–40 rue du Général Leclerc
92794 Issy les Moulineaux, Cedex 9, France

1   Introduction

The origins of eSTREAM can be traced back to the 2004 RSA Data Security Conference. There, as part of the *Cryptographer's Panel*, Adi Shamir made some insightful comments on the state of stream ciphers. In particular, with AES [8] deployment being so wide-spread, Shamir wondered whether there remained a need for a stream cipher of dedicated design. As arguments against, one might observe that for most applications, the use of the AES in an appropriate stream cipher mode [9] frequently offers a perfectly adequate solution. Some also doubt our understanding of how best to design a dedicated stream cipher, a view somewhat supported by the lack of surviving stream ciphers in the NESSIE project [1]. However, as counter-arguments Shamir went on to identify two areas where a dedicated stream cipher might conceivably offer some advantage over block ciphers: (1) where exceptionally high throughput is required in software and (2) where exceptionally low resource consumption is required in hardware.

Shamir's comments were widely reported and, to help explore the state of stream ciphers, ECRYPT launched the eSTREAM project [2] later the same year. The primary goal of eSTREAM was to help the community develop its know-how of stream cipher analysis and design. The project began with the first of a series of workshops entitled *The State of the Art of Stream Ciphers*. During an initial study period, which included input from industry, it became clear that one of the best ways to promote research in stream ciphers would be for eSTREAM to make a call for new proposals. These new stream ciphers could be either *synchronous* or *self-synchronising* and they would then be subject to several years of analysis in a process co-ordinated by ECRYPT. The final outcome would be a small portfolio of promising stream cipher designs. To aid designers, and reflecting Shamir's comments, two specific goals or stream cipher *Profiles* were identified:

- Profile 1: Stream ciphers for software applications with high throughput.
- Profile 2: Stream ciphers for hardware applications with highly restricted resources.

Some experts also emphasized the importance of providing an authentication method along with encryption and so two further profiles were proposed:

- Profile 1A: Stream ciphers satisfying Profile 1 with an associated authentication method.

M. Robshaw and O. Billet (Eds.): New Stream Cipher Designs, LNCS 4986, pp. 1–6, 2008.

– Profile 2A: Stream ciphers satisfying Profile 2 with an associated authentication method.

As is common with stream ciphers, designs were required to use an *initialisation vector* as well as a secret key. For Profiles 1A and 2A the authentication method would provide an *authentication tag* and, it was suggested that any authentication mechanism should allow for what is termed *associated data*; that is auxiliary data that might be authenticated but not necessarily encrypted.

To give designers as much design space as possible there were few restrictions. The target security levels were set by the must-satisfy values for the length of the keys. However several designers submitted algorithms that had greater flexibility than this single value implies. The lengths of the initialisation vector (IV) and authentication tag were also given though designs that offered greater flexibility without performance penalty were welcomed.

	key length (bits)	IV length (bits)	tag length (bits)
Profile 1	128	64 and 128	-
Profile 1A	128	64 and 128	32, 64, 96, or 128
Profile 2	80	32 and 64	-
Profile 2A	80	32 and 64	32 or 64

Over the course of eSTREAM the most significant evaluation criteria were

1. security,
2. performance when compared to the AES in an appropriate mode,
3. performance when compared to other submissions,
4. justification and supporting analysis,
5. simplicity and flexibility, and
6. completeness and clarity of submission.

Clearly security takes precedence. To assess software performance a range of environments were considered over the course of eSTREAM. The development of a software testing framework by Christophe De Cannière was a particular success and it has since been used by other researchers outside of eSTREAM. For hardware performance, the results for both FPGA and ASIC implementations were of interest though, as we will see in a later chapter, it is not always easy to isolate the most relevant metric when judging hardware performance. For both profiles, a candidate cipher was compared to its companion submissions and to existing primitives. In particular a submission needed to be demonstrably superior to the AES in at least one significant aspect, where it was assumed that the AES would be used in an appropriate, *e.g.* counter mode.

The original call for proposals generated considerable interest and 34 ciphers were submitted by the deadline of April 29, 2005. Many were presented at the SKEW workshop [3] in the same year. The submissions are listed in Table 1 where they are separated into the different profiles. While many designers naturally strived to design an algorithm with both profiles in mind, it is notable that no finalist algorithm is considered to be simultaneously suitable for both the software and hardware profile.

Table 1. The candidates to the first round of eSTREAM. Ciphers offering an authentication mechanism are indicated with a letter A.

Profile 1		Profile 1 and 2		Profile 2	
ABC		F-FCSR		Achterbahn	
CryptMT/Fubuki		Hermes8		DECIM	
DICING		LEX		Edon-80	
DRAGON		MAG		Grain	
Frogbit	A	NLS	A	MICKEY	
HC-256		Phelix	A	MOSQUITO	
Mir-1		Polar Bear		SFINKS	A
Py		POMARANCH		Trivium	
SOSEMANUK		Rabbit		TSC-3	
		SSS	A	VEST	A
		TRBDK3 YAEA		WG	
		Yamb		ZK-Crypt	
		Salsa20			

2 eSTREAM: Phase 1

The difficulty of stream cipher design was soon made clear and after a year more than half the initial proposals had a demonstrated weakness. However at the start of eSTREAM the administrators had decided on a flexible first round and all designers had the option to tweak their designs at the end of this first phase. This was even allowed if substantial cryptographic flaws had been discovered. This flexibility in the process reflected the concern that the cryptographic community might lose out on a good design idea if a cipher were rejected because of a careless oversight. While this flexibility generated many administrational difficulties, the result was much stronger candidates later in the project.

By considering the public discussions at SASC 2006 [5], postings on the discussion forum [2] and all available analysis, the internal committee decided which algorithms would be advanced to the second phase. The algorithms Frogbit, MAG, Mir-1, SFINKS , SSS, TRBDK3 YAEA, and Yamb were archived. These were ciphers for which no tweaks were proposed despite substantial deficiencies in security or performance, or for which updated code and documentation had not been received.

3 eSTREAM: Phase 2

The algorithms moved forward to the second phase of eSTREAM are listed in Table 2. It is immediately clear that there was only a small reduction in the number of candidates under consideration. This was a side-product of allowing substantial tweaks and the number of algorithms in the second phase was a point of some concern given the limited cryptanalysis time available.

After another opportunity for the submission of optimised code along with many new results on cryptanalysis and implementation, the SASC 2007 workshop [6] provided the starting point for the final round of eSTREAM. Submissions with identified security issues such as (partial) key or state recovery

Table 2. Algorithms that were advanced to the second phase of eSTREAM. Ciphers offering an authentication mechanism are indicated with a letter A. For tweaked ciphers we use the version-numbers provided by the authors or the mark (P2) to indicate the version considered in the second phase. Note that some ciphers took keys of different sizes; the reader is referred to the text.

Profile 1		Profile 2	
ABC v3		Achterbahn-128/80	
CryptMT v3		DECIM v2	
DICING (P2)		Edon-80	
DRAGON		Grain v1	
HC-128 (-256)		F-FCSR-H (-16)	
LEX		Hermes8	
NLS v2	A	LEX	
Phelix	A	MICKEY v2	
Polar Bear v2		MICKEY-128 v2	
Py		MOUSTIQUE	
Rabbit		NLS v2	A
Salsa20		Phelix	A
SOSEMANUK		Polar Bear v2	
		POMARANCH v3	
		Rabbit	
		Salsa20	
		Trivium	
		TSC-4	
		VEST (P2)	A
		WG (P2)	
		Zk-Crypt (P2)	A

attacks could not be advanced. And looking to the final stage of eSTREAM, the clear presentation of a cipher that welcomes independent analysis was a very compelling factor. Our final decision for the end of the second phase was completely independent of the IP status of any cipher and depended on the usual eSTREAM criteria. We were also able to gauge the opinion of the broader community since voting forms were distributed to attendees of SASC 2007. While we were not bound by the vote, our final decisions were roughly in line with attendee preference which provided broad confirmation for the final choices.

4   eSTREAM: Phase 3

The ciphers advanced to the final phase of eSTREAM are listed in Table 3. For Profile 1 the focus was on stream ciphers that offered a high throughput for software applications and all the finalists showed sufficient potential, in one way or another, to be a promising alternative to the AES in counter mode. While the focus remained on versions that used 128-bit keys, companion versions supporting 256-bit keys were also considered. The algorithm NLS v2 was moved forward as encryption-only since the authentication component performed poorly.

For Profile 2 the focus was on hardware applications with restricted resources. The primary criteria at this stage of eSTREAM (after security) was the space an implementation might require. There needed to be good evidence that the algorithm could be implemented in at least one configuration that occupied

Table 3. Algorithms that were advanced to the final phase of eSTREAM. Some of the ciphers had variants that allowed keys of different sizes; however we list the 128- and 80-bit key versions for Profile 1 and 2 respectively.

Profile 1	Profile 2
CryptMT v3	DECIM v2
DRAGON	Edon-80
HC-128	F-FCSR-H
LEX	Grain v1
NLS v2	MICKEY v2
Rabbit	MOUSTIQUE
Salsa20	POMARANCH v3
SOSEMANUK	Trivium

less space than the AES. However it seemed likely that the finalists would also permit a range of implementation trade-offs, and this was something that would be explored further in the third phase. While the focus of eSTREAM remained on 80-bit keys for Profile 2 ciphers, companion versions that supported 128-bit keys were also advanced.

The ciphers in the final phase of eSTREAM are the subject of this book. In the chapters that follow they are fully specified in turn. We will also provide two implementation surveys, one for each profile. It goes without saying that all the designers of all the finalist ciphers are to be congratulated. Regardless of whether a particular algorithm appears in the final portfolio, in reaching the third phase of eSTREAM all the algorithms in this book have made a significant advance in the development of stream ciphers.

The eSTREAM Portfolio

The eSTREAM project formally closes with the publication of the eSTREAM portfolio. For the portfolio the committee will select the most promising software and hardware-oriented candidates from among those described in this book. Of course the decisions reflected in the portfolio are based on a snap-shot of a field that will continue to develop long after eSTREAM itself has ended. After only a few years of analysis all the designs are somewhat immature and future cryptanalysis may well have a significant impact. With this in mind the portfolio will be published on the eSTREAM web-pages [2] and these web-pages will be maintained for the foreseeable future. In this way the eSTREAM portfolio can be updated if circumstances dictate and it will continue to reflect our understanding of what appear to be some very promising new stream cipher designs.

References

1. New European Schemes for Signatures, Integrity, and Encryption (NESSIE), http://www.cosic.esat.kuleuven.be/nessie/
2. ECRYPT. The eSTREAM project, http://www.ecrypt.eu.org/stream/

3. eSTREAM. SKEW - Symmetric Key Encryption Workshop (May 26-27, 2005), http://www.ecrypt.eu.org
4. eSTREAM. SASC - The State of the Art of Stream Ciphers (October 14-15, 2004), http://www.ecrypt.eu.org/stvl/sasc/
5. eSTREAM. SASC 2006 - Stream Ciphers Revisited (February 2-3, 2006), http://www.ecrypt.eu.org/stvl/sasc2006/
6. eSTREAM. SASC 2007 - The State of the Art of Stream Ciphers (January 31 - February 1, 2007), http://sasc.crypto.rub.de
7. eSTREAM. SASC 2008 - The State of the Art of Stream Ciphers (February 13-14, 2008), http://www.ecrypt.eu.org/stvl/sasc2008/
8. National Institute of Standards and Technology. FIPS 197: Advanced Encryption Standard (November 2001), http://csrc.nist.gov
9. National Institute of Standards and Technology. SP800-38A: Recommendation for Block Cipher Modes of Operation (December 2001), http://csrc.nist.gov

CryptMT3 Stream Cipher*

Makoto Matsumoto[1], Mutsuo Saito[2], Takuji Nishimura[3], and Mariko Hagita[4]

[1] Dept. of Math., Hiroshima University,
m-mat@math.sci.hiroshima-u.ac.jp
[2] Dept. of Math., Hiroshima University,
saito@math.sci.hiroshima-u.ac.jp
[3] Dept. of Math. Sci., Yamagata University,
nisimura@sci.kj.yamagata-u.ac.jp
[4] Dept. of Info. Sci., Ochanomizu University,
hagita@is.ocha.ac.jp

Abstract. CryptMT version 3 (CryptMT3) is a stream cipher obtained by combining a large LFSR and a nonlinear filter with memory using integer multiplication. Its period is proved to be no less than $2^{19937} - 1$, and the 8-bit output sequence is at least 1241-dimensionally equidistributed. It is one of the fastest stream ciphers on a CPU with SIMD operations, such as Intel Core 2 Duo.

1 Introduction

In this article, we discuss pseudorandom number generators (PRNGs) for stream ciphers. We assume that the PRNG is implemented in software, and the platform is a 32-bit CPU with enough memory and fast integer multiplication.

Our proposal [5][6] is to combine a huge state linear generator (called the mother generator) and a filter with memory, as shown in Figure 1.

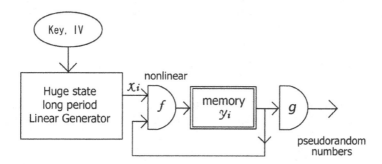

Fig. 1. Combined generator = linear generator + filter with memory

---

* CryptMT is proposed to eSTREAM Project http://www.ecrypt.eu.org/stream/. The reference codes are available there. This work is supported in part by JSPS Grant-In-Aid #16204002, #18654021, #18740044, #19204002 and JSPS Core-to-Core Program No.18005.

M. Robshaw and O. Billet (Eds.): New Stream Cipher Designs, LNCS 4986, pp. 7–19, 2008.

Definition 1. *(Generator with a filter with memory.) Let X be a finite set (typically the set of the word-size integers). The mother generator G generates a sequence $x_0, x_1, x_2, \ldots \in X$. Let Y be a finite set, which is the set of the possible states of the memory in the filter. We take a $y_0 \in Y$. Let $f : Y \times X \to Y$ be the state transition function of the memory of the filter, that is, the content y_i of the memory is changed by the recursion*

$$y_{i+1} := f(y_i, x_i).$$

The output at the i-th step is given by $g(y_i)$, where $g : Y \to O$ is the output function which converts the content of the memory to an output symbol in O.

In a previous manuscript [5], we chose the mother generator to be Mersenne Twister [4], which generates a sequence of 32-bit integers by an $\mathbb{F}_2$-linear recursion. The filter is given by

$$f(y, x) := y \times (x|1) \bmod 2^{32}, \quad g(y) := 8 \text{ MSBs of } y \tag{1}$$

where $(x|1)$ denotes x with LSB set to 1, and 8 MSBs mean the 8 most significant bits of the integer y. Initially, the memory is set to an odd integer y_0. This is CryptMT version 1 (CryptMT1). There has been no attacks reported to this generator (even non-practical attacks). We introduced CryptMT version 2 [7] and version 3 [8], not to improve the security, but to improve the speed of initialization and generation. This manuscript is based on [8]. Theoretical analysis of this type of generators is developed in [9], where the quasigroup property of the filter plays the role of "balanced filter".

2   CryptMT3: A New Variant Based on 128-Bit Operations

Modern CPUs often have single-instruction-multiple-data (SIMD) operations. Typically, a quadruple of 32-bit registers is considered as a single 128-bit register. CryptMT3 proposed here is a modification of the CryptMT version 1, so that it fits to the high-speed SIMD operations.

2.1   Notation

Let us fix the notations for 128-bit integers. A bold italic letter $\mathbf{x}$ denotes a 128-bit integer. It is a concatenation of four 32-bit registers, each of which is denoted by $\mathbf{x}[3], \mathbf{x}[2], \mathbf{x}[1], \mathbf{x}[0]$, respectively, from MSB to LSB.

The notation $\mathbf{x}[3][2]$ denotes the 64-bit integer obtained by concatenating the two 32-bit integers $\mathbf{x}[3]$ and $\mathbf{x}[2]$, in this order. Similarly, $\mathbf{x}[0][3][2][1]$ denotes the 128-bit integer obtained by permuting (actually rotating) the four 32-bit integers in $\mathbf{x}$. Thus, for example, $\mathbf{x} = \mathbf{x}[3][2][1][0]$ holds.

An operation on 128-bit registers that is executed for each 32-bit integer is denoted with the subscript 32. For example,

$$\mathbf{x} +_{32} \mathbf{y} := [(\mathbf{x}[3] + \mathbf{y}[3]), (\mathbf{x}[2] + \mathbf{y}[2]), (\mathbf{x}[1] + \mathbf{y}[1]), (\mathbf{x}[0] + \mathbf{y}[0])],$$

that is, the first 32-bit part is the addition of $\mathbf{x}[3]$ and $\mathbf{y}[3]$ modulo 2^{32}, the second 32-bit is that of $\mathbf{x}[2]$ and $\mathbf{y}[2]$ (without the carry from the second 32-bit part to the first 32-bit part, differently from the addition of 128-bit integers). The outer most [ ] in the right hand side is to emphasize that they are concatenated to give a 128-bit integer.

Similarly, for an integer S,

$$\mathbf{x} >>_{32} S := [(\mathbf{x}[3] >> S), (\mathbf{x}[2] >> S), (\mathbf{x}[1] >> S), (\mathbf{x}[0] >> S)]$$

means the shift right by S bits applied to each of the four 32-bit integers, and

$$\mathbf{x} >>_{64} S := [(\mathbf{x}[3][2] >> S), (\mathbf{x}[1][0] >> S)]$$

means the shifts applied to each of the two 64-bit integers.

In the following, we often use functions such as

$$\mathbf{x} \mapsto \mathbf{x} \oplus (\mathbf{x}[2][1][0][3] >>_{32} S),$$

which we call *perm-shift*. Here $\oplus$ means the bit-wise exclusive-or. The permutation $[2][1][0][3]$ may be an arbitrary permutation, and the shift may be to the left. A function of the form

$$\mathbf{x} \mapsto \mathbf{x}[i_3][i_2][i_1][i_0] \oplus (\mathbf{x} >>_{32} S)$$

is also called a perm-shift, where $i_3 i_2 i_1 i_0$ is a permutation of $3, 2, 1, 0$. A perm-shift is an $\mathbb{F}_2$-linear transformation, and if $S \geq 1$ then it is a bijection. (Since its representation matrix is an invertible triangular matrix times a permutation matrix, under a suitable choice of the basis.)

Let n be a positive integer, and x be a 32-bit integer. The n most significant bits of x are denoted by $\mathrm{MSB}^n(x)$. Similar notation $\mathrm{LSB}^n(x)$ is also used. For a 128-bit integer $\mathbf{x}$, we define

$$\mathrm{MSB}^n_{32}(\mathbf{x}) := [\mathrm{MSB}^n(\mathbf{x}[3]), \mathrm{MSB}^n(\mathbf{x}[2]), \mathrm{MSB}^n(\mathbf{x}[1]), \mathrm{MSB}^n(\mathbf{x}[0])],$$

which is a $(n \times 4)$-bit integer.

A function $f : Y \times X \to Z$ is *bi-bijective* if for any fixed $x \in X$, the mapping $Y \to Z$, $y \mapsto f(y, x)$ is bijective, and for any fixed $y \in Y$, the mapping $X \to Z$, $x \mapsto f(y, x)$ is bijective. It is necessary that the cardinalities coincide: $\#(X) = \#(Y) = \#(Z)$.

2.2 SIMD Fast MT

CryptMT3 adopts the following mother generator, named SIMD-oriented Fast Mersenne Twister (SFMT) [10].

Let N be an integer, and $\mathbf{x}_0, \mathbf{x}_1, \ldots, \mathbf{x}_{N-1}$ be N 128-bit integers given as the initial state. A version of SFMT used here is to generate a sequence of 128-bit integers by the following $\mathbb{F}_2$-linear recursion:

$$\mathbf{x}_{N+j} := (\mathbf{x}_{N+j-1} \ \& \ \text{128-bit MASK}) \oplus \\ (\mathbf{x}_{M+j} >>_{64} S) \oplus (\mathbf{x}_{M+j}[2][0][3][1]) \oplus (\mathbf{x}_j[0][3][2][1]). \tag{2}$$

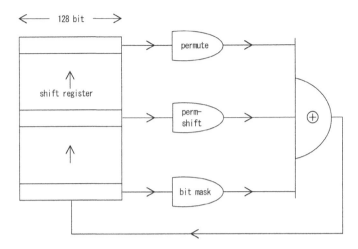

Fig. 2. The mother generator: SIMD Fast Mersenne Twister.
permute: $\mathbf{y} \mapsto \mathbf{y}[0][3][2][1]$.
perm-shift: $\mathbf{y} \mapsto \mathbf{y}[2][0][3][1] \oplus (\mathbf{y} >>_{64} 3)$.
bit-mask: `ffdfafdf f5dabfff ffdbffff ef7bffff`

Here, & denotes the bit-wise-and operation, so the first term is the result of
the bit-mask of $\mathbf{x}_{N+j-1}$ by a constant 128-bit MASK. The second term is the
concatenation of two 64-bit integers $(\mathbf{x}_{M+j}[3][2] >> S)$ and $(\mathbf{x}_{M+j}[1][0] >> S)$,
as explained above. The third term is a permutation of four 32-bit integers in
$\mathbf{x}_{M+j}$, and the last term is a rotation of those in $\mathbf{x}_j$. Thus, the SFMT is based on
the N-th order linear recursion over the 128-dimensional vectors $\mathbb{F}_2{}^{128}$. Figure 2
describes the SFMT.

By a computer search, we found the parameters $N = 156$, $M = 108$, $S = 3$,
and MASK = `ffdfafdf f5dabfff ffdbffff ef7bffff` in the hexa-decimal
notation. Such a mask is necessary to break the symmetry (i.e., without such
asymmetry, if each 128-bit integer $\mathbf{x}_i$ in the initial state array satisfies $\mathbf{x}_i[3] =
\mathbf{x}_i[2] = \mathbf{x}_i[1] = \mathbf{x}_i[0]$, then this equality holds ever after). We selected a mask
with more 1's than 0's, so that we do not lose the information so much.

We proved that, if $\mathbf{x}_0[3] =$ `0x4d734e48`, then the period of the generated
sequence of the SFMT is a multiple of the Mersenne prime $2^{19937} - 1$, and the
output is 155-dimensionally equidistributed, using the method described in [10].

These operations are chosen to fit SIMD instructions in modern CPUs such
as Intel Core 2 Duo. We note that even for CPUs without SIMD, computation
of such a recurring formula is fast since it fits the pipeline processing.

2.3   A New Filter

The previously proposed filter (1) uses integer multiplication in the ring $\mathbb{Z}/2^{32}\mathbb{Z}$.
To avoid the degenerations, we restrict the multiplication to the set of odd
integers in $\mathbb{Z}/2^{32}\mathbb{Z}$, by setting the LSB to be 1 in (1).

In CryptMT3, we use the following binary operation $\tilde{\times}$ on $\mathbb{Z}/2^{32}\mathbb{Z}$ instead of $\times$: for $x, y \in \mathbb{Z}/2^{32}\mathbb{Z}$, we define

$$x \tilde{\times} y := 2xy + x + y \mod 2^{32},$$

which is essentially the multiplication of 33-bit odd integers. Let S be the set of odd integers in $\mathbb{Z}/2^{33}\mathbb{Z}$. By regarding $\mathbb{Z}/2^{32}\mathbb{Z} = \{0, 1, \ldots, 2^{32} - 1\}$, we have a bijection

$$\varphi : \mathbb{Z}/2^{32}\mathbb{Z} \to S, \quad x \mapsto 2x + 1.$$

Then, $\tilde{\times}$ above is defined by

$$x \tilde{\times} y := \varphi^{-1}(\varphi(x) \times \varphi(y)),$$

where $\times$ denotes the multiplication in S. Thus, $\tilde{\times}$ is given by looking at the upper 32 bits of multiplications in S. Consequently, $\tilde{\times}$ is bi-bijective.

Most of modern CPUs have 32-bit integer multiplication but not 64-bit nor 128-bit multiplication. Thus, a simplest parallelization of (1) would be the following: $X = Y = (\mathbb{Z}/2^{32}\mathbb{Z})^4$, and

$$f(\mathbf{y}, \mathbf{x}) := \mathbf{y} \tilde{\times}_{32} \mathbf{x},$$

(that is, $f(\mathbf{y}, \mathbf{x})[i] := \mathbf{y}[i] \tilde{\times} \mathbf{x}[i]$ for $i = 3, 2, 1, 0$), and

$$g(\mathbf{y}) := \mathrm{MSB}^8_{32}(\mathbf{x})$$

is the output of (8×4)-bit integers (for notations, see §2.1).

In CryptMT3, we adopted a modified filter (see Figure 3) as follows. For a given pair of 128-bit integers $\mathbf{x}, \mathbf{y}$, we define

$$f(\mathbf{y}, \mathbf{x}) := (\mathbf{y} \oplus (\mathbf{y}[0][3][2][1] >>_{32} 1)) \tilde{\times}_{32} \mathbf{x}. \tag{3}$$

The operation applied to $\mathbf{y}$ in the right hand side is a perm-shift (see §2.1), hence is bijective. Since $\tilde{\times}$ is bi-bijective, so is f. The purpose to introduce the

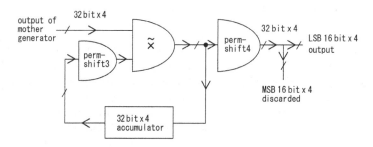

Fig. 3. Filter of CryptMT3.
perm-shift3: $\mathbf{y} \mapsto \mathbf{y} \oplus (\mathbf{y}[0][3][2][1] >>_{32} 1)$.
perm-shift4: $\mathbf{y} \mapsto \mathbf{y} \oplus (\mathbf{y} >>_{32} 16)$.
$\tilde{\times}$: multiplication of 33-bit odd integers.

perm-shift is to mix the information among four 32-bit memories in the filter, and to send the information of the upper bits to the lower bits. This supplements the multiplication, which lacks this direction of transfer of the information.

The output function is

$$g(\mathbf{y}) := \mathrm{LSB}_{32}^{16}(\mathbf{y} \oplus (\mathbf{y} >>_{32} 16)). \tag{4}$$

Thus, the new filter has 128-bit of memory, receives a 128-bit integer, and output a (16×4)-bit integer. The compression ratio of this filter is $(128:64)$, which is smaller than $(32:8)$ in the previously proposed filter. This change of the ratio is for the speed, but might weaken the security. To compensate, the output function takes the exclusive-or of the 16 MSBs and the 16 LSBs of $\mathbf{y}[i]$, $i = 3, 2, 1, 0$.

2.4   Conversion to 8-Bit Integers

Since the outputs of the filter are (16×4)-bit integers and the specification required is 8-bit integer outputs, we need to dissect them into 8-bit integers. Because of the nature of the 128-bit SIMD instructions, the following strategy is adopted for the speed. Let

LOWER16 := $(\texttt{0x0000ffff}, \texttt{0x0000ffff}, \texttt{0x0000ffff}, \texttt{0x0000ffff})$
UPPER16 := $(\texttt{0xffff0000}, \texttt{0xffff0000}, \texttt{0xffff0000}, \texttt{0xffff0000})$

be the 128-bit masks.

Let $\mathbf{y}_0, \mathbf{y}_1, \ldots, \mathbf{y}_{2i}, \mathbf{y}_{2i+1}, \ldots$ be the content of the memory in the filter at every step, i.e., generated by $\mathbf{y}_{i+1} := f(\mathbf{y}_i, \mathbf{x}_i)$ in (3). Then, $\mathbf{y}_{2i}$ and $\mathbf{y}_{2i+1}$ are used to generate the i-th 128-bit integer output $\mathbf{z}_i$, by the formula

$$\mathbf{z}_i := [(\mathbf{y}_{2i} \oplus (\mathbf{y}_{2i} >>_{32} 16))\&\mathrm{LOWER16}] \mid [(\mathbf{y}_{2i+1} \oplus (\mathbf{y}_{2i+1} <<_{32} 16))\&\mathrm{UPPER16}]$$

where $\mid$ denotes the bit-wise-or. Then, $\mathbf{z}_i$ is separated into 16 of 8-bit integers from the lower bits to the upper bits, and used as the 8-bit integer outputs.

2.5   A New Booter for the Initialization

SFMT in §2.2 requires $N = 156$ of 128-bit integers as the initial state. We need to expand the key and IV to an initial state at the initialization, but this is expensive when the message length is much less than $N \times 128$ bits. Our strategy introduced in [7] is to use a smaller PRNG called the booter. Its role is to expand the key and IV to a sequence of 128-bit integers. The output of the booter is passed to the filter discussed above to generate the pseudorandom integer stream, and at the same time, used to fill the state of SFMT. Once the state of SFMT is filled up, then the generation is switched from the booter to SFMT.

The booter we adopted here is described in Figure 4. We choose an integer H later in §2.6 according to the sizes of the Key and IV. The state space of the booter is a shift register consisting of H 128-bit integers. We choose an initial state $\mathbf{x}_0, \mathbf{x}_1, \ldots, \mathbf{x}_{H-1}$ and the initial value $\mathbf{a}_0$ of the accumulator (a 128-bit

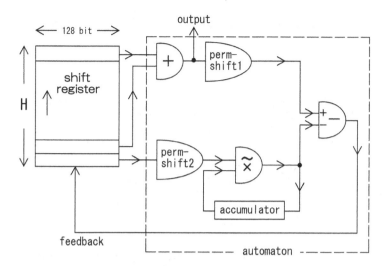

Fig. 4. Booter of CryptMT3.
`perm-shift1`: $\mathbf{x} \mapsto (\mathbf{x}[2][1][0][3]) \oplus (\mathbf{x} >>_{32} 13)$.
`perm-shift2`: $\mathbf{x} \mapsto (\mathbf{x}[1][0][2][3]) \oplus (\mathbf{x} >>_{32} 11)$.
$\tilde{\times}$: multiplication of (a quadruple of) 33-bit odd integers.

memory) as described in the next section. Then, the state transition is given by the recursion

$$\mathbf{a}_j := (\mathbf{a}_{j-1} \ \tilde{\times}_{32} \ \texttt{perm-shift2}(\mathbf{x}_{H+j-1}))$$
$$\mathbf{x}_{H+j} := \texttt{perm-shift1}(\mathbf{x}_j +_{32} \mathbf{x}_{H+j-2}) -_{32} \mathbf{a}_j,$$

where

$$\texttt{perm-shift1}(\mathbf{x}) := (\mathbf{x}[2][1][0][3]) \oplus (\mathbf{x} >>_{32} 13)$$
$$\texttt{perm-shift2}(\mathbf{x}) := (\mathbf{x}[1][0][2][3]) \oplus (\mathbf{x} >>_{32} 11).$$

Similarly to the notation $+_{32}$ (§2.1), $-_{32}$ denotes the subtraction modulo 2^{32} for each of the four 32-bit integers. The output of the j-th step is $\mathbf{x}_j +_{32} \mathbf{x}_{H+j-2}$.

As described in Figure 4, the booter consists of an automaton with three inputs and two outputs of 128-bit integers, with a shift register. In the implementation, the shift register is taken in an array of 128-bit integers with the length $2H + 2 + N$. This redundancy of the length is for idling, as explained below.

2.6 Key and IV Set-Up

We assume that both the IV and the Key are given as arrays of 128-bit integers, of length from 1 to 16 for each. Thus, the Key-size can be flexibly chosen from 128 bits to 2048 bits, as well as the IV-size. We claim the security level that is the same with the minimum of the Key-size and the IV-size.

In the set-up of the IV and the Key, these arrays are concatenated and copied twice to an array, as described in Figure 5. To break the symmetry, we add a

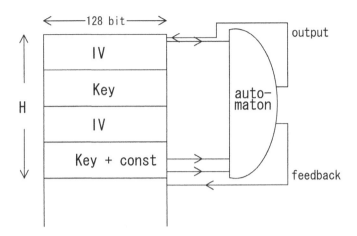

Fig. 5. Key and IV set-up. The IV-array and Key-array are concatenated and copied to an array twice. Then, a constant is added to the bottom of the second copy of the key to break a possible symmetry. The automaton is described in Figure 4.

constant 128-bit integer $(846264, 979323, 265358, 314159)$ (denoting four 32-bit integers in a decimal notation) to the bottom row of the second copy of the key (add means $+_{32}$ modulo 2^{32}). Now, the size H of the shift register in the booter is set, to be:

$$2 \times (\text{IV-size} + \text{Key-size (in bits)})/128,$$

namely, the twice of the number of 128-bit integers contained in the IV and the Key. For example, if the IV-size and the Key-size are both 128 bits, then $H = 2 \times (1 + 1) = 4$. The automaton in the booter described in Figure 4 is equipped on this array, as shown in Figure 5. The accumulator of the booter-automaton is set to

$$(\text{the top row of the key array}) \mid (1, 1, 1, 1),$$

that is, the top row is copied to the accumulator and then the LSB of each of the 32-bit integers in the accumulator is set to 1.

At the first generation, the automaton reads three 128-bit integers from the array, and write the output 128-bit integer at the top of the array. The feedback to the shift register is written into the $(H + 1)$-st entry of the array. For the next generation, we shift the automaton downwards by one, and proceed in the same way.

For idling, we iterate this for $H + 2$ times. Then, the latest modified row in the array is the $(2H + 2)$-nd row, and it is copied to the 128-bit memory in the filter. We discard the top $H + 2$ entries of the array. This completes the Key and IV set-up. Figure 6 shows the state after the set-up.

After the set-up, the booter produces 128-bit integer outputs at most N times. Let L be the number of 8-bit integers in the message. If $L \times 8 \leq N \times 64$, then

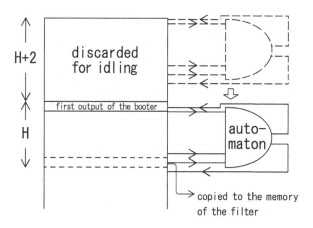

Fig. 6. After the Key and IV set-up

we do not need the mother generator. We generate the necessary number of 128-bit integers by the booter, and pass them to the filter to obtain the required outputs. If $L \times 8 \geq N \times 64$, then, we generate N 128-bit integers by the booter, and pass them to the filter to obtain N 64-bit integers, which are used as the first outputs. At the same time, these N 128-bit integers are recorded in the array, and they are passed to SFMT as the initial state.

To eliminate the possibility of shorter period than $2^{19937} - 1$, we set the 32 MSBs of the first row of the state array of SFMT to the magic number 0x4d734e48 in the hexadecimal representation, as explained in §2.2. This is illustrated in Figure 7. That is, we start the recursion (2) of SFMT with x_0, $x_1, \ldots, x_{N-1}$ being the array of length N indicated in Figure 7, and produces $x_N, x_{N+1}, \ldots$. Since x_N might be easier to guess because of the constant part in the initial state, we skip it and pass the 128-bit integers $x_{N+1}, x_{N+2}, \ldots$ to the filter.

3   Resistance of CryptMT3 to Standard Attacks

The cryptanalysis developed in §4 in [6] for CryptMT is also valid for version 3. We list some properties of the SFMT (§2.2) required in the following cryptanalysis. Algorithms to check these are described in [10].

Proposition 1. *SFMT is an automaton with the state space S being an array of 128-bit integers of the length 156 (hence having $19968 = 128 \times 156$ bits).*

1. *The state-transition function h of SFMT is an $\mathbb{F}_2$-linear bijection, whose characteristic polynomial is factorized as*

$$\chi_h(t) = \chi_{19937}(t) \times \chi_{31}(t),$$

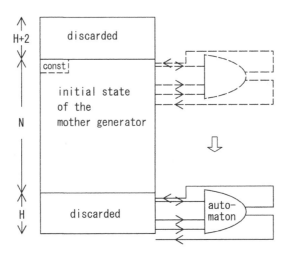

Fig. 7. Initialization of the SFMT mother generator

where $\chi_{19937}(t)$ is a primitive polynomial of degree 19937 and $\chi_{31}(t)$ is a polynomial of degree 31.

2. The state S is uniquely decomposed into a direct sum of h-invariant subspaces of degrees 19937 and 31

$$S = V_{19937} + V_{31},$$

where the characteristic polynomial of h restricted to V_{19937} is $\chi_{19937}(t)$.

3. From any initial state s_0 not contained in V_{31}, the period P of the state transition is a multiple of the 24th Mersenne Prime $2^{19937} - 1$, namely $P = (2^{19937} - 1)q$ holds for some $1 \leq q \leq 2^{31} - 1$ (q may depend on s_0). The period of the output sequence is also P.

In this case, in addition, the output sequence of 128-bit integers of SFMT is at least 155-dimensionally equidistributed with defect q, in the sense of [6, §4.4].

4. Let s_0 be the initial state of the SFMT, i.e., an array of 128-bit integers of length 156. If the 32 MSBs of the first 128-bit integer in s_0 is 0x4d734e48, then $s_0 \notin V_{31}$ (cf. §2.2). In the initialization of SFMT, the corresponding 32 bits in s_0 is set to this (cf. §2.6).

5. $\chi_h(t)$ has 8928 nonzero terms (which is much larger than 135 in the case of MT19937), and $\chi_{19937}(t)$ has 9991 nonzero terms.

3.1   Period

Proposition 2. *Any bit of the 8-bit integer stream generated by CryptMT3 has a period that is a multiple of* $2^{19937} - 1$.

Proof. Put $Q := 2^{19937} - 1$. Assume the converse, so there exists one bit among the 8 bits whose period is not a multiple of Q, which we call a short-period bit.

Let us denote by $h_0, h_1, h_2, \ldots$ the output 8-bit integer sequence of CryptMT3. If we consider CryptMT3 as a 64-bit integer generator (see §2.4), then its outputs $z_0, z_1, z_2, \ldots$ determine $h_0, h_1, h_2, \ldots$ by

$$
\begin{aligned}
z_0 &= (h_{13}, h_{12}, h_9, h_8, h_5, h_4, h_1, h_0) \\
z_1 &= (h_{15}, h_{14}, h_{11}, h_{10}, h_7, h_6, h_3, h_2) \\
z_2 &= (h_{29}, h_{28}, h_{25}, h_{24}, h_{21}, h_{20}, h_{17}, h_{16}) \\
z_3 &= (h_{31}, h_{30}, h_{27}, h_{26}, h_{23}, h_{22}, h_{19}, h_{18})
\end{aligned}
\tag{5}
$$
$$\vdots$$

From this, we see that the bits in $z_0, z_2, z_4, \ldots$ that corresponds to the short-period bit (there are 8 bits for each) has a period not a multiple of Q (since it is obtained by taking every 16-th h's). This implies that each of the corresponding 8 bits in $z_0, z_1, z_2, z_3, \ldots$ have a period not a multiple of Q.

We use Theorem A.1 in [6] (or equivalently Theorem 1 in [9]) to show that any two bits among the 64 bits in z_i have a period that is a multiple of Q (as a 2-bit integer sequence), which proves this proposition. We consider CryptMT3 as a 64-bit integer stream generator. Then it satisfies the conditions in the theorem, with $n = 155$, $Q = 2^{19937} - 1$, $q < 2^{31}$, and $Y = \mathbb{F}_2{}^{128}$. If we define the mapping $g : Y \to B$ in Theorem A.1 by setting $B := \mathbb{F}_2{}^2$ and

$$g : \mathbf{y} \mapsto \text{any fixed two bits in } \mathrm{LSB}^{16}_{32}(\mathbf{y} \oplus (\mathbf{y} >>_{32} 16)),$$

then $r = 1/4$ and the inequality

$$r^{-156} = 2^{312} > q \times \#(Y)^2 \; (< 2^{31} \times 2^{256})$$

implies that any pair of bits in the 64 bits has period of a multiple of Q, by Theorem A.1.

3.2 Time-Memory-Trade-off Attack

A naive time-memory-tradeoff attack consumes the computation time of roughly the square root of the size of the state space, which is $O(\sqrt{2^{19968+128}}) = O(2^{10048})$ for CryptMT3.

3.3 Dimension of Equidistribution

Proposition 1 shows that SFMT satisfies all conditions in §4.2–§4.3 of [6], with period $P = (2^{19937} - 1)q$ $(1 \le q < 2^{31})$ and $n = 155$-dimensional equidistribution with defect $d = q$. Proposition 4.4 in [6] implies that the output 64-bit integer sequence of CryptMT3 is 156-dimensionally equidistributed with defect $q \cdot 2^{128} < 2^{159}$, and hence 1241-dimensionally equidistributed as 8-bit integers. (The argument here appears also in §2.1 of [9].)

3.4 Correlation Attacks and Distinguishing Attacks

By Corollary 4.7 in [6], if we consider a simple distinguishing attack to CryptMT3 of order ≤ 155, then its security level is $2^{19937 \times 2}$, since $P/d = 2^{19937} - 1$.

Because of the 156-dimensional equidistribution property, correlation attacks seem to be non-applicable. See §4.5 of [6] for more detail.

3.5 Algebraic Degree of the Filter

Proposition 4.11 in [6] is about the multiplicative filter, so it is not valid for CryptMT3 as it is. However, since the filter of CryptMT3 introduces more bit-mixing than the original multiplicative filter, we guess that each bit of the output of CryptMT3 would have high algebraic degree, close to the upper bound coming from the number of variables. Algebraic attacks and Berlekamp-Massey attacks would be infeasible, by the same reasons stated in §4.9 and §4.10 of [6].

3.6 Speed Comparison

Comparison of the speed of generation for stream ciphers is a delicate problem: it depends on the platform, compilers, and so on. Here we compare the number of cycles consumed per byte, by CryptMT3, HC256, SOSEMANUK, Salsa20, Dragon (these are the five candidates in eSTREAM software cipher phase 3 permitting 256-bit Key), SNOW2.0 [3] and AES (counter-mode), in three different CPUs: Intel Core 2 Duo, AMD-Athlon X2, and Motorola PowerPC G4, using eSTREAM timing-tool [2]. The data are listed in Table 1. Actually, they are copied from Bernstein's page [1]. The number of cycles in Key set-up and IV set-up are also listed.

CryptMT3 is the fastest in generation in Intel Core 2 Duo CPU, reflecting the efficiency of SIMD operations in this newer CPU. CryptMT3 is slower in Motorola PowerPC. This is because AltiVec (SIMD of PowerPC) lacks 32-bit integer multiplication (so we used non-SIMD multiplication instead). Note that PowerPC is replaced with Intel CPUs in the present version of Mac PCs.

Table 1. Summary from eSTREAM benchmark by Bernstein[1]

Primitive	Core 2 Duo			AMD Athlon 64 X2			Motorola PowerPC G4		
	Stream	Key setup	IV setup	Stream	Key	IV	Stream	Key	IV
CryptMT3	2.95	61.41	514.42	4.73	107.00	505.64	9.23	90.71	732.80
HC-256	3.42	61.31	83805.33	4.26	105.11	88726.20	6.17	87.71	71392.00
SOSEMANUK	3.67	848.51	624.99	4.41	1183.69	474.13	6.17	1797.03	590.47
SNOW-2.0	4.03	90.42	469.02	4.86	110.70	567.00	7.06	107.81	719.38
Salsa20	7.12	19.71	14.62	7.64	61.22	51.09	4.24	69.81	42.12
Dragon	7.61	121.42	1241.67	8.11	120.21	1469.43	8.39	134.60	1567.54
AES-CTR	19.08	625.44	18.90	20.42	905.65	50.00	34.81	305.81	34.11

4   Conclusion

We modified the mother generator, the filter, and the initialization of CryptMT and CryptMT2 so that they fit to the parallelism of modern CPUs, such as single-instruction-multiple-data operations and pipeline processing.

The proposed CryptMT3 is 1.8 times faster than the first version (faster than SNOW2.0 on Core 2 Duo and AMD Athlon platform), while the astronomical period $\geq 2^{19937} - 1$ and the 1241-dimensional equidistribution property (as a 8-bit integer generator) are guaranteed. The Key-size and the IV-size can be flexibly chosen from 128 bits to 2048 bits for each. The size of the state and the length of the period makes time-memory-trade-off attacks infeasible, and the high non-linearity introduced by the integer multiplication would make the algebraic attacks and Berlekamp-Massey attacks impossible. CryptMT has no look-up tables, and hence has resistance to the cache-timing attacks.

A shortcoming of CryptMT3 might be in the size of consumed memory (nearly 2.6KB), but it does not matter in usual computers (of course it does matter in some applications, though).

5   Intellectual Property Status

CryptMT is patent-pending. Its property owners are Hiroshima University and Ochanomizu University. However, the inventors (i.e., the authors of this manuscript) had the following permission from the owners:

– CryptMT is free for non-commercial use.
– If CryptMT survives in the final portfolio of the stream ciphers in eSTREAM competition, then it is free even for commercial use.

The inventors' wish is that this algorithm be freely and widely used in the community, similarly to Mersenne Twister PRNG [4] invented by the first and the third authors.

References

1. Bernstein, D.J. http://cr.yp.to/streamciphers/timings.html
2. eSTREAM – The ECRYPT Stream Cipher Project – Phase 3, http://www.ecrypt.eu.org/stream/index.html
3. Ekdahl, P., Johansson, T.: A New Version of the Stream Cipher SNOW, Selected Areas in Cryptography. In: Nyberg, K., Heys, H.M. (eds.) SAC 2002. LNCS, vol. 2595, pp. 47–61. Springer, Heidelberg (2003)
4. Matsumoto, M., Nishimura, T.: Mersenne Twister: A 623-dimensionally equidistributed uniform pseudo-random number generator. ACM Transactions on Modeling and Computer Simulation 8, 3–30 (1998)
5. Matsumoto, M., Nishimura, T., Saito, M., Hagita, M.: Cryptographic Mersenne Twister and Fubuki stream/block cipher, http://eprint.iacr.org/2005/165, This is an extended version of Mersenne Twister and Fubuki stream/block cipher in, http://www.ecrypt.eu.org/stream/cryptmtfubuki.html
6. Matsumoto, M., Saito, M., Nishimura, T., Hagita, M.: Cryptanalysis of CryptMT: Effect of Huge Prime Period and Multiplicative Filter. In: SASC 2006 Conference Volume (2006), http://www.ecrypt.eu.org/stream/cryptmtfubuki.html
7. Matsumoto, M., Saito, M., Nishimura, T., Hagita, M.: CryptMT Version 2.0: a large state generator with faster initialization. In: SASC 2006 Conference Volume (2006), http://www.ecrypt.eu.org/stream/cryptmtfubuki.html
8. Matsumoto, M., Saito, M., Nishimura, T., Hagita, M.: CryptMT Stream Cipher Version 3. In: SASC 2007 Conference Volume (2007), http://www.ecrypt.eu.org/stream/cryptmtp3.html
9. Matsumoto, M., Saito, M., Nishimura, T., Hagita, M.: A Fast Stream Cipher with Huge State Space and Quasigroup Filter for Software. In: Proceedings of SAC 2007. LNCS, vol. 4876, pp. 245–262 (2007)
10. Saito, M., Matsumoto, M.: SIMD-Oriented Fast Mersenne Twister: a 128-bit Pseudorandom Number Generator. Monte Carlo and Quasi-Monte Carlo Methods 2006, pp. 607–622. Springer, Heidelberg (2008)

The Dragon Stream Cipher: Design, Analysis, and Implementation Issues

Ed Dawson[1], Matt Henricksen[2], and Leonie Simpson[1]

[1] Information Security Research Centre, Queensland University of Technology,
GPO Box 2434, Brisbane Qld 4001, Australia
{e.dawson,lr.simpson}@qut.edu.au
[2] Institute for Infocomm Research,
A*STAR, Singapore
mhenricksen@i2r.a-star.edu.sg

Abstract. Dragon is a word-based stream cipher. It was submitted to the eSTREAM project in 2005 and has advanced to Phase 3 of the software profile. This paper discusses the Dragon cipher from three perspectives: design, security analysis and implementation. The design of the cipher incorporates a single word-based non-linear feedback shift register and a non-linear filter function with memory. This state is initialized with 128- or 256-bit key-IV pairs. Each clock of the stream cipher produces 64 bits of keystream, using simple operations on 32-bit words. This provides the cipher with a high degree of efficiency in a wide variety of environments, making it highly competitive relative to other symmetric ciphers. The components of Dragon were designed to resist all known attacks. Although the design has been open to public scrutiny for several years, the only published attacks to date are distinguishing attacks which require keystream lengths greatly exceeding the stated 2^{64} bit maximum permitted keystream length for a single key-IV pair.

1 Introduction

The word-based stream cipher Dragon was first presented at ICISC in 2004 [5]. It was also submitted as a candidate to the ECRYPT stream cipher project eSTREAM [12] in April 2005 and has advanced to Phase 3 in the software profile. The objective of eSTREAM is to identify stream ciphers that are suitable for widespread adoption for software applications with high throughput requirements. This paper discusses the Dragon cipher from three perspectives: design, security analysis and implementation.

Stream cipher design has traditionally focussed on bit-based linear feedback shift registers (LFSRs), as these are well studied and produce sequences which satisfy common statistical criteria. Non-linearity is introduced into the keystream of these ciphers either by a non-linear combining function or filter function, or by irregular clocking, or both. When implemented in hardware, bit-based stream ciphers can generate high-throughput keystream, but they are notoriously slow in software. LFSR-based ciphers that use sparse feedback functions may be

M. Robshaw and O. Billet (Eds.): New Stream Cipher Designs, LNCS 4986, pp. 20–38, 2008.

vulnerable to attack, but increasing the number of feedback taps decreases the efficiency of the cipher. Finally, the security of some ciphers with linear state update functions is threatened by algebraic attacks [8].

Word-based stream ciphers may exceed the performance of bit-based ciphers in both software and hardware. They produce many times the amount of keystream per iteration than ciphers built using bit-based LFSRs. In software they can outperform even fast block ciphers like the Advanced Encryption Standard [19] by almost an order of magnitude. Although it is easy to assess the speed of these word based stream ciphers, it is difficult to precisely quantify the security they provide.

Dragon was designed with both security and efficiency in mind. It uses a word based non-linear feedback shift register (NLFSR) in conjunction with a non-linear filter to produce keystream as 64-bit words. Dragon has a throughput of gigabits per second and requires little more than four kilobytes of memory, so is suitable for use in many environments including those that are resource-constrained. Not only is Dragon an efficient keystream generator, it is also key agile, making it especially suitable for mobile applications and wireless communications.

Section 2 of this paper presents the specification for Dragon, while Section 3 describes the design decisions behind the algorithm. Sections 4 and 5 provide an analysis of the security related properties of Dragon and discuss the application of current cryptanalytic techniques. Section 6 discusses the performance of Dragon in both software and hardware, and associated implementation issues. Finally, we draw conclusions regarding the security provided by the cipher against all currently known attacks, including both distinguishing and key/state recovery attacks.

2 Dragon Design Specification

Dragon can be used with a 128-bit key and 128-bit IV, or with a 256-bit key and 256-bit IV. We term the former version *Dragon-128*, and the latter *Dragon-256*. Keystream generation for both versions is identical, but key initialization differs slightly.

Both versions of Dragon are constructed using a single 1024-bit word based NLFSR and 64-bit memory M, giving a state size of 1088 bits. The initial state is populated using the key and IV in conjunction with the state's update function F. The update function is also used in keystream generation.

2.1 Dragon's State Update Function (F Function)

Dragon-128 and Dragon-256 both use the same F function. As shown in Figure 1, F is an invertible mapping from 192 to 192 bits: it takes 6×32 bits as input (denoted a, b, c, d, e, f) and produces 6×32 bits as output (denoted a', b', c', d', e', f'). The network consists of three layers: a initial mixing layer, an s-box layer, and a final mixing layer. The mixing layers use addition modulo 2^{32}

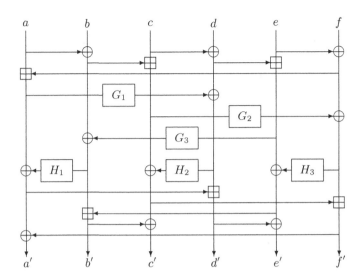

Fig. 1. F function

($\boxplus$) and binary addition ($\oplus$). The s-box layer contains G and H functions which in turn contain multiple 8×32 s-boxes.

G and H functions. The G and H functions are highly non-linear virtual 32×32 s-boxes, constructed from two 8×32-bit s-boxes. These smaller s-boxes, S_1 and S_2, are fully specified in Appendix B. The output of G and H is calculated as described below, where the 32-bit input x is broken into four bytes, $x = x_0 \| x_1 \| x_2 \| x_3$, where $a \| b$ denotes the concatenation of a and b.

$$G_1(x) = S_1(x_0) \oplus S_1(x_1) \oplus S_1(x_2) \oplus S_2(x_3)$$

$$G_2(x) = S_1(x_0) \oplus S_1(x_1) \oplus S_2(x_2) \oplus S_1(x_3)$$

$$G_3(x) = S_1(x_0) \oplus S_2(x_1) \oplus S_1(x_2) \oplus S_1(x_3)$$

$$H_1(x) = S_2(x_0) \oplus S_2(x_1) \oplus S_2(x_2) \oplus S_1(x_3)$$

$$H_2(x) = S_2(x_0) \oplus S_2(x_1) \oplus S_1(x_2) \oplus S_2(x_3)$$

$$H_3(x) = S_2(x_0) \oplus S_1(x_1) \oplus S_2(x_2) \oplus S_2(x_3)$$

2.2   Initialization

For key initialization the NLFSR is partitioned into eight 128-bit words, labelled W_0 to W_7. Dragon-128 and Dragon-256 have simple two-phase initialization strategies that differ only in the first phase.

Phase 1: populating the cipher state. In the first phase, the initial 1024-bit NLFSR state and the 64-bit memory M are populated using a key (K) and (IV).

Dragon-128 takes a 128-bit key and 128-bit IV and populates the NLFSR state such that $(W_0 \parallel ... \parallel W_7) = (K \parallel K' \oplus IV' \parallel IV \parallel K \oplus IV' \parallel K' \parallel K \oplus IV \parallel IV' \parallel K' \oplus IV)$, where x' denotes the swapping of the upper and lower 64-bit halves of x.

Dragon-256 takes a 256-bit key and 128-bit IV and populates the NLFSR state such that $W_0 \parallel ... \parallel W_7 = K \parallel K \oplus IV \parallel \overline{K \oplus IV} \parallel IV$ (256-bit), where where $\overline{x}$ denotes the complement of x.

In both cases, the 64-bit memory M is loaded with the constant value 0x0000447261676F6E , an ASCII representation of 'Dragon'.

Phase 2: mixing the cipher state. In the second phase, the state update function is iterated sixteen times to mix the contents of the NLFSR and the 64-bit memory M, as shown in Figure 2. The update function provides the F function with a 128-bit input formed from the linear combination of three of the NLFSR's words, and a 64-bit input directly from M. Specifically,

$$a \parallel b \parallel c \parallel d = (W_0 \oplus W_6 \oplus W_7)$$
$$e \parallel f = M$$

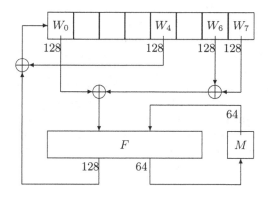

Fig. 2. Dragon: initialisation state update function

After each application of the F function, the NLFSR is updated. The internal state is clocked such that W_7 at time t is discarded and $W_i^{t+1} = W_{i-1}^t, 1 \leq i \leq 7$. The 128-bit NLFSR feedback word which forms the contents of W_0^{t+1} is formed by adding W_4^t to $(a' \parallel b' \parallel c' \parallel d')$ using binary addition. The remaining two 32-bit output words are concatenated and used to update the memory, $M = e' \parallel f'$. The initialization algorithm is given in Table 1.

To protect against attacks that require large amounts of keystream and against unknown future attacks, a maximum of 2^{64} bits of keystream should be produced for any pairing of a specific key and IV.

Table 1. Dragon key initialization algorithm

Input $= \{\ K, IV\ \}$
1. $M = \text{0x0000447261676F6E}$
2. $W_0 \parallel \ldots \parallel W_7 =$
128-bit key and IV
$K \parallel K' \oplus IV' \parallel IV \parallel K \oplus IV' \parallel K' \parallel K \oplus IV \parallel IV' \parallel K' \oplus IV$
256-bit key and IV
$K \parallel K \oplus IV \parallel \overline{K \oplus IV} \parallel IV$
Perform steps 3-8 16 times
3. $a \parallel b \parallel c \parallel d\ = (W_0 \oplus W_6 \oplus W_7)$
4. $e \parallel f\ = M$
5. $\{a', b', c', d', e', f'\} = F(a, b, c, d, e, f)$
6. $t = (a' \parallel b' \parallel c' \parallel d'\ ) \oplus W_4$
7. $W_i = W_{i-1}, 1 \leq i \leq 7$
8. $W_0 = t$
9. $M = e' \parallel f'$
Output $= \{\ W_0 \parallel \ldots \parallel\ W_7\ \}$

2.3   Keystream Generation

During keystream generation, the 1024-bit NLFSR state is divided into thirty-two 32-bit words $B_i, 0 \leq i \leq 31$. Keystream generation also makes use of the F function to update the state.

During each iteration, four 32-bit inputs to F are taken from the NLFSR at stages B_0, B_9, B_{16}, and B_{19}. The remaining two 32-bit inputs are formed from the binary addition of B_{30} and B_{31} with M_L and M_R, respectively, where $M = M_L \parallel M_R$.

The NLFSR is shifted by two stages, and B_0 and B_1 are filled with feedback from the F function output words b' and c' respectively. The 64-bit keystream word z is formed from the concatenation of a' and e'. The remaining two output words of F, d' and f' are discarded. The 64-bit memory M acts as a counter during keystream generation and is incremented at the end of every cycle. Table 2 outlines one iteration of the keystream generation process.

Table 2. Dragon's keystream generation process

Input $= \{\ B_0 \parallel \ldots \parallel\ \ B_{31}, M\ \}$
1. $(M_L \parallel M_R) = M$
2. $a = B_0, b = B_9, c = B_{16}, d = B_{19}, e = B_{30} \oplus M_L, f = B_{31} \oplus M_R$
3. $(a', b', c', d', e', f') = F(a, b, c, d, e, f)$
4. $B_i = B_{i-2}, 2 \leq i \leq 31$
5. $B_0 = b', B_1 = c'$
6. $M = M + 1$
7. $z = a' \parallel e'$
Output $= \{\ z, B_0 \parallel \ldots \parallel\ B_{31}, M\ \}$

3   Design Principles of Dragon

Dragon is designed to provide efficient and secure encryption for confidentiality.

3.1   Design of the F Function

The Dragon F function updates the internal state during both initialization and keystream generation. The reuse of a component for multiple tasks in a cipher both simplifies analysis and increases implementation efficiency by decreasing the size of the code footprint.

The F function consists of three successive layers, as shown in Table 3. Each of the three layers – pre-mixing, s-box, and post-mixing – of the F function is designed to allow parallelisation, giving Dragon its speed. Each of steps 1 through 6 of Table 3 consists of three operations. Each set of three operations can be performed in parallel. Dependencies exist between, but not within, steps.

Table 3. Dragon's three-layered F Function

Input = { a, b, c, d, e, f }			
Pre-mixing Layer:			
1. $b = b \oplus a$;	$d = d \oplus c$;	$f = f \oplus e$;	
2. $c = c \boxplus b$;	$e = e \boxplus d$;	$a = a \boxplus f$;	
S-box Layer:			
3. $d = d \oplus G_1(a)$;	$f = f \oplus G_2(c)$;	$b = b \oplus G_3(e)$;	
4. $a = a \oplus H_1(b)$;	$c = c \oplus H_2(d)$;	$e = e \oplus H_3(f)$;	
Post-mixing Layer:			
5. $d' = d \boxplus a$;	$f' = f \boxplus c$;	$b' = b \boxplus e$;	
6. $c' = c \oplus b$;	$e' = e \oplus d$;	$a' = a \oplus f$;	
Output = { a', b', c', d', e', f' }			

During keystream generation, both keystream and feedback words are dependent on all input words, both at the bit level and word level. A single bit change in any of the six input words results in completely different keystream and feedback words.

Design of the G and H Functions. The G and H functions are non-linear mappings of 32-bit inputs to 32-bit outputs. Storing a 32×32 s-box requires sixteen gigabytes, which is inefficient. Virtual 32-bit s-boxes that retain good properties and use small amounts of memory can be constructed from 8×32 32 s-boxes. Therefore the G and H functions are constructed from two 8×32 s-boxes, S_1 and S_2. These s-boxes were designed to provide a range of important security related properties.

Both s-boxes were designed to have balanced component Boolean functions with:

– best known non-linearity of 116,
– optimum algebraic degree 6 or 7 according to Siegenthaler's tradeoff [22],

- low autocorrelation,
- distinct equivalence classes,
- all XOR pairs satisfying:
  - better than random non-linearity with 102 minimum,
  - almost balanced (the imbalance is not more than 16),
  - distinct equivalence classes,
  - same optimal degree as the components.

A standard notation (n, t, d, x, y) is used to describe boolean function properties; where n is the number of variables, t is the order of resiliency (where $t = 0$ indicates a balanced function), d is the algebraic degree, x is the non-linearity and y is the largest magnitude in the autocorrelation function. All the component functions of S_1 are $(8, 1, 6, 116, y)$ where $32 \leq y \leq 48$ which is considered sufficiently low. S_1 functions achieve the highest non-linearity possible for resilient functions. All the component functions of S_2 are $(8, 0, 7, 116, 24)$. Note that the achieved autocorrelation of 24 is the lowest currently known for balanced functions of this size.

The s-boxes were created using heuristic techniques. Existing methods [18] were adopted to generate individual boolean functions. These were compared to the existing s-box functions and the above-listed requirements were checked for the XOR pairs. Acceptable candidate functions were appended to the s-box. Otherwise, the function was discarded and another function created and tested.

The simple construction of the G and H functions (shown in Section 2.1) allows the non-linearity of the boolean functions producing the output bits of G and H to be calculated exactly from S_1 and S_2. The Dragon virtual s-boxes G and H have higher non-linearity (at 116) than sboxes such as the SBOX/MIXCOL operation from AES [19] and Mugi [23], which use functions with a non-linearity of 112. The Dragon s-boxes also avoid the linear redundancy weakness that is intrinsic to finite field operation based s-boxes [13] which are used in the international standard ciphers AES [19] and Camellia [2].

3.2   Design of the Key Initialisation Process

The initialisation and keystream generation processes of Dragon both use the F function to optimize implementation and ease of analysis. However, the state update functions during the initialization process and during keystream generation have three main differences. These relate to the use of the 64-bit component M, the size of the feedback word and the FPDS selection.

The component M is used as memory during initialisation: the contents are used as input to F and M is updated with outputs from F. During keystream generation, there is no feedback to M from F: M is an independent counter.

During initialization, the 1024-bit NLFSR state is partitioned into words of 128 bits, and during each iteration is updated with a new word formed by four 32-bit outputs of the F function. During keystream generation, the NLFSR is partitioned into words of 32 bits, and updated with two new word formed from two 32-bit outputs of F.

A different FPDS is chosen for the initialization process because of the change in the size of the feedback. The taps from the internal state, $\{0,4,6,7\}$, form a FPDS both in the forward and reverse direction. This is designed to frustrate the cryptanalysis of key setup by guess and determine techniques.

The use of the large word size during the initialization process results in an effective mix of the key and initialization vector in a minimum number of iterations. A smaller number of iterations during initialisation translates directly into high rekeying performance. This makes Dragon very competitive for practical applications that require frequent rekeying, such as mobile and wireless transmissions that usually use the frame number as the IV.

From Section 3.1, F is a reversible mapping, and the design of the initialisation network uses this property of F to produce a bijective process. For any unique (key, IV) pair, the procedure initialises the NLFSR and M to unique values. Dragon-128 and Dragon-256 are designed to have very similar initialization processes so that rekeying speeds are identical. However, another important design consideration is the use of 128-bit and 256-bit (key, IV) pairs. We ensured that no pair of 256-bit (K, IV) initialises Dragon to the same state as any arbitrary 128-bit (K, IV) pair. This avoids the cryptanalyst reducing the search space in a brute force attack from 256-bit to 128-bit.

4   Cipher Analysis

Necessary, but not suficient, conditions for cryptographically useful pseudo-random binary sequences are good statistical properties and a large period. The design of the Dragon cipher aims to produce sequences to meet these conditions.

4.1   Statistical Tests

Statistical tests provided by the CRYPT-X [10] package were performed on keystream produced by the Dragon cipher. The frequency, binary derivative, change point, subblock and runs tests were executed with thirty streams of Dragon output, each eight megabits in length. The sequence and linear complexity tests were executed for the thirty streams with two hundred kilobits each. Dragon passed all pertinent statistical tests.

4.2   Period Length

The expected period for the sequence produced by a 1024-bit NLFSR is 2^{512}, assuming the sequence is pseudo-random [4]. However, when producing sequences for cryptographic use, a lower bound rather than an expected value for the period is critical. During keystream generation, each iteration of Dragon is under the influence of a 64-bit counter, M. Since the counter M has a period of 2^{64}, this provides a lower bound for the period of the keystream sequence produced. Taken together, the NLFSR and the counter M give Dragon an expected period of 2^{576}.

In the specification of Dragon (Section 2.2) the maximum amount of key-stream produced by a unique (key, IV) pair is limited to 2^{64} bits. This does not exceed the lower bound on the period, and is a very small fraction of the expected period, so therefore avoids the possibility of keystream collision attacks. In many applications the actual keystream required is much smaller than this, so this limitation should not restrict the applications for which Dragon may be used.

4.3   Weak Keys

Weak keys are those keys that bypass some operations of the cipher. That is, for weak keys these operations have no effect in the calculation of the feedback or the output keystream. Dragon is designed to avoid weak keys. The use of a NLFSR removes the restriction against the use of the all zero state which must be applied to LFSRs. The state update functions of Dragon are designed to avoid fixed points.

Although it is easy to bypass the pre-mixing phase of the F function when considering a single iteration (for example, by having repetitive inputs such as all zeros or all ones), this is only possible for the first of the 16 iterations of F performed during initialisation. In any case, during initialisation, selected values are limited to the first four inputs of the F function, as the last two inputs take the value of M. The network of G and H functions ensures that the initial states which bypass the pre-mixing phase cannot bypass any later operations in F. We believe that the above design features provide a strong guarantee that there are no weak keys for Dragon.

5   Cryptanalysis of Dragon

Although good statistical properties and a large period are necessary conditions for cryptographically useful pseudo-random binary sequences, they are not suf-ficient. An acceptable cipher should also be resistant to all known attacks. In this section we discuss the resistance provided by Dragon against known attack types. These attacks can be broadly grouped, based on their objective, as either distinguishing attacks or key/state recovery attacks.

5.1   Distinguishing Attacks

The objective of a distinguishing attack is to successfully distinguish between the output sequence of a stream cipher and a truly random binary sequence. To date, the only published attacks on Dragon have been distingushing attacks [11,6], although in both cases the keystream requirements greatly exceed the permitted maximum keystream length of 2^{64} bits. They do not consistute a security breach, but do highlight some interesting observations about the Dragon cipher.

In [11], Englund and Maximov describe a distinguishing attack for Dragon-256 which requires 2^{155} keystream words produced from a single key-initialisation vector pair. There are two variants of the attack, one with a complexity of 2^{187} operations and memory requirements of 2^{32} words, and the other with a complexity of 2^{155} operations and a memory requirement of 2^{96} words. The attacks are based upon empirical measurements of biases in the G and H s-boxes. Even disregarding the excessive keystream requirements, neither of these attacks can be applied to distinguish the keystream of Dragon-128 any faster than exhaustive search. Also, the attacks cannot be extended to permit state or key recovery.

In [6], Cho and Pieprzyk describe a distinguishing attack against Dragon which requires $2^{150.6}$ keystream words and has a memory requirement of 2^{59}. The attack arises as a result of three separate aspects of the Dragon cipher:

1. for particular input and output masks, the 8×32 s-boxes S_1 and S_2 have biases as strong as $2^{-2.09}$ rather than the expected optimal value of 2^{-3}.
2. the outputs of the 8×32 s-boxes are combined linearly to produce the 32×32 s-box, which may have a bias as great as $2^{-8.58}$. This contradicts the statement in our original specification paper that the greatest affine approximation has a bias no greater than $2^{-14.66}$.
3. the choice of FPDS indices permits one 32-bit output word to be associated with another output word fifteen cycles later.

Although this attack is an improvement on the distinguisher presented in [11], the authors of [6] conclude that it is of theoretical interest only, due to the excessive keystream requirements. The requirements of the attack can be further exacerbated by improving any of the three aspects noted above.

5.2 Key/State Recovery Attacks

The objective of many attacks on keystream generators for stream ciphers is to recover either the internal state of the cipher at a specified time, or to recover the secret key. Where the state is recovered, but not the secret key, it is possible to produce the remainder of the keystream for that session, but the attack must be repeated when the cipher is rekeyed. If the secret key can be determined, then the attacker is able to reproduce keystream sequences for all keystreams even after rekeying with a new initialisation vector.

Key/state recovery attacks may be conducted where the attacker has access to a single keystream, or where an attacker has access to multiple keystreams generated from multiple key-initialisation vector pairs which are related in some way. For example, there may be multiple keystreams produced using the same secret key but multiple known initialisation vectors. In this section we consider possible attacks where either multiple keystreams are known, or single keystreams.

Related Key and *IV* Attacks. The use of an initialisation process to combine a secret master key with a known initialisation vector provides a means for reusing keys without generating identical keystreams. The Dragon initialisation and rekeying strategy is simple, and prevents related key and *IV* attacks by mixing each bit of the key and the initialisation vector into all words of the initial state. This comprehensive mixing is accomplished by performing 16 iterations of the initialisation state update function, which makes use of the highly non-linear F function.

Of the six 32-bit inputs to the F function, four words are taken directly from the NLFSR, and the remaining two are taken from a 64-bit memory M. The contents of M are initially known, since they are determined by a published constant. As this value is not variable, it can not be manipulated by an attacker. Two outputs from the F function form the new value for M, making its value hard to determine after the first iteration. All output words of F are affected by the value of M, increasing the difficulty that an attacker faces in controlling inputs to F in subsequent iterations.

In each iteration, four of the six 32-bit outputs of F are used to update 128 bits of the 1024 bit NLFSR. Thus, after eight iterations, all of the initial key material in the internal state has been replaced by highly nonlinear combinations of the key and IV values obtained as outputs from the F function.

Differential attacks. One attack strategy is to observe how differences in inputs affect the output of a cipher. For a fixed key, a number of different initialisation vectors can be chosen so that the initial internal states are similar, and differences in the keystreams can be used to determine information about the key bits. For Dragon, an attacker may observe multiple keystreams, but must allow for the initialisation process when computing differentials.

Even a single iteration of the Dragon F function prevents high probability differentials due to its use of the G and H functions, and high diffusion. A single input difference is propagated to differences in each of the outputs. The F function consists of three layers: pre-mixing, confusion through s-box application, and post-mixing. Using the notation from Section 2.1, only inputs a, b, c and d can be initially and indirectly controlled by an attacker, since e and f come from internal and inaccessible memory.

An attacker may try to use the fact that b and d are mixed with only one other word in the pre-mixing phase, while a and c are mixed with two others. For the input $-(e \oplus f), b, -(b \oplus e \oplus f), -(b \oplus e \oplus f), e, e \oplus f$ the pre-mixing stage produces the output $(0, b \oplus -(e \oplus f), 0, 0, e, e \oplus f)$. For difference input Δb, this produces the difference $(0, \Delta b, 0, 0, 0, 0)$ since e and f are at this stage constants. This bypasses the G row of s-boxes and activates a single s-box in the second row to produce the post-mixing input $(\Delta H_1(\Delta b), \Delta b, 0, 0, 0, 0)$. The post-mixing output is $(\Delta H_1(\Delta b), \Delta b, \Delta b, (\Delta H_1(\Delta b), 0, 0))$. At this stage, all of the feedback words to the NLFSR are non-zero but the difference in the feedback to the NLFSR is still zero. This fact cannot be exploited by the attacker since the input differences to this iteration are not reproducible in later iterations, and thus the difference of the internal memory cannot be maintained.

The initialisation and rekeying procedure for Dragon is designed so that after 12 iterations, an initial difference of a single word in the NLFSR is propagated to all words in the NLFSR (see Table 4). As 16 iterations of the state update function are performed during initialisation, an attacker is unlikely to be able

Table 4. Propagation of non-zero difference in internal state of the rekeying

1	0	ΔA	0	0	0	0	0	0
2	0	0	ΔA	0	0	0	0	0
3	0	0	0	ΔA	0	0	0	0
4	0	0	0	0	ΔA	0	0	0
5	ΔA	0	0	0	0	ΔA	0	0
6	ΔB	ΔA	0	0	0	0	ΔA	0
7	ΔC	ΔB	ΔA	0	0	0	0	ΔA
8	ΔD	ΔC	ΔB	ΔA	0	0	0	0
9	ΔE	ΔD	ΔC	ΔB	ΔA	0	0	0
10	ΔF	ΔE	ΔD	ΔC	ΔB	ΔA	0	0
11	ΔG	ΔF	ΔE	ΔD	ΔC	ΔB	ΔA	0
12	ΔH	ΔG	ΔF	ΔE	ΔD	ΔC	ΔB	ΔA

determine useful relationships between the NLFSR contents after rekeying. The speed of this diffusion is aided by the fact that the first word of the NLFSR is used as input to the F function, and the output of the F function is used to replace that word. Consequently related key attacks on Dragon based on finding differentials do not seem to be any more efficient than a brute force search of the 128 or 256-bit key.

Time-Memory Tradeoff Attacks. Time-Memory tradeoff attacks [3] rely on pre-computation to reduce the effort required for a key recovery attack on a keystream. The attack comprises two steps. The first, the preprocessing step, sees the attacker calculating a table of keys or internal states and corresponding keystream prefixes. The table is ordered upon the prefix. The second step involves observing keystreams and attempting to match each against a prefix in the table. If the match is successful, then with some likelihood the internal state is known by reading the opposing entry in the table. When the internal state is recovered, some further effort may be applied to recover the key. The difficulty of performing key recovery from a known state depends on the initialisation process.

The parameters in an attack are time (T), memory (M), and amount of data (D). Generally, $T \times M^2 \times D^2 = S^2$ where S is the state space of the cipher, and $D^2 \leq T$ [3]. The pre-computation time P is equal to $S \div D$.

Dragon has an internal state space of 1088 bits (consisting of the 1024 bit NLFSR and the 64-bit M). For Dragon-256, the time-memory tradeoff attack to recover the internal state is infeasible: for a brute-force equivalent attack, with $T = 2^{256}$, the limitation on maximum keystream length of 2^{64} bits results in a lower bound on required memory for the attack of 2^{896} bits. A TMD attack to recover the internal state of Dragon-128 is similarly infeasible.

Guess and Determine Attacks. The indices $\{0, 9, 16, 19, 30, 31\}$ of the NLFSR stages used as inputs to Dragon's state update function form a full positive difference set. This design decision is a deliberate attempt to prevent guess and determine attacks [14] on the cipher.

During keystream generation, guessing six inputs (192 bits) to F in an iteration allows an attacker to calculate the feedback words b' and c' and the keystream words a' and e'. This knowlege can be used to discard many incorrect guesses. At this point the attacker has knowledge of the contents of the NLFSR stages at indices $\{0, 1, 10, 17, 20\}$ and some information about the value of B_{31} and M. However, the FPDS selection of the internal state means that to obtain the next pair of keystream words, guessing a further five inputs (160 bits) is necessary. The attacker can attempt to jump ahead to a future keystream word pair, but again the FPDS means that the attacker needs to guess five inputs. This rapid increase in the number of possible guess pathways makes the attack infeasible. In addition, the interplay of B_{30}, B_{31} and M means there will be more than one set of possible values for these three elements for a unique pair of e and f. This further complicates any guess and determine attack.

An attacker is also unable to reduce the complexity of a guess and determine attack by guessing bytes rather than words of the NLFSR state contents. The use of large s-boxes (G and H functions are effectively 32×32 s-boxes) means that guessing three of the four input bytes is insufficient to deduce any byte of the s-box output.

To calculate keystream words from two iterations of Dragon, the attacker is required to guess more than 256 bits of the internal state. This is worse than exhaustive key search on Dragon-256, and makes guess and determine attacks on Dragon infeasible. Similarly, for Dragon-128, the attack is infeasible, as the approach required guessing the contents of three NLFSR words (192 bits), which is worse than exhaustive key search. The feedback and keystream words rely on all six inputs, consequently there is no way for the attacker to use even a single keystream word to verify guesses using fewer bits than this.

Algebraic Attacks. Successful algebraic attacks on keystream generators [8] have so far been restricted mainly to LFSR based generators. The general attack model consists of the internal state S, the linear update function L and the output function f. Let S_0 denote the internal state at time $t = 0$, and $L^t(S_0)$ denote the internal state at time t. The attacker constructs a system of equations relating the initial internal state bits with the observed keystream bits, where $z_t = f(L^t(S_0))$ at time t. The attacker can set up a large number of equations in terms of the initial state values by merely collecting keystream bits, since the internal state at time t can easily be derived from the initial internal state due to the linear nature of LFSRs.

Dragon's nonlinear state update function prevents the application of algebraic attacks. Let N denote the non-linear update function. Then the kestream output at time t is $z_t = f(N^t(S_0))$. When constructing the system of equations relating the initial internal state to the keystream ouput for Dragon, the degree of the equations grows exponentially as t increases. This is easy to see as any output of G or H is a degree 7 function of the inputs since S_2 has algebraic order 7. If we approximate $\boxplus$ with $\oplus$, we can then write equations of degree $7^2 = 49$ that maps the 192 input bits to the first 64 output keystream bits. However, the feedback is used immediately in the production of the next 64 bits of keystream, and results in equations of degree $7^4 = 2,401$. Note that at this point, the inputs consist of only 352 bits, and therefore the equations would be limited to degree 352. The degree of the equations would grow to the full 1024 bits of the internal state after 8 iterations of the F function, or 512 bits of keystream have been produced.

The use of a nonlinear update function provides the resistance to algebraic attacks. Note that the nonlinear state update function N has a poor linear approximation of $2^{-73.3}$. Using the technique published in [9] to describe the 8×32 s-boxes of Dragon using quadratic equations results in 565 quadratic equations in 256 monomials for each s-box (identical to the analysis of CAST [1]). Again, let us approximate $\boxplus$ with $\oplus$, then after 8 iterations of F, the system of equations has degree 1,024 as well. This is to say, even if there existed some annihilators [17] that reduce Dragon's Boolean functions right down to quadratic, the degree of the overall equations would still grow to unmanageable sizes.

It is clear that the system of equations relating the internal state of Dragon and the keystream bits will be very difficult to solve, if it is solvable at all. Furthermore, it will require far more effort than exhaustive key search since solving techniques all have complexities exponential in the degree of the equations. It is interesting to note that in the above analysis modular addition was replaced by XOR, and thus resulting in a weaker version of Dragon. With the modular addition in place, it will be even more difficult for algebraic attacks to succeed against Dragon (see similar example of the effect of modular addition in CAST [1]).

6   Implementation and Performance

Dragon is designed to be efficient in both software and hardware, in terms of throughput and a small implementation footprint. Its 32-bit word size is chosen to match that of the ubiquitous Intel Pentium family, since this leads to the best software efficiency on that platform. Note that the results presented in this Section apply to both Dragon-128 and Dragon-256.

6.1   Software

Dragon is very efficient in software. Most operations are expected to perform with latencies of $\frac{1}{2}$ or 1 cycles on modern processors, such as the Intel Pentium family. There is some pressure generated by the need to trade security and efficiency. For example, Dragon relies heavily upon consecutive and serial invocations of s-boxes, which by depending upon a single type of operation do not fully utilize the superscalar nature of processors.

On an Intel Pentium 4, an optimized implementation of Dragon produces one byte of keystream every 6.74 clock cycles, and 1,395 cycles per rekeying operation. On a 3.2GHz Pentium 4, the throughput of Dragon is 3.8Gbps. This is competitive with many of its peers, including SNOW 2 (5.5 cycles/byte), Turing (6.1 cycles/byte) and RC4 (7.1 cycles/byte). When used with the eSTREAM API, the performance figures of Dragon are more conservative but remain competitive.

Storage requirements include 2,048 bytes to store Dragon's two 8×32 s-boxes, 1,024 bits (128 bytes) for the internal state, and a further 8 bytes for the 64-bit counter. Including temporary variables and an object code size of 2,810 bytes, Dragon has memory requirements totalling 4,994 bytes. This is suitable for even very constrained environments.

6.2   Hardware

The design of Dragon allows high degree of parallelisation in hardware. The operations on the six inputs of the F function can be divided into three groups, each operating on two inputs. The pre-mixing and the post-mixing are implemented using 32-bit modular adders. The G and H functions are implemented using look-up tables and XOR operations. The hardware complexity is about 6,524 gates and 196,672 bits of memory. On Samsung 0.13um ASIC running at 2.6GHz, the minimum delay is 2.774ns with a throughput of 23Gbps.

The speed in hardware can be improved by using m-parallel-structure proposed in [16]. This hardware implementation strategy applies to all shift registers, and achieves an m times increase in efficiency with m times increase in hardware complexity. On Altera FPGA/CPLD running at 16.67MHz, an implementation of Dragon achieves a throughput of 1.06Gbps with 16 times hardware complexity.

7   Conclusion

Dragon is a word based stream cipher constructed using a word based non-linear feedback shift register. It was first presented at ICISC in 2004 [5] and later submitted as a candidate to eSTREAM, where it is currently one of the Phase 3 focus ciphers. In this paper the Dragon cipher is discussed from three perspectives: design, security analysis and implementation.

Dragon may be used with two possible key and initialisation vector sizes: the key and initialisation vector are 128 bits for Dragon-128 and 256 bits for Dragon-256. The cipher was designed with both security and implementation efficiency in mind. To date, the only published attacks on Dragon are distinguishing attacks which require amounts of keystream greatly exceeding the specified maximum keystream length. Thus the cipher may be considered secure for all practical applications.

References

1. Adams, C.: Designing Against the 'Overdefined System of Equations' Attack (May 2004), http://eprint.iacr.org/2004/110/
2. Aoki, K., Ichikawa, T., Kanda, M., Matsui, M., Moriai, S., Nakajima, J., Tokita, T.: Camellia: A 128-Bit Block Cipher Suitable for Multiple Platforms - Design and Analysis. In: Stinson, D.R., Tavares, S. (eds.) SAC 2000. LNCS, vol. 2012, pp. 39–56. Springer, Heidelberg (2001)
3. Biryukov, A., Shamir, A.: Cryptanalytic Time/Memory/Data Tradeoffs for Stream Ciphers. In: Okamoto, T. (ed.) ASIACRYPT 2000. LNCS, vol. 1976, pp. 1–13. Springer, Heidelberg (2000)

4. Chambers, W.: On Random Mappings and Random Permutations. In: Preneel, B. (ed.) FSE 1994. LNCS, vol. 1008, pp. 22–28. Springer, Heidelberg (1995)
5. Chen, K., Millan, W., Fuller, J., Simpson, L., Dawson, E., Lee, H., Moon, S.: Dragon: A Fast Word Based Stream Cipher. In: Park, C.-s., Chee, S. (eds.) ICISC 2004. LNCS, vol. 3506, pp. 33–50. Springer, Heidelberg (2005), http://www.ecrypt.eu.org/stream/dragonp3.html
6. Cho, J., Pieprzyk, J.: An improved distinguisher for Dragon (Date accessed: September 28, 2007), http://eprint.iacr.org/2007/108.pdf
7. Coppersmith, D., Halevi, S., Jutla, C.: Cryptanalysis of Stream Ciphers with Linear Masking. In: Yung, M. (ed.) CRYPTO 2002. LNCS, vol. 2442, pp. 515–532. Springer, Heidelberg (2002)
8. Courtois, N.: Higher Order Correlation Attacks, XL Algorithm and Cryptanalysis of Toyocrypt. In: Lee, P., Lim, C. (eds.) ICISC 2002. LNCS, vol. 2587, pp. 182–199. Springer, Heidelberg (2003)
9. Courtois, N., Pieprzyk, J.: Cryptanalysis of Block Ciphers with Overdefined Systems of Equations. In: Zheng, Y. (ed.) ASIACRYPT 2002. LNCS, vol. 2501, pp. 267–287. Springer, Heidelberg (2002)
10. Dawson, E., Clark, A., Gustafson, G., May, L.: CRYPT-X 1998 User Manual (1999)
11. Englund, H., Maximov, A.: Attack the Dragon. ECRYPT eSTREAM submission (submitted, September 2005), http://www.ecrypt.eu.org/stream/papersdir/062.pdf
12. eSTREAM, the ECRYPT Stream Cipher Project, http://www.ecrypt.eu.org/stream
13. Fuller, J., Millan, W.: Linear Redundancy in S-Boxes. In: Johansson, T. (ed.) FSE 2003. LNCS, vol. 2887, pp. 74–86. Springer, Heidelberg (2003)
14. Hawkes, P., Rose, G.: Guess-and-Determine Attacks on SNOW. In: Nyberg, K., Heys, H. (eds.) SAC 2002. LNCS, vol. 2595, pp. 37–46. Springer, Heidelberg(2003)
15. Kam, J., Davida, G.: Structured Design of Substitution-Permutation Encryption Networks. IEEE Transactions on Computers 28(10), 747–753 (1979)
16. Lee, H., Moon, S.: Parallel Stream Cipher for Secure High-Speed Communications. Signal Processing 82(2), 137–143 (2002)
17. Meier, W., Pasalic, E., Carlet, C.: Algebraic Attacks and Decomposition of Boolean Functions. In: Cachin, C., Camenisch, J.L. (eds.) EUROCRYPT 2004. LNCS, vol. 3027, pp. 474–491. Springer, Heidelberg (2004)
18. Millan, W., Fuller, J., Dawson, E.: New Concepts in Evolutionary Search for Boolean Functions in Cryptology. In: The 2003 Congress on Evolutionary Computation, 2003. CEC 2003, vol. 3, pp. 2157–2164. IEEE, Los Alamitos (2003)
19. National Institute of Standards and Technology. Federal Information Processing Standards Publication 197 (2001)
20. Rose, G., Hawkes, P.: Turing: A Fast Stream Cipher. In: Johansson, T. (ed.) FSE 2003. LNCS, vol. 2887, pp. 290–306. Springer, Heidelberg (2003)
21. Seberry, J., Zhang, X., Zheng, Y.: Nonlinearly Balanced Boolean Functions and Their Propagation Characteristics. In: Stinson, D.R. (ed.) CRYPTO 1993. LNCS, vol. 773, pp. 49–60. Springer, Heidelberg (1994)
22. Siegenthaler, T.: Correlation Immunity of Nonlinear Combining Functions for Cryptographic Applications. IEEE Transactions on Information Theory 30(5), 776–780 (1984)
23. Watanabe, D., Furuya, S., Yoshida, H., Takaragi, K., Preneel, B.: A New Keystream Generator MUGI. In: Daemen, J., Rijmen, V. (eds.) FSE 2002. LNCS, vol. 2365, pp. 179–194. Springer, Heidelberg (2002)

A   Test Vectors

128-BIT KEY AND IV

KEY:
00001111 22223333 44445555 66667777
IV:
00001111 22223333 44445555 66667777
KEYSTREAM:
99B3AA14 B63BD02F E14358A4 54950425 F4B0D3FD 8BA69178 E0392938 A718C165
2E3BEB1E 11613D58 9EABB9F5 43A1C51C 73C1F227 9D1CAEA8 5C55F539 BAFD3C59
ECAC88BD 17EB1C9D A28DD63E 9093C913 3032D918 3A9B33BC 2933A79D 75669827
20EF3004 C53B0253 7A1BE796 29F8D9A3 8DC1FD31 ED9D1100 B07DFFB1 AC75EB31

KEY:
00112233 44556677 8899AABB CCDDEEFF
IV:
00112233 44556677 8899AABB CCDDEEFF
KEYSTREAM:
98821506 0E87E695 EB7AEF36 313FF910 E6C7312F 30357424 4922043D 98146EE2
202D4D49 6C602ECC 937DD3F4 E39BE26C 849DB415 F04C540E 88588C7A A3C65A31
E2156229 1E86028B 3F5A21B9 4A94C135 B3A01527 747E6521 FFEE14F0 FA1FCC73
74C8B204 4009F57D 1D63007E F1D8D221 E429EBA8 60F56098 45891D74 716694B2

256-BIT KEY AND IV

KEY:
00001111 22223333 44445555 66667777 88889999 AAAABBBB CCCCDDDD EEEEFFFF
IV:
00001111 22223333 44445555 66667777 88889999 AAAABBBB CCCCDDDD EEEEFFFF
KEYSTREAM:
BC020767 DC48DAE3 14778D8C 927E8B32 E086C6CD E593C008 600C9D47 A488F622
3A2B94D6 B853D644 27E93362 ABB8BA21 751CAAF7 BD316595 2A37FC1E A3F12FE2
5C133BA7 4C15CE4B 3542FDF8 93DAA751 F5710256 49795D54 31914EBA 0DE2C2A7
8013D29B 56D4A028 3EB6F312 7644ECFE 38B9CA11 1924FBC9 4A0A30F2 AFFF5FE0

KEY:
00112233 44556677 8899AABB CCDDEEFF 00112233 44556677 8899AABB CCDDEEFF
IV:
00112233 44556677 8899AABB CCDDEEFF 00112233 44556677 8899AABB CCDDEEFF
KEYSTREAM:
8D3AB9BA 01DAA3EB 5CBD0F6D E3ECFCAB 619AF808 CF9C4A42 E2877766 6D2D7037
EE6F94AC 29D1EEE5 340DB047 8E91A679 480D8D88 2367CE2A 31C96AD4 49E70756
815EBEB2 290DBA7A 3CCB76A2 257BD122 2B0B7AED 917FAFFF 6B58B2B2 B05F24F6
E271A016 9E897BEF F5C22451 DA6F9E40 52B78BE5 6C97C1A5 C6F8E791 0F7B9C98

B   Dragon's S-Boxes

sbox1[256]={
0x393BCE6B,0x232BA00D,0x84E18ADA,0x84557BA7,0x56828948,0x166908F3,
0x414A3437,0x7BB44897,0x2315BE89,0x7A01F224,0x7056AA5D,0x121A3917,
0xE3F47FA2,0x1F99D0AD,0x9BAD518B,0x99B9E75F,0x8829A7ED,0x2C511CA9,
0x1D89BF75,0xF2F8CDD0,0x2DA2C498,0x48314C42,0x922D9AF6,0xAA6CE00C,
0xAC66E078,0x7D4CB0C0,0x5500C6E8,0x23E4576B,0x6B365D40,0xEE171139,
0x336BE860,0x5DBEEEFE,0x0E945776,0xD4D52CC4,0x0E9BB490,0x376EB6FD,
0x6D891655,0xD4078FEE,0xE07401E7,0xA1E4350C,0xABC78246,0x73409C02,
0x24704A1F,0x478ABB2C,0xA0849634,0x9E9E5FEB,0x77363D8D,0xD350BC21,
0x876E1BB5,0xC8F55C9D,0xD112F39F,0xDF1A0245,0x9711B3F0,0xA3534F64,
0x42FB629E,0x15EAD26A,0xD1CFA296,0x7B445FEE,0x88C28D4A,0xCA6A8992,
0xB40726AB,0x508C65BC,0xBE87B3B9,0x4A894942,0x9AEECC5B,0x6CA6F10B,
0x303F8934,0xD7A8693A,0x7C8A16E4,0xB8CF0AC9,0xAD14B784,0x819FF9F0,
0xF20DCDFA,0xB7CB7159,0x58F3199F,0x9855E43B,0x1DF6C2D6,0x46114185,
0xE46F5D0F,0xAAC70B5B,0x48590537,0x0FD77B28,0x67D16C70,0x75AE53F4,
0xF7BFECA1,0x6017B2D2,0xD8A0FA28,0xB8FC2E0D,0x80168E15,0x0D7DEC9D,
0xC5581F55,0xBE4A2783,0xD27012FE,0x53EA81CA,0xEBAA07D2,0x54F5D41D,
0xABB26FA6,0x41B9EAD9,0xA48174C7,0x1F3026F0,0xEFBADD8E,0x387E9014,
0x1505AB79,0xEADF0DF7,0x67755401,0xDA2EF962,0x41670B0E,0x0E8642F2,
0xCE486070,0xA47D3312,0x4D7343A7,0xECDA58D0,0x1F79D536,0xD362576B,
0x9D3A6023,0xC795A610,0xAE4DF639,0x60C0B14E,0xC6DD8E02,0xBDE93F4E,
0xB7C3B0FF,0x2BE6BCAD,0xE4B3FDFD,0x79897325,0x3038798B,0x08AE6353,
0x7D1D20EB,0x3B208D21,0xD0D6D104,0xC5244327,0x9893F59F,0xE976832A,
0xB1EB320B,0xA409D915,0x7EC6B543,0x66E54F98,0x5FF805DC,0x599B223F,
0xAD78B682,0x2CF5C6E8,0x4FC71D63,0x08F8FED1,0x81C3C49A,0xE4D0A778,
0xB5D369CC,0x2DA336BE,0x76BC87CB,0x957A1878,0xFA136FBA,0x8F3C0E7B,
0x7A1FF157,0x598324AE,0xFFBAAC22,0xD67DE9E6,0x3EB52897,0x4E07E855,
0x87CE73F5,0x8D046706,0xD42D18F2,0xE71B1727,0x38473B38,0xB37B24D5,
0x381C6AE1,0xE77D6589,0x6018CBFF,0x93CF3752,0x9B6EA235,0x504A50E8,
0x464EA180,0x86AFBE5E,0xCC2D6AB0,0xAB91707B,0x1DB4D579,0xF9FAFD24,
0x2B28CC54,0xCDCFD6B3,0x68A30978,0x43A6DFD7,0xC81DD98E,0xA6C2FD31,
0x0FD07543,0xAFB400CC,0x5AF11A03,0x2647A909,0x24791387,0x5CFB4802,
0x88CE4D29,0x353F5F5E,0x7038F851,0xF1F1C0AF,0x78EC6335,0xF2201AD1,
0xDF403561,0x4462DFC7,0xE22C5044,0x9C829EA3,0x43FD6EAE,0x7A42B3A7,
0x5BFAAAEC,0x3E046853,0x5789D266,0xE1219370,0xB2C420F8,0x3218BD4E,
0x84590D94,0xD51D3A8C,0xA3AB3D24,0x2A339E3D,0xFEE67A23,0xAF844391,
0x17465609,0xA99AD0A1,0x05CA597B,0x6024A656,0x0BF05203,0x8F559DDC,
0x894A1911,0x909F21B4,0x6A7B63CE,0xE28DD7E7,0x4178AA3D,0x4346A7AA,
0xA1845E4C,0x166735F4,0x639CA159,0x58940419,0x4E4F177A,0xD17959B2,
0x12AA6FFD,0x1D39A8BE,0x7667F5AC,0xED0CE165,0xF1658FD8,0x28B04E02,
0x1FA480CF,0xD3FB6FEF,0xED336CCB,0x9EE3CA39,0x9F224202,0x2D12D6E8,
0xFAAC50CE,0xFA1E98AE,0x61498532,0x03678CC0,0x9E85EFD7,0x3069CE1A,
0xF115D008,0x4553AA9F,0x3194BE09,0xB4A9367D,0x0A9DFEEC,0x7CA002D6,
0x8E53A875,0x965E8183,0x14D79DAC,0x0192B555};

sbox2[256]={
0xA94BC384,0xF7A81CAE,0xAB84ECD4,0x00DEF340,0x8E2329B8,0x23AF3A22,
0x23C241FA,0xAED8729E,0x2E59357F,0xC3ED78AB,0x687724BB,0x7663886F,

```
0x1669AA35,0x5966EAC1,0xD574C543,0xDBC3F2FF,0x4DD44303,0xCD4F8D01,
0x0CBF1D6F,0xA8169D59,0x87841E00,0x3C515AD4,0x708784D6,0x13EB675F,
0x57592B96,0x07836744,0x3E721D90,0x26DAA84F,0x253A4E4D,0xE4FA37D5,
0x9C0830E4,0xD7F20466,0xD41745BD,0x1275129B,0x33D0F724,0xE234C68A,
0x4CA1F260,0x2BB0B2B6,0xBD543A87,0x4ABD3789,0x87A84A81,0x948104EB,
0xA9AAC3EA,0xBAC5B4FE,0xD4479EB6,0xC4108568,0xE144693B,0x5760C117,
0x48A9A1A6,0xA987B887,0xDF7C74E0,0xBC0682D7,0xEDB7705D,0x57BFFEAA,
0x8A0BD4F1,0x1A98D448,0xEA4615C9,0x99E0CBD6,0x780E39A3,0xADBCD406,
0x84DA1362,0x7A0E984B,0xBED853E6,0xD05D610B,0x9CAC6A28,0x1682ACDF,
0x889F605F,0x9EE2FEBA,0xDB556C92,0x86818021,0x3CC5BEA1,0x75A934C6,
0x95574478,0x31A92B9B,0xBFE3E92B,0xB28067AE,0xD862D848,0x0732A22D,
0x840EF879,0x79FFA920,0x0124C8BB,0x26C75B69,0xC3DAAAC5,0x6E71F2E9,
0x9FD4AFA6,0x474D0702,0x8B6AD73E,0xF5714E20,0xE608A352,0x2BF644F8,
0x4DF9A8BC,0xB71EAD7E,0x6335F5FB,0x0A271CE3,0xD2B552BB,0x3834A0C3,
0x341C5908,0x0674A87B,0x8C87C0F1,0xFF0842FC,0x48C46BDB,0x30826DF8,
0x8B82CE8E,0x0235C905,0xDE4844C3,0x296DF078,0xEFAA6FEA,0x6CB98D67,
0x6E959632,0xD5D3732F,0x68D95F19,0x43FC0148,0xF808C7B1,0xD45DBD5D,
0x5DD1B83B,0x8BA824FD,0xC0449E98,0xB743CC56,0x41FADDAC,0x141E9B1C,
0x8B937233,0x9B59DCA7,0xF1C871AD,0x6C678B4D,0x46617752,0xAAE49354,
0xCABE8156,0x6D0AC54C,0x680CA74C,0x5CD82B3F,0xA1C72A59,0x336EFB54,
0xD3B1A748,0xF4EB40D5,0x0ADB36CF,0x59FA1CE0,0x2C694FF9,0x5CE2F81A,
0x469B9E34,0xCE74A493,0x08B55111,0xEDED517C,0x1695D6FE,0xE37C7EC7,
0x57827B93,0x0E02A748,0x6E4A9C0F,0x4D840764,0x9DFFC45C,0x891D29D7,
0xF9AD0D52,0x3F663F69,0xD00A91B9,0x615E2398,0xEDBBC423,0x09397968,
0xE42D6B68,0x24C7EFB1,0x384D472C,0x3F0CE39F,0xD02E9787,0xC326F415,
0x9E135320,0x150CB9E2,0xED94AFC7,0x236EAB0F,0x596807A0,0x0BD61C36,
0xA29E8F57,0x0D8099A5,0x520200EA,0xD11FF96C,0x5FF47467,0x575C0B39,
0x0FC89690,0xB1FBACE8,0x7A957D16,0xB54D9F76,0x21DC77FB,0x6DE85CF5,
0xBFE7AEE9,0xC49571A9,0x7F1DE4DA,0x29E03484,0x786BA455,0xC26E2109,
0x4A0215F4,0x44BFF99C,0x711A2414,0xFDE9CDD0,0xDCE15B77,0x66D37887,
0xF006CB92,0x27429119,0xF37B9784,0x9BE182D9,0xF21B8C34,0x732CAD2D,
0xAF8A6A60,0x33A5D3AF,0x633E2688,0x5EAB5FD1,0x23E6017A,0xAC27A7CF,
0xF0FC5A0E,0xCC857A5D,0x20FB7B56,0x3241F4CD,0xE132B8F7,0x4BB37056,
0xDA1D5F94,0x76E08321,0xE1936A9C,0x876C99C3,0x2B8A5877,0xEB6E3836,
0x9ED8A201,0xB49B5122,0xB1199638,0xA0A4AF2B,0x15F50A42,0x775F3759,
0x41291099,0xB6131D94,0x9A563075,0x224D1EB1,0x12BB0FA2,0xFF9BFC8C,
0x58237F23,0x98EF2A15,0xD6BCCF8A,0xB340DC66,0x0D7743F0,0x13372812,
0x6279F82B,0x4E45E519,0x98B4BE06,0x71375BAE,0x2173ED47,0x14148267,
0xB7AB85B5,0xA875E314,0x1372F18D,0xFD105270,0xB83F161F,0x5C175260,
0x44FFD49F,0xD428C4F6,0x2C2002FC,0xF2797BAF,0xA3B20A4E,0xB9BF1A89,
0xE4ABA5E2,0xC912C58D,0x96516F9A,0x51561E77};
```

The Stream Cipher HC-128

Hongjun Wu

Katholieke Universiteit Leuven, ESAT/SCD-COSIC and IBBT
Kasteelpark Arenberg 10, B-3001 Leuven-Heverlee, Belgium
wu.hongjun@esat.kuleuven.be

Abstract. We present the 128-bit version of the stream cipher HC-256.

1 Introduction

The stream cipher HC-128 is a simplified version of HC-256 [15] for 128-bit security. HC-128 is a simple, secure, software-efficient cipher[1] and it is freely-available. HC-128 consists of two secret tables, each one with 512 32-bit elements. At each step we update one element of a table with non-linear feedback function. All the elements of the two tables get updated every 1024 steps. At each step, one 32-bit output is generated from the non-linear output filtering function. HC-128 is suitable for the modern (and future) super-scalar microprocessors. The dependency between operations in HC-128 is very small: three consecutive steps can be computed in parallel; at each step, the feedback and output functions can be computed in parallel. The high degree of parallelism allows HC-128 to run efficiently on modern processors. We implemented HC-128 in C, and the encryption speed of HC-128 reaches 3.05 cycles/byte on the Intel Pentium M processors.

HC-128 is very secure. Our analysis shows that recovering the key of HC-128 is as difficult as exhaustive key search. To distinguish the keystream from random, we expect that more than 2^{64} keystream bits are required (our current analysis shows that about 2^{151} outputs are needed in the distinguishing attack). This report is organized as follows. We introduce HC-128 in Section 2. The security analysis of HC-128 is given in Section 3 and Section 4. Section 5 discusses the implementation and performance of HC-128. Section 6 concludes this report.

2 Cipher Specifications

In this section, we describe the stream cipher HC-128. From a 128-bit key and a 128-bit initialization vector, it generates keystream with length up to 2^{64} bits.

---

[1] This description of the cipher was prepared by the editor using the version available at http://www.ecrypt.eu.org/stream/ as a source. Any transcription errors are the fault of the editor and the reader is recommended to consult the original.

M. Robshaw and O. Billet (Eds.): New Stream Cipher Designs, LNCS 4986, pp. 39–47, 2008.

2.1   Operations, Variables, and Functions

The following operations are used in HC-128:

$+$	$x + y$ means $x + y$ mod 2^{32}, where $0 \le x < 2^{32}$ and $0 \le y < 2^{32}$
$\boxminus$	$x \boxminus y$ means $x - y$ mod 512
$\oplus$	bit-wise exclusive OR
$\parallel$	concatenation
$\gg$	right shift operator: $x \gg n$ means x being right shifted n bits
$\ll$	left shift operator: $x \ll n$ means x being left shifted n bits
$\ggg$	right rotation operator: $x \ggg n$ means $((x \gg n) \oplus (x \ll (32 - n)))$, where $0 \le n < 32$, $0 \le x < 2^{32}$
$\lll$	left rotation operator: $x \lll n$ means $((x \ll n) \oplus (x \gg (32 - n)))$, where $0 \le n < 32$, $0 \le x < 2^{32}$

Two tables P and Q are used in HC-128. The key and the initialization vector of HC-128 are denoted as K and IV. We denote the keystream being generated as s.

P	a table with 512 elements of 32-bits denoted by $P[i]$ for $0 \le i \le 511$
Q	a table with 512 elements of 32-bits denoted by $Q[i]$ for $0 \le i \le 511$
K	the 128-bit key of HC-128
IV	the 128-bit initialization vector of HC-128
s	the keystream being generated from HC-128; The 32-bit output of the ith step is denoted as s_i. Then $s = s_0 \parallel s_1 \parallel s_2 \parallel \cdots$

There are six functions being used in HC-256. $f_1(x)$ and $f_2(x)$ are the same as the $\sigma_0^{256}(x)$ and $\sigma_1^{256}(x)$ being used in the message schedule of SHA-256 [14]. For $h_1(x)$, the table Q is used as S-box. For $h_2(x)$, the table P is used as S-box.

$$f_1(x) = (x \ggg 7) \oplus (x \ggg 18) \oplus (x \gg 3) \ ,$$
$$f_2(x) = (x \ggg 17) \oplus (x \ggg 19) \oplus (x \gg 10) \ ,$$
$$g_1(x, y, z) = ((x \ggg 10) \oplus (z \ggg 23)) + (y \ggg 8) \ ,$$
$$g_2(x, y, z) = ((x \lll 10) \oplus (z \lll 23)) + (y \lll 8) \ ,$$
$$h_1(x) = Q[x_0] + Q[256 + x_2] \ ,$$
$$h_2(x) = P[x_0] + P[256 + x_2] \ ,$$

where $x = x_3 \parallel x_2 \parallel x_1 \parallel x_0$, x is a 32-bit word, x_0, x_1, x_2, and x_3 are four bytes. The bytes x_3 and x_0 respectively denote the most and least significant byte of x.

2.2   Initialization Process (Key and IV Setup)

The initialization process of HC-128 consists of expanding the key and initialization vector into P and Q (similar to the message setup in SHA-256) and running the cipher 1024 steps (with the outputs being used to update P and Q).

The initialization process is as follows:

- Let $K = K_0||K_1||K_2||K_3$ and $IV = IV_0||IV_1||IV_2||IV_3$, where each K_i and IV_i denotes a 32-bit value. Let $K_{i+4} = K_i$, and $IV_{i+4} = IV_i$ for $0 \le i < 4$. The key and IV are expanded into an array W_i ($0 \le i \le 1279$) as:

$$W_i = \begin{cases} K_i & 0 \le i \le 7 \\ IV_{i-8} & 8 \le i \le 15 \\ f_2(W_{i-2}) + W_{i-7} + f_1(W_{i-15}) + W_{i-16} + i & 16 \le i \le 1279 \end{cases}$$

- Update the tables P and Q with the array W:

$$P[i] = W_{i+256} \quad \text{for } 0 \le i \le 511$$
$$Q[i] = W_{i+768} \quad \text{for } 0 \le i \le 511$$

- Run the cipher 1024 steps and use the outputs to replace the table elements as follows ('$\boxminus$' denotes '$-$' modulo 512):

for $i = 0$ to 511, do
$\quad P[i] = (P[i] + g_1(P[i \boxminus 3], P[i \boxminus 10], P[i \boxminus 511])) \oplus h_1(P[i \boxminus 12]);$

for $i = 0$ to 511, do
$\quad Q[i] = (Q[i] + g_2(Q[i \boxminus 3], Q[i \boxminus 10], Q[i \boxminus 511])) \oplus h_2(Q[i \boxminus 12]);$

The initialization process completes and the cipher is ready to generate keystream.

2.3   The Keystream Generation Algorithm

At each step, one element of a table is updated and one 32-bit output is generated. Each S-box is used to generate only 512 outputs, then it is updated in the next 512 steps. The keystream generation algorithm of HC-128 is given below ("$\boxminus$" denotes "-" modulo 512, s_i denotes the output of the i-th step).

$\quad i = 0;$
repeat until (enough keystream bits are generated)
$\{$
$\qquad j = i \bmod 512;$
$\qquad$ **if** ($i \bmod 1024$) < 512
$\qquad \{$
$\qquad\qquad P[j] = P[j] + g_1(P[j \boxminus 3], P[j \boxminus 10], P[j \boxminus 511]);$
$\qquad\qquad s_i = h_1(P[j \boxminus 12]) \oplus P[j];$
$\qquad \}$
$\qquad$ **else**
$\qquad \{$
$\qquad\qquad Q[j] = Q[j] + g_2(Q[j \boxminus 3], Q[j \boxminus 10], Q[j \boxminus 511]);$
$\qquad\qquad s_i = h_2(Q[j \boxminus 12]) \oplus Q[j];$
$\qquad \}$
$\qquad i = i + 1;$
$\}$

3   Security Analysis of HC-128

The security analysis of HC-128 is similar to that of HC-256. The output and feedback functions of HC-128 are non-linear, so it is impossible to apply the fast correlation attacks [12,9,13,5,11] and algebraic attacks [1,6,7,8] to recover the secret key of HC-128. The large secret S-box of HC-128 is updated during the keystream generation process, so it is very difficult to develop linear relations linking the input and output bits of the S-box.

In this section, we will analyze the period of HC-128, the security of the secret key and the security of the initialization process. The randomness of the keystream will be analyzed separately in Section 4.

3.1   Period

The 32778-bit state of HC-128 ensures that the period of the keystream is extremely large. But the exact period of HC-128 is difficult to predict. The average period of the keystream is estimated to be much more than 2^{256}. The large number of states also eliminates the threat of the time-memory-data tradeoff attack on stream ciphers [4] (also [2,10]).

3.2   Security of the Secret Key

We note that the output function and the feedback function of HC-128 are non-linear. The non-linear output function leaks small amount of partial information at each step. The non-linear feedback function ensures that the secret key can not be recovered from those leaked partial information.

3.3   Security of the Initialization Process (Key/IV Setup)

The initialization process of the HC-128 consists of two stages, as given in Subsection 2.2. We expand the key and IV into P and Q. At this stage, every bit of the key/IV affects all the bits of the two tables and any difference in the related keys/IVs results in uncontrollable differences in P and Q. Note that the constants in the expansion function at this stage play significant role in reducing the effect of related keys/IVs. After the expansion, we run the cipher 1024 steps and using the outputs to update the P and Q. After the initialization process, we expect that any difference in the keys/IVs would not result in biased keystream.

3.4   Randomness of the Keystream

Our initial analysis shows that the distinguishing attack on HC-128 requires more than 2128 outputs. The analysis is given below.

Recall that if, at the i-th step, $(i \bmod 1024) < 512$, table P is updated as:

$$P[i \bmod 512] = P[i \bmod 512] + g_1(P[i \boxminus 3], P[i \boxminus 10], P[i \boxminus 511])$$

We know that $s_i = h_1(P[i \boxminus 12]) \oplus P[i \bmod 512]$. For $10 \leq (i \bmod 1024) < 511$, this feedback function can be written alternatively as:

$$s_i \oplus h_1(z_i) = (s_{i-1024} \oplus h_1'(z_{i-1024})) +$$
$$g_1(s_{i-3} \oplus h_1(z_{i-3}), s_{i-10} \oplus h_1(z_{i-10}), s_{i-1023} \oplus h_1'(z_{i-1023})) \quad (1)$$

where $h_1(x)$ and $h_1'(x)$ indicate two different functions since they are related to different S-boxes; z_j denotes $P[j \boxminus 12]$ at the j-th step.

We note that there are two '+' operations in the feedback function. We will first investigate the least significant bits in the feedback function since they are not affected by the '+' operations. Denote the i-th least significant bit of a as a^i. From (1), we obtain that for $10 \leq (i \bmod 1024) < 511$,

$$s_i^0 \oplus s_{i-1024}^0 \oplus s_{i-3}^{10} \oplus s_{i-10}^8 \oplus s_{i-1023}^{23} = (h_1(z_i))^0 \oplus$$
$$\oplus (h_1'(z_{i-1024}))^0 \oplus (h_1(z_{i-3}))^{10} \oplus (h_1(z_{i-10}))^8 \oplus (h_1'(z_{i-1023}))^{23} \quad (2)$$

Similarly, for $1024 \times \alpha + 10 \leq i, j < 1024 \times \alpha + 511$ and $j \neq i$, we obtain:

$$s_j^0 \oplus s_{j-1024}^0 \oplus s_{j-3}^{10} \oplus s_{j-10}^8 \oplus s_{j-1023}^{23} = (h_1(z_j))^0 \oplus$$
$$\oplus (h_1'(z_{j-1024}))^0 \oplus (h_1(z_{j-3}))^{10} \oplus (h_1(z_{j-10}))^8 \oplus (h_1'(z_{j-1023}))^{23} \quad (3)$$

For the left sides of (2) and (3) to be equal, i.e., for the following equation:

$$s_i^0 \oplus s_{i-1024}^0 \oplus s_{i-3}^{10} \oplus s_{i-10}^8 \oplus s_{i-1023}^{23} =$$
$$s_j^0 \oplus s_{j-1024}^0 \oplus s_{j-3}^{10} \oplus s_{j-10}^8 \oplus s_{j-1023}^{23} \quad (4)$$

to hold, we require that:

$$(h_1(z_i))^0 \oplus (h_1'(z_{i-1024}))^0 \oplus (h_1(z_{i-3}))^{10} \oplus (h_1(z_{i-10}))^8 \oplus (h_1'(z_{i-1023}))^{23} =$$
$$(h_1(z_j))^0 \oplus (h_1'(z_{j-1024}))^0 \oplus (h_1(z_{j-3}))^{10} \oplus (h_1(z_{j-10}))^8 \oplus (h_1'(z_{j-1023}))^{23} \quad (5)$$

Approximate (5) as

$$H(x_1) = H(x_2) \quad (6)$$

where H denotes a random secret 80-bit to 1-bit S-box, x_1 and x_2 are two 80-bit random inputs, $x_1 = \bar{z}_i||\bar{z}_{i-3}||\bar{z}_{i-10}||\bar{z}_{i-1023}||\bar{z}_{i-1024}$ and $x_2 = \bar{z}_j||\bar{z}_{j-3}||\bar{z}_{j-10}|| \bar{z}_{j-1023}||\bar{z}_{j-1024}$, where $\bar{z}$ indicates the concatenation of the least significant byte and the second most significant byte of z. The following theorem gives the collision rate of the outputs of $H(x)$.

Theorem 1. *Let H be an m-bit to n-bit S-box and all those n-bit elements are randomly generated, where $m \geq n$. Let x_1 and x_2 be two m-bit random inputs to H. Then $H(x_1) = H(x_2)$ with probability $2^{-m} + 2^{-n} - 2^{-m-n}$.*

Proof. If $x_1 = x_2$, then $H(x_1) = H(x_2)$. If $x_1 \neq x_2$, then $H(x_1) = H(x_2)$ with probability $2^{-n} \cdot x_1 = x_2$ with probability 2^{-m} and $x_1 \neq x_2$ with probability $1 - 2^{-m}$. The probability that $H(x_1) = H(x_2)$ is $2^{-m} + (1 - 2^{-m}) \cdot 2^{-n}$.

According to Theorem 1, (6) holds with probability $\frac{1}{2}+2^{-81}$. So (4) holds with probability $\frac{1}{2}+2^{-81}$. After testing the validity of 2^{164} equations (4), the output of the cipher can be distinguished from random signal with success rate 0.9772 (with false negative rate and false positive rate as 0.0228). Note that only about 2^{17} equations (4) can be obtained from every 512 outputs, this distinguishing attack requires about 2^{156} outputs.

We note that the attack above only deals with the least significant bit in (1). It may be possible to consider the rest of the 31 bits bit-by-bit. But due to the effect of the two '+' operations in the feedback function, the attack exploiting those 31 bits is not as effective as that exploiting the least significant bit. Thus more than 2^{151} outputs are needed in this distinguishing attack.

It may be possible that the distinguishing attack against HC-128 can be improved in the future. However, it is very unlikely that our security goal can be breached since the security margin is extremely large. We thus conjecture that it is computationally impossible to distinguish 2^{64} bits keystream of HC-128 from random.

4   Implementation and Performance of HC-128

The optimized implementation of HC-128 is similar to that of HC-256. On the Pentium M processor, the speed of HC-128 reaches 3.05 cycles/bye, while the speed of HC-256 is about 4.4 cycles/byte.

4.1   The Optimized Implementation of HC-128

In the optimized code, loop unrolling is used and only one branch decision is made for every 16 steps. The details of the implementation are given below. The feedback function of P is given as:

$$P[i \bmod 512] = P[i \bmod 512] + P[i \boxminus 10] + g_1(P[i \boxminus 3], P[i \boxminus 511]).$$

A register X containing 16 elements is introduced for P. If $(i \bmod 1024) < 512$ and $i \bmod 16 = 0$, then at the beginning of step i, $X[j] = P[(i-16+j) \bmod 512]$ for $j = 0, 1, \ldots, 15$, i.e. X contains the values $P[i \boxminus 16]$, $P[i \boxminus 15]$, $\ldots$, $P[i \boxminus 1]$. During the 16 steps starting from step i, the P and X are updated as:

$$P[i] = P[i] + g_1(X[13], X[6], P[i+1]);$$
$$X[0] = P[i];$$
$$P[i+1] = P[i+1] + g_1(X[14], X[7], P[i+2]);$$
$$X[1] = P[i+1];$$
$$P[i+2] = P[i+2] + g_1(X[15], X[8], P[i+3]);$$
$$X[2] = P[i+2];$$
$$P[i+3] = P[i+3] + g_1(X[0], X[9], P[i+4]);$$
$$X[3] = P[i+3];$$

$$\vdots$$

$$P[i+14] = P[i+14] + g_1(X[11], X[4], P[i+15]);$$
$$X[14] = P[i+14];$$
$$P[i+15] = P[i+15] + g_1(X[12], X[5], P[(i+1) \bmod 512]);$$
$$X[15] = P[i+15];$$

Note that at step i, two elements of $P[i \boxminus 10]$ and $P[i \boxminus 3]$ can be obtained directly from X. Also for the output function $s_i = h_1(P[i \boxminus 12]) \oplus P[i \bmod 1024]$, the value $P[i \boxminus 12]$ can be obtained from X. In this implementation, there is no need to compute $i \boxminus 3$, $i \boxminus 10$, and $i \boxminus 12$.

A register Y with 16 elements is used in the implementation of the feedback function of Q in the same way as that given above.

4.2   The Performance of HC-128

Encryption Speed. We use the C codes submitted to the eSTREAM to measure the encryption speed. The processor used in the measurement is the Intel Pentium M (1.6 GHz, 32 KB Level 1 cache, 2 MB Level 2 cache).

Using the eSTREAM performance testing framework, the highest encryption speed of HC-128 is 3.05 cycles/byte with the compiler gcc (there are three optimization options leading to this encryption speed: k8 O3-ual-ofp, prescott O2-ofp, and athlon O3-ofp). Using the Intel C++ Compiler 9.1 in Windows XP (SP2), the speed is 3.3 cycles/byte. Using the Microsoft Visual C++ 6.0 in Windows XP (SP2), the speed is 3.6 cycles/byte.

Initialization Process. The key setup of HC-128 requires about 27,300 clock cycles. There are two large S-boxes in HC-128. In order to eliminate the threat of related key/IV attack, the tables should be updated with the key and IV thoroughly and this process requires a lot of computations. It is thus undesirable to use HC-128 in the applications where key (or IV) is updated very frequently.

5   Conclusion

In this report, a software-efficient stream cipher HC-128 is illustrated. Our analysis shows that HC-128 is very secure. However, the extensive security analysis of any new cipher requires a lot of efforts from many researchers. We encourage the readers to analyze the security of HC-128.

References

1. Armknecht, F., Krause, M.: Algebraic Attacks on Combiners with Memory. In: Boneh, D. (ed.) CRYPTO 2003. LNCS, vol. 2729, pp. 162–175. Springer, Heidelberg (2003)
2. Babbage, S.: A Space/Time Tradeoff in Exhaustive Search Attacks on Stream Ciphers. In: European Convention on Security and Detection, IEE Conference publication, May 1995, vol. 408 (1995)

3. Biham, E., Shamir, A.: Differential Cryptanalysis of DES-like Cryptosystems. In: Menezes, A., Vanstone, S.A. (eds.) CRYPTO 1990. LNCS, vol. 537, pp. 2–21. Springer, Heidelberg (1991)

4. Biryukov, A., Shamir, A.: Cryptanalytic Time/Memory/Data Tradeoffs for Stream Ciphers. In: Okamoto, T. (ed.) ASIACRYPT 2000. LNCS, vol. 1976, pp. 1–13. Springer, Heidelberg (2000)

5. Chepyzhov, V.V., Johansson, T., Smeets, B.: A Simple Algorithm for Fast Correlation Attacks on Stream Ciphers. In: Schneier, B. (ed.) FSE 2000. LNCS, vol. 1978, pp. 181–195. Springer, Heidelberg (2001)

6. Courtois, N.: Higher Order Correlation Attacks, XL algorithm and Cryptanalysis of Toyocrypt. In: Lee, P.J., Lim, C.H. (eds.) ICISC 2002. LNCS, vol. 2587, pp. 182–199. Springer, Heidelberg (2003)

7. Courtois, N., Meier, W.: Algebraic Attacks on Stream Ciphers with Linear Feedback. In: Biham, E. (ed.) EUROCRYPT 2003. LNCS, vol. 2656, pp. 345–359. Springer, Heidelberg (2003)

8. Courtois, N.: Fast Algebraic Attacks on Stream Ciphers with Linear Feedback. In: Boneh, D. (ed.) CRYPTO 2003. LNCS, vol. 2729, pp. 176–194. Springer, Heidelberg (2003)

9. Golić, J.D.: Towards Fast Correlation Attacks on Irregularly Clocked Shift Registers. In: Guillou, L.C., Quisquater, J.-J. (eds.) EUROCRYPT 1995. LNCS, vol. 921, pp. 248–262. Springer, Heidelberg (1995)

10. Golić, J.D.: Cryptanalysis of Alleged A5 Stream Cipher. In: Fumy, W. (ed.) EUROCRYPT 1997. LNCS, vol. 1233, pp. 239–255. Springer, Heidelberg (1997)

11. Johansson, T., Jönsson, F.: Fast Correlation Attacks through Reconstruction of Linear Polynomials. In: Bellare, M. (ed.) CRYPTO 2000. LNCS, vol. 1880, pp. 300–315. Springer, Heidelberg (2000)

12. Meier, W., Staffelbach, O.: Fast Correlation Attacks on Certain Stream Ciphers. Journal of Cryptography 1(3), 159–176 (1989)

13. Mihaljević, M., Fossorier, M.P.C., Imai, H.: A Low-Complexity and High- Performance Algorithm for Fast Correlation Attack. In: Schneier, B. (ed.) FSE 2000. LNCS, vol. 1978, pp. 196–212. Springer, Heidelberg (2001)

14. National Institute of Standards and Technology, Secure Hash Standard (SHS), Federal Information Processing Standards Publication (FIPS), 180–182, http://csrc.nist.gov/publications/ps/

15. Wu, H.: A New Stream Cipher HC-256. In: Roy, B., Meier, W. (eds.) FSE 2004. LNCS, vol. 3017, pp. 226–244. Springer, Heidelberg (2004), http://eprint.iacr.org/2004/092.pdf

A Test Vectors of HC-128

Let $K = K_0||K_1||\cdots||K_7$ and $IV = IV_0||IV_1||\cdots||IV_7$. The first 512 bits of keystream are given for different values of key and IV. Note that for each 32-bit output given below, the least significant byte leads the most significant byte in the keystream. For example, if S and T are 32-bit words, and $S = s_3||s_2||s_1||s_0$, $T = t_3||t_2||t_1||t_0$, where each s_i and t_i is one byte, and s_0 and t_0 denote the least significant bytes, then the keystream S, T is related to the keystream $s_0, s_1, s_2, s_3, t_0, t_1, t_2, t_3$.

1. The key and IV are set as 0:

   ```
   73150082 3bfd03a0 fb2fd77f aa63af0e
   de122fc6 a7dc29b6 62a68527 8b75ec68
   9036db1e 81896005 00ade078 491fbf9a
   1cdc3013 6c3d6e24 90f664b2 9cd57102
   ```

2. The key is set as 0, the IV is set as 0 except that $IV_0 = 1$:

   ```
   c01893d5 b7dbe958 8f65ec98 64176604
   36fc6724 c82c6eec 1b1c38a7 c9b42a95
   323ef123 0a6a908b ce757b68 9f14f7bb
   e4cde011 aeb5173f 89608c94 b5cf46ca
   ```

3. The IV is set as 0, the key is set as 0 except that $K_0 = \text{0x55}$:

   ```
   518251a4 04b4930a b02af931 0639f032
   bcb4a47a 5722480b 2bf99f72 cdc0e566
   310f0c56 d3cc83e8 663db8ef 62dfe07f
   593e1790 c5ceaa9c ab03806f c9a6e5a0
   ```

4. Let $A_i = \bigoplus_{j=0}^{\text{0xfffff}} s_{16j+i}$ for $i = 0, 1, \ldots, 15$, i.e. set a 512-bit buffer as 0 and encrypt it repeatedly for 2^{20} times. Set the key and IV as 0, the value of $A_0 \| A_1 \| \cdots \| A_{15}$ is given below:

   ```
   a4eac026 7e491126 6a2a384f 5c4e1329
   da407fa1 55e6b1ae 05c6fdf3 bbdc8a86
   7a699aa0 1a4dc117 63658ccc d3e62474
   9cf8236f 0131be21 c3a51de9 d12290de
   ```

Design of a New Stream Cipher—LEX

Alex Biryukov

University of Luxembourg, FSTC,
6, rue Richard Coudenhove-Kalergi,
L-1359 Luxembourg-Kirchberg Luxembourg

Abstract. In this paper we define a notion of leak extraction from a block cipher. We demonstrate this new concept on an example of AES. A result is LEX: a simple AES-based stream cipher which is at least 2.5 times faster than AES both in software and in hardware.

1 Introduction

In this paper we suggest a simple notion of a *leak extraction* from a block cipher. The idea is to extract parts of the internal state at certain rounds and give them as the output key stream (possibly after passing an additional filter function). This idea applies to any block cipher but a careful study by cryptanalyst is required in each particular case in order to decide which parts of the internal state may be given as output and at what frequency. This mainly depends on the strength of the cipher's round function and on the strength of the cipher's key-schedule. For example, ciphers with good diffusion might allow to output larger parts of the internal state at each round than ciphers with weak diffusion.

In this paper we describe our idea on an example of 128/192/256 bit key AES. Similar approach may be applied to the other block-ciphers, for example to Serpent. Interesting lessons learnt from LEX so far are that: LEX setup and resynchronization which are just a single AES key-setup and a single AES encryption are much faster than for most of the other stream ciphers (see performance evaluation of eSTREAM candidates [8]). This is due to the fact that many stream ciphers aimed at fast encryption speed have a huge state which takes very long time to initialize. Also, the state of the stream ciphers has to be at least double of the keysize in order to avoid tradeoff attacks, but on the other hand it does not have to be more than that. Moreover unlike in a typical stream cipher, where the whole state changes with time, in LEX as much as half of the state does not need to be changed or may evolve only very slowly.

2 Description of LEX

In this section we describe a 128-bit key stream cipher LEX (which stands for Leak EXtraction, and is pronounced "leks"). In what follows we assume that the reader is familiar with the Advanced Encryption Standard Algorithm (AES) [7]. The LEX design is very simple and is using AES in a natural way: at each

M. Robshaw and O. Billet (Eds.): New Stream Cipher Designs, LNCS 4986, pp. 48–56, 2008.

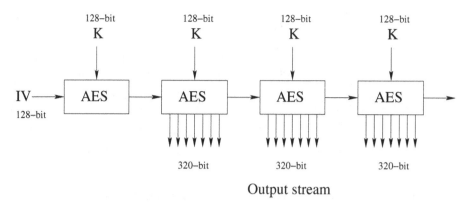

Fig. 1. Initialization and stream generation

AES round we output certain four bytes from the intermediate state. The AES with all three different key lengths (128, 192, 256) can be used. The difference with AES is that the attacker never sees the full 128-bit ciphertext but only portions of the intermediate state. Similar principle can be applied to any other block-cipher.

In Fig. 1 we show how the cipher is initialized and chained[1]. First a standard AES key-schedule for some secret 128-bit key K is performed. Then a given 128-bit IV is encrypted by a single AES invocation: $S = AES_K(IV)$. The 128-bit result S together with the secret key K constitute a 256-bit secret state of the stream cipher.[2] S is changed by a round function of AES every round and K is kept unchanged (or in a more secure variant is changing every 500 AES encryptions).

The most crucial part of this design is the exact location of the four bytes of the internal state that are given as output as well as the frequency of outputs (every round, every second round, etc.). So far we suggest to use the bytes $b_{0,0}, b_{2,0}, b_{0,2}, b_{2,2}$ at every odd round and the bytes $b_{0,1}, b_{2,1}, b_{0,3}, b_{2,3}$ at every even round. We note that the order of bytes is not relevant for the security but is relevant for the fast software implementation. The order of bytes as given above allows to extract a 32-bit value from two 32-bit row variables t_0, t_2 in just four operations (that can be pipelined):

$$out32 = ((t_0 \& 0xFF00FF) << 8) \oplus (t_2 \& 0xFF00FF),$$

while each round of AES uses about 40 operations. Here t_i is a row of four bytes: $t_i = (b_{i,0}, b_{i,1}, b_{i,2}, b_{i,3})$. So far we do not propose to use any filter function and output the bytes as they are. The choice of the output byte locations (see also Fig. 2) is motivated by the following: both sets constitute an invariant subset of

---

[1] There is a small caveat: we use full AES to encrypt the IV, but we use AES with slightly modified last round for the stream generation, as will be explained further in this section.

[2] In fact the K part is expanded by the key-schedule into ten 128-bit subkeys.

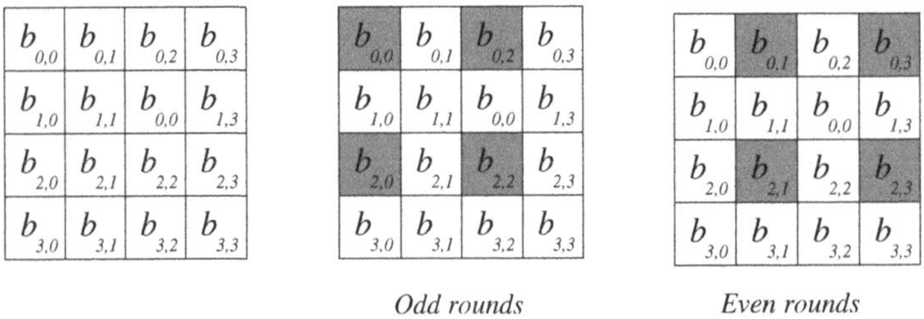

$b_{0,0}$	$b_{0,1}$	$b_{0,2}$	$b_{0,3}$
$b_{1,0}$	$b_{1,1}$	$b_{0,0}$	$b_{1,3}$
$b_{2,0}$	$b_{2,1}$	$b_{2,2}$	$b_{2,3}$
$b_{3,0}$	$b_{3,1}$	$b_{3,2}$	$b_{3,3}$

Odd rounds

Even rounds

Fig. 2. The positions of the leak in the even and in the odd rounds

the ShiftRows operation (the first row is not shifted and the third is rotated by two bytes). By alternating the two subsets in even and odd rounds we ensure that the attacker does not see input and output bytes that are related by a single SubBytes and a single MixColumn. This choice ensures that the attacker will have to analyze two consecutive rounds. The two rounds of AES have full diffusion thus limiting divide-and-conquer capabilities of the attacker. Note also that in AES the 10th round differs from the rest, there is no MixColumn and there is a XOR of the last (11th) subkey. In LEX there is no need to make the 10th round different from any other round. Any LEX encryption round consists of:

```
Round(State, i)
{ SubBytes(State);
  ShiftRows(State);
  MixColumns(State);
  AddRoundKey(State, ExpandedKey[i mod N_r]);
}
```

Here N_r is the number of rounds and is equal to 10 for 128-bit key AES. The full T iterations of LEX would then look like:

```
LEX(State, SecretKey)
{
AESKeyExpansion(SecretKey, ExpandedKey);
State = AESEncrypt(IV, ExpandedKey);
AddroundKey(State, ExpandedKey[0]);
for (i=1; i < T; i++){
  Round(State, i);
  Output[i] = LeakExtract(State, i mod 2);
 }
}
```

It is advisable to change the $SecretKey$ at least every 2^{32} IV setups, and to change the IV every $T = 500$ iterations.

Note also that IV setup is performed by full AES encryption and the subtle difference in the last round of AES and absence of such difference in encryption rounds of LEX is crucial to break similarity which otherwise could be exploited by slide attacks [5, 11] (see Section 3.8 for a discussion).

The speed of this cipher is more than 2.5 times faster than 128-bit key AES, 3 times faster than 192-bit key AES, and 3.5 times faster than 256-bit key AES. So far there are no weaknesses known to the designers as well as there are no hidden weaknesses inserted by the designers.

3 Analysis of LEX

In this section we analyze resistance of LEX to various attacks.

3.1 Period of the Output Sequence

The way we use AES is essentially an Output Feedback Mode (OFB), in which instead of using the ciphertexts as a key-stream we use the leaks from the intermediate rounds as a key-stream. The output stream will eventually cycle when we traverse the full cycle of the AES-generated permutation. If one assumes that AES is indistinguishable from a random permutation for any fixed key, one would expect the cycle size to be of the order $O(2^{128})$ since the probability of falling into one of the short cycles is negligible[3].

3.2 Tradeoff Attacks

For a stream cipher to be secure against time-memory and time-memory-data tradeoff attacks [1, 9, 4] the following conditions are necessary: $|K| = |IV| = |State|/2$. This ensures that the best tradeoff attack has complexity roughly the same as the exhaustive key-search. The IV's may be public, but it is very important that full-entropy IV's are used to avoid tradeoff-resynchronization attacks [3, 10]. In the case of LEX $|K| = |IV| = |Block| = 128$ bits, where $Block$ denotes an intermediate state of the plaintext block during the encryption. Internal state is the pair (IV, K) at the start and $(Block, Key)$ during the stream generation, and thus $|K| + |IV| = |K| + |S| = 256$ bits which is enough to avoid the tradeoff attacks. Note that if one uses LEX construction with larger key variants of AES this might be a "problem". For example for 192-bit key AES the state would consist of 128-bit internal variable and the 192-bit key. This would allow to apply a time-memory-data tradeoff attack with roughly 2^{160} stream, memory and time. For 256-bit key AES it would be 2^{192} stream, memory and time. Such attack is absolutely impractical but may be viewed as a certificational weakness.

---

[3] A random permutation over n-bit integers typically consists of only about $O(n)$ cycles, the largest of them spanning about 62% of the space.

3.3   Algebraic Attacks

Algebraic attack on stream ciphers [6] is a recent and a very powerful type of attack. Applicability of these to LEX is to be carefully investigated. If one could write a non-linear equation in terms of the outputs and the key – that could lead to an attack. Re-keying every 500 AES encryptions may help to avoid such attacks by limiting the number of samples the attacker might obtain while target-ing a specific subkey. We expect that after the re-keying the system of non-linear equations collected by the attacker would become obsolete. Shifting from AES key-schedule to a more robust one might be another precaution against these at-tacks. Note also that unlike in LFSR-based stream ciphers we expect that there do not exist simple relations that connect internal variables at distances of 10 or more steps. Such relations if they would exist would be useful in cryptanalysis of AES itself.

3.4   Differential, Linear, or Multiset Resynchronization Attacks

If mixing of IV and the key is weak the cipher might be prone to chosen or known IV attacks similar to the chosen plaintext attacks on the block-ciphers. However in our case this mixing is performed via a single AES encryption. Since AES is designed to withstand such differential, linear or multiset attacks we believe that such attacks pose no problem for our scheme either.

3.5   Potential Weakness — AES Key-Schedule

There is a simple way to overcome weaknesses in AES key-schedule (which is almost linear) and which might be crucial for our construction. One might use ten consecutive encryptions of the IV as subkeys, prior to starting the encryption. This method will however loose in key agility, since key-schedule time will be 11 AES encryptions instead of one. If better key-agility is required a faster dedicated key-schedule may be designed.

   If bulk encryption is required then it might be advisable to replace the static key with a slowly time-varying key. One possibility would be to perform an addi-tional 10 AES encryptions every 500 AES encryptions and to use the 10 results as subkeys. This method is quite efficient in software but might not be suitable for small hardware due to the requirement to store 1280 bits (160 bytes) of the subkeys. The overhead of such key-change is only 2% slowdown, while it might stop potential attacks which require more than 500 samples gathered for a spe-cific subkey. An alternative more gate-efficient solution would be to perform a single AES encryption every 100 steps without revealing the intermediate values and use the result as a new 128-bit key. Then use the keyschedule of AES to generate the subkeys. Note, that previously by iterating AES with the same key we explored a single cycle of AES, which was likely to be of length $O(2^{128})$ due to the cipher being a permutation of 2^{128} values. However by doing intermediate key-changes we are now in a random mapping scenario. Since state size of our random mapping is 256 bits (key + internal state), one would expect to get into a "short cycle" in about $O(2^{128})$ steps, which is the same as in the previous case and poses no security problem.

3.6   No Weak Keys

Since there are no weak keys known for the underlying AES cipher we believe that weak keys pose no problem for this design either. This is especially important since we suggest frequent rekeying to make the design more robust against other cryptanalytic attacks.

3.7   Dedicated Attacks

An obvious line of attack would be to concentrate on every 10th round, since it reuses the same subkey, and thus if the attacker guesses parts of this subkey he still can reuse this information $10t, t = 1, 2, \ldots$ rounds later. Note however that unlike in LFSR or LFSM based stream ciphers the other parts of the intermediate state have hopelessly changed in a complex non-linear manner and any guesses spent for those are wasted (unless there is some weakness in a full 10-round AES).

3.8   The Slide Attack

In [11] a slide attack [5] on resynchronization mechanism of LEX (as it was described for the eSTREAM project) is shown. The attack requires the ability to perform 2^{61} resynchronizations and uses 2^{75} bytes of output stream data produced under a single key and different IVs, which need to be stored and sorted in 2^{75} bytes of memory. This attack is comparable in complexity to time-memory-key tradeoff attacks which are applicable to any block cipher in popular modes of operation like ECB, CBC (time-memory-data complexity of $O(2^{64})$ for any 128-bit cipher) [2, 3][4] This attack thus does not make LEX weaker than 128-bit key AES.

However the observation leading to the attack is of interest since it can be easily generalized and would apply to any leak-extraction cipher in which resynchronization and encryption are performed by the same function. The idea of the attack is simple: iterations of LEX explore a cycle of the size about 2^{128} starting from IV. Random IV selections would sample random points on this cycle. If the IV setup is performed by the same function as the subsequent stream generation

---

[4] One may argue that attack on a single key is more interesting than the tradeoff attack that breaks one key out of 2^{64}. Firstly we think that it is subjective and depends on the appliation. Secondly, if we limit the amount of stream produced per key to 2^{32} as is typical for many other stream-ciphers, this argument will not be valid any more. The slide attack will have 2^{96} complexity and will need to try the same amount of keys as the tradeoff attack – 2^{64}, before it succeeds.

then one may pick an IV which is equal to the block-state just after the IV setup of another sample. This causes the attacker to know the full block input of the cipher and the result of the leak one round later, which clearly leaks lots of information about the secret subkey of that round. In order to find such colliding block-states the attacker needs at least 2^{65} block samples stored and sorted in memory. The attack assumes the ability to perform about 2^{64} resynchronizations for the same key.

A natural way to increase resistance against the attack would be to require a change of keys every 2^{32} IV's. There would still remain a chance of 2^{-64} to find colliding block-states in a collection of 2^{32} IV samples. However the complexity of the attack would increase to 2^{96} and the attacker would need to try the attack for 2^{64} different keys – the same number as in the tradeoff attack. Such high complexity should be a sufficient protection for most of the practical purposes. In addition, in order to completely get rid of the sliding property one should use two different functions for the resynchronization and the encryption. Moreover even a small difference between the two would suffice. For example, if one uses the full AES with the XOR of the last subkey for the IV setup and AES without the XOR of this subkey for the encryption – this is enough to break the similarities used by sliding.

4   Implementation

As one may observe from software performance test done by ECRYPT [8], LEX holds to its promise and runs 2.5 times faster than 128-bit key AES. We expect that the same holds for hardware implementations. It is also somewhat pleasantly surprising that LEX is one of the fastest ciphers out of the 32 candidates on many of the platforms: 6th on Intel Pentium M, 1700MHz; 4th on Intel Pentium 4, 2.40GHz; 6th on AMD Athlon 64 3000+, 1.80GHz; 7th on PowerPC G4 533MHz; 6th on Alpha EV5.6, 400MHz; 5th on HP 9000/785, 875MHz; 5th on UltraSPARC-III, 750MHz). It is also one of the best in terms of agility of the key-setup, the IV-setup, and the combined Internet packet metric IMIX. LEX is thus very well suited for the short packet exchanges typical for the Internet environment.

Since LEX could reuse existing AES implementations it might provide a simple and cheap speedup option in addition to the already existing base AES encryption. For example, if one uses a fast software AES implementation which runs at 14-15 clocks per byte we may expect LEX to be running at about 5-6 clocks per byte. The same leak extraction principle naturally applies to 192 and 256-bit AES resulting in LEX-192 and LEX-256. LEX-192 should be 3 times faster than AES-192, and LEX-256 is 3.5 times faster than AES-256. Note that unlike in AES the speed penalty for using larger key versions is much smaller in LEX (a slight slowdown for a longer keyschedule and resynchronization but not for the stream generation).

5   Strong Points of the Design

Here we list some benefits of using this design:

- AES hardware/software implementations can be reused with few simple modifications. The implementors may use all their favorite AES implementation tricks.
- The cipher is at least 2.5 times faster than AES. In order to get an idea of the speed of LEX divide cycles-per-byte performance figures of AES by a factor 2.5. The speed of key and IV setup is equal to the speed of AES keyschedule followed by a single AES encryption. In hardware the area and gate count figures are essentially those of the AES.
- Unlike in the AES the key-setup for encryption and decryption in LEX are the same.
- The cipher may be used as a speedup alternative to the existing AES implementation and with only minor changes to the existing software or hardware.
- Security analysis benefits from existing literature on AES.
- The speed/cost ratio of the design is even better than for the AES and thus it makes this design attractive for both fast software and fast hardware implementations. The design will also perform reasonably well in restricted resource environments.
- Since this design comes with explicit specification of IV size and resynchronization mechanism it is secure against time-memory-data tradeoff attacks. This is not the case for the AES in ECB mode or for the AES with IV's shorter than 128-bits.
- Side-channel attack countermeasures developed for the AES will be useful for this design as well.

6   Summary

In this paper we have suggested a new concept of conversion of block ciphers into stream ciphers via *leak extraction*. As an example of this approach we have described efficient extensions of AES into the world of stream ciphers, which we called LEX. We expect that (if no serious weaknesses would be found) LEX may provide a very useful speedup option to the existing base implementations of AES. We hope that there are no attacks on this design faster than $O(2^{128})$ steps. The design is rather bold and of course requires further study.

Acknowledgment

This paper is a result of several inspiring discussions with Adi Shamir. We would like to thank Christophe De Cannière, Joseph Lano, Ingrid Verbauwhede and other cosix for the exchange of views on the stream cipher design. We also would like to thank anonymous reviewers for comments that helped to improve this paper.

References

[1] Babbage, S.: Improved "exhaustive search" attacks on stream ciphers. In: Babbage, S. (ed.) ECOS 1995 (European Convention on Security and Detection). IEE Conference Publication, vol. 408 (May 1995)

[2] Biham, E.: How to decrypt or even substitute DES-encrypted messages in 2^{28} steps. Information Processing Letters 84, 117–124 (2002)

[3] Biryukov, A., Mukhopadhyay, S., Sarkar, P.: Improved Time-Memory Trade-offs with Multiple Data. In: Preneel, B., Tavares, S. (eds.) SAC 2005. LNCS, vol. 3897, pp. 110–127. Springer, Heidelberg (2006)

[4] Biryukov, A., Shamir, A.: Cryptanalytic time/memory/data tradeoffs for stream ciphers. In: Okamoto, T. (ed.) ASIACRYPT 2000. LNCS, vol. 1976, pp. 1–13. Springer, Heidelberg (2000)

[5] Biryukov, A., Wagner, D.: Slide attacks. In: Knudsen, L.R. (ed.) FSE 1999. LNCS, vol. 1636, pp. 245–259. Springer, Heidelberg (1999)

[6] Courtois, N.T., Meier, W.: Algebraic attacks on stream ciphers with linear feedback. In: Biham, E. (ed.) Advances in Cryptology – EUROCRYPT 2003. LNCS, pp. 345–359. Springer, Heidelberg (2003)

[7] Daemen, J., Rijmen, V.: The design of Rijndael: AES — The Advanced Encryption Standard. Springer, Heidelberg (2002)

[8] eSTREAM, eSTREAM Optimized Code HOWTO (2005),
http://www.ecrypt.eu.org/stream/perf/

[9] Golic, J.D.: Cryptanalysis of alleged A5 stream cipher. In: Fumy, W. (ed.) EUROCRYPT 1997. LNCS, vol. 1233, pp. 239–255. Springer, Heidelberg (1997)

[10] Hong, J., Sarkar, P.: Rediscovery of time memory tradeoffs (2005),
http://eprint.iacr.org/2005/090

[11] Wu, H., Preneel, B.: Attacking the IV Setup of Stream Cipher LEX. In: Robshaw, M.J.B. (ed.) FSE 2006. LNCS, vol. 4047. Springer, Heidelberg (2006)

Specification for NLSv2

Philip Hawkes, Cameron McDonald, Michael Paddon, Gregory G. Rose,
and Miriam Wiggers de Vries

Qualcomm Australia
Level 3, 230 Victoria Rd
Gladesville NSW 2111, Australia
Tel.: +61-2-9817-4188; Fax: +61-2-9817-5199
{phawkes,cameronm,mwp,ggr,miriamw}@qualcomm.com

1 Introduction

NLSv2 is a synchronous stream cipher with message authentication functionality, submitted to the ECrypt Network of Excellence call for stream cipher primitives, profile 1A. NLSv2 is an updated version of NLS [19]. The minor change between NLS and NLSv2 increases resistance to attacks utilizing large amounts of keystream. NLS stands for Non-Linear SOBER, and the NLS ciphers are members of the SOBER family of stream ciphers [12],[16],[23] and [24].

NLSv2 is a synchronous stream cipher designed for a secret key that may be up to 128 bits in length. The cipher outputs the key stream in 32-bit blocks. NLSv2 is a software-oriented cipher based on simple 32-bit operations (such as 32-bit XOR and addition modulo 2^{32}), and references to small fixed arrays. Consequently, NLSv2 is at home in many computing environments, from smart cards to large computers. Source code for NLSv2 is freely available and use of this source code, or independent implementations, is allowed free for any purpose.

NLSv2 includes a facility for simple re-synchronization without the sender and receiver establishing new secret keys through the use of a nonce (a number used only once). This facility does not always need to be used. For example, NLSv2 may be used to generate a single encryption keystream of arbitrary length. In this mode it would be possible to use NLSv2 as a replacement for the commonly deployed RC4 cipher in, for example, SSL/TLS. In this mode, no nonce is necessary. In practice though, much communication is done in messages where multiple encryption keystreams are required. NLSv2 achieves this using a single secret key for the entire (multi-message) communication, with a nonce distinguishing individual messages. NLSv2 is intended to provide security under the condition that no nonce is ever reused with a single key, that no more than 2^{80} words of data are processed with one key, and that no more than 2^{48} words of data are processed with one key/nonce pair. There is no requirement that nonces be random; this allows use of a counter, and makes guaranteeing uniqueness much easier.

This document is arranged as follows. Section 2 introduces the history of NLSv2 and some of the design principles used in the construction. Section 5 contains a complete description of NLSv2. An analysis of the security characteristics, and corresponding design rationale of NLSv2 is found in Section 6.

M. Robshaw and O. Billet (Eds.): New Stream Cipher Designs, LNCS 4986, pp. 57–68, 2008.

2   Design Considerations

2.1   Heritage

Much of the design of NLSv2 can be traced back through the line of SOBER stream ciphers to the original SOBER [23] stream cipher, proposed by Rose in 1998. The algorithm for SOBER is based on 8-bit operations, versus the 32-bit operations used in NLSv2. SOBER was superseded by SOBER-II [24] when various weaknesses were found in the original design. S16 was proposed as 16-bit extension of SOBER-II: S16 copies the structure of SOBER-II and uses 16-bit operations.

However, there were opportunities for strengthening SOBER-II and S16 that could not be ignored. Consequently, replacements for SOBER-II, S16 and a 32-bit version were created. These replacements were called the t-class of SOBER ciphers [12]. The t-class contains three ciphers based on 8-bit, 16-bit and 32-bit operations. The ciphers SOBER-t16 and SOBER-t32 were submitted to the NESSIE program [21]; SOBER-t16 as a stream cipher with 128-bit key strength and SOBER-t32 as a stream cipher with 256-bit key strength. SOBER-t16 and SOBER-t32 proved to be among the strongest stream cipher submissions to NESSIE. However, both ciphers were found to fall short of the stringent NESSIE requirements.

Turing [16] is an adventurous stream cipher proposal that evolved from SOBER-t32. In comparison to other SOBER ciphers, Turing produces five words of output for each internal state update, which is five times more than other SOBER ciphers. The key setup of Turing was found to be lacking [20], but otherwise the design appears strong. However, SOBER proposals since the Turing cipher have returned to the original approach of producing one word of output for each internal state update.

SOBER-128 [17] uses the internal state update function from Turing, but with a very conservative output filter function. SOBER-128 also included an innovative (and flawed [25]) message integrity functionality. Mundja [18], a message integrity primitive based on SHA-256 designed to cooperate with a stream cipher, was developed to rectify the flawed message integrity of SOBER-128.

All these ciphers (SOBER through to SOBER-128) utilize a Linear Feedback Shift Register (LFSR) to produce a changing internal state, with a Non-Linear Filter (NLF) applied to the internal state to produce a word of NLF output. The LFSR provided an internal state with guaranteed cycle period but, on the other hand, the use of an LFSR also enhanced a range of attacks against the ciphers. This suggested that there may be an advantage to replacing the LFSR with a nonlinear feedback shift register. This resulted in NLS [19]: an improved version of SOBER-128 that is based on a nonlinear feedback shift register instead of an LFSR, and with a simplified and more efficient filter function. NLS also incorporates the Mundja primitive for message integrity. NLS was then submitted to the eSTREAM project. NLS was subsequently found to be susceptible to distinguishing attack [5].

As a result, NLS was tweaked to become NLSv2. The only change from NLS is the inclusion of periodic updating of the Konst variable (in NLS, Konst is a key-dependent variable that remains constant for the duration of keystream generation), to resist the distinguishing attack on NLS [5]. NLSv2 was chosen as a Phase III finalist for the eSTREAM project, but only in "encrypt-only" mode (that is, without the message integrity functionality of the Mundja primitive). This paper discusses only on the encryption functionality of NLSv2. The reader is directed to [18] for more details on Mundja.

3   Notation

- A 32-bit block is called a *word*.
- $f16$ is the 16th Fermat number, $2^{16} + 1 = 65537$.
- $a \lll b$(resp. $\ggg$) means rotation of the word a to the left (respectively right) by b bits.
- $\oplus$ is simply exclusive-or of words.
- $+$ is addition modulo 2^{32}.

For NLSv2, conversion between 4-byte chunks and 32-bit words is done in "little-endian" fashion irrespective of the byte ordering of the underlying machine.

4   Design Considerations

4.1   Similarities with Preceding SOBER Designs

In updating NLSv2 from SOBER-128, there were various features of SOBER-128 that were desirable to maintain:

Word Size: A word size of 32-bits was suitable for a variety of implementations. This word size also allowed the f function of SOBER-128 to be utilized in NLSv2.

Choice of Filter and Feedback taps: The position of the words (within the internal state) used in the feedback function and the output filter function has been common to the last few generations of SOBER ciphers. This choice was optimized (during development of the t-class SOBER ciphers) to give maximum resistance to Guess and Determine attacks [2,15]: the best Guess and Determine attacks appear to have complexity greater than 2^{256}. This aspect of the design is considered a strength and is used in NLSv2.

The non-linear f function from SOBER-128: This function is a combination of the Skipjack [22] S-box (called "F-table" in the definition of Skipjack) and an S-box tailor-designed by the Information Security Research Centre (ISRC) at the Queensland University of Technology [9]. The Skipjack S-box has no known weaknesses. The ISRC S-box has been used in SOBER-stream ciphers dating back to the t-class SOBER ciphers, and also has no known weaknesses. The designers saw no need to generate a new non-linear function for NLSv2, so the existing function is utilized.

Choice of Operations: Timing attacks and power attacks can exploit data-dependent rotations and other data-dependent conditional executions. In Turing and SOBER-128 there is no data-dependent conditional execution after initial keying. Instructions that commonly take a variable amount of time, such as data-dependent shifts, or which are difficult to implement in hardware or often not implemented on low-end microprocessors, such as integer multiplication, have been avoided. NLS continues this design philosophy.

Key loading: The *LoadKey()* function (employed in loading the key and/or nonce) also dates back to the t-class ciphers. This function was extensively analyzed during development of the t-class ciphers to ensure that (after all key material has been included), the following properties hold:

- Every bit of the initial state is a non-linear function of every bit of the key and nonce [10].
- No initial state word is algebraically related to any subset of other words.
- The key/nonce length is included to prevent equivalent secret keys/nonces.
- No two secret keys (up to 128-bits in length) can result in the same initial key state. Also, given a key state, no two nonces (up to 128-bits in length) can result in the same initial state.
- There is no initial state of the registers that is known to be weak in any sense, so it follows that there are no known weak keys.

We believe that these properties ensure that the key loading cannot be exploited.

4.2   Changes from Preceding SOBER Designs

Stuttering: Prior to the Turing cipher, SOBER ciphers applied irregular decimation to the NLF outputs to produce the keystream (this was called *stuttering*). The stuttering did not appear to provide significant resistance to attacks, and slowed the output rate of the ciphers. In evolving from the t-class ciphers to Turing, the SOBER designs stopped using stuttering.

Non-linear Feedback Function: The linear feedback functions of the preceding SOBER cipher have some weaknesses. First, every word of internal state is always a linear function of the initial state, which enhances the effect of algebraic attacks [8] and Correlation-based attacks [4]. Second, there is always a linear relationship between corresponding bits of internal state which can be exploited using linear distinguishers [7]. To counter these attacks, it was decided that the NLSv2 internal state should be updated using a non-linear function that incorporated the non-linear f function.

Reducing the Non-linearity of the Output Filter: The linear feedback function of the preceding SOBER cipher necessitated a strongly non-linear filter function to resist the aforementioned attacks. Using a non-linear feedback function in NLSv2 reduced the requirement for such a strong non-linearity. To increase the speed of NLSv2 compared to SOBER-128, it was decided that only one S-box look up would be allowed. This lookup was already used in the feedback function, so the non-linear filter chosen for NLSv2 had to rely only on addition and XOR operations. The resulting function is significantly less non-linear than preceding non-linear filters, but the NLSv2 non-linear filter is significantly faster.

Incorporating a *Counter* into the Internal State: One advantage of the linear feedback functions in earlier SOBER ciphers is that the cycle length can be predicted. For NLS, the cycle length is no longer guaranteed. The designers wished to guarantee a minimum cycle length for NLSv2. This is achieved using a counter that increments with every word generated, and every $(2^{16} - 1)$ words, the value of this counter is added to one of the internal state words. This ensures that the internal state (and thus the output stream) has a minimum cycle length of $C = 2^{48} + 2^{32}$, and any cycle must be a multiple of this value. We have no reason to believe that there are a significant number of cycles of length less than 2^{80}. Our studies with the inclusion of the counter value disabled (thus removing any minimum cycle length) have been unable to demonstrate any cycle. Algebraic methods for constructing such a cycle have eluded us.

Updating *Konst*: A final change is the periodic updating of the *Konst*, as a measure against a distinguishing attack found on NLS [5].

5   Description

5.1   Summary of Keystream Generation

NLSv2's stream generator is constructed from a *non-linear feedback shift register* (NLFSR) and a non-linear filter (NLF), with assistance from a *counter*. The vector $\sigma_t = (r_t[0], \ldots, r_t[16])$ of words is known as the *state* of the register at time t, and the state $\sigma_0 = (r_0[0], \ldots, r_0[16])$ is called the *initial state*. The *key state* and a 32-bit, key-dependent word called *Konst* are initialized from the secret key by the *key loading*. If a nonce is being used, then the key state is further perturbed by the nonce loading process to form the initial state, otherwise the key state is used directly as the initial state. During nonce-loading, the stream generator performs a new calculation of *Konst*, in order to make *Konst* dependent on both the key and the *nonce*. Once initialized, the stream generator produces 32-bit *keystream words* denoted v_j that combine to form the keystream $\{v_j\}$.

5.2   Generating Output

The NLFSR (described below) transforms state σ_t into state σ_{t+1}. Successive states σ_t from the NLFSR are fed through the non-linear filter to produce 32-bit *output words* denoted out_t. Each output word out_t is obtained using the NLF as

$$out_t = NLF(\sigma_t) = (r_t[0] + r_t[16]) \oplus (r_t[1] + r_t[13]) \oplus (r_t[6] + Konst).$$

When $t \equiv 0 (\text{modulo } f16)$, then out_t is used as a new value for *Konst* and the value of out_t is not output as keystream. Otherwise, out_t is used directly as keystream. The mapping to keystream words $\{v_j\}$ from output words $\{out_t\}$ is $v_j = out_{j-(j \ div \ f16)}$ where $(j \ div \ f16)$ denotes the integer part of $(j \div f16)$.

The NLFSR uses the following process to transform state σ_t into state σ_{t+1}:

1. $r_{t+1}[i] = r_t[i+1]$, for $0 \leq i \leq 15$.
2. $r_{t+1}[16] = f((r_t[0] \lll 19) + (r_t[15] \lll 9) + Konst) \oplus r_t[4]$.
3. $r_t[0]$ is abandoned.
4. If $t \equiv 0 (\text{modulo } f16)$, then the following special actions are applied:
   (a) $r_{t+1}[2]$ is modified by adding t (modulo 2^{32});
   (b) $out_{t+1} = NLF(\sigma_{t+1})$ is computed,
   (c) $Konst$ is changed to the resulting value of out_{t+1}; and
   (d) the state σ_{t+1} is transformed into σ_{t+2} prior to producing out_{t+2}, as in steps 1 to 3.

The nonlinear function f is defined in section 5.3 below.

NLSv2 allows for encryption/decryption of plaintext of any length, but most of the operations are designed to act on 32-bit blocks of plaintext or transmission message. If the last portion of the plaintext (or the last portion of the transmission message bits) does not form a full 32-bit word, then the generated keystream word v_j is truncated to a keystream of suitable length.

5.3 The S-Box Function f

Notation: The most significant 8 bits of 32-bit word a is denoted a_H.

The function f employs XOR, and an 8×32-bit substitution box (S-box) denoted $SBox$. For a 32-bit value a, the function is $f(a) = SBox[a_H] \oplus a$.

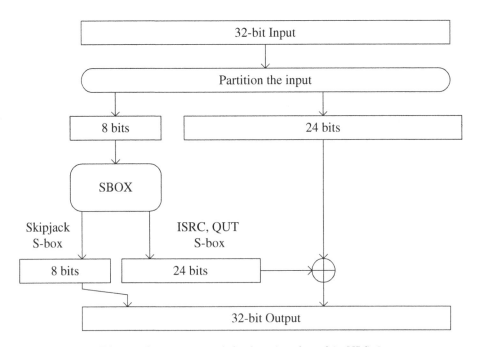

Fig. 1. The structure of the function f used in NLSv2

The S-box is a combination of the Skipjack [22] S-box (called "F-table" in the definition of Skipjack) and an S-box tailor-designed by the Information Security Research Centre (ISRC) at the Queensland University of Technology [9]. The ISRC S-box was constructed as 24 mutually uncorrelated, balanced and highly non-linear single bit functions. Suppose that the S-box has the input a_H. The eight most significant bits (MSBs) of the output of the S-box, XORed with a_H, are equal to the output of the Skipjack S-box, given the input a_H. The 24 least significant bits (LSBs) of the output of the S-box are the output of the S-box constructed by the ISRC, given the input a_H. The entire S-box is given in Appendix A of this document. (Note: the NLSv2 f yields the same output as the SOBER-t32 f, but does not require a masking operation. The SBox table differs only in the high byte of each word.)

Thus, the eight most significant bits of the output of f is the output of the Skipjack S-box, while the 24 LSBs are obtained by XORing the 24 bits of the output of the ISRC S-box with the 24 LSBs of the input (see Figure 1). The function f is defined this way to ensure that it is one-to-one and highly non-linear, while using only a single, small S-box. The function f also serves to transfer the non-linearity from the high bits of its input to the low bits of its output.

5.4   Key and Nonce Loading

NLSv2 is keyed and re-keyed using operations that transform the values in the register under the influence of key material. Two principle operations are employed:

- Include(X): this operation adds the word X to $r[15]$ modulo 2^{32}.
- Diffuse(): this operation clocks the NLFSR, obtains the output v of the NLF and replaces the value of $r[4]$ with the value of $(r[4] \oplus v)$.

The main function used to load the key and nonce is the *Loadkey(k[], keylen)* operation, where $k[]$ is an array containing the *keylen* bytes of the key with one byte stored in each entry of $k[]$. The *Loadkey()* operation uses the values in $k[]$ to transform the current state of the register. All keys must be a multiple of 4 bytes in length; *keylen* is the length of the key in bytes.

Algorithm for *Loadkey(k[], keylen)*

1. Convert $k[]$ into $kwl = keylen/4$ words and store in an array $kw[]$ of kwl "little-endian" words
2. For each i, $0 \leq i \leq (kwl - 1)$: Include($kw[i]$) and apply Diffuse().
3. Include(*keylen*).
4. Apply Diffuse() 17 more times.   □

The 17 applications of Diffuse() are designed to ensure that every bit of input affects every bit of the resulting register state in a nonlinear fashion, as discussed in Section 4.1. Including *keylen* ensures that keys and nonces of different lengths result in distinct initial states.

NLSv2 is keyed using a secret, t-byte session key $K[0], \ldots, K[t-1]$ (and optional m-byte nonce $nonce[0], \ldots, nonce[m-1]$) as follows:

Algorithm for Keying

1. The 17 words of state information are initialized to the first 17 Fibonacci numbers by setting $R[0] = R[1] = 1$, and computing $R[i] = R[i-1] + R[i-2]$, for $2 \leq i \leq 16$. The value of $Konst$ is set to the word $0x6996c53a$ (called INITKONST).
2. The cipher applies $Loadkey(K[],t)$ which includes the key bytes and key length into the register, and diffuses the information through the register.
3. The NLFSR is clocked and the NLF output is calculated and $Konst$ is then set to the resulting value.
4. If the cipher is going to be used for multiple messages, then the 17 word state of the register, $(R[0], \ldots, R[16])$, (which we call the *key state*) can be saved at this point for later use, and the key discarded. However, for shorter keys, the key could be saved and the keying procedure repeated as necessary, trading additional computation time for some extra memory.
5. If the cipher is not being used with nonces, then the cipher produces a key stream with the register starting in the key state. That is, the key state is used as the initial state. However, if the application uses nonces, then the cipher first resets the register state to the initial key state and resets $Konst$ to INITKONST. The cipher then loads the m-byte nonce $nonce[0], \ldots, nonce[m-1]$ using $Loadkey(nonce[],m)$. The NLFSR is clocked and the NLF output is calculated and $Konst$ is then set to the resulting value. The resulting state of the register is taken as the initial state $r_0[i]$, $0 \leq i \leq 16$, and the cipher produces a key stream with the register starting in this state. Note that a zero-length nonce is allowed, and is distinct from all other nonces and also distinct from the key state.

6 Security Analysis of NLSv2

NLSv2 is intended to provide 128-bit security, although we believe it provides significantly more than that. NLSv2 is believed to be susceptible only to distinguishing attacks, which we address below. Otherwise, all other attacks on NLSv2 are believed to either require the owner of the secret key(s) to generate more than 2^{80} key stream words, or the computational complexity of the attack is equivalent to the attacker rekeying the cipher 2^{128} times and generating at least 5 words of output each time. This claim is subject to the condition that no key/nonce pair is ever reused.

6.1 Heuristic Analysis of NLSv2

Most of the components of NLSv2 have been subjected to scrutiny when they appeared in earlier members of the SOBER family of stream ciphers. The two major changes that we now address briefly are (1) the effect of making the feedback function non-linear and (2) the effect of making the output function less non-linear.

The feedback function of the stream cipher is highly nonlinear, through use of the SBox. Rotation of the words used in the feedback function inputs ensures that all bits in the register have nonlinear effect on the register contents quite rapidly (within 26 words of output). The nonlinear effects also compound quite rapidly. Since the register employs nonlinear feedback, little can be proven about its cycle length, so a regular modification of the state is used to guarantee a minimum cycle length in excess of 2^{48}. This should be more than ample in practice. In the absence of any reason to believe that the feedback function behaves in a significantly non-random fashion, the average cycle length is approximately 2^{542}.

The output filter function is quite simple, and serves mostly to ensure that no exploitable combination of input words appears before many applications of the nonlinear SBox have been applied. The nonlinearity of the feedback function, and the selection of the taps for the output filter function, should adequately disguise any short-distance correlations. The regular modification of the state should enhance this effect for long-distance correlations.

6.2   Distinguishing Attacks and NLSv2

The Crossword Puzzle distinguisher attack [5] on the first version of NLS relies on detecting a *Konst*-dependent bias in a linear combination of keystream bits. The attack has a complexity of around 2^{60} keystream observations. For some values of *Konst* the bias tends towards the linear combination equaling zero, while for other values of *Konst* the bias tends towards the linear combination equaling one. When averaged over *Konst*, these biases cancel out and the average bias is zero (or very close to zero).

In the attack on the first version of NLS, the attacker can rely on getting a large amount of keystream generated from a single value of *Konst* for which the linear combinations of keystream bits will all have the same bias. In considering the same attack on NLSv2, since *Konst* changes periodically in NLSv2, the attacker is unable to find enough keystream with the identical values of *Konst*. The attacker must use keystream generated from multiple values of *Konst*. The resulting overall bias in the linear combination of keystream bits will (on average) tend to zero.

However, Cho [6] has shown since that it is possible to form other distinguishing equations for NLSv2 in which the bits of *Konst* can be canceled out so that *Konst* has no effect on the bias. Cho also obtained more accurate estimations of the bias, and showed that distinguisher appears to have a bias of around 2^{-37} and a complexity of around 2^{74} keystream observations, which is less than the limit of 2^{80} keystream observations imposed by the designers.

References

1. Babbage, S., De Cannière, C., Lano, J., Preneel, B., Vandewalle, J.: Cryptanalysis of SOBER-t32. In: Pre-proceedings of Fast Software Encryption FSE2003, pp. 119-136 (February 1999)
2. Blackburn, S., Murphy, S., Piper, F., Wild, P.: A SOBERing Remark. Information Security Group, Royal Holloway University of London, Egham, Surrey TW20 0EX, U. K (1998) (unpublished report)
3. De CanniÅre, C.: Guess and Determine Attack on SOBER. NESSIE Public Document NES/DOC/SAG/WP5/010/a (November 2001) See [21]
4. Chepyzhov, V., Smeets, B.: On a fast correlation attack on certain stream ciphers. In: Davies, D.W. (ed.) EUROCRYPT 1991. LNCS, vol. 547, pp. 176–185. Springer, Heidelberg (1991)
5. Cho, J., Pieprzyk, J.: Crossword Puzzle Attack on NLS, IACR Cryptology ePrint Archive, http://eprint.iacr.org/2006/049.pdf
6. Cho, J., Pieprzyk, J.: Multiple Modular Additions and Crossword Puzzle Attack on NLSv2. IACR Cryptology ePrint Archive (2007), http://eprint.iacr.org/2007/038.pdf
7. Coppersmith, D., Haveli, S., Jutla, C.: Cryptanalysis of stream ciphers with linear masking. In: Yung, M. (ed.) CRYPTO 2002. LNCS, vol. 2442, pp. 515–532. Springer, Heidelberg (2002)
8. Courtois, N.: Fast Algebraic Attacks on Stream Ciphers with Linear Feedback. Awaiting publication, http://www.minrank.org/~courtois/myresearch.html
9. Dawson, E., Millan, W., Burnett, L., Carter, G.: On the Design of 8*32 S-boxes. By the Information Systems Research Centre, Queensland University of Technology (1999) (unpublished report)
10. Dichtl, M., Schafheutle, M.: Linearity Properties of the SOBER-t32 Key Loading. NESSIE Public Document NES/DOC/SAG/WP5/046/1 (November 2001) See [21]
11. Ekdahl, P., Johansson, T.: Distinguishing Attacks on SOBER-t16 and t32. In: Daemen, J., Rijmen, V. (eds.) Fast Software Encryption Workshop (FSE) 2002. LNCS, vol. 1976, pp. 210–224. Springer, Heidelberg (2002)
12. Hawkes, P., Rose, G.: The t-class of SOBER stream ciphers. Technical report, QUALCOMM Australia (1999), http://www.qualcomm.com.au
13. Hawkes, P., Rose, G.: Primitive Specification and Supporting Documentation for SOBER-t16 Submission to NESSIE (submitted, 2000) See [21]
14. Hawkes, P., Rose, G.: Primitive Specification and Supporting Documentation for SOBER-t32 submission to NESSIE (submitted, 2000) See[21]
15. Hawkes, P., Rose, G.: Exploiting multiples of the connection polynomial in word-oriented stream ciphers. In: Okamoto, T. (ed.) ASIACRYPT 2000. LNCS, vol. 1976, pp. 303–316. Springer, Heidelberg (2000)
16. Hawkes, P., Rose, G.: Turing, a Fast Stream Cipher. In: Johansson, T. (ed.) FSE 2003. LNCS, vol. 2887, pp. 290–306. Springer, Heidelberg (2003)
17. Hawkes, P., Rose, G.: Primitive Specification for SOBER-128, 2003. IACR Cryptology ePrint Archive, http://eprint.iacr.org/2003/081.pdf
18. Hawkes, P., Paddon, M., Rose, G.: The Mundja Streaming MAC. IACR Cryptology ePrint Archive (2004), http://eprint.iacr.org/2004/271.pdf
19. Hawkes, P., Paddon, M., Rose, G., Wiggers de Vries, M.: Primitive Specification for NLS (2005), www.ecrypt.eu.org/stream/nls.html
20. Joux, A., Muller, F.: A Chosen IV Attack Against Turing. In: Matsui, M., Zuccherato, R. (eds.) SAC 2003. LNCS, vol. 3006, pp. 194–207. Springer, Heidelberg (2004)

21. NESSIE: New European Schemes for Signatures, Â Integrity, and Encryption,
    http://www.cryptonessie.org
22. National Institute of Standards and Technology, FIPS 185- Escrowed Encryption
    Standard (EES), Federal Information Processing Standards 185,
    http://www.itl.nist.gov/fipspubs/fip185.htm
23. Rose, G.: A Stream Cipher based on Linear Feedback over GF(28). In: Boyd, C.
    (ed.) Proc. Australian Conference on Information Security and Privacy. Springer,
    Heidelberg (1998)
24. Rose, G.: SOBER: A Stream Cipher based on Linear Feedback over GF(28). Un-
    published report, QUALCOMM Australia (1998), http://www.qualcomm.com.au
25. Watanabe, D., Furuya, S.: A MAC forgery attack on SOBER-128. In: Proc. Fast
    Software Encryption 2004. Springer, Heidelberg (2004)

7   Appendix

7.1   The S-Box

The entries in the NLF S-box are given below in hexadecimal form.

```
unsigned long SBox[256] = {
0xa3aa1887, 0xd65e435c, 0x0b65c042, 0x800e6ef4,
0xfc57ee20, 0x4d84fed3, 0xf066c502, 0xf354e8ae,
0xbb2ee9d9, 0x281f38d4, 0x1f829b5d, 0x735cdf3c,
0x95864249, 0xbc2e3963, 0xa1f4429f, 0xf6432c35,
0xf7f40325, 0x3cc0dd70, 0x5f973ded, 0x9902dc5e,
0xda175b42, 0x590012bf, 0xdc94d78c, 0x39aab26b,
0x4ac11b9a, 0x8c168146, 0xc3ea8ec5, 0x058ac28f,
0x52ed5c0f, 0x25b4101c, 0x5a2db082, 0x370929e1,
0x2a1843de, 0xfe8299fc, 0x202fbc4b, 0x833915dd,
0x33a803fa, 0xd446b2de, 0x46233342, 0x4fcee7c3,
0x3ad607ef, 0x9e97ebab, 0x507f859b, 0xe81f2e2f,
0xc55b71da, 0xd7e2269a, 0x1339c3d1, 0x7ca56b36,
0xa6c9def2, 0xb5c9fc5f, 0x5927b3a3, 0x89a56ddf,
0xc625b510, 0x560f85a7, 0xace82e71, 0x2ecb8816,
0x44951e2a, 0x97f5f6af, 0xdfcbc2b3, 0xce4ff55d,
0xcb6b6214, 0x2b0b83e3, 0x549ea6f5, 0x9de041af,
0x792f1f17, 0xf73b99ee, 0x39a65ec0, 0x4c7016c6,
0x857709a4, 0xd6326e01, 0xc7b280d9, 0x5cfb1418,
0xa6aff227, 0xfd548203, 0x506b9d96, 0xa117a8c0,
0x9cd5bf6e, 0xdcee7888, 0x61fcfe64, 0xf7a193cd,
0x050d0184, 0xe8ae4930, 0x88014f36, 0xd6a87088,
0x6bad6c2a, 0x1422c678, 0xe9204de7, 0xb7c2e759,
0x0200248e, 0x013b446b, 0xda0d9fc2, 0x0414a895,
0x3a6cc3a1, 0x56fef170, 0x86c19155, 0xcf7b8a66,
0x551b5e69, 0xb4a8623e, 0xa2bdfa35, 0xc4f068cc,
0x573a6acd, 0x6355e936, 0x03602db9, 0x0edf13c1,
0x2d0bb16d, 0x6980b83c, 0xfeb23763, 0x3dd8a911,
```

```
0x01b6bc13, 0xf55579d7, 0xf55c2fa8, 0x19f4196e,
0xe7db5476, 0x8d64a866, 0xc06e16ad, 0xb17fc515,
0xc46feb3c, 0x8bc8a306, 0xad6799d9, 0x571a9133,
0x992466dd, 0x92eb5dcd, 0xac118f50, 0x9fafb226,
0xa1b9cef3, 0x3ab36189, 0x347a19b1, 0x62c73084,
0xc27ded5c, 0x6c8bc58f, 0x1cdde421, 0xed1e47fb,
0xcdcc715e, 0xb9c0ff99, 0x4b122f0f, 0xc4d25184,
0xaf7a5e6c, 0x5bbf18bc, 0x8dd7c6e0, 0x5fb7e420,
0x521f523f, 0x4ad9b8a2, 0xe9da1a6b, 0x97888c02,
0x19d1e354, 0x5aba7d79, 0xa2cc7753, 0x8c2d9655,
0x19829da1, 0x531590a7, 0x19c1c149, 0x3d537f1c,
0x50779b69, 0xed71f2b7, 0x463c58fa, 0x52dc4418,
0xc18c8c76, 0xc120d9f0, 0xafa80d4d, 0x3b74c473,
0xd09410e9, 0x290e4211, 0xc3c8082b, 0x8f6b334a,
0x3bf68ed2, 0xa843cc1b, 0x8d3c0ff3, 0x20e564a0,
0xf8f55a4f, 0x2b40f8e7, 0xfea7f15f, 0xcf00fe21,
0x8a6d37d6, 0xd0d506f1, 0xade00973, 0xefbbde36,
0x84670fa8, 0xfa31ab9e, 0xaedab618, 0xc01f52f5,
0x6558eb4f, 0x71b9e343, 0x4b8d77dd, 0x8cb93da6,
0x740fd52d, 0x425412f8, 0xc5a63360, 0x10e53ad0,
0x5a700f1c, 0x8324ed0b, 0xe53dc1ec, 0x1a366795,
0x6d549d15, 0xc5ce46d7, 0xe17abe76, 0x5f48e0a0,
0xd0f07c02, 0x941249b7, 0xe49ed6ba, 0x37a47f78,
0xe1cfffbd, 0xb007ca84, 0xbb65f4da, 0xb59f35da,
0x33d2aa44, 0x417452ac, 0xc0d674a7, 0x2d61a46a,
0xdc63152a, 0x3e12b7aa, 0x6e615927, 0xa14fb118,
0xa151758d, 0xba81687b, 0xe152f0b3, 0x764254ed,
0x34c77271, 0x0a31acab, 0x54f94aec, 0xb9e994cd,
0x574d9e81, 0x5b623730, 0xce8a21e8, 0x37917f0b,
0xe8a9b5d6, 0x9697adf8, 0xf3d30431, 0x5dcac921,
0x76b35d46, 0xaa430a36, 0xc2194022, 0x22bca65e,
0xdaec70ba, 0xdfaea8cc, 0x777bae8b, 0x242924d5,
0x1f098a5a, 0x4b396b81, 0x55de2522, 0x435c1cb8,
0xaeb8fe1d, 0x9db3c697, 0x5b164f83, 0xe0c16376,
0xa319224c, 0xd0203b35, 0x433ac0fe, 0x1466a19a,
0x45f0b24f, 0x51fda998, 0xc0d52d71, 0xfa0896a8,
0xf9e6053f, 0xa4b0d300, 0xd499cbcc, 0xb95e3d40,
};
```

The Rabbit Stream Cipher

Martin Boesgaard[1], Mette Vesterager[1], and Erik Zenner[2]

[1] Cryptico A/S
info@cryptico.com
[2] Technical University of Denmark
e.zenner@mat.dtu.dk

Abstract. The stream cipher Rabbit was first presented at FSE 2003 [3], and no attacks against it have been published until now. With a measured encryption/decryption speed of 3.7 clock cycles per byte on a Pentium III processor, Rabbit does also provide very high performance. This paper gives a concise description of the Rabbit design and some of the cryptanalytic results available.

Keywords: Stream cipher, fast, non-linear, coupled, counter.

1 Introduction

Rabbit was first presented at the Fast Software Encryption workshop in 2003 [3]. Since then, an IV-setup function has been designed [18], and additional security analysis has been completed [16,2], but no cryptographical weaknesses have been revealed. The cipher is currently amongst the finalists of the stream cipher project eSTREAM.

The Rabbit algorithm can briefly be described as follows. It takes a 128-bit secret key and a 64-bit IV (if desired) as input and generates for each iteration an output block of 128 pseudo-random bits from a combination of the internal state bits. Encryption/decryption is done by XOR'ing the pseudo-random data with the plaintext/ciphertext. The size of the internal state is 513 bits divided between eight 32-bit state variables, eight 32-bit counters and one counter carry bit. The eight state variables are updated by eight coupled non-linear functions. The counters ensure a lower bound on the period length for the state variables.

Rabbit was designed to be faster than commonly used ciphers and to justify a key size of 128 bits for encrypting up to 2^{64} blocks of plaintext. This means that for an attacker who does not know the key, it should not be possible to distinguish up to 2^{64} blocks of cipher output from the output of a truly random generator, using less steps than would be required for an exhaustive key search over 2^{128} keys.

1.1 Organization and Notation

In Section 2, we describe the design of Rabbit in detail. We discuss the cryptanalysis of Rabbit in Section 3, and in Section 4 the performance results are presented.

M. Robshaw and O. Billet (Eds.): New Stream Cipher Designs, LNCS 4986, pp. 69–83, 2008.
© Springer-Verlag Berlin Heidelberg 2008

We use the following notation: $\oplus$ denotes logical XOR, $\ll$ and $\gg$ denote left and right logical bit-wise shift, $\lll$ and $\ggg$ denote left and right bit-wise rotation, and $\diamond$ denotes concatenation of two bit sequences. $A^{[g..h]}$ means bit number g through h of variable A. When numbering bits of variables, the least significant bit is denoted by 0. Hexadecimal numbers are prefixed by "0x". Finally, we use integer notation for all variables and constants. Note that the description below is specified for little-endian processors (e.g. most Intel processors).

2   The Rabbit Stream Cipher

The internal state of the stream cipher consists of 513 bits. 512 bits are divided between eight 32-bit state variables $x_{j,i}$ and eight 32-bit counter variables $c_{j,i}$, where $x_{j,i}$ is the state variable of subsystem j at iteration i, and $c_{j,i}$ denotes the corresponding counter variable. There is one counter carry bit, $\phi_{7,i}$, which needs to be stored between iterations. This counter carry bit is initialized to zero. The eight state variables and the eight counters are derived from the key at initialization.

2.1   Key Setup Scheme

The algorithm is initialized by expanding the 128-bit key into both the eight state variables and the eight counters such that there is a one-to-one correspondence between the key and the initial state variables, $x_{j,0}$, and the initial counters, $c_{j,0}$.

The key, $K^{[127..0]}$, is divided into eight subkeys: $k_0 = K^{[15..0]}$, $k_1 = K^{[31..16]}$, ..., $k_7 = K^{[127..112]}$. The state and counter variables are initialized from the subkeys as follows:

$$x_{j,0} = \begin{cases} k_{(j+1 \bmod 8)} \diamond k_j & \text{for } j \text{ even} \\ k_{(j+5 \bmod 8)} \diamond k_{(j+4 \bmod 8)} & \text{for } j \text{ odd} \end{cases} \qquad (1)$$

and

$$c_{j,0} = \begin{cases} k_{(j+4 \bmod 8)} \diamond k_{(j+5 \bmod 8)} & \text{for } j \text{ even} \\ k_j \diamond k_{(j+1 \bmod 8)} & \text{for } j \text{ odd.} \end{cases} \qquad (2)$$

The system is iterated four times, according to the next-state function defined in section 2.3, to diminish correlations between bits in the key and bits in the internal state variables. Finally, the counter variables are modified according to:

$$c_{j,4} = c_{j,4} \oplus x_{(j+4 \bmod 8),4} \qquad (3)$$

for all j, to prevent recovery of the key by inversion of the counter system.

2.2   IV Setup Scheme

Let the internal state after the key setup scheme be denoted the master state, and let a copy of this master state be modified according to the IV scheme. The

IV setup scheme works by modifying the counter state as function of the IV. This is done by XORing the 64-bit IV on all the 256 bits of the counter state. The 64 bits of the IV are denoted $IV^{[63..0]}$. The counters are modified as:

$$c_{0,4} = c_{0,4} \oplus IV^{[31..0]} \qquad c_{1,4} = c_{1,4} \oplus (IV^{[63..48]} \diamond IV^{[31..16]})$$
$$c_{2,4} = c_{2,4} \oplus IV^{[63..32]} \qquad c_{3,4} = c_{3,4} \oplus (IV^{[47..32]} \diamond IV^{[15..0]})$$
$$c_{4,4} = c_{4,4} \oplus IV^{[31..0]} \qquad c_{5,4} = c_{5,4} \oplus (IV^{[63..48]} \diamond IV^{[31..16]}) \qquad (4)$$
$$c_{6,4} = c_{6,4} \oplus IV^{[63..32]} \qquad c_{7,4} = c_{7,4} \oplus (IV^{[47..32]} \diamond IV^{[15..0]}).$$

The system is then iterated four times to make all state bits non-linearly dependent on all IV bits. The modification of the counter by the IV guarantees that all 2^{64} different IVs will lead to unique keystreams.

2.3   Next-State Function

The core of the Rabbit algorithm is the iteration of the system defined by the following equations:

$$x_{j,i+1} = \begin{cases} g_{j,i} + (g_{j-1 \bmod 8,i} \lll 16) + (g_{j-2 \bmod 8,i} \lll 16) & \text{for } j \text{ even} \\ g_{j,i} + (g_{j-1 \bmod 8,i} \lll 8) + g_{j-2 \bmod 8,i} & \text{for } j \text{ odd} \end{cases} \qquad (5)$$

$$g_{j,i} = \left((x_{j,i} + c_{j,i})^2 \oplus ((x_{j,i} + c_{j,i})^2 \ggg 32) \right) \bmod 2^{32}, \qquad (6)$$

where all additions are modulo 2^{32}. This coupled system is illustrated in Fig. 1. Before an iteration the counters are incremented as described below.

2.4   Counter System

The dynamics of the counters is defined as follows:

$$c_{0,i+1} = \begin{cases} c_{0,i} + a_0 + \phi_{7,i} \bmod 2^{32} & \text{for } j = 0 \\ c_{j,i} + a_j + \phi_{j-1,i+1} \bmod 2^{32} & \text{for } j > 0, \end{cases} \qquad (7)$$

where the carry $\phi_{j,i+1}$ is given by

$$\phi_{j,i+1} = \begin{cases} 1 & \text{if } c_{0,i} + a_0 + \phi_{7,i} \geq 2^{32} \wedge j = 0 \\ 1 & \text{if } c_{j,i} + a_j + \phi_{j-1,i+1} \geq 2^{32} \wedge j > 0 \\ 0 & \text{otherwise}, \end{cases} \qquad (8)$$

Furthermore, the a_j constants are defined as:

$$a_0 = a_3 = a_6 = \text{0x4D34D34D},$$
$$a_1 = a_4 = a_7 = \text{0xD34D34D3}, \qquad (9)$$
$$a_2 = a_5 = \text{0x34D34D34}.$$

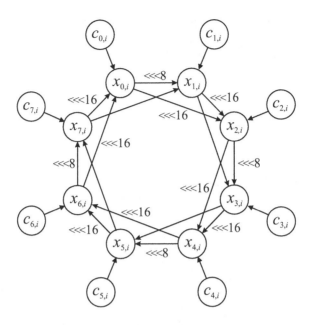

Fig. 1. Graphical illustration of the next-state function

2.5   Extraction Scheme

After each iteration, four 32-bit words of pseudo-random data are generated as follows:

$$
\begin{aligned}
s_{j,i}^{[15..0]} &= x_{2j,i}^{[15..0]} \oplus x_{2j+5 \bmod 8,i}^{[31..16]}, \\
s_{j,i}^{[31..16]} &= x_{2j,i}^{[31..16]} \oplus x_{2j+3 \bmod 8,i}^{[15..0]}.
\end{aligned}
\tag{10}
$$

where $s_{j,i}$ is word j at iteration i. The four pseudorandom words are then XOR'ed with the plaintext/ciphertext to encrypt/decrypt.

3   Security Analysis

In this section we first discuss the key setup function, IV setup function, and periodic properties. We then present an algebraic analysis of the cipher, approximations of the next-state function, differential analysis, and the statistical properties.

3.1   Key Setup Properties

Design Rationale: The key setup can be divided into three stages: Key expansion, system iteration, and counter modification.

- The *key expansion stage* guarantees a one-to-one correspondence between the key, the state and the counter, which prevents key redundancy. It also distributes the key bits in an optimal way to prepare for the the system iteration.
- The *system iteration* makes sure that after one iteration of the next-state function, each key bit has affected all eight state variables. It also ensures that after two iterations of the next-state function, all state bits are affected by all key bits with a measured probability of 0.5. A safety margin is provided by iterating the system four times.
- Even if the counters are presumed known to the attacker, the *counter modification* makes it hard to recover the key by inverting the counter system, as this would require additional knowledge of the state variables. It also destroys the one-to-one correspondence between key and counter, however, this should not cause a problem in practice (see below).

Attacks on the Key Setup Function: After the key setup, both the counter bits and the state bits depend strongly and highly non-linearly on the key bits. This makes attacks based on guessing parts of the key difficult. Furthermore, even if the counter bits were known after the counter modification, it is still hard to recover the key. Of course, knowing the counters would make other types of attacks easier.

As the non-linear map in Rabbit is many-to-one, different keys could potentially result in the same keystream. This concern can basically be reduced to the question whether different keys result in the same counter values, since different counter values will almost certainly lead to different keystreams[1]. Note that key expansion and system iteration were designed such that each key leads to unique counter values. However, the counter modification might result in equal counter values for two different keys. Assuming that after the four initial iterations, the inner state is essentially random and not correlated with the counter system, the probability for counter collisions is given by the birthday paradox, i.e. for all 2^{128} keys, one collision is expected in the 256-bit counter state. Thus, counter collisions should not cause a problem in practice.

Another possibility for related key attacks is to exploit the symmetries of the next-state and key setup functions. For instance, consider two keys, K and $\tilde{K}$ related by $K^{[i]} = \tilde{K}^{[i+32]}$ for all i. This leads to the relation, $x_{j,0} = \tilde{x}_{j+2,0}$ and $c_{j,0} = \tilde{c}_{j+2,0}$. If the a_j constants were related in the same way, the next-state function would preserve this property. In the same way this symmetry could lead to a set of bad keys, i.e. if $K^{[i]} = K^{[i+32]}$ for all i, then $x_{j,0} = x_{j+2,0}$ and $c_{j,0} = c_{j+2,0}$. However, the next-state function does not preserve this property due to the counter system as $a_j \neq a_{j+2}$.

---

[1] The reason is that when the periodic part of the functional graph has been reached, the next-state function, including the counter system, is one-to-one on the set of points in the period.

3.2   IV Setup Properties

Design Rationale: The security goal of the IV scheme of Rabbit is to justify an IV length of 64 bits for encrypting up to 2^{64} plaintexts with the same 128-bit key, i.e. by requesting up to 2^{64} IV setups, no distinguishing from random should be possible. There are two stages: IV addition and system iteration.

– The *IV addition* modifies the counter values in such a way that it can be guaranteed that under an identical key, all 2^{64} possible different IVs will lead to unique keystreams. Note that each IV bit will affect the input of four different g-functions in the first iteration, which is the maximal possible influence for a 64-bit IV. The expansion of the bits also takes the specific rotation scheme of the g-functions into account, preparing for the system iteration.
– The *system iteration* guarantees that after just one iteration, each IV bit has affected all eight state variables. The system is iterated four times in total in order to make all state bits non-linearly dependent on all IV bits.

A full security analysis of the IV setup is given in [10]. It concludes that the good diffusion and non-linearity properties (see below) of the Rabbit next-state function seem to prevent all known attacks against the IV setup scheme.

3.3   Period Length

A central property of counter assisted stream ciphers [19] is that strict lower bounds on the period lengths can be provided. The counter system adopted in Rabbit has a period length of $2^{256} - 1$ [3]. Since it can be shown that the input to the g-functions has at least the same period, a very pessimistic lower bound of 2^{215} can be guaranteed on the period of the state variables [18].

3.4   Partial Guessing

Guess-and-Verify Attack: Such attacks become possible if output bits can be predicted from a small set of inner state bits. The attacker will guess the relevant part of the state, predict the output bits and compare them with actually observed output bits, thus verifying whether his guess was correct.

In [3], it was shown that the attacker must guess at least $2 \cdot 12$ input bytes for the different g-functions in order to verify against one byte. This is equivalent to guessing 192 bits and is thus harder than exhaustive key search. It was also shown that even if the attacker verifies against less than one byte of output, the work required is still above exhaustive key search. Finally, when replacing all additions by XORs, all byte-wise combinations of the extracted output still depend on at least four different g-functions (see section 3.6). To conclude, it seems to be impossible to verify a guess of fewer than 128 bits against the output.

Guess-and-Determine Attack: The strategy for this attack is to guess a few of the unknown variables of the cipher and from those deduce the remaining unknowns.

The system is then iterated a few times, producing output that can be compared with the actual cipher output, verifying the guess.

In the following, we sketch an attack based on guessing bytes, with the counters being considered as static for simplicity. The attacker tries to reconstruct 512 bit of inner state, i.e. he observes 4 consecutive 128-bit outputs of the cipher and proceeds as follows:

- Divide the 32-bit counter and state variables into 8-bit variables.
- Construct an equation system that models state transition and output. For each of the 4 outputs, he obtains $8 \cdot 2 = 16$ equations. For each of the 3 state transitions, he obtains $8 \cdot 4 = 32$ equations. Thus, he has an overall of 160 equations and 160 variables ($4 \cdot 32$ state and 32 counter variables).
- Solve this equation system by guessing as few variables as possible.

The efficiency of such a strategy depends on the amount of variables that must be guessed before the determining process can begin. This amount is lower bounded by the 8-bit subsystem with the smallest number of input variables. Neglecting the counters, the results of [3] illustrate that each byte of the next-state function depends on 12 input bytes. When the counters are included, each output byte of a subsystem depends on 24 input bytes. Consequently, the attacker must guess more than 128 bits before the determining process can begin, thus making the attack infeasible. Dividing the system into smaller blocks than bytes results in the same conclusion.

3.5 Algebraic Attacks

Known Algebraic Attacks: The algebraic attacks on stream ciphers discussed in the literature [1,5,6,4,7] target ciphers whose internal state is mainly updated in a linear way, with only a few memory bits having a nonlinear update function. This, however, is not the case for Rabbit, where 256 inner state bits are updated in a strongly nonlinear fashion. In the following, we will discuss in some detail the nonlinearity properties of Rabbit, demonstrating why the known algebraic attacks are not applicable against the cipher.

The Algebraic Normal Form (ANF) of the g-function: A convenient way of representing Boolean functions is through its algebraic normal form (see, e.g., [17]). Given a Boolean function $f : \{0,1\}^n \to \{0,1\}$, the ANF is the representation of f as a multivariate polynomial (i.e., a sum of monomials in the input variables). Both a large number of monomials in the ANF and a good distribution of their degrees are important properties of nonlinear building blocks in ciphers.

For a random Boolean function in 32 variables, the average total number of monomials is 2^{31}, and the average number of monomials including a given variable is 2^{30}. If we consider 32 such random functions, then the average number of monomials that are not present in any of the 32 functions is 1 and the corresponding variance is also 1. For more details, see [8].

For the g-function of Rabbit, the ANFs for the 32 Boolean subfunctions have an algebraic degree of at least 30. The number of monomials in the functions

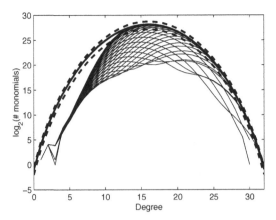

Fig. 2. The number of monomials of each degree in each of the 32 Boolean functions of the g-function. The thick solid line and the two dashed lines denote the average and variance for an ideal random function.

range from $2^{24.5}$ to $2^{30.9}$, where for a random function it should be 2^{31}. The distribution of monomials as function of degree is presented in Fig. 2. Ideally the bulk of the distribution should be within the dashed lines that illustrate the variance for ideal random functions. Some of the Boolean functions deviate significantly from the random case, however, they all have a large number of monomials of high degree.

Furthermore, the overlap between the 32 Boolean functions that constitute the g-function was investigated. The total number of monomials that only occur once in the g-function is $2^{26.03}$, whereas the number of monomials that do not occur at all is $2^{26.2}$. This should be compared to the random result which has a mean value of 1 and a variance of 1.

To conclude, the results for the g-function were easily distinguishable from random. However, the properties of the ANFs for the output bits of the g-function are highly complex, i.e. containig more than 2^{24} monomials per output bit, and with an algebraic degree of at least 30. Furthermore, no obvious exploitable structure seems present.

The Algebraic Normal Form (ANF) of the full cipher: It is clearly not feasible to calculate the full ANF of the output bits for the complete cipher. But reducing the word size from 32 bits to 8 bits makes it possible to study the 32 output Boolean functions as function of the 32-bit key.

For this scaled-down version of Rabbit, the setup function for different numbers of iterations was investigated. In the setup of Rabbit, four iterations of next-state are applied, plus one extra before extraction. We have determined the ANFs after 0+1, 1+1, 2+1, 3+1 and 4+1 iterations, where the +1 denotes the iteration in the extraction.

The results were much closer to random than in the case of the g-function. For 0+1 iterations, we found that the number of monomials is very close to

2^{31} as expected for a random function. Already after two iterations the result seems to stabilize, i.e. the amount of fluctuations around 2^{31} does not change when increasing the number of iterations. We also made an investigation of the number of missing monomials for all 32 output bits. It turned out that for the 0+1, 1+1, 2+1, 3+1 and 4+1 iterations, the numbers were 0, 1, 2, 3 and 1, respectively. This seems in accordance with the mean value of 1 and variance of 1 for a random function. So after a few iterations, basically all possible monomials are present in the full cipher output functions.

Concluding, for the down-scaled version of the full cipher, no non-random properties were identified. For full details of the analysis, including statistical data, the reader may refer to [8].

Overdefined Equation Systems in the State: For simplicity, we ignore the counters and consider only the 256 inner state bits. Furthermore, we replace all arithmetical additions by XOR and omit the rotations. The use of XOR is a severe simplification as this will guarantee that the algebraic degree of the complete cipher will never exceed 32 for one iteration (but, of course, grow for more iterations).

With the inner state consisting of 256 bit, we need the output of at least two (ideally consecutive) iterations, giving us a non-linear system of 256 equations in 256 variables. Note that in the modified Rabbit design, everything is linear with the exception of the g-functions. Thus, we can calculate the number of monomials when expressing the output as a function of the state bits as follows:

- The output of the first iteration can be modelled as a linear function in the inner state, according to Equ. (10). Thus, we obtain 128 very simple linear equations, containing all 256 monomials of degree 1.
- In order to generate the output of the next iteration, however, the inner state bits are run through the g-functions. Remember that $2^{32} - 2^{26.2} \approx 2^{31.97}$ monomials (are contained in the output of each g-functions. Thus, the second set of equations contains approximately $8 \cdot 2^{31.97} = 2^{34.97}$ monomials.

In particular, this means that the non-linear system of equations is neither sparse, nor is it of low degree. Linearizing it increases the number of variables to about 2^{35}, and in order to solve it, an extra $2^{35} - 2^8$ equations are required. These can not be obtained by using further iterations, because this way, the number of monomials increases beyond 2^{128}. Analysis conducted in [8] indicates that they can not be obtained by using implicit equations, either. If, however, it would be possible to find such equations, the non-linear additions and the counter system would most likely destroy their benefit. Thus, we do not expect a algebraic attack using the inner state bits as variables to be feasible.

Overdefined Equation Systems in the Key: An algebraic attack targeting the key bits is even more difficult, since there are at least five rounds iterations of the non-linear layer before the first output bits can be observed (nine rounds if IV is used). Thus, the ANF of the full cipher has to be considered. Remembering that for the 8-bit version of the cipher, the ANF of the cipher is equivalent to a random function after just two iterations, it becomes obvious that the number of monomials in the equation system would be close to the maximum of 2^{128}. Solving such a system of equations would be well beyond a brute force search over the key space.

3.6 Correlation Attacks

Linear Approximations: In [3], at thorough investigation of linear approximations by use of the Walsh-Hadamard Transform [17,11] was made. The best linear approximation between bits in the input to the next-state function and the extracted output found in this investigation had a correlation coefficient of $2^{-57.8}$.

In a distinguishing attack, the attacker tries to distinguish a sequence generated by the cipher from a sequence of truly random numbers. A distinguishing attack using less than 2^{64} blocks of output cannot be applied using only the best linear approximation because the corresponding correlation coefficient is $2^{-57.8}$. This implies that in order to observe this particular correlation, output from 2^{114} iterations must be generated [13].

The independent counters have very simple and almost linear dynamics. Therefore, large correlations to the counter bits may cause a possibility for a correlation attack (see e.g. [14]) for recovering the counters. It is not feasible to exploit only the best linear approximation in order to recover a counter value. However, more correlations to the counters could be exploited. As this requires that there exist many such large and useable correlations, we do not believe such an attack to be feasible[2].

Second Order Approximations: However, it was found that truncating the ANFs of the g-functions after second order terms proposes relatively good approximations under the right circumstances.

We denote by $f^{[j]}$ the functions that contain the terms of first and second order of the ANF of $g^{[j]}$. Measurements of the correlation between $f^{[j]}$ and $g^{[j]}$ revealed correlation coefficients of less than $2^{-9.5}$, which is relatively poor compared to the corresponding linear approximations. However, the XOR sum of two neighbor bits, i.e. $g^{[j]} \oplus g^{[j+1]}$ was found to be correlated with $f^{[j]} \oplus f^{[j+1]}$ with correlation coefficients as large as $2^{-2.72}$. This could indicate that some terms of higher degree vanish when two neighbor bits are XOR'ed.

These results can be applied to construct second order approximations of the cipher. The best one is correlated to the real function with a correlation coefficient of $2^{-26.4}$, and a number of approximations with correlation coefficients of similar size. Preliminary investigations were made with other XOR sums. In general, sums of two bits can be approximated significantly better than single bits. The sum of neighboring bits does, however, seem to be the best

---

[2] Knowing the values of the counters may significantly improve both the Guess-and-Determine attack, the Guess-and-Verify attack as well as a Distinguishing attack even though obtaining the key from the counter values is prevented by the counter modification in the setup function.

approximation. Preliminary investigations show that approximations of sums of more than two bits have relatively small correlation coefficients.

It is not trivial to use second-order relations in linear cryptanalysis, and even the improved correlation values are not high enough for an attack as we know it. In an attack it would be necessary to include the counter, and set up relations between two consecutive outputs. We expect this to seriously complicate such an attack and make it infeasible.

3.7 Differential Analysis

Difference scheme: Given two inputs x' and x'', and their corresponding outputs y' and y'' (all in $\{0,1\}^n$), the following difference schemes were used:

- The *subtraction modulus* input and output differences are defined by $\Delta x = x' - x'' \mod 2^n$ and $\Delta y = y' - y'' \mod 2^n$, respectively.
- The *XOR* difference scheme is defined by $\Delta x = x' \oplus x''$ and $\Delta y = y' \oplus y''$.

Other differences are in principle possible, however, none of them were found to be better than the above ones.

Differentials of the g-function: Differentials of the g-function are investigated in [9]. While in principle, it would be necessary to calculate the probabilities of all 2^{64} possible differentials (which is not feasible given standard equipment), valuable insights can be gained by considering smaller versions of the g-functions. This way, 8-, 10-, 12-, 14-, 16- and 18-bit g-functions were considered.

For the XOR difference operator, the investigation of reduced g-functions revealed a simple structure of the most likely differential that persisted for all sizes. The input differences were characterized by a block of ones of size of approximately $\frac{3}{4}$ of the word length[3]. Making the reasonable assumption that these properties will be maintained in the 32-bit g-function, all input differences constituted by single blocks of ones were considered. The largest probability, and most likely the largest of all, found in this investigation was $2^{-11.57}$ for the differential (0x007FFFFE, 0xFF001FFF).

For the subtraction modulus difference, no such clear structure was observed, so the differentials with the largest probabilities could not be determined for the 32-bit g-function. However, the probabilities scale nicely with word length. Assuming that this scaling continues to 32-bit, the differential with the largest probability is expected to be of the order 2^{-17}. The probabilities are significantly lower compared those available for the XOR difference operator.

Higher order differentials were also briefly investigated, but due to the huge complexity, only g-functions with very small word length could be examined. This revealed that in order to obtain a differential with probability 1, the differential has to be of order equal to the word length, meaning that the non-linear order of the g-function is maximal, for the small word length g-functions examined.

---

[3] Other structural properties are also present, they are described in [8] in more detail.

Differentials of the full cipher: The differentials of the full cipher were extensively investigated in [8]. It was shown that any characteristic will involve at least 8 g-functions[4].

From analyzing the transition matrices for smaller word length g-functions it was found that after about four iterations of those, there resulted a steady state distribution of matrix elements close to uniform for both the XOR and subtraction modulus difference schemes. Using this and that the probability for the best characteristic, P_{max}, satisfies $P_{max} < 2^{-11.57\cdot 8} \ll 2^{-64}$, we do not expect any exploitable differential.

For a very simplified version of Rabbit, without rotations and with the XOR operation in the g-function replaced by an addition mod 2^{32}, higher order differentials can be used to break the IV setup scheme even for a relatively large number of iterations. If we consider another simplified version, with rotations, third order differential still has a high probability for one round. However, for more iterations, the security increases very quickly. Finally, using the XOR in the g-function completely destroys the applicability of higher order differentials based on modular subtraction and XOR.

3.8   Statistical Tests

The statistical tests on Rabbit were performed using the NIST Test Suite [15], the DIEHARD battery of tests [12] and the ENT test [20]. Tests were performed on the internal state as well as on the extracted output. Furthermore, we also conducted various statistical tests on the key setup function. Finally, we performed the same tests on a version of Rabbit where each state variable and counter variable was reduced to 8 bit. No weaknesses were found in any of these cases.

4   Performance

4.1   Software Performance

Encryption speeds for the specific processors were obtained by encrypting 8 kilobytes of data stored in RAM and measuring the number of clock cycles passed. For convenience, all 513 bits of the internal state are stored in an instance structure, occupying a total of 68 bytes. The presented memory requirements show the amount of memory allocated on the stack related to the calling convention (function arguments, return address and saved registers) and for temporary data. Memory for storing the key, instance, ciphertext and plaintext has not been included. All performance results, code size and memory requirements are listed in Table 1 below.

Intel Pentium Architecture: The performance was measured on a 1.0 GHz Pentium III processor and on a 1.7 GHz Pentium 4 processor. The speed-optimized

---

[4] probably it can be shown that 16 g-functions are the true minimum.

Table 1. Performance (in clock cycles or clock cycles per byte), code size and memory requirements (in bytes) for encryption / key setup / IV setup.

Processor	Performance	Code size	Memory
Pentium III	3.7/278/253	440/617/720	40/36/44
Pentium 4	5.1/486/648	698/516/762	16/36/28
ARM7	9.6/610/624	368/436/408	48/80/80
MIPS 4Kc	10.9/749/749	892/856/816	40/32/32

version of Rabbit was programmed in assembly language (using MMX instructions) inlined in C and compiled using the Intel C++ 7.1 compiler. A memory-optimized version can eliminate the need for memory, since the entire instance structure and temporary data can fit into the CPU registers.

ARM7 Architecture: A speed optimized ARM implementation was compiled and tested using ARM Developer Suite version 1.2 for ARM7TDMI. Performance was measured using the integrated ARMulator.

MIPS 4Kc Architecture: An assembly language version of Rabbit has been written for the MIPS 4Kc processor[5]. Development was done using The Embedded Linux Development Kit (ELDK), which includes GNU cross-development tools. Performance was measured on a 150 MHz processor running a Linux operating system.

8-bit Processors: The simplicity and small size of Rabbit makes it suitable for implementations on processors with limited resources such as 8-bit microcontrollers. Multiplying 32-bit integers is rather resource demanding using plain 32-bit arithmetics. However, squaring involves only ten 8-bit multiplications which reduces the workload by approximately a factor of two. Finally, the rotations in the algorithm have been chosen to correspond to simple byte-swapping.

4.2   Hardware Estimates

ASIC Performance: The toughest operation from a hardware point of view is the 32-bit squaring. If no separate squaring unit is available, the nature of squaring allows for some simplification over an ordinary 32×32 multiplication. It can be implemented as three 16×16 multiplications followed by addition. Being the most complex part of the algorithm, it determines the overall speed and contributes significantly to the gate count.

The eight internal state and counter words can be computed using between 1 and 8 parallel pipelines. Estimates for different versions are given in Table 2, giving gate count, die area and performance on a .18 micron technology. If greater

---

[5] The MIPS 4Kc processor has a reduced instruction set compared to other MIPS 4K series processors, which decreases performance.

Table 2. Hardware estimates for Rabbit on .18 micron technology

Pipelines	Gate count	Die area	Performance
1	28K	0.32 mm^2	3.7 GBit/s
2	35K	0.40 mm^2	6.2 GBit/s
4	57K	0.66 mm^2	9.3 GBit/s
8	100K	1.16 mm^2	12.4 GBit/s

speed is needed and if the gate count is of less importance, more advanced multiplication methods can be used. The gate count and die area numbers include key and IV setup.

FPGA Performance: When implementing Rabbit in an FPGA, the challenges will be similar to those in an ASIC implementation. Again the squaring operation will be the most complex element. Several FPGA families have dedicated multiplication units available (e.g., Xilinx Spartan 3 or Altera Cyclone II). In these architectures the latencies of the multiplier units are given to be 2.4 and 4.0 ns respectively. Based on a 2-pipeline design using 6 muliplier units, this will give us decryption performance of 8.9 Gbit/s and 5.3 Gbit/s respectively. If more multipliers are available, the number of pipelines can be increased, and throughputs of 17.8 Gbit/s and 10.7 Gbit/s will be achievable.

5   Conclusion

The stream cipher Rabbit was first presented at FSE 2003 [3], and no attacks against it have been published until now. With a measured encryption/decryption speed of 3.7 clock cycles per byte on a Pentium III processor, Rabbit does also provide very high performance. In this paper, we gave a concise description of the Rabbit design and some of the cryptanalytic results available.

Acknowledgements

The authors would like to thank Thomas Pedersen, Ove Scavenius, Jesper Christiansen, and Thomas Christensen for their contributions to the development, cryptanalysis, and implementation of the cipher Rabbit. In addition, we would like to thank Vincent Rijmen for several ideas and suggestions, and Ivan Damgaard and Tomas Bohr for many helpful inputs.

References

1. Armknecht, F., Krause, M.: Algebraic attacks on combiners with memory. In: Boneh, D. (ed.) CRYPTO 2003. LNCS, vol. 2729, pp. 162–175. Springer, Heidelberg (2003)
2. Aumasson, J.-P.: On a bias of Rabbit. In: Proc. SASC (2007),
   http://www.ecrypt.eu.org/stream/papersdir/2007/033.pdf

3. Boesgaard, M., Vesterager, M., Pedersen, T., Christiansen, J., Scavenius, O.: Rabbit: A new high-performance stream cipher. In: Johansson, T. (ed.) FSE 2003. LNCS, vol. 2887, pp. 307–329. Springer, Heidelberg (2003)
4. Courtois, N.: Fast algebraic attacks on stream ciphers with linear feedback. In: Boneh, D. (ed.) CRYPTO 2003. LNCS, vol. 2729, pp. 176–194. Springer, Heidelberg (2003)
5. Courtois, N.: Higher order correlation attacks, XL algorithm and cryptoanalysis of toyocrypt. In: Lee, P.J., Lim, C.H. (eds.) ICISC 2002. LNCS, vol. 2587, pp. 182–199. Springer, Heidelberg (2003)
6. Courtois, N., Meier, W.: Algebraic attacks on stream ciphers with linear feedback. In: Biham, E. (ed.) EUROCRYPT 2003. LNCS, vol. 2656, pp. 345–359. Springer, Heidelberg (2003)
7. Courtois, N., Pieprzyk, J.: Cryptanalysis of block ciphers with overdefined systems of equations. In: Zheng, Y. (ed.) ASIACRYPT 2002. LNCS, vol. 2501, pp. 267–287. Springer, Heidelberg (2002)
8. Cryptico A/S. Algebraic analysis of Rabbit. white paper (2003),
   `http://www.cryptico.com`
9. Cryptico A/S. Differential properties of the g-function. white paper (2003),
   `http://www.cryptico.com`
10. Cryptico A/S. Security analysis of the IV-setup for Rabbit. white paper (2003),
    `http://www.cryptico.com`
11. Daemen, J.: Cipher and hash function design strategies based on linear and differential cryptanalysis. PhD thesis, KU Leuven (March 1995)
12. Masaglia, G.: A battery of tests for random number generators (1996),
    `http://stat.fsu.edu/~geo/diehard.html`
13. Matsui, M.: Linear cryptanalysis method for DES cipher. In: Helleseth, T. (ed.) EUROCRYPT 1993. LNCS, vol. 765, pp. 386–397. Springer, Heidelberg (1994)
14. Meier, W., Staffelbach, O.: Fast correlation attacks on stream ciphers. In: Günther, C.G. (ed.) EUROCRYPT 1988. LNCS, vol. 330, pp. 301–314. Springer, Heidelberg (1988)
15. National Institute of Standards and Technology. A statistical test suite for the validation of random number generators and pseudo random number generators for cryptographic applications. NIST Special Publication 800–822 (2001),
    `http://csrc.nist.gov/rng`
16. Rijmen, V.: Analysis of Rabbit (September 2003),
    `http://www.cryptico.com/Files/filer/security_report.pdf`
17. Rueppel, R.: Analysis and Design of Stream Ciphers. Springer, Heidelberg (1986)
18. Scavenius, O., Boesgaard, M., Pedersen, T., Christiansen, J., Rijmen, V.: Periodic properties of counter assisted stream cipher. In: Okamoto, T. (ed.) CT-RSA 2004. LNCS, vol. 2964, pp. 39–53. Springer, Heidelberg (2004)
19. Shamir, A., Tsaban, B.: Guaranteeing the diversity of number generators. Information and Computation 171(2), 350–363 (2001)
20. Walker, J.: A pseudorandom number sequence test program (1998),
    `http://www.fourmilab.ch/random`

The Salsa20 Family of Stream Ciphers

Daniel J. Bernstein[*]

Department of Mathematics, Statistics, and Computer Science (M/C 249)
The University of Illinois at Chicago
Chicago, IL 60607–7045
snuffle6@box.cr.yp.to

Abstract. Salsa20 is a family of 256-bit stream ciphers designed in 2005 and submitted to eSTREAM, the ECRYPT Stream Cipher Project. Salsa20 has progressed to the third round of eSTREAM without any changes. The 20-round stream cipher Salsa20/20 is consistently faster than AES and is recommended by the designer for typical cryptographic applications. The reduced-round ciphers Salsa20/12 and Salsa20/8 are among the fastest 256-bit stream ciphers available and are recommended for applications where speed is more important than confidence. The fastest known attacks use $\approx 2^{153}$ simple operations against Salsa20/7, $\approx 2^{249}$ simple operations against Salsa20/8, and $\approx 2^{255}$ simple operations against Salsa20/9, Salsa20/10, etc. In this paper, the Salsa20 designer presents Salsa20 and discusses the decisions made in the Salsa20 design.

1 Introduction

A sender and receiver share a short secret key. They use the secret key to encrypt a series of messages. A message could be short, just a few bytes, but it could be much longer, perhaps gigabytes. The series of messages could be short, just one message, but it could be much longer, perhaps billions of messages.

The sender and receiver encrypt messages using an **encryption function**: a function that produces the first ciphertext from the key and the first plaintext, that produces the second ciphertext from the key and the second plaintext, etc.

An encryption function has to be fast. Many senders have to encrypt large volumes of data in very little time using limited resources. Many receivers are faced with even larger volumes of data—not just the legitimate messages but also a flood of forgery attempts. A slow encryption function can satisfy some senders and receivers, but my focus is on encryption functions suitable for a wider range of applications.

An encryption function also has to be secure. Many users are facing, or at least think that they are facing, years of cryptanalytic computations by well-funded attackers equipped with millions of fast parallel processors. Some users

[*] Permanent ID of this document: 31364286077dcdff8e4509f9ff3139ad. Date of this document: 2007.12.25. This work was supported by the National Science Foundation under grants CCR–9983950 and ITR–0716498, and by the Alfred P. Sloan Foundation.

M. Robshaw and O. Billet (Eds.): New Stream Cipher Designs, LNCS 4986, pp. 84–97, 2008.
© Springer-Verlag Berlin Heidelberg 2008

Table 1. Salsa20 software speeds; measured by the official eSTREAM benchmarking framework; sorted by final column. "576" means single-core cycles/byte to encrypt a 576-byte packet; "long" means single-core cycles/byte to encrypt a long stream.

				Cycles/byte					
			Salsa20	Salsa20/8		Salsa20/12		Salsa20/20	
Arch	MHz	Machine	software	long	576	long	576	long	576
amd64	3000	Xeon 5160 (6f6)	amd64-xmm6	1.88	2.07	2.80	3.25	3.93	4.25
amd64	2137	Core 2 Duo (6f6)	amd64-xmm6	1.88	2.07	2.57	2.80	3.91	4.33
ppc32	533	PowerPC G4 7410	ppc-altivec	1.99	2.14	2.74	2.88	4.24	4.39
x86	2137	Core 2 Duo (6f6)	x86-xmm5	2.06	2.28	2.80	3.15	4.32	4.70
amd64	2000	Athlon 64 X2 (15,75,2)	amd64-3	3.47	3.65	4.86	5.04	7.64	7.84
ppc64	2000	PowerPC G5 970	ppc-altivec	3.28	3.48	4.83	4.87	7.82	8.04
amd64	2391	Opteron (f5a)	amd64-3	3.78	3.96	5.33	5.51	8.42	8.62
amd64	2192	Opteron (f58)	amd64-3	3.82	4.18	5.35	5.73	8.42	8.78
x86	2000	Athlon 64 X2 (15,75,2)	x86-1	4.50	4.78	6.27	6.55	9.80	10.07
x86	900	Athlon (622)	x86-athlon	4.61	4.84	6.44	6.65	10.04	10.24
ppc64	1452	POWER4	merged	6.83	7.00	8.35	8.51	11.29	11.47
hppa	1000	PA-RISC 8900	merged	5.82	5.97	7.68	7.85	11.39	11.56
amd64	3000	Pentium D (f64)	amd64-xmm6	5.38	5.87	7.19	7.84	10.69	11.73
x86	1300	Pentium M (695)	x86-xmm5	5.30	5.53	7.44	7.70	11.70	11.98
x86	3000	Xeon (f26)	x86-xmm5	5.30	5.86	7.41	8.21	11.64	12.55
x86	3200	Xeon (f25)	x86-xmm5	5.30	5.84	7.40	8.15	11.63	12.59
x86	2800	Xeon (f29)	x86-xmm5	5.33	5.95	7.44	8.20	11.67	12.65
x86	3000	Pentium 4 (f41)	x86-xmm5	5.76	6.92	8.12	9.33	11.84	13.40
x86	1400	Pentium III (6b1)	x86-mmx	6.37	6.79	8.88	9.29	13.88	14.29
sparc	1050	UltraSPARC IV	sparc	6.65	6.76	9.21	9.33	14.34	14.45
x86	3200	Pentium D (f47)	x86-athlon	7.13	7.66	9.90	10.31	15.29	15.94
ia64	1500	Itanium II	merged	8.49	8.87	12.42	12.62	18.07	18.27
ia64	1400	Itanium II	merged	8.28	8.65	12.56	12.76	18.21	18.40

are satisfied with lower levels of security, but again my focus is on encryption functions suitable for a wider range of applications.

There is a conflict between these desiderata. One can reasonably conjecture, for example, that every function that encrypts data in 0.5 Core-2 cycles/byte is breakable. One can also conjecture that *almost every* function that encrypts data in 5 Core-2 cycles/byte is breakable. On the other hand, several unbroken submissions to eSTREAM, the ECRYPT Stream Cipher Project, encrypt data in fewer than 5 Core-2 cycles/byte.

In particular, my 20-round stream cipher Salsa20/20 encrypts data in 3.93 Core-2 cycles/byte. (For comparison: Matsui and Nakajima recently reported 9.2 Core-2 cycles/byte for 10-round AES using a pre-expanded 128-bit key. See [18].) The fastest known attack against Salsa20/20 is a 256-bit brute-force search. I recommend Salsa20/20 for encryption in typical cryptographic applications.

Reduced-round ciphers in the Salsa20 family are attractive options for users who value speed more highly than confidence. The 12-round stream cipher Salsa20/12 encrypts data in 2.80 Core-2 cycles/byte; the fastest known attack against Salsa20/12 is a 256-bit brute-force search. The 8-round stream cipher

Salsa20/8 encrypts data in 1.88 Core-2 cycles/byte; as discussed in Section 5, papers by several cryptanalysts have culminated in an attack against Salsa20/8 taking "only" 2^{249} operations, but this is far beyond any computation that will be carried out in the foreseeable future. Perhaps better attacks will be developed, but competing ciphers at similar speeds seem to be much more easily broken!

I hadn't heard of the Core 2 when I designed Salsa20. I was aiming for high speed on a wide variety of platforms; I don't find it surprising that Salsa20 is able to take advantage of a new platform. Table 1 shows Salsa20's software speeds on various CPUs.

This paper defines Salsa20 and explains the decisions that I made in the Salsa20 design. Section 2 discusses the selection of low-level operations used in Salsa20—a deliberately limited set, in particular with no S-boxes. Section 3 discusses the high-level data flow in Salsa20—again quite limited, in particular with no communication across blocks aside from a simple block counter. Section 4 discusses the middle-level structure of Salsa20. Section 5 reviews known attacks on Salsa20.

2   Low Level: Which Operations Are Used?

2.1   What Does Salsa20 Do?

The Salsa20 encryption function is a long chain of three simple operations on 32-bit words:

- 32-bit addition, producing the sum $a + b \bmod 2^{32}$ of two 32-bit words a, b;
- 32-bit exclusive-or, producing the xor $a \oplus b$ of two 32-bit words a, b; and
- constant-distance 32-bit rotation, producing the rotation $a \lll b$ of a 32-bit word a by b bits to the left, where b is constant.

On occasion I encounter the superstitious notion that these operations are "too simple." In fact, these operations can easily simulate any circuit, and are therefore capable of reaching the same security level as any other selection of operations. The real question for the cipher designer is whether a different mix of operations could achieve the same security level *at higher speed*.

2.2   Should There Be Integer Multiplications?

Some popular CPUs can quickly compute $xy \bmod 2^{64}$, given x, y. Some ciphers are designed to take advantage of this operation. Sometimes one of x, y is a constant; sometimes x, y are both variables.

The basic argument for integer multiplication is that the output bits are complicated functions of the input bits, mixing the inputs more thoroughly than a few simple integer operations.

The basic counterargument is that integer multiplication takes several cycles on the fastest CPUs, and many more cycles on other CPUs. For comparison, a comparably complex series of simple integer operations is always reasonably fast.

Multiplication might be slightly faster on some CPUs but it is not *consistently* fast.

I do like the amount of mixing provided by multiplication, and I'm impressed with the fast multiplication circuits included (generally for non-cryptographic reasons) in many CPUs, but the potential speed benefits don't seem big enough to outweigh the massive speed penalty on other CPUs. Similar comments apply to 64-bit additions, to 32-bit multiplications, and to variable-distance ("data-dependent") rotations.

A further argument against integer multiplication is that it increases the risk of timing leaks. What really matters is not the speed of integer multiplication, but the speed of *constant-time* integer multiplication, which is often much slower.

Example: On the Motorola PowerPC 7450 (G4e), a fairly common general-purpose CPU, the `mull` multiplication instruction usually takes 2 cycles (with 4-cycle latency), but it takes only 1 cycle (with 3-cycle latency) if "the 15 msbs of the B operand are either all set or all cleared." See [1, page 6.45]. The same is true for the 8641D, the newest CPU in the same family. It is possible to eliminate the timing leak on these CPUs by, e.g., using the floating-point multiplier, but moving data back and forth to floating-point registers costs CPU cycles, not to mention extra programming effort.

2.3   Should There Be S-Box Lookups?

An **S-box lookup** is an array lookup using an input-dependent index. Most ciphers are designed to take advantage of this operation. For example, typical high-speed AES software has several 1024-byte S-boxes, each of which converts 8-bit inputs to 32-bit outputs.

The basic argument for S-boxes is that a single table lookup can mangle its input quite thoroughly—more thoroughly than a chain of a few simple integer operations taking the same amount of time.

The basic counterargument is that a simple integer operation takes one or two 32-bit inputs rather than one 8-bit input, so it effectively mangles several 8-bit inputs at once. It is not obvious that a series of S-box lookups—even with rather large S-boxes, as in AES, increasing L1 cache pressure on large CPUs and forcing different implementation techniques for small CPUs—is faster than a comparably complex series of integer operations.

A further argument against S-box lookups is that, on most platforms, they are vulnerable to timing attacks. NIST's statement to the contrary in [19, Section 3.6.2] (table lookup is "not vulnerable to timing attacks") is erroneous. It is extremely difficult to work around this problem without sacrificing a tremendous amount of speed. See my paper [5] for much more information on this topic, including an example of successful remote extraction of a complete AES key.

For me, the timing-attack problem is decisive. For any particular security level, I'm not sure whether adding S-box lookups would gain speed, but I'm sure that adding *constant-time* S-box lookups would *not* gain speed.

Salsa20 is certainly not the first cipher without S-boxes. The Tiny Encryption Algorithm, published by Wheeler and Needham in [23], is a classic example of a reduced-instruction-set cipher: it is a long chain of 32-bit shifts, 32-bit xors, and 32-bit additions. IDEA, published by Lai, Massey, and Murphy in [17], is even older and almost as simple: it is a long chain of 16-bit additions, 16-bit xors, and multiplications modulo $2^{16} + 1$.

2.4   Should There Be Fewer Rotations?

Rotations account for about $1/3$ of the integer operations in Salsa20. If rotations are simulated by shift-shift-xor (as they are on the UltraSPARC and with XMM instructions) then they account for about $1/2$ of the integer operations in Salsa20. Replacing some of the rotations with a comparable number of additions might achieve comparable diffusion in less time.

The reader may be wondering why I used rotations rather than shifts. The basic argument for rotations is that one xor of a rotated quantity provides as much diffusion as two xors of shifted quantities. There does not appear to be a counterargument. Rotate-xor is faster than shift-shift-xor-xor on many CPUs and is never slower.

3   High Level: How Do Blocks Interact?

3.1   What Does Salsa20 Do?

Salsa20 expands a 256-bit key and a 64-bit nonce (unique message number) into a 2^{70}-byte stream. It encrypts a b-byte plaintext by xor'ing the plaintext with the first b bytes of the stream and discarding the rest of the stream. It decrypts a b-byte ciphertext by xor'ing the ciphertext with the first b bytes of the stream. There is no feedback from the plaintext or ciphertext into the stream.

Salsa20 generates the stream in 64-byte (512-bit) blocks. Each block is an independent hash of the key, the nonce, and a 64-bit block number; there is no chaining from one block to the next. The Salsa20 output stream can therefore be accessed randomly, and any number of blocks can be computed in parallel.

There are no hidden preprocessing costs in Salsa20. In particular, Salsa20 does not preprocess the key before generating a block; each block uses the key directly as input. Salsa20 also does not preprocess the nonce before generating a block; each block uses the nonce directly as input.

3.2   Should Encryption and Decryption Be Different?

The most common model of a stream cipher is that each ciphertext block is the xor of the plaintext block and the stream block at the same position. Each stream block is determined by its position, the nonce, the key, and the previous blocks of plaintext—equivalently, the previous blocks of ciphertext. Salsa20 follows this model, as does any block cipher in counter mode, OFB mode, CFB mode, et al.

Some ciphers mangle plaintext in a more complicated way. Consider, for example, AES in CBC mode: the nth plaintext block p_n is converted into the nth ciphertext block c_n by the formula $c_n = \mathrm{AES}_k(c_{n-1} \oplus p_n)$.

The popularity of CBC appears to be a historical accident. I have found very few people arguing for CBC over counter mode, and none of the arguments are even marginally convincing. On occasion I encounter the superstitious notion that encryption by xor is "too simple"; but a one-time pad (in conjunction with, for example, a Gilbert/MacWilliams/Sloane authenticator) provably achieves perfect secrecy (and any desired level of integrity), so there is obviously nothing wrong with xor.

There are several clear arguments against CBC. One disadvantage of CBC is that it requires different code for encryption and decryption, increasing costs in many contexts. Another disadvantage of CBC is that the extra communication from the cryptanalyst into the cipher state is a security threat; regaining the original level of confidence means adding rounds, taking additional time.

There is a security proof for CBC. How, then, can I claim that CBC is less secure than counter mode? One answer is that CBC's security guarantee assumes that the block cipher outputs *for attacker-controlled inputs* are indistinguishable from uniform, whereas counter mode applies the block cipher to *highly restricted* inputs, with many input bits forced to be 0. There are many examples in the literature of block ciphers for which CBC has been broken but counter mode is unbroken.

3.3   Should the Stream Depend on the Plaintext?

A more restricted model of a stream cipher is that ciphertext is plaintext xor stream, where the stream is determined by the nonce and the key. The plaintext and ciphertext do not affect the stream. Salsa20 follows this model, as does any block cipher in counter mode.

Some stream ciphers violate this model: they produce a stream that depends on the plaintext. One example is Helix, published in [13] by Ferguson, Whiting, Schneier, Kelsey, Lucks, and Kohno. The tweaked cipher Phelix was submitted to eSTREAM by Whiting, Schneier, Lucks, and Muller.

The basic argument for incorporating plaintext into the stream (specifically, incorporating plaintext blocks into subsequent blocks of the stream) is that this allows message authentication "for free." After encrypting the plaintext, one can generate a constant number of additional stream blocks and output those blocks as an authenticator of the plaintext.

One counterargument is that "free" is a wild exaggeration. Incorporating the plaintext into the stream takes time for every block, and generating an authenticator takes time for every message.

Another counterargument is that the incorporation of plaintext, being extra communication from the cryptanalyst into the cipher state, is a security threat. Regaining the original level of confidence means adding rounds, which takes additional time for every block.

Another counterargument is that state-of-the-art 128-bit authenticators can be computed in just a few cycles per byte. This may exceed the cost of "free" authentication for *legitimate* packets, but it is much less expensive than "free" authentication for *forged* packets, because it skips the cost of decryption.

For me, the cost of rejecting forged packets is decisive. Consider a denial-of-CPU-service attack in which an attacker floods a CPU with forged packets through a large network. In this situation, a traditional authenticator, such as Poly1305 from [4], is capable of handling a substantially larger flood than a "free" authenticator. See [9] for a new strategy to compute authenticators at even higher speeds.

The idea of incorporating plaintext into the stream clearly deserves further study for users who value authenticated-encryption performance more highly than forgery-rejection performance. In [8] I reported speed measurements for many authenticated-encryption methods; Phelix provided impressive speeds for authenticated encryption and verified decryption. Phelix was later eliminated from eSTREAM for reasons I consider frivolous, namely an "attack" against users who have trouble counting $1, 2, 3, \ldots$; I have no idea why this "attack" should eliminate an attractive option for users who *are* able to count $1, 2, 3, \ldots$.

3.4   Should There Be More State?

Salsa20 carries minimal state between blocks. Each block of the stream is a separate hash of the key, the nonce, and the block counter.

Most stream ciphers use a larger state, reusing portions of the first-block computation as input to the second-block computation, reusing portions of the second-block computation as input to the third-block computation, etc.

The argument for a larger state is that one does not need as many cipher rounds to achieve the same conjectured security level. Copying state across blocks seems to provide just as much mixing as the first few cipher rounds. A larger state therefore saves some time after the first block.

One counterargument is that a larger state reduces the number of communication channels that can be handled simultaneously by limited hardware. Ciphers that chain between blocks typically use 64 or more bytes for each channel. With Salsa20, each channel uses just 32 bytes for a key (less if several channels share a key), at most 8 bytes for a nonce, and at most 8 bytes for a block counter.

Another counterargument is that reuse forces serialization. Chaining between blocks prohibits random access to the stream (unless the stream is precomputed and saved, consuming memory). Chaining between blocks means that one cannot take advantage of extra hardware to reduce the latency of computing a long stream.

For me, the serialization problem is decisive. Inability to exploit parallelism is often a disaster. A few extra rounds are often undesirable but are never a disaster.

Case study (due to Wei Dai): As discussed in Section 4, there are 4 parallel 32-bit operations in each step of computing a Salsa20 block. The Core 2 CPU has more parallelism than this: it can carry out (in each core) 12 parallel 32-bit arithmetic operations. Fortunately, thanks to the lack of chaining, there are 16 parallel 32-bit operations in each step of computing 4 consecutive Salsa20 blocks.

3.5   Should Blocks Be Larger Than 64 Bytes?

Salsa20 hashes its key, nonce, and block counter into a 64-byte block. Similar structures could easily produce a larger block.

The basic argument for a larger block size, say 256 bytes, is that one does not need as many cipher rounds to achieve the same conjectured security level. Using a larger block size, like copying state across blocks, seems to provide just as much mixing as the first few cipher rounds. A larger state therefore saves time.

The basic counterargument is that a larger block size also loses time. On most CPUs, the communication cost of sweeping through a 256-byte block is a bottleneck; CPUs are designed for computations that don't involve so much data.

Another way that a larger block size loses time is by increasing the overhead for inconvenient message sizes. Expanding a 300-byte message to 512 bytes is much more expensive than expanding it to 320 bytes.

3.6   Should Keys Be Smaller Than 256 Bits?

The original eSTREAM call for submissions asked for 128-bit software ciphers and 80-bit hardware ciphers. Salsa20 is a 256-bit cipher; it allows smaller keys as options, but I recommend 256-bit keys.

Larger keys are more expensive than smaller keys, especially in hardware. Are they necessary for security?

The basic argument for 128-bit keys is that they will never be found by a brute-force attack. If checking about 2^{20} keys per second requires a CPU costing about 2^6 euros, then searching 2^{128} keys in a year will cost an inconceivable 2^{89} euros.

The basic counterargument is that 128-bit keys *will* be found by a brute-force attack. Here are three reasons that 2^{89} euro-years is a wild exaggeration, even without any improvements in computer technology:

- The attacker can succeed in far fewer than 2^{128} computations. He reaches success probability p after just $2^{128}p$ computations.
- More importantly, each key-checking circuit costs far less than 2^6 euros, at least in bulk: 2^{10} or more key-checking circuits can fit into a single chip, effectively reducing the attacker's costs by a factor of 2^{10}.
- Even more importantly, if the attacker simultaneously attacks (say) 2^{40} keys, he can effectively reduce his costs by a factor of 2^{40}.

One can counter the third cost reduction by putting extra randomness into nonces, but putting the same extra randomness into keys is less expensive. See [7] for a much more detailed discussion of these issues.

I predict that future cryptographers will settle on 256-bit keys as providing a comfortable security level. They will regard 80-bit keys as a silly historical mistake, and 128-bit keys as uncomfortably risky.

4   Medium Level: How Is a Block Generated?

4.1   What Does Salsa20 Do?

The goal of the Salsa20 core, as discussed in Section 3, is to produce a 64-byte block given a key, nonce, and block counter. The tools available to the Salsa20 core, as discussed in Section 2, are addition, xor, and constant-distance rotation of 32-bit words.

The Salsa20 core builds an array of 16 words containing the constant word 0x61707865, the first 4 key words, the constant word 0x3320646e, the 2 nonce words, the 2 block-counter words, the constant word 0x79622d32, the remaining 4 key words, and the constant word 0x6b206574. Strings are always interpreted in little-endian form. (Most current CPUs take extra time for big-endian accesses, while big-endian CPUs generally have good support for little-endian accesses.)

For example, here is the starting array for key $(1, 2, 3, 4, 5, \ldots, 32)$, nonce $(3, 1, 4, 1, 5, 9, 2, 6)$, and block 7:

> 0x61707865, 0x04030201, 0x08070605, 0x0c0b0a09,
>
> 0x100f0e0d, 0x3320646e, 0x01040103, 0x06020905,
>
> 0x00000007, 0x00000000, 0x79622d32, 0x14131211,
>
> 0x18171615, 0x1c1b1a19, 0x201f1e1d, 0x6b206574.

The diagonal constants are the same for every block, every nonce, and every 32-byte key. As an extra (non-recommended) option, Salsa20 can use a 16-byte key, repeated to form a 32-byte key; in this case the diagonal constants change to 0x61707865, 0x3120646e, 0x79622d36, 0x6b206574. Salsa20 can also use a 10-byte key, zero-padded to form a 16-byte key; in this case the diagonal constants change to 0x61707865, 0x3120646e, 0x79622d30, 0x6b206574.

Salsa20 now modifies each below-diagonal word as follows: add the diagonal and above-diagonal words, rotate left by 7 bits, and xor into the below-diagonal words. The result is the following array:

> 0x61707865, 0x04030201, 0x08070605, 0x95b0c8b6,
>
> 0xd3c83331, 0x3320646e, 0x01040103, 0x06020905,
>
> 0x00000007, 0x91b3379b, 0x79622d32, 0x14131211,
>
> 0x18171615, 0x1c1b1a19, 0x130804a0, 0x6b206574.

The underlined words were added, and the next word was modified.

Salsa20 then modifies each below-below-diagonal word as follows: add the diagonal and below-diagonal words, rotate left by 9 bits, and xor into the below-below-diagonal words. The result is the following array:

> 0x61707865, 0x04030201, 0xdc64a31d, 0x95b0c8b6,
>
> 0xd3c83331, 0x3320646e, 0x01040103, 0xa45e5d04,
>
> 0x71572c6d, 0x91b3379b, 0x79622d32, 0x14131211,
>
> 0x18171615, 0xbb230990, 0x130804a0, 0x6b206574.

Salsa20 continues down each column, rotating left by 13 bits:

> 0x61707865, 0xcc266b9b, <u>0xdc64a31d</u>, <u>0x95b0c8b6</u>,
>
> <u>0xd3c83331</u>, 0x3320646e, 0x95f3bcee, <u>0xa45e5d04</u>,
>
> <u>0x71572c6d</u>, <u>0x91b3379b</u>, 0x79622d32, 0xf0a45550,
>
> 0xf3e4deb6, <u>0xbb230990</u>, <u>0x130804a0</u>, 0x6b206574.

Salsa20 then modifies the diagonal words, this time rotating left by 18 bits:

> 0x4dfdec95, <u>0xcc266b9b</u>, <u>0xdc64a31d</u>, 0x95b0c8b6,
>
> 0xd3c83331, 0xe78e794b, <u>0x95f3bcee</u>, <u>0xa45e5d04</u>,
>
> <u>0x71572c6d</u>, 0x91b3379b, 0xf94fe453, <u>0xf0a45550</u>,
>
> <u>0xf3e4deb6</u>, <u>0xbb230990</u>, 0x130804a0, 0xa272317e.

Salsa20 finally transposes the array:

> 0x4dfdec95, 0xd3c83331, 0x71572c6d, 0xf3e4deb6,
>
> 0xcc266b9b, 0xe78e794b, 0x91b3379b, 0xbb230990,
>
> 0xdc64a31d, 0x95f3bcee, 0xf94fe453, 0x130804a0,
>
> 0x95b0c8b6, 0xa45e5d04, 0xf0a45550, 0xa272317e.

That's the end of one round.

In the second round, Salsa20 performs exactly the same modifications, with the same rotation counts, again starting with the below-diagonal words and finishing with the diagonal words, and finally transposing the array:

> 0xba2409b1, 0x1b7cce6a, 0x29115dcf, 0x5037e027,
>
> 0x37b75378, 0x348d94c8, 0x3ea582b3, 0xc3a9a148,
>
> 0x825bfcb9, 0x226ae9eb, 0x63dd7748, 0x7129a215,
>
> 0x4effd1ec, 0x5f25dc72, 0xa6c3d164, 0x152a26d8.

That's the end of two rounds. Note that implementors can eliminate the transposes and perform the second round on rows instead of columns.

Salsa20/r continues for a total of r rounds, modifying each word r times. For example, Salsa20/20 produces the following array:

> 0x58318d3e, 0x0292df4f, 0xa28d8215, 0xa1aca723,
>
> 0x697a34c7, 0xf2f00ba8, 0x63e9b0a1, 0x27250e3a,
>
> 0xb1c7f1f3, 0x62066edc, 0x66d3ccf1, 0xb0365cf3,
>
> 0x091ad09e, 0x64f0c40f, 0xd60d95ea, 0x00be78c9.

After these r rounds, Salsa20 adds the final 4×4 array to the original array to obtain its 64-byte output block. For example, here is the 64-byte output block for Salsa20/20:

0xb9a205a3, 0x0695e150, 0xaa94881a, 0xadb7b12c,

0x798942d4, 0x26107016, 0x64edb1a4, 0x2d27173f,

0xb1c7f1fa, 0x62066edc, 0xe035fa23, 0xc4496f04,

0x2131e6b3, 0x810bde28, 0xf62cb407, 0x6bdede3d.

4.2   Should Key Words and Nonce Words Be Separated?

Salsa20 puts its key k and its nonce/counter n into a single array. It uses the k words to modify the k words, the k words to modify the n words, the n words to modify the n words, and the n words to modify the k words. After a few rounds there is no reasonable distinction between the k parts of the array and the n parts of the array. Both the k words and the n words are used as output. The final addition prevents the cryptanalyst from inverting the computation.

For comparison, a "block cipher" uses the k words to modify the k words, the k words to modify the n words, and the n words to modify the n words; but it *never* uses the n words to modify the k words. The k words are kept separate from the n words through the entire computation. Only the n words are used as output. The omission of k prevents the cryptanalyst from inverting the computation.

The basic argument for a block cipher—for keeping the k words independent of the n words—is that, for fixed k, it is easy to make a block cipher be an invertible function of n. But this feature seems to be of purely historical interest. Invertible stream generation is certainly not necessary for encryption.

The basic disadvantage of a block cipher is that the k words consume valuable communication resources. A 64-byte block cipher with a 32-byte key would need to repeatedly sweep through 96 bytes of memory (plus a few bytes of temporary storage) for its 64 bytes of output; in contrast, Salsa20 repeatedly sweeps through just 64 bytes of memory (plus a few bytes of temporary storage) for its 64 bytes of output.

I also see each use of a k word as a missed opportunity to spread changes through the n words. The time wasted is not very large—in AES, for example, 80% of the table lookups and most of the xor inputs are n-dependent—and can be reduced by precomputation in contexts where the cost of memory is unnoticeable; but dropping the barrier between k and n achieves the same conjectured security level at higher speed.

4.3   Should There Be More Code?

Salsa20 can be implemented as a loop of identical rounds, where each round modifies each word once and then transposes the result. Or it can be implemented as a loop of identical double-rounds, where each double-round modifies each word twice, without any transposition. Either way, the Salsa20 code is very short.

Some ciphers have more code: e.g., using different structures for the first and last rounds, or even using different code in every round. MARS, published by

Burwick et al. in [10], has about one third of its operations in initial and final rounds that look quite different from the remaining rounds.

The basic argument for using two different kinds of rounds is the idea that attacks will have some extra difficulty passing through the switch from one kind to another. This extra difficulty would allow the cipher to reach the same security level with fewer rounds.

The basic counterargument is that extra code is expensive in many contexts. It increases pressure on a CPU's L1 cache, for example, and it increases the minimum size of a hardware implementation.

Even if larger code were free, I wouldn't feel comfortable reducing the number of rounds. The cryptanalytic literature contains a huge number of examples of how extra rounds increase security; it's much less clear how much benefit is obtained from switching round types.

4.4   Should There Be Faster Diffusion Among Words?

During the first round of Salsa20, there is no communication between words in different columns; each column has its own chain of 12 operations modifying the words in that column. During the second round, there is no communication between words that were in different rows; each (transposed) row has its own chain of 12 operations modifying the words in that row. Et cetera.

There are pairs (i, j) such that a change in word i has no opportunity to affect word j until the third round. A different communication structure would allow much faster diffusion of changes through all 16 words. On the other hand, it doesn't appear to be possible to achieve much faster diffusion of changes through all 512 *bits*.

The current communication structure has speed benefits on CPUs that do not have many fast registers. For example, my software for the Pentium III relies on the ability to operate locally within 4 words for a little while.

4.5   Should There Be Modifications Other Than Xor-a-Rotated-Sum?

There are many plausible ways to modify each word in a column using other words in the same column. I settled on "xor a rotated sum" as bouncing back and forth between incompatible structures on the critical path. I chose "xor a rotated sum" over "add a rotated xor" for simple performance reasons: the x86 architecture has a three-operand addition (LEA) but not a three-operand xor.

4.6   Should There Be Other Rotation Distances?

I chose the Salsa20 rotation distances 7, 11, 13, 18 as doing a good job of spreading every low-weight change across bit positions within a few rounds. The exact choice of distances doesn't seem very important.

My software uses SIMD vector operations for the Pentium 4, the Core 2, et al. These operations rely on the fact that each column uses the same sequence of distances.

5   Cryptanalysis

This section briefly reviews the history of third-party cryptanalysis of Salsa20.

2005.05 [6]: I presented Salsa20 at the ECRYPT Symmetric-Key Encryption Workshop in Aarhus. I offered a $1000 prize for the most interesting Salsa20 cryptanalysis made public that year.

2005.10 [11]: Crowley posted a 2^{165}-operation attack on Salsa20/5. Crowley received the $1000 prize and presented his attack at the 2006.02 ECRYPT State of the Art of Stream Ciphers workshop in Leuven. The attack works forwards from a small known input difference to a biased bit 3 rounds later, and works 2 rounds backwards from an output after guessing 160 relevant key bits.

2006.12 [14]: Fischer, Meier, Berbain, Biasse, and Robshaw reported a 2^{177}-operation attack on Salsa20/6 (and a much faster attack on Salsa20/5, clearly breaking Salsa20/5) at the Indocrypt conference in Calcutta. The attack works forwards from a small known input difference to a biased bit 4 rounds later, and works 2 rounds backwards from an output after guessing 160 relevant key bits.

2007.01 [22]: Tsunoo, Saito, Kubo, Suzaki, and Nakashima reported a 2^{184}-operation attack on Salsa20/7 (and a much faster attack on Salsa20/6, clearly breaking Salsa20/6) at the ECRYPT State of the Art of Stream Ciphers workshop in Bochum. The attack works forwards from a small known input difference to a biased bit 4 rounds later, and works 3 rounds backwards from an output after guessing 171 highly relevant key bits.

2007.12 [2]: Aumasson, Fischer, Khazaei, Meier, and Rechberger reported a 2^{249}-operation attack on Salsa20/8 and a 2^{153}-operation attack on Salsa20/7. The Salsa20/8 attack works forwards from a small known input difference to a biased bit 4 rounds later, and works 4 rounds backwards from an output after guessing 228 extremely relevant key bits.

References

1. MPC7450 RISC microprocessor family reference manual, Freescale Semiconductor (2005),
   http://www.freescale.com/files/32bit/doc/refmanual/MPC7450UM.pdf
2. Aumasson, J.-P., Fischer, S., Khazaei, S., Meier, W., Rechberger, C.: New features of Latin dances: analysis of Salsa, ChaCha, and Rumba (2007),
   http://eprint.iacr.org/2007/472
3. Barua, R., Lange, T. (eds.): INDOCRYPT 2006. LNCS, vol. 4329. Springer, Heidelberg (2006) See [14]
4. Bernstein, D.J.: The Poly1305-AES message-authentication code in [15], pp. 32–49 (2005) (ID 0018d9551b5546d97c340e0dd8cb5750),
   http://cr.yp.to/papers.html#poly1305
5. Bernstein, D.J.: Cache-timing attacks on AES (2005) (ID cd9faae9bd5308c440df50fc26a517b4),
   http://cr.yp.to/papers.html#cachetiming
6. Bernstein, D.J.: The Salsa20 stream cipher, slides of talk. In: ECRYPT STVL Workshop on Symmetric Key Encryption (2005),
   http://cr.yp.to/talks.html#2005.05.26

7. Bernstein, D.J.: Understanding brute force. In: Workshop Record of ECRYPT STVL Workshop on Symmetric Key Encryption, eSTREAM report 2005/036 (2005) (ID 73e92f5b71793b498288efe81fe55dee), http://cr.yp.to/papers.html#bruteforce

8. Bernstein, D.J.: Cycle counts for authenticated encryption. In: Workshop Record of SASC 2007: The State of the Art of Stream Ciphers, eSTREAM report 2007/015 (2007) (ID be6b4df07eb1ae67aba9338991b78388), http://cr.yp.to/papers.html#aecycles

9. Bernstein, D.J.: Polynomial evaluation and message authentication (2007) (ID b1ef3f2d385a926123e1517392e20f8c), http://cr.yp.to/papers.html#pema

10. Burwick, C., Coppersmith, D., D'Avignon, E., Gennaro, R., Halevi, S., Jutla, C., Matyas Jr., S.M., OĆonnor, L., Peyravian, M., Safford, D., Zunic, N.: MARS: a candidate cipher for AES (1999), www.research.ibm.com/security/mars.pdf

11. Crowley, P.: Truncated differential cryptanalysis of five rounds of Salsa20. In: Workshop Record of SASC 2006: Stream Ciphers Revisted, eSTREAM technical report 2005/073 (2005), http://www.ecrypt.eu.org/stream/papers.html

12. Davies, D.W. (ed.): EUROCRYPT 1991. LNCS, vol. 547. Springer, Heidelberg (1991) See [17]

13. Ferguson, N., Whiting, D., Schneier, B., Kelsey, J., Lucks, S., Kohno, T.: Helix: fast encryption and authentication in a single cryptographic primitive, in [16], pp. 330–346 (2003), http://www.macfergus.com/helix/

14. Fischer, S., Meier, W., Berbain, C., Biasse, J.-F., Robshaw, M.J.B.: Non-randomness in eSTREAM candidates Salsa20 and TSC-4, in [3], pp. 2–16 (2006)

15. Gilbert, H., Handschuh, H. (eds.): FSE 2005. LNCS, vol. 3557. Springer, Heidelberg (2005), See [4]

16. Johansson, T. (ed.): FSE 2003. LNCS, vol. 2887. Springer, Heidelberg (2003), See [13]

17. Lai, X., Massey, J.L., Murphy, S.: Markov ciphers and differential cryptanalysis, in [12], pp. 17–38 (1991)

18. Matsui, M., Nakajima, J.: On the power of bitslice implementation on Intel Core2 Processor, in [20], pp. 121–134 (2007)

19. Nechvatal, J., Barker, E., Bassham, L., Burr, W., Dworkin, M., Foti, J., Roback, E.: Report on the development of the Advanced Encryption Standard (AES). Journal of Research of the National Institute of Standards and Technology 106 (2001), http://nvl.nist.gov/pub/nistpubs/jres/106/3/cnt106-3.htm

20. Paillier, P., Verbauwhede, I. (eds.): CHES 2007. LNCS, vol. 4727. Springer, Heidelberg (2007) See [18]

21. Preneel, B. (ed.): FSE 1994. LNCS, vol. 1008. Springer, Heidelberg (1995) See [23]

22. Tsunoo, Y., Saito, T., Kubo, H., Suzaki, T., Nakashima, H.: Differential cryptanalysis of Salsa20/8. In: Workshop Record of SASC 2007: The State of the Art of Stream Ciphers, eSTREAM report 2007/010 (2007), http://www.ecrypt.eu.org/stream/papers.html

23. Wheeler, D.J., Needham, R.M.: TEA, a tiny encryption algorithm, in [21], pp. 363–366 (1995)

SOSEMANUK, a Fast Software-Oriented Stream Cipher*

Côme Berbain[1], Olivier Billet[1], Anne Canteaut[2], Nicolas Courtois[3],
Henri Gilbert[1], Louis Goubin[4], Aline Gouget[5], Louis Granboulan[6],
Cédric Lauradoux[2], Marine Minier[7], Thomas Pornin[8], and Hervé Sibert[9]

[1] Orange Labs, France,
{come.berbain,olivier.billet,henri.gilbert}@orange-ftgroup.com
[2] INRIA-Rocquencourt, projet CODES, France
{anne.canteaut,cedric.lauradoux}@inria.fr
[3] University College of London, UK
n.courtois@ucl.ac.uk
[4] Université de Versailles, France
louis.goubin@prism.uvsq.fr
[5] Gemalto, France
aline.gouget@gemalto.com
[6] EADS, France
louis.granboulan@eads.net
[7] INSA de Lyon, France
marine.minier@insa-lyon.fr
[8] Cryptolog International, France
thomas.pornin@cryptolog.com
[9] NXP Semiconductors, France
herve.sibert@nxp.com

Abstract. SOSEMANUK is a new synchronous software-oriented stream
cipher, corresponding to Profile 1 of the ECRYPT call for stream cipher
primitives. Its key length is variable between 128 and 256 bits. It accommodates a 128-bit initial value. Any key length is claimed to achieve
128-bit security. The SOSEMANUK cipher uses both some basic design
principles from the stream cipher SNOW 2.0 and some transformations
derived from the block cipher SERPENT. SOSEMANUK aims at improving SNOW 2.0 both from the security and from the efficiency points of
view. Most notably, it uses a faster IV-setup procedure. It also requires
a reduced amount of static data, yielding better performance on several
architectures.

1 Introduction

This paper presents a proposal for a new synchronous software-oriented stream
cipher, named SOSEMANUK. The SOSEMANUK cipher uses both basic design principles from the stream cipher SNOW 2.0 [12] and transformations derived from

---

* Work partially supported by the French Ministry of Research RNRT Project "X-
CRYPT" and by the European Commission via ECRYPT network of excellence
IST-2002-507932.

M. Robshaw and O. Billet (Eds.): New Stream Cipher Designs, LNCS 4986, pp. 98–118, 2008.

the block cipher SERPENT [3]. For this reason, its name should refer both to SERPENT and SNOW. However, it is well-known that snow snakes do not exist since snakes either hibernate or move to warmer climes during the winter.Instead SOSEMANUK is a popular sport played by the Eastern Canadian tribes. It consists in throwing a wooden stick along a snow bank as far as possible. Its name means snowsnake in the Cree language, since the stick looks like a snake in the snow. *Kwakweco-cime win* is a variant of the same game but does not sound like an appropriate cipher name. More details on the SOSEMANUK game and a demonstration can be found in [19] and [24].

The SOSEMANUK stream cipher is a new synchronous stream cipher dedicated to software applications. Its key length is variable between 128 and 256 bits. Any key length is claimed to achieve 128-bit security. It is inspired by the design of SNOW 2.0 which is very elegant and achieves a very high throughput on a Pentium 4. SOSEMANUK aims at improving SNOW 2.0 from two respects. First, it avoids some structural properties which may appear as potential weaknesses, even if the SNOW 2.0 cipher with a 128-bit key resists all known attacks. Second, efficiency is improved on several architectures by reducing the internal state size, thus allowing for a more direct mapping of data on the processor registers. SOSEMANUK also requires a reduced amount of static data; this lower data cache pressure yields better performance on several architectures. Another strength of SOSEMANUK is that its key setup procedure is based on a reduced version of the well-known block cipher SERPENT, improving classical initialization procedures both from an efficiency and a security point of view.

2   Specification

2.1   SERPENT and Derivatives

SERPENT [3] is a block cipher proposed as an AES candidate. SERPENT operates over blocks of 128 bits which are split into four 32-bit words, which are then combined in so-called "bitslice" mode. SERPENT can thus be defined as working over quartets of 32-bit words. We number SERPENT input and output quartets from 0 to 3, and write them in the order: (Y_3, Y_2, Y_1, Y_0). Y_0 is the least significant word, and contains the least significant bits of the 32 4-bit inputs to the SERPENT S-boxes. When SERPENT output is written into 16 bytes, the Y_i values are written following the little-endian convention (least significant byte first), and Y_0 is output first, then Y_1, and so on.

From SERPENT, we define two primitives called *Serpent1* and *Serpent24*.

Serpent1. A SERPENT rounds consist of, in that order:

- a subkey addition, by bitwise exclusive or;
- S-box application (which is expressed as a set of bitwise combinations between the four running 32-bit words, in bitslice mode);
- a linear bijective transformation (which amounts to a few XORs, shifts and rotations in bitslice mode), see Appendix A.2.

Serpent1 is one round of SERPENT, without the key addition and the linear transformation. SERPENT uses eight distinct S-boxes (see A.1 for details), numbered from S_0 to S_7 on 4-bit words. We define *Serpent1* as the application of S_2, in bitslice mode. This is the third S-box layer of SERPENT. *Serpent1* takes four 32-bit words as input, and provides four 32-bit words as output.

Serpent24. *Serpent24* is SERPENT reduced to 24 rounds, instead of the full version of SERPENT which counts 32 rounds. *Serpent24* is equal to the first 24 rounds of SERPENT, where the last round (the 24th) is a complete one and includes a complete round with the linear transformation and an XOR with the 25th subkey. In other words, the 24th round of *Serpent24* is thus equivalent to the thirty-second round of SERPENT, except that it contains the linear transformation and that the 24th and 25th subkeys are used (32nd and 33rd subkeys in SERPENT). Thus, the last round equation on Page 224 in [3] is

$$R_{23}(X) = L\left(\hat{S}_{23}(X \oplus \hat{K}_{23})\right) \oplus \hat{K}_{24} .$$

Serpent24 uses only 25 128-bit subkeys, which are the first 25 subkeys produced by the SERPENT key schedule. In SOSEMANUK, *Serpent24* is used for the initialization step, only in encryption mode. Decryption is not used.

2.2   The LFSR

Underlying finite field. Most of the stream cipher internal state is held in a LFSR containing 10 elements of $\mathbb{F}_{2^{32}}$, the field with 2^{32} elements. The elements of $\mathbb{F}_{2^{32}}$ are represented exactly as in SNOW 2.0. We recall this representation here. Let $\mathbb{F}_2$ denote the finite field with 2 elements. Let β be a root of the primitive polynomial:

$$Q(X) = X^8 + X^7 + X^5 + X^3 + 1$$

on $\mathbb{F}_2[X]$. We define the field $\mathbb{F}_{2^8}$ as the quotient $\mathbb{F}_2[X]/Q(X)$. Each element in $\mathbb{F}_{2^8}$ is represented using the basis $(\beta^7, \beta^6, ...\beta, 1)$. Since the chosen polynomial is primitive, then β is a multiplicative generator of all invertible elements of $\mathbb{F}_{2^8}$: every non-zero element in $\mathbb{F}_{2^8}$ is equal to β^k for some integer k $(0 \leq k \leq 254)$. Any element in $\mathbb{F}_{2^8}$ is identified with an 8-bit integer by the following bijection:

$$\phi: \quad \mathbb{F}_{2^8} \quad \rightarrow \{0, 1, \ldots, 255\}$$
$$x = \textstyle\sum_{i=0}^{7} x_i \beta^i \mapsto \quad \textstyle\sum_{i=0}^{7} x_i 2^i$$

where each x_i is either 0 or 1. For instance, β^{23} is represented by the integer $\phi(\beta^{23}) = \mathtt{0xE1}$ (in hexadecimal).Therefore, the addition of two elements in $\mathbb{F}_{2^8}$ corresponds to a bitwise XOR between the corresponding integer representations. The multiplication by β is a left shift by one bit of the integer representation, followed by an XOR with a fixed mask if the most significant bit dropped by the shift equals 1.

Let α be a root of the primitive polynomial

$$P(X) = X^4 + \beta^{23} X^3 + \beta^{245} X^2 + \beta^{48} X + \beta^{239}$$

on $\mathbb{F}_{2^8}[X]$. The field $\mathbb{F}_{2^{32}}$ is then defined as the quotient $\mathbb{F}_{2^8}[X]/P(X)$, i.e., its elements are represented with the basis $(\alpha^3, \alpha^2, \alpha, 1)$. Any element in $\mathbb{F}_{2^{32}}$ is identified with a 32-bit integer by the following bijection:

$$\psi: \quad \begin{array}{ccc} \mathbb{F}_{2^{32}} & \to & \{0, 1, \ldots, 2^{32} - 1\} \\ y = \sum_{i=0}^{3} y_i \alpha^i & \mapsto & \sum_{i=0}^{3} \phi(y_i) 2^{8i} \end{array}$$

Thus, the addition of two elements in $\mathbb{F}_{2^{32}}$ corresponds to a bitwise XOR between their integer representations. This operation will hereafter be denoted by $\oplus$. SOSEMANUK also uses multiplications and divisions of elements in $\mathbb{F}_{2^{32}}$ by α. Multiplication of $z \in \mathbb{F}_{2^{32}}$ by α corresponds to a left shift by 8 bits of $\psi(z)$, followed by an XOR with a 32-bit mask which depends only on the most significant byte of $\psi(z)$. Division of $z \in \mathbb{F}_{2^{32}}$ by α is a right shift by 8 bits of $\psi(z)$, followed by an XOR with a 32-bit mask which depends only on the least significant byte of $\psi(z)$.

Definition of the LFSR. The LFSR operates over elements of $\mathbb{F}_{2^{32}}$. The initial state, at $t = 0$, entails the ten 32-bit values s_1 to s_{10}. At each step, a new value is computed, with the following recurrence:

$$s_{t+10} = s_{t+9} \oplus \alpha^{-1} s_{t+3} \oplus \alpha s_t, \quad \forall t \geq 1$$

and the register is shifted (see Figure 1 for an illustration of the LFSR).

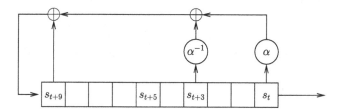

Fig. 1. The LFSR

The LFSR is associated with the following feedback polynomial:

$$\pi(X) = \alpha X^{10} + \alpha^{-1} X^7 + X + 1 \in \mathbb{F}_{2^{32}}[X]$$

Since the LFSR is non-singular and since π is a primitive polynomial, the sequence of 32-bit words $(s_t)_{t \geq 1}$ is periodic and has maximal period $(2^{320} - 1)$.

2.3   The Finite State Machine

The Finite State Machine (FSM) is a component with 64 bits of memory, corresponding to two 32-bit registers $R1$ and $R2$. At each step, the FSM takes as inputs some words from the LFSR state; it updates the memory bits and produces a 32-bit output. The FSM operates on the LFSR state at time $t \geq 1$ as follows:

$$FSM_t : (R1_{t-1}, R2_{t-1}, s_{t+1}, s_{t+8}, s_{t+9}) \mapsto (R1_t, R2_t, f_t)$$

where

$$R1_t = (R2_{t-1} + \text{mux}(\text{lsb}(R1_{t-1}), s_{t+1}, s_{t+1} \oplus s_{t+8})) \bmod 2^{32} \tag{1}$$
$$R2_t = Trans(R1_{t-1}) \tag{2}$$
$$f_t = (s_{t+9} + R1_t \bmod 2^{32}) \oplus R2_t \tag{3}$$

where $\text{lsb}(x)$ is the least significant bit of x, $\text{mux}(c, x, y)$ is equal to x if $c = 0$, or to y if $c = 1$. The internal transition function $Trans$ on $\mathbb{F}_{2^{32}}$ is defined by

$$Trans(z) = (M \times z \bmod 2^{32})_{<<<7}$$

where M is the constant value $0x54655307$ (the hexadecimal expression of the first ten decimals of π) and $<<<$ denotes bitwise rotation of a 32-bit value (by 7 bits here).

2.4   Output Transformation

The outputs of the FSM are grouped by four, and *Serpent1* is applied to each group; the result is then combined by XOR with the corresponding dropped values from the LFSR, to produce the output values z_t:

$$(z_{t+3}, z_{t+2}, z_{t+1}, z_t) = Serpent1(f_{t+3}, f_{t+2}, f_{t+1}, f_t) \oplus (s_{t+3}, s_{t+2}, s_{t+1}, s_t)$$

Four consecutive rounds of SOSEMANUK are depicted in Figure 2.

2.5   SOSEMANUK **Workflow**

The SOSEMANUK cipher combines the FSM and the LFSR to produce the output values z_t. Time $t = 0$ designates the internal state after initialization; the first output value is z_1. Figure 3 gives a graphical overview of SOSEMANUK.

At time $t \geq 1$, we perform the following operations:

- The FSM is updated: $R1_t$, $R2_t$ and the intermediate value f_t are computed from $R1_{t-1}$, $R2_{t-1}$, s_{t+1}, s_{t+8} and s_{t+9}.
- The LFSR is updated: s_{t+10} is computed, from s_t, s_{t+3} and s_{t+9}. The value s_t is sent to an internal buffer, and the LFSR is shifted.

Once every four steps, four output values z_t, z_{t+1}, z_{t+2} and z_{t+3} are produced from the accumulated values $f_t, f_{t+1}, f_{t+2}, f_{t+3}$ and $s_t, s_{t+1}, s_{t+2}, s_{t+3}$. Thus, SOSEMANUK produces 32-bit values. We recommend encoding them into groups of four bytes using the little-endian convention, because it is faster on the most widely used high-end software platform (x86-compatible PC), and because SERPENT uses that convention.

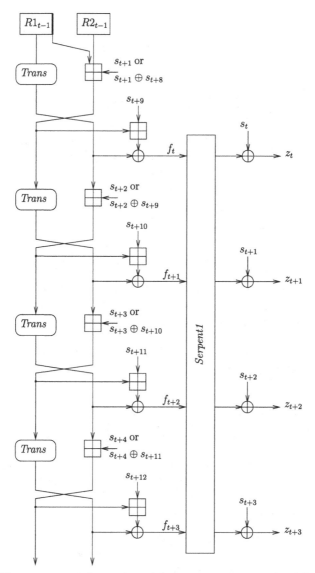

Fig. 2. The output transformation on four consecutive rounds of SOSEMANUK

Therefore, the first four iterations of SOSEMANUK are as follows.

- The LFSR initial state contains values s_1 to s_{10}; no value s_0 is defined. The FSM initial state contains $R1_0$ and $R2_0$.
- During the first step, $R1_1$, $R2_1$ and f_1 are computed from $R1_0$, $R2_0$, s_2, s_9 and s_{10}.
- The first step produces the buffered intermediate values s_1 and f_1.

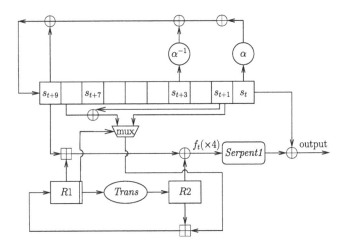

Fig. 3. An overview of SOSEMANUK

- During the first step, the feedback word s_{11} is computed from s_{10}, s_4 and s_1, and the internal state of the LFSR is updated, leading to a new state composed of s_2 to s_{11}.
- The first four output values are z_1, z_2, z_3 and z_4, and are computed using one application of *Serpent1* over (f_4, f_3, f_2, f_1), whose output is combined by XORs with (s_4, s_3, s_2, s_1).

2.6   Key Initialization and IV Injection

The SOSEMANUK initialization process is split into two steps:

- the key schedule, which processes the secret key but does not depend on the IV; and
- the IV injection, which uses the output of the key schedule and the IV. This initializes the stream cipher internal state.

Key schedule. The key setup corresponds to the *Serpent24* key schedule, which produces 25 128-bit subkeys, as 100 32-bit words. These 25 128-bit subkeys are identical to the first 25 128-bit subkeys produced by the plain SERPENT key schedule.

SERPENT accepts any key length from 1 to 256 bits; hence, SOSEMANUK may work with exactly the same keys. However, since SOSEMANUK aims at 128-bit security; its key length must then be at least 128 bits. Therefore, 128 bits is the standard key length. Any key length from 128 bits to 256 bits is supported. But, the security level still corresponds to 128-bit security. In other words, using a longer secret key does not guarantee to provide the security level usually expected from such a key.

IV injection. The IV is a 128-bit value. It is used as input to the *Serpent24* block cipher, as initialized by the key schedule. *Serpent24* consists of 24 rounds and the outputs of the 12th, 18th and 24th rounds are used. We denote those outputs as follows:

- $(Y_3^{12}, Y_2^{12}, Y_1^{12}, Y_0^{12})$: output of the 12th round;
- $(Y_3^{18}, Y_2^{18}, Y_1^{18}, Y_0^{18})$: output of the 18th round;
- $(Y_3^{24}, Y_2^{24}, Y_1^{24}, Y_0^{24})$: output of the 24th round.

The output of each round consists of the four 32-bit words just after the linear transformation, except for the 24th round, for which the output is taken just after the addition of the 25th subkey.

These values are used to initialize the SOSEMANUK internal state, with the following values:

$$(s_7, s_8, s_9, s_{10}) = (Y_3^{12}, Y_2^{12}, Y_1^{12}, Y_0^{12})$$
$$(s_5, s_6) = (Y_1^{18}, Y_3^{18})$$
$$(s_1, s_2, s_3, s_4) = (Y_3^{24}, Y_2^{24}, Y_1^{24}, Y_0^{24})$$
$$R1_0 = Y_0^{18}$$
$$R2_0 = Y_2^{18}$$

3   Design Rationale

3.1   Key Initialization and IV Injection

Underlying principle. A first property of the initialization process is that it is split into two distinct steps: the key schedule which does not depend on the IV, and the IV injection which generates the initial state of the generator from the IV and from the output of the key schedule. Then, the IV setup for a fixed key is less expensive than a complete key setup, improving the common design since changing the IV is more frequent than changing the secret key.

A second characteristic of SOSEMANUK is that the IV setup is derived from the application of a block cipher over the IV. If we consider the function F_K which maps a n-bit IV to the first n bits of output stream generated from the key K and the IV, then F_K must be computationaly indistinguishable from a random function over $\mathbb{F}_2^n$. Hence, the computation of F_K cannot "morally" be faster than the best known PRF over n-bit blocks. It so happens that the fastest known PRF use the same implementation techniques that the fastest known Pseudo-Random Permutations (which are block ciphers), and amount to the equivalent performance.

Since SOSEMANUK stream generation is very fast, the generation of n stream bits takes little time compared to a computation of a robust PRP over a block of n bits. Following this path of reasoning, we decided to use a block cipher as the fundation of the IV setup for SOSEMANUK: the IV setup itself cannot be much faster than the application of a block cipher, and the security requirements for that step are much similar to what is expected from a block cipher.

Choice of the block cipher. The block cipher used in the IV setup is derived from SERPENT for the following reasons:

- SERPENT has been thoroughly analyzed during the AES selection process and its security is well-understood.
- SERPENT needs no static data tables, and hence adds little or no data cache pressure.
- The SERPENT round function is optimized for operation over data represented as 32-bit words, which is exactly how data is managed within SOSEMANUK. Using SERPENT implies no tedious byte extraction from 32-bit words, or recombinations into such words.
- We needed a block cipher for the key schedule and IV injection; using something other else than AES seems good for "biodiversity".

Design of Serpent24. The IV injection uses a reduced version of SERPENT because SERPENT aimed at 256-bit security, whereas SOSEMANUK is meant for 128-bit security. The best linear bias and differential bias for a 6-round version of SERPENT are 2^{-28} and 2^{-58} respectively [3]. Thus, 12 rounds should provide appropriate security. Twelve more rounds are added in order to generate enough data (three 128-bit words are needed for initializing SOSEMANUK), hence 24 rounds for *Serpent24*. We rely on the SOSEMANUK core itself to provide some security margins (the output of *Serpent24* is not available directly to the attacker). Two consecutive outputs of data are spaced with six inner rounds in order to prevent the existence of relations between the bits of the initial state and the secret key bits which could be used in an attack.

3.2 LFSR

The SNOW 2.0 LFSR contains 16 elements, which means 512 bits of internal state. Since we aim only at 128-bit security, we can accommodate a shorter LFSR. To defeat time-memory-data trade-off attacks, 256 bits of internal state at least should be used; we wanted some security margin, hence an LFSR length a bit more than six words.

LFSR length. The LFSR length n must be as small as possible: the bigger the state, the more difficult it is to map the state values on the processor registers. Ideally, the total state should fit in the 16 general-purpose registers that the new AMD64 architecture offers.

For efficient LFSR implementation, the LFSR must not be physically shifted; moving data around contributes nothing to actual security, and takes time. If n is the LFSR length, then kn steps (for some integer k) must be "unrolled", so that at each step only one LFSR cell is modified. Moreover, since *Serpent1* operates over four successive output values, kn corresponds to $\mathrm{lcm}(4, n)$ and it should be kept as small as possible, since a higher code size increases code cache pressure.

These considerations led us to $n = 8$ or 10. But, an LFSR of length eight presents potential weaknesses which may be exploited in a guess-and-determine attack (see Section 4.3). Therefore, a LFSR of length 10 is a suitable choice: the 384-bit internal state length should be enough; only 20 steps need to be unrolled for an efficient implementation. The total internal state fits in 12 registers, which should map fine on the new AMD64 architecture.

Feedback polynomial. The design criteria for the feedback polynomial are similar to those used in SNOW 2.0. Since the feedback polynomial must be as sparse as possible, we chose as in SNOW 2.0 a primitive polynomial of the form

$$\pi(X) = c_0 X^{10} + c_a X^{n-a} + c_b X^{n-b} + 1 \ ,$$

where $0 < a < b < 10$. The coefficients c_0, c_a and c_b preferably lie in $\{1, \alpha, \alpha^{-1}\}$ which are the elements corresponding to an efficient multiplication in $\mathbb{F}_{2^{32}}$. Moreover, $\{c_0, c_a, c_b\}$ must contain at least two distinct non-binary elements; otherwise, a multiple of π with binary coefficients can be easily constructed [11,16], providing an equation which holds for each single bit position.

We also want a and b to be coprime with the LFSR length. Otherwise, for instance if $d = \gcd(a, 10) > 1$, the corresponding recurrence relation

$$s_{t+10} = c_b s_{t+b} + c_a s_{t+a} + c_0 s_t$$

involves three terms of a decimated sequence $(s_{dt+i})_{t>0}$ (for some integer i), which can be generated by an LFSR of length n/d [23]. These conditions led us to $a = 3$ and $b = 9$. Since a and b are not coprime, c_a and c_b must be different; otherwise, some simplified relations may be exhibited by manipulating the feedback polynomial as shown in [16,9]. The values $c_0 = \alpha$, $c_3 = \alpha^{-1}$ and $c_9 = 1$ correspond to a suitable primitive polynomial that fulfills all previously mentioned conditions.

3.3   FSM

The Trans *function.* The *Trans* function is chosen according to the following implementation criteria: no static data tables in order to reduce the cache pressure and the function must be fast on modern processors. For these reasons, the *Trans* function is composed of a 32-bit multiplication and a bitwise rotation which are both very fast. The 32-bit multiplication provides excellent "data mixing" compared to the number of clock cycles it consumes. The bitwise rotation avoids the existence of a linear relation between the least-significant bits of the inputs and the output of the FSM.

The operations involved in the *Trans* functions are incompatible with the other operations used in the FSM (addition over $\mathbb{Z}_{2^{32}}$, XOR operation). Actually, mixing operations on the ring and on the vector space disables associativity and commutativity laws. For instance,

$$(M \times (R2_{t-1} + s_{t+1} \bmod 2^{32}) \bmod 2^{32})_{<<<7}$$
$$\neq$$
$$(M \times (R2_{t-1}) \bmod 2^{32})_{<<<7} + (M \times (s_{t+1}) \bmod 2^{32})_{<<<7} \bmod 2^{32}.$$

The mux *operation.* The mux operation aims at increasing the complexity of fast correlation and algebraic attacks, since it decimates the FSM input sequence in an irregular fashion. Moreover, this operation can be implemented efficiently with either control bit extension and bitwise operations, or an architecture specific "conditional move" opcode. Modern C compilers know how to perform those optimizations when compiling the C conditional ternary operator "?:". This multiplexer is quite fast and requires no jump.

It is fitting that both LFSR elements s_{t+c} and s_{t+d} (with $c \leq d$) in the mux operation are not involved in the recurrence relation. Otherwise the complexity of guess-and-determine attacksmight be reduced. The distance $(d - c)$ between those elements must be coprime with the LFSR length since they must not be expressed as a decimated sequence with a lower linear complexity. Here, we choose $d - c = 7$. Finally, it must be impossible for the inputs of the mux operation at two different steps correspond to the same element in the LFSR sequence. For this reason, the mux operation outputs either s_{t+c} or $s_{t+c} \oplus s_{t+d}$. If $s_{t+c} \oplus s_{t+d}$ is the input of the FSM at time t, the possible inputs at time $(t+d-c)$ are s_{t+d} and $s_{t+d} \oplus s_{t+2d-c}$, which do not match any previous input. It is worth noticy that this property does not hold anymore if the mux outputs either s_{t+c} or s_{t+d}.

3.4   The Output Transformation

The output transformation derived from *Serpent1* aims at mixing four successive outputs of the FSM in a nonlinear way. As a consequence, any 32-bit keystream word produced by SOSEMANUK depends on four consecutive intermediate values f_t. As a result, recovering any single output of the FSM, f_t, in a guess-and-determine attack requires the knowledge of at least four consecutive words from the LFSR sequence, $s_t, s_{t+1}, s_{t+2}, s_{t+3}$ (see Section 4.3 for details).

The following properties have also been taken into account in the choice of output transformation.

- Both nonlinear mixing operations involved in SOSEMANUK (the *Trans* operation and the *Serpent1* used in bitslice mode) do not provide any correlation probability or linear property on the least significant bits that could be used to mount an attack (see Section 4.4 for further details).
- From an algebraic point of view, those operations are combined to produce nonlinear equations (see Section 4.6).
- No linear relation can be directly exploited on the least significant bit of the values $(f_t, f_{t+1}, f_{t+2}, f_{t+3})$, only quadratic equations with more variables than the number of possible equations (see Section 4.4).
- The linear relation between s_t and *Serpent1* $(f_t, f_{t+1}, f_{t+2}, f_{t+3})$ prevents SOSEMANUK from SQUARE-like attacks.

Finally, the fastest SERPENT S-box (S_2) has been chosen in *Serpent1* from an efficiency point of view [22]. But, S_2 also guarantees that there is no differential-linear relation on the least significant bit (the "most linear" one in the output of the FSM).

4   Resistance Against Known Attacks

Our stream cipher Sosemanuk offers a 128-bit security, based on the following security model.

4.1   Security Model

The attacker is a probabilistic Turing Machine with access to a black box (oracle) that accepts the following three instructions: Reset, Init with a 128-bit input, GetStream with a 1-bit output. The attacker's goal is to distinguish with probability 2/3 between a black box that generates random output, and a black box that implements the stream cipher, where Reset generates a random key, Init initializes the internal state of the stream cipher with a new chosen IV, and GetStream generates the next bit of keystream. The attacker is allowed to do 2^{128} elementary operations, an instruction to the black box being an elementary operation.

This security model falls under remarks made by Hong and Sarkar [18], because the precomputation time is not bounded by our model. Therefore our claim is that the 256-bit key variant of Sosemanuk provide a 128-bit security. We do not know of a formal security model that restricts the precomputation time, i.e. that only allows the attacker one of the probabilistic Turing machines that can be built in a reasonable time from the current content of today's computers. Therefore, our claim is that the 128-bit key variant of Sosemanuk, and all variants with larger keys, provide a 128-bit security against an attacker that is not allowed to benefit from large precomputation.

The following sections focus on the security of Sosemanuk against known attacks. It is important to note that the secret key of the cipher cannot be easily recovered from the initial state of the generator. Once the initial state is recovered, the attacker is only able to generate the output sequence for a particular key and a given IV. Recovering the secret key or generating the output for a different IV additionally requires the cost of an attack on *Serpent24* with a certain number of plaintext/ciphertext pairs.

4.2   Time-Memory-Data Tradeoff Attacks

Due to the choice of the length of the LFSR (more than twice the key length), the time-memory-data tradeoff attacks described in [2,14,5] are impracticable. Moreover, since these TMDTO attacks aim at recovering the internal state of the cipher, recovering the secret key requires the additional cost of an attack against *Serpent24*. The best time-memory data tradeoff attack is the Hellman's one [17] which aims at recovering a pair (K, IV). For a 128-bit secret key and a 128-bit IV, its time complexity is equal to 2^{128} cipher operations (see [18] for further details).

4.3   Guess and Determine Attacks

The main weaknesses of SNOW 1.0 are related to this type of attacks (two at least have been exhibited [16], [9]). They essentially exploit a particular weakness in the linear recurrence equation. This does not hold anymore for the new polynomial choice in SNOW 2.0 and for the polynomial used in SOSE-MANUK which involve non-binary multiplications by two different constants. The first attack [16] also exploited a "trick" coming from the dependence between the values $R1_{t-1}$ and $R1_t$. This trick is avoided in SNOW 2.0 (because there is no direct link between those two register values anymore) and in SOSEMANUK.

The best guess and determine attack we have found on SOSEMANUK is the following.

- Guess at time t, $s_t, s_{t+1}, s_{t+2}, s_{t+3}$, $R1_{t-1}$ and $R2_{t-1}$ (6 words).
- Compute the corresponding outputs of the FSM $(f_t, f_{t+1}, f_{t+2}, f_{t+3})$.
- Compute $R2_t = Trans(R1_{t-1})$ and $R1_t$ from Equation (1) if $\mathrm{lsb}(R1_{t-1}) = 1$ (this can be done only with probability $1/2$).
- From $f_t = (s_{t+9} + R1_t \bmod 2^{32}) \oplus R2_t$, compute s_{t+9}.
- Compute $R1_{t+1}$ from the knowledge of both s_{t+2} and s_{t+9}; compute $R2_{t+1}$. Compute s_{t+10} from f_{t+1}, $R1_{t+1}$ and $R2_{t+1}$.
- Compute $R1_{t+2}$ from s_{t+3} and s_{t+10}; compute $R2_{t+2}$. Compute s_{t+11} from f_{t+2}, $R1_{t+2}$ and $R2_{t+2}$. Now, s_{t+4} can be recovered due to the feedback relation at time $t+1$:

$$\alpha^{-1} s_{t+4} = s_{t+11} \oplus s_{t+10} \oplus \alpha s_{t+1} .$$

- Compute $R1_{t+3}$ from s_{t+4} and s_{t+11}; compute $R2_{t+2}$. Compute s_{t+12} from f_{t+3}, $R1_{t+3}$ and $R2_{t+3}$. Compute s_{t+5} by the feedback relation at time $t+2$:

$$\alpha^{-1} s_{t+5} = s_{t+12} \oplus s_{t+11} \oplus \alpha s_{t+2} .$$

At this point, the LFSR words $s_t, s_{t+1}, s_{t+2}, s_{t+3}, s_{t+4}, s_{t+5}, s_{t+9}$ are known. Three elements $(s_{t+6}, s_{t+7}, s_{t+8})$ remain unknown. To complete the full 10 words state of the LFSR, we need to guess 2 more words, s_{t+6} and s_{t+7} since each f_{t+i}, $4 \le i \le 7$, depends on all 4 words s_{t+4}, s_{t+5}, s_{t+6} and s_{t+7}. Therefore, this attack requires the guess of 8 32-bit words, leading to a complexity of 2^{256}.

Note that in [1] and in [25] the authors respectively proposed two guess and determine attacks against SOSEMANUK that have a complexity approximatively equal to 2^{226} and 2^{224} computations. However, as stated in paragraphs 2.6, 3.2 and 4.1, we never intended to have more than 128-bit security. The internal state of SOSEMANUK is 384-bit long, which would be bad practice if we aimed at 256-bit security. Therefore, those guess-and-determine attacks, while being interesting theoretical studies, do not compromise the security of SOSEMANUK.

4.4   Correlation Attacks

In order to find a relevant correlation in SOSEMANUK, the following questions can be addressed:

- does there exist a linear relation at bit level between some input and output bits?

- does there exist a particular relation between some input bit vector and some output bit vector?

In the first case, two linear relations could be exhibited at the bit level. In the first, the least significant bit of s_{t+9} was "conserved", since the modular addition over $\mathbb{Z}_{2^{32}}$ is a linear operation on the least significant bit. The second linear relation induced by the FSM concerns the least significant bit of s_{t+1} or of $s_{t+1} \oplus s_{t+8}$ (used to compute $R1_t$) or the seventh bit of $R2_t$ computed from s_t or of $s_t \oplus s_{t+7}$. We here use that $R2_t = Trans(R1_{t-1})$ and $R1_{t-1} = R2_{t-2} + (s_t \text{ or } (s_t \oplus s_{t+7})) \bmod 2^{32}$.

No linear relation holds after applying $Serpent1$ and there are too many unknown bits to exploit a relation on the outputs words due to the bitslice design. Moreover, a fast correlation attack seems to be impracticable because the mux operation prevents certainty in the dependence between the LFSR states and the observed keystream.

4.5 Distinguishing Attacks

A distinguishing attack by D. Coppersmith, S. Halevi and C. Jutla (see [10]) against the first version of SNOW used a particular weakness of the feedback polynomial built on a single multiplication by α. This property does not hold for the choice of the new polynomial in SNOW 2.0 and for the polynomial used in SOSEMANUK where multiplication by α^{-1} is also included.

In [26], D. Watanabe, A. Biryukov and C. De Cannire have mounted a new distinguishing attack on SNOW 2.0 with a complexity about 2^{225} operations using multiple linear masking method. They construct 3 different masks $\Gamma_1 = \Gamma$, $\Gamma_2 = \Gamma \cdot \alpha$ and $\Gamma_3 = \Gamma \cdot \alpha^{-1}$ based on the same linear relation Γ.

The linear property deduced from the masks Γ_i ($i = 1, 2$ or 3) must hold with a high probability on the both following quantities: $\Gamma_i \cdot S'(x) = \Gamma_i \cdot x$ and $\Gamma_i \cdot z \oplus \Gamma_i \cdot t = \Gamma_i \cdot (z \boxplus t)$ for $i=1,2$ and 3, where S' is the transition function of the FSM in SNOW 2.0. In the case of SNOW 2.0, the hardest hypothesis to satisfy is the first one defined on $y = S'(x)$. In the case of SOSEMANUK, we need $Pr(\Gamma_i \cdot Trans(x) = \Gamma_i \cdot x)_{i=1,2,3}$ to be high. But, we also need that $\forall i = 1, 2, 3$, the relation

$$(\Gamma_i', \Gamma_i', \Gamma_i', \Gamma_i') \cdot (x_1, x_2, x_3, x_4) = Serpent1((\Gamma_i, \Gamma_i, \Gamma_i, \Gamma_i) \cdot (x_1, x_2, x_3, x_4)).$$

for some $\Gamma_i' \in \mathbb{F}_2^{32}$, holds with a high probability.

Due to the bitslice design chosen for $Serpent1$, it seems very difficult to find such a mask. Therefore, the attack described in [26] could not be applied directly on SOSEMANUK.

4.6 Algebraic Attacks

Let us consider, as in [4], the initial state of the LFSR at bit level:

$$(s_{10}, \cdots, s_1) = (s_{10}^{31}, \cdots, s_{10}^0, \cdots, s_1^{31}, \cdots, s_1^0)$$

Then, the outputs of SOSEMANUK at time $t \geq 1$ could be written:

$$F^t((s_{31}^{10}, \cdots, s_0^1)) = (z_t, z_{t+1}, z_{t+2}, z_{t+3})$$

where F is a vectorial Boolean function from $\mathbb{F}_2^{320}$ into $\mathbb{F}_2^{128}$ that could be seen as 128 Boolean functions F_j, $\forall j \in [0..127]$ from $\mathbb{F}_2^{320}$ into $\mathbb{F}_2$.

Let us study the degree of an F_j function depending on a particular bit of the output or on a linear combination of output bits because it is not possible to directly compute the algebraic immunity of each function F_j due to the very large number of variables (320 input bits). We think that the following remarks prevent the existence of low degree relations between the inputs and the outputs of F_j.

- The output bit i after the modular addition on $\mathbb{Z}_{2^{32}}$ is of degree $i + 1$ (as described in [6]).
- The output bit i after the *Trans* mapping is of degree $i+1-7 \bmod 32$, $\forall i \neq 6$ and equal to 32 for $i = 6$ (as described in [6]).
- The mux operation does not enable to determine with probability one the exact number of bits of the initial state involved in the algebraic relation.
- The algebraic immunity of the SERPENT S-box S_2 at 4-bit word level is equal to 2 (see [21] for a definition of the algebraic immunity and more details).

Under those remarks, we think that an algebraic attack against SOSEMANUK is intractable.

5   Implementation

The reference C implementation is also an optimized implementation. When compiled with the `SOSEMANUK_VECTOR` macro defined, it is a full program (with its own `main()` function) which outputs two detailed test vectors. Since the LFSR length is ten, we unroll the C code on 20 rounds (see 3.2 for details); each test vector contains:

- A copy of the secret key (a sequence of bytes, expressed in hexadecimal).
- The expanded secret key, as described by the SERPENT specification: the key is expanded to 256 bits, then read as a 256-bit number with the little endian convention. The test vector outputs that key as a big hexadecimal number, with some digit grouping.
- The 25 *Serpent24* subkeys, each of them consisting of four 32-bit words (in the (K_3, K_2, K_1, K_0) order).
- The 128-bit IV, as a sequence of 16 bytes.
- The IV, once transformed into four 32-bit words, in the (I_3, I_2, I_1, I_0) order.
- The initial LFSR state (s_1 to s_{10}, in that order).
- The initial FSM state ($R1_0$ and $R2_0$).
- Ten times the following data:

- Four times the following:
  * the new FSM state ($R1_t$ and $R2_t$);
  * the new LFSR state, after the update (the dropped value s_t is also output);
  * the intermediate output f_t.
- The *Serpent1* input.
- The *Serpent1* output.
- 16 bytes of SOSEMANUK output.
− The total stream output (160 bytes).

6 Performance

6.1 Software Implementation

This section is devoted to the software performance of SOSEMANUK. It compares the performance of SOSEMANUK with the other candidates selected in the Phase 3 (Software Profile), SNOW 2.0 and AES-CTR using the eSTREAM testing framework and the provided reference C implementations [7]. The three tables Table 1, Table 2 and Table 3 sum up the results (for the keystream generation, the *IV* setup and the key setup) given in [8] for three different architectures: an Intel Pentium 4 (CISC target), an AMD Athlon64 X2 4200+ (CISC target) and an Alpha EV6 (RISC target).

All the results presented for SOSEMANUK have been computed using the supplied reference C implementation.

Code size. The main unrolled loop implies a code size between 2 and 5 KB depending on the platform and the compiler. Therefore, the entire code fits in the L1 cache.

Static data. The reference C implementation uses static data tables with a total size equal to 4 KB. This amount is 3 times smaller than the size of static data required in SNOW 2.0, leading to a lower date cache pressure.

Key setup. We recall that the key setup (the subkey generation given by *Serpent24*) is made once and that each new IV injection for a given key corresponds to a small version of the block cipher SERPENT.

The performance of the key setup and of the IV setup in SOSEMANUK are directly derived from the performance of SERPENT [13]. Due to intellectual property aspects, our reference implementation does not re-use the best implementation of SERPENT. However, the performance given in [20] (i.e., computed on the Gladman's code written in assembly language [13]) leads to the following results on a Pentium 4:

− key setup ≃ 900 cycles;
− IV setup ≃ 480 cycles.

These estimations for the IV setup (resp. key setup) performance corresponds to about 3/4 of the best published performance for SERPENT encryption (resp. for SERPENT key schedule).

Performance results. Table 1, Table 2 and Table 3 present the performance of the keystream generation (using four performance measures), the agility, the *IV* setup and the key setup to test the most relevant implementation properties. The four elementary tests for keystream generation are: the encryption rate for long streams by ciphering a long stream in chunks of about 4Kb; the packet encryption rate for three packet lengths (40, 576 and 1500 bytes) including an *IV* setup; the agility test initiates a large number of sessions (filling 16MB of RAM), and then encrypts streams of plaintexts in short blocks of around 256 bytes, each time jumping from one session to another.

Table 1. Number of CPU cycles for the stream ciphers using a Pentium 4 at 2.80GHz, Model 15/2/9

		cycles/byte					cycles/key	cycles/IV
Algo.	*IV*	Stream	40 bytes	576 bytes	1500 bytes	agility	Key setup	IV setup
AES CTR	128	17.81	29.19	18.35	18.04	20.77	393.45	76.16
SNOW v2.0	128	5.04	35.60	6.92	5.92	7.95	85.44	1000.54
CryptMT v3	128	5.27	39.12	12.09	11.55	11.35	53.71	849.25
DRAGON	128	11.37	74.09	26.07	23.23	15.00	256.04	1925.54
HC-128	128	3.76	1458.58	104.86	42.64	19.02	78.81	56929.45
HC-256	128	4.39	2596.20	184.25	73.59	26.27	76.66	104341.33
LEXv1	128	9.46	20.78	10.88	10.01	12.30	486.57	449.00
NLSv2	128	6.64	38.94	8.52	6.97	12.10	823.74	704.68
Rabbit	64	9.46	34.45	11.77	10.76	12.89	984.27	825.55
Salsa20	64	16.61	42.21	17.63	18.57	18.71	90.32	78.19
SOSEMANUK	64	5.81	52.37	12.52	9.62	7.40	1287.55	1245.71

Table 2. Number of CPU cycles for the stream ciphers using an AMD Athlon 64 X2 4200+ at 2.20GHz, Model 15/75/2

		cycles/byte					cycles/key	cycles/IV
Algo.	*IV*	Stream	40 bytes	576 bytes	1500 bytes	agility	Key setup	IV setup
AES CTR	128	13.39	18.09	13.39	13.35	15.03	152.81	15.58
SNOW v2.0	128	4.83	23.18	5.77	5.34	6.46	43.37	528.04
CryptMT v3	128	4.65	19.26	8.47	7.64	8.82	25.47	384.33
DRAGON	128	7.76	60.20	25.90	24.31	10.01	89.90	1449.74
HC-128	128	2.86	587.00	43.19	18.43	13.07	37.85	23308.78
HC-256	128	4.72	1420.99	103.10	42.83	21.13	41.31	56725.89
LEXv1	128	6.84	14.19	7.78	7.20	9.19	226.41	268.31
NLSv2	128	10.69	53.24	13.45	11.48	14.13	453.35	1293.15
Rabbit	64	4.98	14.60	5.55	5.25	6.34	288.21	292.38
Salsa20	64	7.64	16.10	7.74	7.91	8.93	24.57	14.29
SOSEMANUK	64	4.07	25.26	7.20	6.10	5.12	759.06	560.63

Table 3. Number of CPU cycles for the stream ciphers using an Alpha EV6 at 500MHz, Model 21264

Algo.	IV	cycles/byte					cycles/key	cycles/IV
		Stream	40 bytes	576 bytes	1500 bytes	agility	Key setup	IV setup
AES CTR	128	15.53	24.63	15.94	15.82	17.80	633.65	37.58
SNOW v2.0	128	5.17	23.74	6.11	5.73	6.37	69.00	489.35
CryptMT v3	128	6.90	24.74	11.64	11.75	12.86	37.49	422.17
DRAGON	128	8.46	74.94	41.89	40.52	10.13	234.33	1542.46
HC-128	128	3.90	1029.93	77.41	31.59	14.80	54.67	42130.00
HC-256	128	5.18	2414.77	171.48	69.34	23.53	52.96	95937.00
LEXv1	128	7.99	16.87	9.15	8.44	9.53	198.49	334.58
NLSv2	128	5.93	24.26	6.44	5.59	7.94	530.39	421.66
Rabbit	64	5.27	14.49	5.69	5.53	6.32	318.57	280.63
Salsa20	64	13.61	39.93	13.77	14.34	14.46	33.60	20.16
SOSEMANUK	64	4.63	28.80	7.66	6.26	5.32	1301.09	692.71

As shown in these tables, SOSEMANUK remains among the fastest algorithms on several platforms due to a good design for the mappings of data on the processor registers and a low data cache pressure.

6.2   Hardware Implementation

In [15], the authors propose hardware implementations and performance metrics for several stream cipher candidates and especially SOSEMANUK. They remark that even if the design of SOSEMANUK is a little bit complex to implement, it leads to an impressive performance. The required number of gates for designing SOSEMANUK on 0.13 μm Standard Cell CMOS with a key of length 256 bits is 18819 considering that 32 bits are outputted at each cycle. Moreover, the corresponding leakage power is 33.55 μW for a total power at 10MHz equal to 812.47 μW. The authors also derive the metrics for maximum clock frequency and for an output rate at 10 Mbps (estimated typical future wireless LAN). In this last case, the corresponding clock frequency is equal to 0.313 MHz for a Power-Area-Time equal to 564.8 nJ-um2. In conclusion, they recommend SOSE-MANUK for WLAN applications with a key length equal to 256 bits. They say that "with regard to SOSEMANUK, the utility as a hardware cipher is clear thus in our opinion requires adding to the hardware focus profile."

7   Strengths and Advantages of SOSEMANUK

The new synchronous stream cipher SOSEMANUK based upon the SNOW 2.0 design improves it from several points of view. From a security point of view, SOSEMANUK avoids some potential weaknesses as the distinguishing attack proposed in [26] due to the particular use of *Serpent1* in bitslice mode. The chosen LFSR is designed to eliminate all potential weaknesses (particular decimation properties, linear relations,...). The mappings used in the Finite State Machine have been carefully designed in the following way:

- The *Trans* function guarantees good properties of confusion and diffusion for a low cost in software. Moreover, this mapping prevents SOSEMANUK from algebraic attacks.
- The mux operation, that could be efficiently implemented, protects SOSE-MANUK from fast correlation attacks and algebraic attacks.

The *Serpent1* output transformation, very efficient in bitslice mode, provides nonlinear equations, a good diffusion and it improves the resistance to guess-and-determine attacks.

The new design chosen for the key setup and the IV injection allows to split the initialization procedure into two distinct parts, without any loss of security. It leads to a much faster resynchronization mechanism.

From an efficiency point of view, due to a reduced amount of static data and a reduced internal state size, the exploitation of the processor registers is enhanced and the data cache pressure is improved on several platforms, especially on RISC architectures.

Acknowledgments. The authors would like to thank Matt Robshaw for valuable comments.

Note that this work has been performed while the 4th author was affiliated to Axalto/Gemalto (France), the 7th and the 12th authors were affiliated to France Télécom R&D/Orange Labs (France), the 8th author was affiliated to the École Normale Supérieure (France), the 10th author was affiliated to INRIA Rocquencourt (France).

References

1. Ahmadi, H., Eghlidos, T., Khazaei, S.: Improved guess and determine attack on SOSEMANUK. eSTREAM, ECRYPT Stream Cipher Project, Report 2005/085 (2005), http://www.ecrypt.eu.org/stream
2. Babbage, S.: A space/time trade-off in exhaustive search attacks on stream ciphers. In: European Convention on Security and Detection, vol. 408. IEEE Conference Publication (1995)
3. Biham, E., Anderson, R., Knudsen, L.: SERPENT: A new block cipher proposal. In: Vaudenay, S. (ed.) FSE 1998. LNCS, vol. 1372, pp. 222–238. Springer, Heidelberg (1998)
4. Billet, O., Gilbert, H.: Resistance of SNOW 2.0 against algebraic attacks. In: Menezes, A. (ed.) CT-RSA 2005. LNCS, vol. 3376, pp. 19–28. Springer, Heidelberg (2005)
5. Biryukov, A., Shamir, A.: Cryptanalytic time-memory-data trade-offs for stream ciphers. In: Okamoto, T. (ed.) ASIACRYPT 2000. LNCS, vol. 1976, pp. 1–14. Springer, Heidelberg (2000)
6. Braeken, A., Semaev, I.: The ANF of the composition of $\times$ and $+$ mod 2^n with a Boolean function. In: Gilbert, H., Handschuh, H. (eds.) FSE 2005. LNCS, vol. 3557, pp. 112–125. Springer, Heidelberg (2005)

7. De Cannière, C.: estream optimized code HOWTO. eSTREAM, ECRYPT Stream Cipher Project (2005), http://www.ecrypt.eu.org/stream/perf/
8. De Cannière, C.: Software performance of the phase 3 candidates. eSTREAM, ECRYPT Stream Cipher Project (2007), http://www.ecrypt.eu.org/stream/phase3perf.html
9. De Cannière, C.: Guess and determine attack on SNOW - NESSIE public reports (2001), https://www.cosic.esat.kuleuven.ac.be/nessie/reports/
10. Coppersmith, D., Halevi, S., Jutla, C.: Cryptanalysis of stream ciphers with linear masking. In: Yung, M. (ed.) CRYPTO 2002. LNCS, vol. 2442. Springer, Heidelberg (2002)
11. Ekdahl, P., Johannson, T.: Distinguishing attacks on SOBER. In: Daemen, J., Rijmen, V. (eds.) FSE 2002. LNCS, vol. 2365, pp. 210–224. Springer, Heidelberg (2002)
12. Ekdahl, P., Johansson, T.: A new version of the stream cipher SNOW. In: Kuich, W., Rozenberg, G., Salomaa, A. (eds.) DLT 2001. LNCS, vol. 2295, pp. 47–61. Springer, Heidelberg (2002)
13. Gladman, B.: SERPENT performance, http://fp.gladman.plus.com/cryptography_technology/serpent/
14. Golić, J.: Cryptanalysis of alleged A5 stream cipher. In: Fumy, W. (ed.) EURO-CRYPT 1997. LNCS, vol. 1233, pp. 239–255. Springer, Heidelberg (1997)
15. Good, T., Benaissa, M.: Hardware results for selected stream cipher candidates. eSTREAM, ECRYPT Stream Cipher Project, SASC, Report 2007/023 (2007), http://www.ecrypt.eu.org/stream
16. Hawkes, P., Rose, G.: Guess-and-determine attacks on SNOW. In: Nyberg, K., Heys, H.M. (eds.) SAC 2002. LNCS, vol. 2595, pp. 37–46. Springer, Heidelberg (2003)
17. Hellman, M.E.: A cryptanalytic time-memory trade-off. IEEE Transactions on Information Theory 26(4), 401–406 (1980)
18. Hong, J., Sarkar, P.: Rediscovery of time memory tradeoffs (2005), http://eprint.iacr.org/2005/090.ps
19. Howard, K.: Snow snake demonstration gives history lesson, http://www.turtletrack.org/Issues01/Co02102001/CO_02102001_Snowsnake.htm
20. Matsui, M., Fukuda, S.: How to maximize software performance of symmetric primitives on Pentiums. In: Gilbert, H., Handschuh, H. (eds.) FSE 2005. LNCS, vol. 3557, pp. 398–412. Springer, Heidelberg (2005)
21. Meier, W., Pasalic, E., Carlet, C.: Algebraic attacks and decomposition of Boolean functions. In: Cachin, C., Camenisch, J.L. (eds.) EUROCRYPT 2004. LNCS, vol. 3027, pp. 474–491. Springer, Heidelberg (2004)
22. Osvik, D.: Speeding up SERPENT. In: Second AES Candidate Conference (2000), http://www.ii.uib.no/~osvik/
23. Rueppel, R.A.: Analysis and Design of stream ciphers. Springer, Heidelberg (1986)
24. The story of Snowsnake, http://www.members.shaw.ca/dmacauley/story_of_snowsnake.htm
25. Tsunoo, Y., Saito, T., Shigeri, M., Suzaki, T., Ahmadi, H., Eghlidos, T., Khaz-aei, S.: Evaluation of SOSEMANUK with regard to guess-and-determine attacks. eSTREAM, ECRYPT Stream Cipher Project, Report 2006/009 (2005), http://www.ecrypt.eu.org/stream
26. Watanabe, D., Biryukov, A., De Cannière, C.: A distinguishing attack of SNOW 2.0 with linear masking method. In: Matsui, M., Zuccherato, R.J. (eds.) SAC 2003. LNCS, vol. 3006, pp. 222–233. Springer, Heidelberg (2004)

A   Specifications of SERPENT

In this appendix, a recall on the specifications of SERPENT given in [3] is made. First, the S-boxes definition is given and the linear part is also defined again.

A.1   S-Boxes Definitions

The eight SERPENT S-boxes act on 4-bit words and are defined as permutations of $\mathbb{Z}_{16}$:

$$S0 : 3, 8, 15, 1, 10, 6, 5, 11, 14, 13, 4, 2, 7, 0, 9, 12$$
$$S1 : 15, 12, 2, 7, 9, 0, 5, 10, 1, 11, 14, 8, 6, 13, 3, 4$$
$$S2 : 8, 6, 7, 9, 3, 12, 10, 15, 13, 1, 14, 4, 0, 11, 5, 2$$
$$S3 : 0, 15, 11, 8, 12, 9, 6, 3, 13, 1, 2, 4, 10, 7, 5, 14$$
$$S4 : 1, 15, 8, 3, 12, 0, 11, 6, 2, 5, 4, 10, 9, 14, 7, 13$$
$$S5 : 15, 5, 2, 11, 4, 10, 9, 12, 0, 3, 14, 8, 13, 6, 7, 1$$
$$S6 : 7, 2, 12, 5, 8, 4, 6, 11, 14, 9, 1, 15, 13, 3, 10, 0$$
$$S7 : 1, 13, 15, 0, 14, 8, 2, 11, 7, 4, 12, 10, 9, 3, 5, 6$$

A.2   Linear Part of SERPENT Round Function

The linear part of a one round version of SERPENT acts on 4 32-bit words (X_3, X_2, X_1, X_0) where X_0 is the least significant word and is defined as follows:

$$X_0 = X_0 \lll 13$$
$$X_2 = X_2 \lll 3$$
$$X_1 = X_1 \oplus X_0 \oplus X_2$$
$$X_3 = X_3 \oplus X_2 \oplus (X_0 \lll 3)$$
$$X_1 = X_1 \lll 1$$
$$X_3 = X_3 \lll 7$$
$$X_0 = X_0 \oplus X_1 \oplus X_3$$
$$X_2 = X_2 \oplus X_3 \oplus (X_1 \lll 7)$$
$$X_0 = X_0 \lll 5$$
$$X_2 = X_2 \lll 22$$

eSTREAM Software Performance[*]

Christophe De Cannière[1,2]

[1] Katholieke Universiteit Leuven, Dept. ESAT/SCD-COSIC and IBBT,
Kasteelpark Arenberg 10, B-3001 Heverlee, Belgium
[2] Département d'Informatique École Normale Supérieure,
45, rue d'Ulm, F-75230 Paris cedex 05
christophe.decanniere@{esat.kuleuven.be,ens.fr}

Abstract. In order to evaluate their performance in software, all Profile 1 candidates were subjected to benchmark tests. This chapter briefly describes the testing framework developed by eSTREAM for this purpose, and summarizes the results of the performance tests conducted on the eight Profile 1 finalists.

1 Introduction

One of the requirements imposed on all eSTREAM stream cipher submissions was that they should demonstrate the potential to be superior to the AES in at least one significant aspect. An aspect which is particularly significant for Profile 1 candidates is software performance.

Software performance can be measured in many different ways, and in order to make comparisons as fair as possible, eSTREAM decided to develop a testing framework. The framework had two objectives:

1. assuring that all stream cipher proposals were submitted to the same tests under the same circumstances
2. automating the test procedure as much as possible such that new optimized implementations, new testing platforms, and new tests (statistical tests, for instance) could be included with as little effort as possible.

2 The Testing Framework

The eSTREAM testing framework consists of a collection of shell scripts and C-code which test three aspects of the submitted code: API compliance, correctness, and performance. Many of these tests were inspired by the NESSIE Test Suite.

---

[*] The work described in this chapter has been partly supported by the European Commission under contract IST-2002-507932 (ECRYPT), by the Fund for Scientific Research – Flanders (FWO), and the Chaire France Telecom pour la sécurité des réseaux de télécommunications.

M. Robshaw and O. Billet (Eds.): New Stream Cipher Designs, LNCS 4986, pp. 119–139, 2008.

2.1 API Compliance

The eSTREAM API is specified in the files `ecrypt-sync.h` and `ecrypt-sync-ae.h`, which can be downloaded from the eSTREAM web page. The framework verifies whether the code complies to this API by performing the following tests:

1. It checks that the code provides the necessary interfaces, i.e., that it compiles and links correctly with the test code (`ecrypt-test.c`).
2. It checks that the `ECRYPT_KEYSIZE(i)` and `ECRYPT_MAXKEYSIZE` macros allow key sizes to be enumerated as specified by the API. Idem for IV and MAC sizes.
3. It checks that calls to the same functions with the same parameters produce the same results, no matter how they are interleaved. When this test fails, this is often an indication that the code stores data in static variables, or that it uses uninitialized variables.
4. It checks that the incremental encryption functions `ECRYPT_encrypt_blocks` and `ECRYPT_encrypt_bytes` produce the same ciphertext as `ECRYPT_encrypt_packet` when fed with the same plaintext. It also verifies that this ciphertext decrypts to the original plaintext.

2.2 Correctness

The correctness of the code on different platforms is verified by generating and comparing test vectors. For convenience, eSTREAM has chosen to use the same format as the NESSIE test vectors.

2.3 Performance

Stream ciphers can be deployed in various situations, each imposing specific requirements on the efficiency of the primitive. Hence, defining a small set of performance criteria which reflects all relevant implementation properties of a stream cipher is not an easy task. In the final version of the framework, eSTREAM has limited itself to four performance measures. More detailed tests can be found in [2], though.

1. **Encryption rate for long streams.** This is where stream ciphers have the biggest potential advantage over block ciphers, and hence this figure is likely to be the most important criterion in many applications. The testing framework measures the encryption rate by encrypting a long stream in chunks of about 4KB using the `ECRYPT_encrypt_blocks` function. The encryption speed, in cycles/byte, is calculated by measuring the number of bytes encrypted in 250 μsec. Note that the time to setup the key or the IV is not considered in this test.
2. **Packet encryption rate.** While a block cipher is likely to be a better choice when encrypting very short packets, it is still interesting to determine at which length a stream cipher starts to take the lead. Moreover, stream

ciphers whose encryption speeds do not deteriorate too much for small packets could have a distinct advantage in applications which use a wide range of packet sizes. The packet encryption rate is measured by applying the ECRYPT_encrypt_packet function to packets of different lengths. Each call to ECRYPT_encrypt_packet includes a separate IV setup and, if authenticated encryption is supported, a MAC finalization step. The packet lengths (40, 576, and 1500 bytes) were chosen to be representative for the traffic seen on the Internet [1].

3. **Agility.** When an application needs to encrypt many streams in parallel on a single processor, its performance will not only depend on the encryption speed of the cipher, but also on the time spent switching from one session to another. This overhead is typically determined by the number of bytes of ECRYPT_ctx that need to be stored or restored during each context switch. In order to build a picture of the agility of the different submissions, the testing framework performs the following test: it first initiates a large number of sessions (filling 16MB of RAM with ECRYPT_ctx structures), and then encrypts streams of plaintext in short blocks of around 256 bytes using ECRYPT_encrypt_blocks, each time jumping from one session to another.

4. **Key and IV setup (+ MAC generation).** The last test in the testing framework separately measures the efficiency of the key setup (ECRYPT_key setup) and the IV setup (ECRYPT_ivsetup). Given that each call to ECRYPT_ AE_ivsetup comes together with a call to ECRYPT_AE_finalize, both functions are benchmarked together in case of authenticated stream ciphers. This is probably the least critical of the four tests, considering that the efficiency of the IV setup is already reflected in the packet encryption rate, and that the time for the key setup will typically be negligible compared to the work needed to generate and exchange the key.

3 Platforms

The eSTREAM testing framework has been run on a large number of platforms (see [2] and [3]), but in this chapter we limit ourselves to two little-endian 32-bit platforms (Pentium 4 and Pentium M), two little-endian 64-bit platforms (Intel Core 2 Duo and AMD Athlon 64), and a (somewhat outdated) big-endian 64-bit platform (HP 9000). The specifications of these platforms are listed in Table 1.

Table 1. Selected test platforms

CPU	Model	Clock frequency	Architecture
Intel Pentium 4	15/ 2 /9	2.80 GHz	x86
Intel Pentium M	6/ 9 /5	1.70 GHz	x86
Intel Core 2 Duo E6550	6/15/11	2.33 GHz	AMD64
AMD Athlon 64 X2 4200+	15/75/2	2.20 GHz	AMD64
HP 9000/785	J6750	875 MHz	PA-RISC 2.0

4   Results

The detailed results of all performance tests can be found on the eSTREAM web page. In this chapter, we restrict ourselves to a series of graphs showing the relative performance of the candidates.

4.1   Profile 1 Candidates with 128-Bit Keys

We first focus on the performance of the eight Profile 1 finalists with standard 128-bit key sizes. For comparison, we also include three benchmark ciphers (AES in counter mode, RC4, and SNOW 2.0), and a number of Profile 2 candidates (with 80-bit keys). The complete list is shown in Table 2.

Table 2. List of considered stream ciphers

Cipher	Profile	Key	IV	MAC
CryptMT-v3	1	128	128	-
Dragon	1	128	128	-
HC-128	1	128	128	-
HC-256	1	128	128	-
LEX-v2	1	128	128	-
NLS-v2	1	128	64	-
NLS-v2	1	128	64	64
Rabbit	1	128	64	-
Salsa20	1	128	64	-
Salsa20/12	1	128	64	-
Salsa20/8	1	128	64	-
SOSEMANUK	1	128	64	-
AES-CTR	-	128	128	-
RC4	-	128	-	-
SNOW-2.0	-	128	128	-
DECIM-v2	2	80	64	-
Edon80	2	80	64	-
Grain-v1	2	80	64	-
MICKEY-v2	2	80	64	-
TRIVIUM	2	80	80	-

The graphs in Figs. 1–10 show the relative speed of the different stream ciphers on different platforms, both for long streams and for short (40-byte) packets. The next series of graphs (Figs. 11–21), consider each finalist separately, and show how each of them performs for each individual test on each platform. The radii of the disks represent the performance of the ciphers compared to the fastest cipher for each specific test.

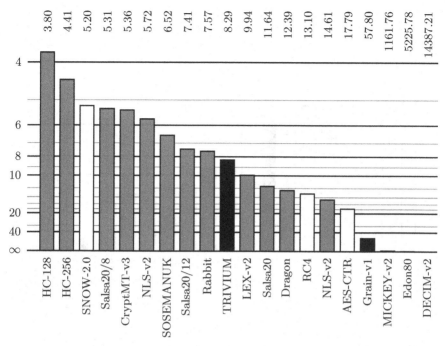

Fig. 1. Pentium 4, encryption speed (in cycles/byte) for long streams

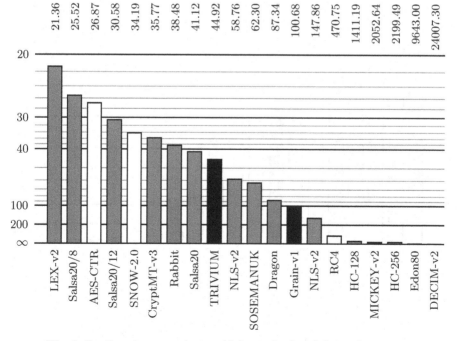

Fig. 2. Pentium 4, encryption speed (in cycles/byte) for 40-byte packets

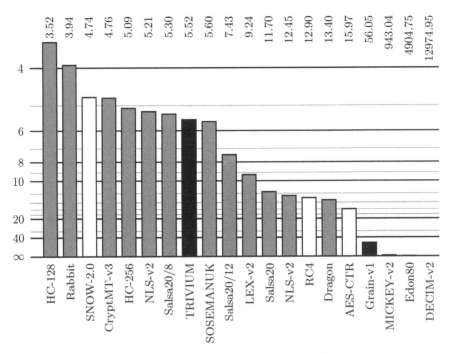

Fig. 3. Pentium M, encryption speed (in cycles/byte) for long streams

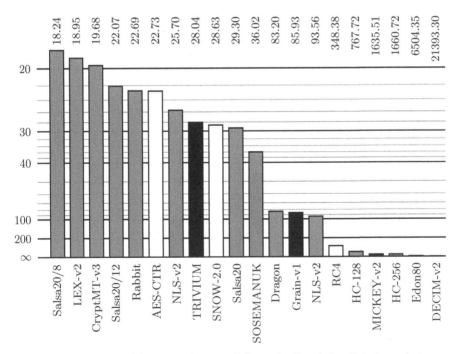

Fig. 4. Pentium M, encryption speed (in cycles/byte) for 40-byte packets

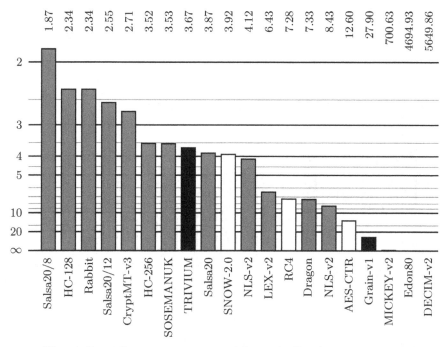

Fig. 5. Core 2 Duo, encryption speed (in cycles/byte) for long streams

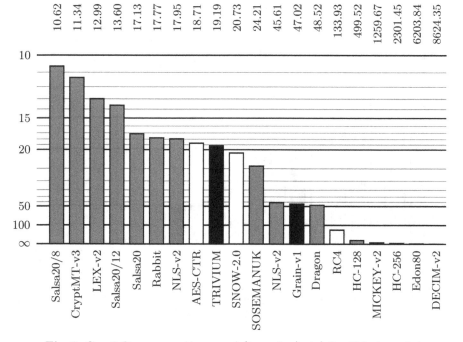

Fig. 6. Core 2 Duo, encryption speed (in cycles/byte) for 40-byte packets

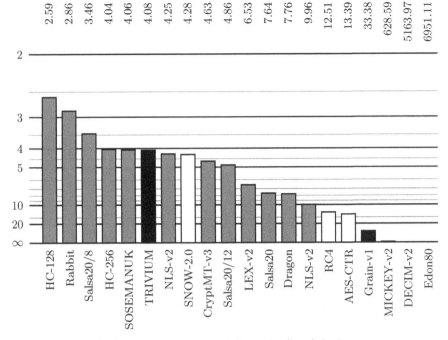

Fig. 7. AMD64, encryption speed (in cycles/byte) for long streams

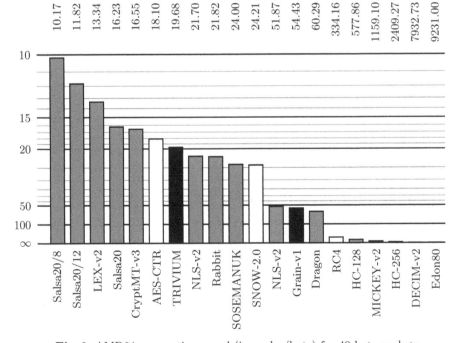

Fig. 8. AMD64, encryption speed (in cycles/byte) for 40-byte packets

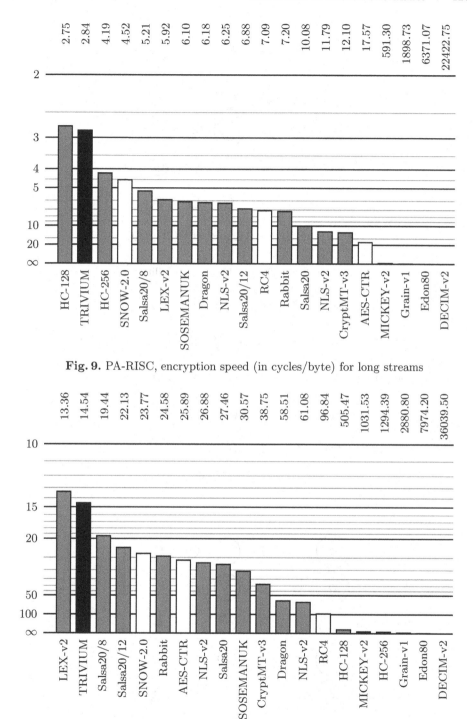

Fig. 9. PA-RISC, encryption speed (in cycles/byte) for long streams

Fig. 10. PA-RISC, encryption speed (in cycles/byte) for 40-byte packets

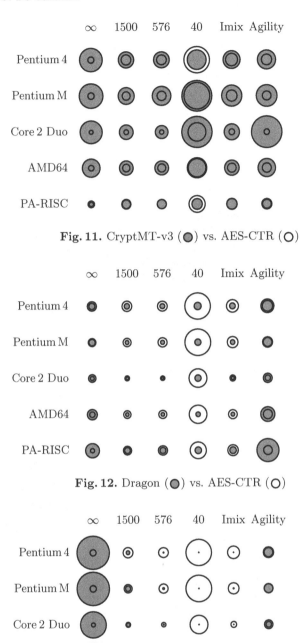

Fig. 11. CryptMT-v3 (●) vs. AES-CTR (○)

Fig. 12. Dragon (●) vs. AES-CTR (○)

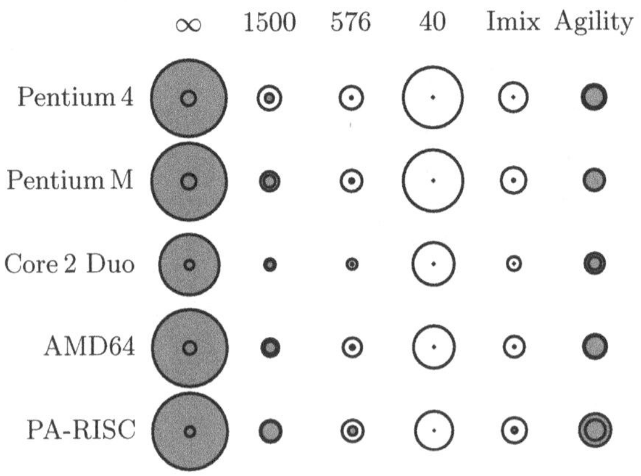

Fig. 13. HC-128 (●) vs. AES-CTR (○)

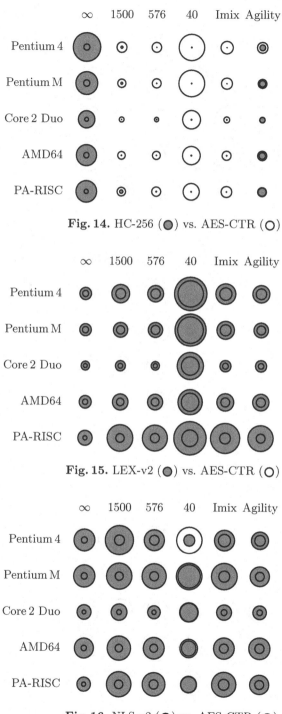

Fig. 14. HC-256 (⬤) vs. AES-CTR (◯)

Fig. 15. LEX-v2 (⬤) vs. AES-CTR (◯)

Fig. 16. NLS-v2 (⬤) vs. AES-CTR (◯)

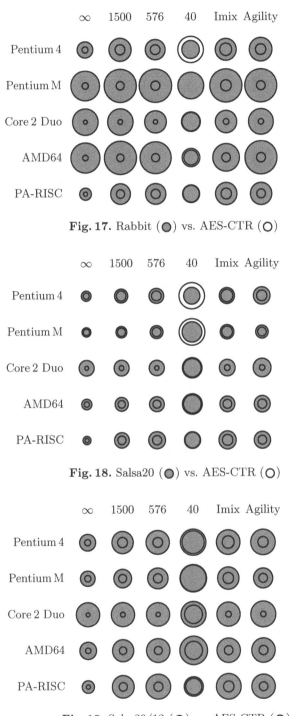

Fig. 17. Rabbit (●) vs. AES-CTR (○)

Fig. 18. Salsa20 (●) vs. AES-CTR (○)

Fig. 19. Salsa20/12 (●) vs. AES-CTR (○)

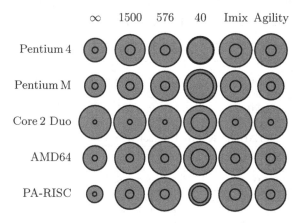

Fig. 20. Salsa20/8 (●) vs. AES-CTR (○)

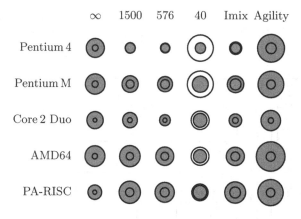

Fig. 21. SOSEMANUK (●) vs. AES-CTR (○)

4.2 Profile 1 Candidates with 256-Bit Keys

In addition to the initial target key length of 128 bit (or 80 bit in Profile 2), several eSTREAM finalists were designed to support longer keys as well. The stream ciphers for which this feature was implemented are listed in Table 3. Their performance is compared in Figs. 22–37.

Table 3. List of considered stream ciphers

Cipher	Profile	Key	IV	MAC
CryptMT-v3	1	256	128	-
Dragon	1	256	128	-
HC-256	1	256	128	-
Salsa20	1	256	64	-
Salsa20/12	1	256	64	-
SOSEMANUK	1	256	128	-
AES-CTR	-	256	128	-
RC4	-	256	-	-
SNOW-2.0	-	256	128	-
F-FCSR-16	2	128	128	-
Grain-128	2	128	96	-
MICKEY-128-v2	2	128	64	-

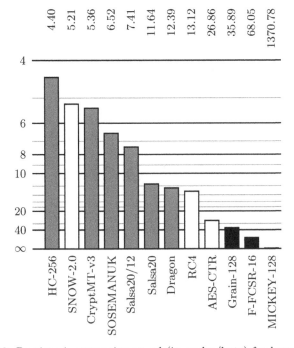

Fig. 22. Pentium 4, encryption speed (in cycles/byte) for long streams

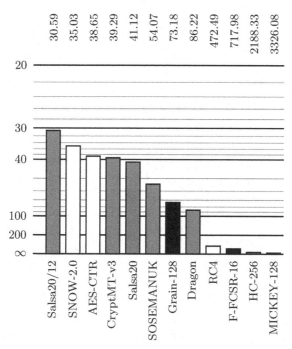

Fig. 23. Pentium 4, encryption speed (in cycles/byte) for 40-byte packets

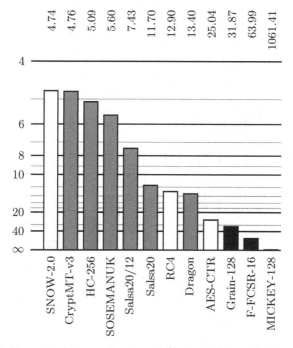

Fig. 24. Pentium M, encryption speed (in cycles/byte) for long streams

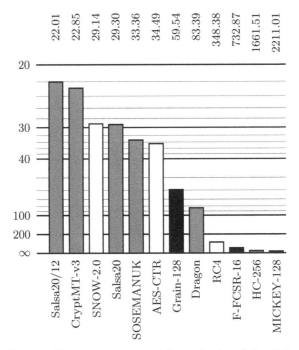

Fig. 25. Pentium M, encryption speed (in cycles/byte) for 40-byte packets

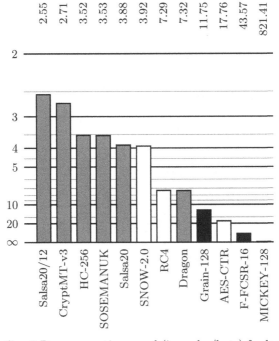

Fig. 26. Core 2 Duo, encryption speed (in cycles/byte) for long streams

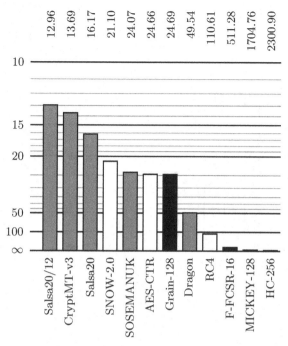

Fig. 27. Core 2 Duo, encryption speed (in cycles/byte) for 40-byte packets

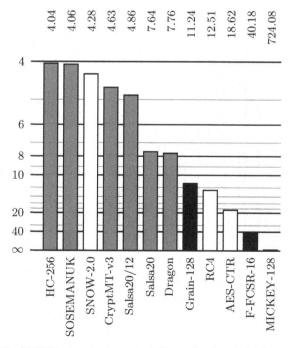

Fig. 28. AMD64, encryption speed (in cycles/byte) for long streams

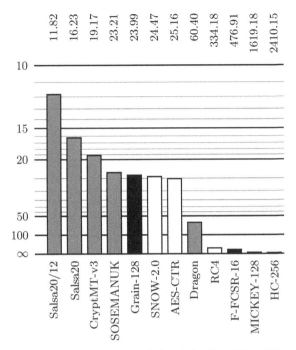

Fig. 29. AMD64, encryption speed (in cycles/byte) for 40-byte packets

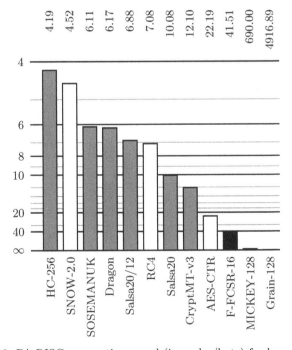

Fig. 30. PA-RISC, encryption speed (in cycles/byte) for long streams

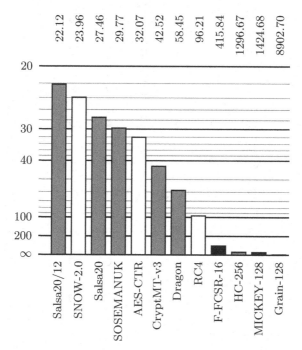

Fig. 31. PA-RISC, encryption speed (in cycles/byte) for 40-byte packets

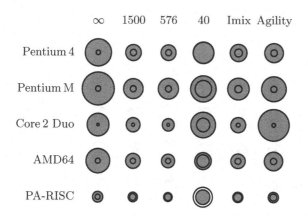

Fig. 32. CryptMT-v3 (⊙) vs. AES-CTR (○)

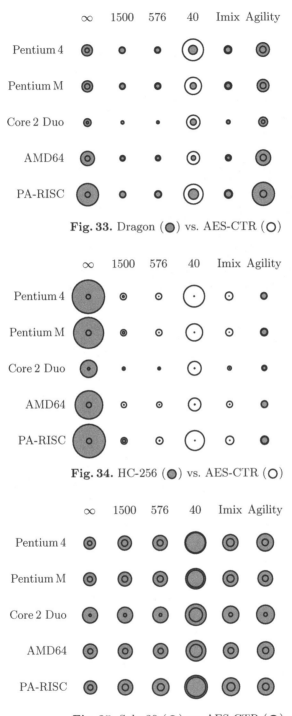

Fig. 33. Dragon (⚫) vs. AES-CTR (◯)

Fig. 34. HC-256 (⚫) vs. AES-CTR (◯)

Fig. 35. Salsa20 (⚫) vs. AES-CTR (◯)

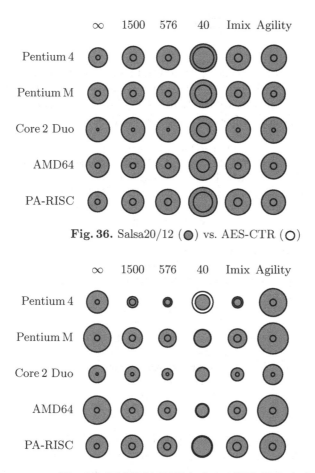

Fig. 36. Salsa20/12 (●) vs. AES-CTR (○)

Fig. 37. SOSEMANUK (●) vs. AES-CTR (○)

References

1. Agilent Technologies, Mixed Packet Size Throughput, Insight Edition 1 (08/2001),
   http://advanced.comms.agilent.com/n2x/docs/insight/2001-08/
2. Bernstein, D.J.: Notes on the ECRYPT Stream Cipher Project (eSTREAM). Software Timings, http://cr.yp.to/streamciphers/timings.html
3. De Cannière, C.: eSTREAM Optimized Code HOWTO,
   http://www.ecrypt.eu.org/stream/perf/

DECIM^{v2}

Côme Berbain[1], Olivier Billet[1], Anne Canteaut[2], Nicolas Courtois[3],
Blandine Debraize[4,5], Henri Gilbert[1], Louis Goubin[4,5], Aline Gouget[4],
Louis Granboulan[6], Cédric Lauradoux[2], Marine Minier[7],
Thomas Pornin[8], and Hervé Sibert[9]

[1] Orange Labs, France
{come.berbain,olivier.billet,henri.gilbert}@orange-ftgroup.com
[2] INRIA Rocquencourt, France
{anne.canteaut,cedric.lauradoux}@inria.fr
[3] University College of London, United Kingdom
n.courtois@ucl.ac.uk
[4] Gemalto, France
{blandine.debraize,aline.gouget}@gemalto.com
[5] Université de Versailles, France
louis.goubin@prism.uvsq.fr
[6] EADS, France
louis.granboulan@eads.net
[7] INSA Lyon, France
marine.minier@insa-lyon.fr
[8] Cryptolog International, France
thomas.pornin@cryptolog.com
[9] NXP Semiconductors, France
herve.sibert@nxp.com

Abstract. In this paper, we present DECIM^{v2}, a stream cipher hardware-oriented selected for the Phase 3 of the ECRYPT stream cipher project eSTREAM. As required by the initial call for hardware-oriented stream cipher contribution, DECIM^{v2} manages 80-bit secret keys and 64-bit public initialization vectors. The design of DECIM^{v2} combines two filtering mechanisms: a nonlinear Boolean filter over a LFSR, followed by an irregular decimation mechanism called the ABSG. Since designers have been invited to demonstrate flexibility of their design by proposing variants that take 128-bit keys, we also present a 128-bit security version of DECIM called DECIM-128.

1 Introduction

DECIM^{v2} is a hardware-oriented stream cipher selected for the Phase 3 of the ECRYPT Stream Cipher Project [1]. DECIM^{v2} is the tweaked version of the original submission DECIM [3]. DECIM^{v2} manages 80-bit secret keys and 64-bit public initialization as required by the initial eSTREAM call for contribution for the hardware-oriented profile. DECIM^{v2} has been developed around the ABSG mechanism [9, 12] which provides a method for irregular decimation of pseudorandom sequences. The ABSG mechanism consists of compressing the input

M. Robshaw and O. Billet (Eds.): New Stream Cipher Designs, LNCS 4986, pp. 140–151, 2008.

sequence in a very simple way and it operates a highly nonlinear transformation. Being an irregular decimation, it prevents algebraic attacks and some fast correlation attacks.

The general running of DECIM^{v2} consists first in generating a binary sequence **y** in a regular way from a Linear Feedback Shift Register (LFSR) which is filtered by a Boolean function. Next, the sequence **y** is filtered by the ABSG mechanism. Wu and Preneel found two weaknesses [15] in the original design of DECIM that have been fixed in DECIM^{v2}. Note that the attacks presented in [15] do not question the main ideas behind DECIM, namely, to filter and then decimate the output of an LFSR using the ABSG mechanism. Since designers have been invited to demonstrate flexibility of their design by proposing variants that take 128-bit keys, we present a 128-bit security version of DECIM called DECIM-128.

The outline of the paper is as follows. In Section 2, we give an overview of DECIM^{v2} and we detail the differences between DECIM and DECIM^{v2}. In Section 3, we provide a full description of DECIM^{v2}. In Section 4, we explain the design rationale. In Section 5, we discuss the hardware implementation. Section 6 is dedicated to the description of DECIM-128. Finally, we conclude in Section 7.

2   Overview of Decim^{v2}

In accordance with the requirements given by the ECRYPT stream cipher project, DECIM^{v2} takes as an input a 80-bit secret key and a 64-bit public initialization vector.

2.1   Keystream Generation

The size of the inner state of DECIM^{v2} is 192 bits. The keystream generation mechanism is described in Figure 1. The bits of the internal state of the LFSR are numbered from 0 to 191, and they are denoted by $(x_0, \ldots, x_{191})$.

The Boolean function f is a 13-variable quadratic symmetric function which is balanced. The whole filter F is a 14-variable Boolean function. The output of the function F at time t is denoted by y_t. The ABSG takes as an input the sequence **y** = $(y_t)_{t \geq 0}$. The sequence output by the ABSG is denoted by **z** = $(z_t)_{t \geq 0}$. The buffer mechanism guarantees a constant throughput for the keystream; we choose a 32 bit-length buffer and the buffer outputs one bit for every four shifts by one position of the LFSR.

2.2   Key/IV Setup

The Key/IV setup mechanism consists in clocking $4 \times 192 = 768$ times the LFSR using the nonlinear feedback described in Figure 2.

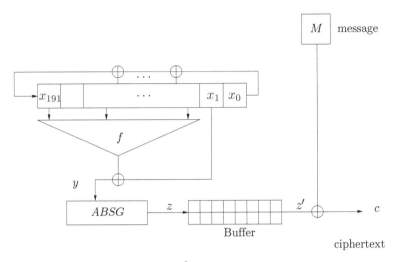

Fig. 1. DECIM^{v2} keystream generation

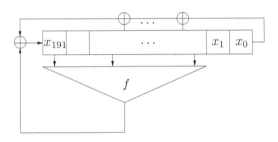

Fig. 2. Key/IV setup mechanism

2.3 Differences between Decim and Decim^{v2}

We do not recall in this paper the full description of the original design of DECIM
(see [3] for details). However, we briefly describe the two flaws in DECIM found by
Wu and Preneel [15], and we explain how DECIM^{v2} fixed these two weaknesses.

The first flaw lies in the initialization stage, i.e. the computation of the initial
inner state for starting the keystream generation. In DECIM, at each clock of
the initialization process, one of two 7-variables permutations π_1 and π_2 was
applied over the internal state in order to break the linearity of the process faster.
However, this mechanism could be exploited to retrieve the key. In DECIM^{v2}, we
use an initialization procedure that is both simpler and more secure than the
one of DECIM. In particular, the permutations are removed in DECIM^{v2} (we
refer to [5] for more details). Moreover, the number of clocks of the register
during the initialization phase is increased in DECIM^{v2} in order to ensure that
the nonlinearity of the initialization stage is sufficient.

The second flaw lies in the keystream generation algorithm. More precisely,
there is a flaw in DECIM in the generation of the sequence **y** which is the output

of the filter (the sequence **y** is next decimated by the ABSG mechanism). This flaw is due to the fact that the sequence **y** is directly the output of a symmetric Boolean function. Indeed, the outputs of the function associated to two input vectors which have one element in common are correlated. It was then shown in [11] that the filter criterion to avoid such correlation is the quasi-immunity criterion. The choice of the filter in DECIM^{v2} takes this design criterion into account.

3   Specification

In this section, we describe each component of DECIM^{v2}.

3.1   The Filtered LFSR

This section describes the filtered LFSR that generates the sequence **y** (the sequence **y** is the input of the ABSG mechanism).

The LFSR. The underlying LFSR is a maximum-length LFSR of length 192 over $\mathbf{F}_2$. It is defined by the following primitive feedback polynomial:

$$P(X) = X^{192} + X^{189} + X^{188} + X^{169} + X^{156} + X^{155} + X^{132} + X^{131}$$
$$+ X^{94} + X^{77} + X^{46} + X^{17} + X^{16} + X^5 + 1 .$$

The sequence of the linear feedback values of the LFSR is denoted by $\mathbf{s} = (s_t)_{t \geq 0}$ and the recursion that corresponds to P for the LFSR is

$$s_{192+n} = s_{187+n} \oplus s_{176+n} \oplus s_{175+n} \oplus s_{146+n} \oplus s_{115+n} \oplus s_{98+n} \oplus s_{61+n}$$
$$\oplus s_{60+n} \oplus s_{37+n} \oplus s_{36+n} \oplus s_{23+n} \oplus s_{4+n} \oplus s_{3+n} \oplus s_n .$$

The filter. The filter function is the 14-variable Boolean function defined by:

$$F : \mathbb{F}_2^{14} \longrightarrow \mathbb{F}_2; \quad a_1, \ldots, a_{14} \mapsto f(a_1, \ldots, a_{13}) \oplus a_{14}$$

where f is the symmetric quadratic Boolean function defined by:

$$f(a_1, \ldots, a_{13}) = \bigoplus_{1 \leq i < j \leq 13} a_i a_j \bigoplus_{1 \leq i \leq 13} a_i$$

The tap positions of the filter are:

$$191 - 186 - 178 - 172 - 162 - 144 - 111 - 104 - 65 - 54 - 45 - 28 - 13 - 1$$

and the input of the ABSG at the stage t is:

$$y_t = f(s_{t+191}, s_{t+186}, s_{t+178}, s_{t+172}, s_{t+162}, s_{t+144},$$
$$s_{t+111}, s_{t+104}, s_{t+65}, s_{t+54}, s_{t+45}, s_{t+28}, s_{t+13}) \oplus s_{t+1} .$$

3.2 Decimation

We now describes how the keystream sequence $\mathbf{z}$ is obtained from the sequence $\mathbf{y}$.

The action of the ABSG on $\mathbf{y}$ consists in splitting $\mathbf{y}$ into subsequences of the form $(\bar{b}, b^i, \bar{b})$, with $i \geq 0$ and $b \in \{0, 1\}$; $\bar{b}$ denotes the complement of b in $\{0, 1\}$. For every subsequence $(\bar{b}, b^i, \bar{b})$, the output bit is b for $i = 0$, and $\bar{b}$ otherwise. The ABSG algorithm is given in Figure 3.

```
Input: (y0, y1, ...)
Set: i ← 0; j ← 0;
Repeat the following steps:
    1.  e ← yi, zj ← yi+1;
    2.  i ← i + 1;
    3.  while (yi = ē) i ← i + 1;
    4.  i ← i + 1;
    5.  output zj;
    6.  j ← j + 1;
```

Fig. 3. ABSG Algorithm

3.3 Buffer Mechanism

The rate of the ABSG mechanism is irregular and therefore we use a buffer in order to guarantee a constant throughput. We choose a buffer of length 32 and for every 4 bits that are input into the ABSG, the buffer is supposed to output one bit exactly. With these parameters, the probability that the buffer is empty while it has to output one bit is less than 2^{-89}.

If the ABSG outputs one bit when the buffer is full, then the newly computed bit is not added into the queue, i.e. it is dropped. The initial filling of the buffer is part of the initialization process detailed in 3.4.

3.4 Key/IV Setup

This subsection describes the computation of the initial inner state for starting the keystream generation. Notice that the ABSG mechanism is not used during the initialization stage.

Initial filling of the LFSR. The secret key K is a 80-bit key denoted by $K = K_0, \ldots, K_{79}$ and the initialization vector IV is a 64-bit IV denoted by $IV_0, \ldots, IV_{63}$. The initial filling of the LFSR is done as follows:

$$x_i = \begin{cases} K_i & 0 \leq i \leq 79, \\ K_{i-80} \oplus IV_{i-80} & 80 \leq i \leq 143, \\ K_{i-80} \oplus IV_{i-144} \oplus IV_{i-128} \oplus IV_{i-112} \oplus IV_{i-96} & 144 \leq i \leq 159, \\ IV_{i-160} \oplus IV_{i-128} \oplus 1 & 160 \leq i \leq 191. \end{cases}$$

The number of possible initial values of the LFSR state is $2^{80+64} = 2^{144}$.

Update of the LFSR state. The LFSR is clocked $4 \times 192 = 768$ times using a nonlinear feedback relation. Let y_t denote the output of f at time t and let lv_t denote the linear feedback value at time $t > 0$. Then, the value of x_{191} at time t is computed using the equation:

$$x_{191} = lv_t \oplus y_t .$$

Notice that there is no bit of the LFSR state output during this step.

Initial filling of the buffer. After the previous step, the buffer has to be filled before starting keystream generation. In order to fill the buffer, we repeat the keystream generation process until the buffer is full. During this step, the buffer is not shifted. In particular, the buffer does not output any bit until it is completely filled. Then, the buffer is filled on average after 96 steps, and it is filled after 234 steps with probability bigger than $1 - 2^{-80}$. Thus, if a constant duration initialization process is required, one can choose to execute 234 steps and throw away the ABSG output bits when the buffer is full.

4   Design Rationale

In this section, we give the rationale for every component of DECIM^{v2}.

4.1   The Filtered LFSR

The LFSR. The length of the LFSR, which corresponds to the size of the internal state of the cipher, must be at least 160 in order to avoid time-memory-date trade-off attacks [13, 6]. Nevertheless, we add a security margin to the LFSR length in order to deal with a reduction of the size of the potential initial state due to the initialization procedure (see Section 4.3). Therefore, we choose a 192-bit LFSR.

The choice of the primitive feedback polynomial P must be made in accordance with the following constraints. The differences between two consecutive positions of the inputs of the feedback polynomial are pairwise coprime. Furthermore, the weight of P must be large enough in order to prevent the existence of sparse multiples with low degree that could be exploited in fast correlation attacks or in distinguishing attacks. However, we do not want the weight of P to be too large, in order to reduce both the overall computational time of the cipher and its hardware size.

The feedback polynomial has been chosen carefully, i.e. it has not low Hamming weight multiples at least for the first 2^{40} next degrees. However, we mention the possibility of a distinguishing attack similar to the distinguishing attack on the Self-Shrinking Generator given in [8].

The filtering function. An important property for the filter is that the output of the filter must be uniformly distributed. Moreover, the filtering function must satisfy some other well-known cryptographic properties. Indeed, it is expected to be far from an affine function (using the Hamming distance). Moreover, the attack presented by Wu and Preneel against DECIM [15] revealed that the filtering function must also fulfil the *quasi-immunity criterion* [11], which is a criterion weaker than being correlation-immune of order 1.

Since DECIM^{v2} is a hardware-oriented cipher, the Boolean filtering function must have a low-cost hardware implementation. In order to get an efficient computation of the function, the Boolean function f has been chosen to be symmetric, i.e. the value of f only depends on the Hamming weight of the input.

The symmetric Boolean functions that best fulfils the previous mentioned criteria are quadratic and have an odd number of input variables. The whole filter F of DECIM^{v2}, constructed from a balanced 13-variable symmetric function, is balanced and correlation-immune of order 1.

The tap positions: filter and feedback polynomial. Assuming knowledge of the keystream $\mathbf{z}$, an attacker will have to guess some bits of the sequence $\mathbf{y}$ in order to attack the function f. The knowledge of the bits of $\mathbf{y}$ directly yields equations in the bits of the initial state of the LFSR. Thus, the number of monomials in the bits of the initial state of the LFSR that are involved in these equations has to be maximized. Moreover, this number has to grow quickly during the first clocks of the LFSR. This implies the following two conditions:

1. Each difference between two positions of bits that are input to f should appear only once;
2. Some inputs of f should be taken at positions near the one of the feedback bit (which means that some inputs should be leftmost on Figure 1).

Finally, the tap positions of the inputs of the Boolean function f and the inputs of the feedback relation should be independent.

4.2   Decimation

The ABSG mechanism was first presented at the ECRYPT Workshop State of the art of stream ciphers [9] and next published in [12]. The ABSG is a scheme that, like the Shrinking Generator (SG) [7] and the Self-Shrinking Generator (SSG) [14], provides a method for irregular decimation of pseudorandom sequences. The ABSG has the advantage on the one hand over the SG that it operates on a single input sequence instead of two and on the other hand over the SSG that it operates at a rate $1/3$ instead of $1/4$ (i.e. producing n bits of the output sequence requires on average $3n$ bits of the input sequence instead of $4n$ bits).

The best known attack on the ABSG filtering a single maximum-length LFSR [12, 10] is based on a guess of the most favorable case. Such a guess requires ℓ output bits in order to guess 2ℓ inputs bits. The guess is correct with probability $\frac{1}{2^\ell}$. In order to check the correctness of his guess, the attacker should try to solve the equations in the bits of the initial state of the LFSR that arise from the bits of $\mathbf{y}$ he has guessed. This attack can be used in order to reconstruct $2L$ consecutive bits of the sequence y from L consecutive bits of the sequence z; it costs $\mathcal{O}(2^{\frac{L}{2}})$ and requires $\mathcal{O}(L2^{\frac{L}{2}})$ bits of z.

Let $\Lambda(\mathbf{y})$ denote the linear complexity of $\mathbf{y}$. Then, the minimal length of a linear feedback shift register which generates the sequence $\mathbf{y}$ is $\Lambda(\mathbf{y})$. The previous attack can be used to reconstruct the initial state of the equivalent LFSR that generates the sequence $\mathbf{y}$. Then, this attack costs $\mathcal{O}(2^{\frac{\Lambda(\mathbf{y})}{2}})$ to recover $\Lambda(\mathbf{y})$ consecutive bits of $\mathbf{y}$.

We have checked that the linear complexity of $\mathbf{y}$ is the best linear complexity expected according to the choice of the Boolean function and the primitive polynomial, that is, $\Lambda(\mathbf{y}) = 18528$.

4.3 Key/IV Setup

The components of the keystream generation are re-used for the key/IV setup; we do not introduce new components.

By using a 80-bit key and a 64-bit IV, the number of possible initial states is at most 2^{144} which is the case in DECIM^{v2}. The key schedule includes a non-linear feedback mechanism that is repeated L times, where L is the length of the register. Thus, in order to deal with the reduction of the potential internal state of the register during this phase, and considering that this non-linear feedback behaves randomly, we chose $L = 192$ to ensure that the final internal state is at least twice the key length, that is, 160.

4.4 The Buffer Mechanism

The buffer mechanism guarantees a constant throughput for the keystream. However, the buffer must have a reasonable length since the keystream generation process starts when the buffer is full.

Recall that for every α bits that are input into the ABSG, the buffer is supposed to output one bit exactly. The output rate of the ABSG is $1/3$ in average. Then, the value of α is greater than 3. For $\alpha = 4$ and a buffer of length 32, the probability that the buffer is empty while it has to output one bit is less than 2^{-89} (the analysis of the buffer mechanism is detailed in [3]).

Timing measurements at the output of the keystream generator is useless since a buffer is used and the throughput is constant. However, if the attacker gets timing information from the internal keystream generator, then timing attacks apply.

5 Hardware Implementation

There is a trade-off between the size of the hardware implementation and the throughput of the cipher. Indeed, the 32-bit length of the buffer has been chosen to ensure that the buffer is ready with probability $(1 - 2^{-89})$ to output one bit every 4 bits entered into the ABSG.

Since each LFSR clock contributes one bit to the sequence entering the ABSG mechanism, one solution is to clock four times the LFSR before outputting one bit. The number of gates involved in an hardware implementation can be estimated as follows, based on the estimation for elementary components given in [2], i.e., 12 gates for a flip-flop, 2.5 gates for an XOR, 1.5 gates for an AND and 5 gates for a MUX.

- LFSR: 2339 gates corresponding to 192 flip-flops and 14 XORs.
- Filtering function: 86.5 gates corresponding to 6 Full Adders and 7 XORs (details on the hardware implementation of quadratic symmetric functions are given in [3]).
- 1-input ABSG, as described in Figure 4: 67 gates corresponding to 2 MUX, 3 XORs, 1 AND, and 4 flip-flops.

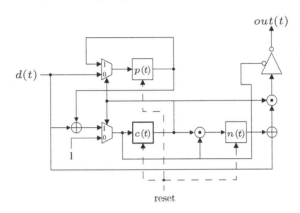

Fig. 4. Hardware implementation of the ABSG

Moreover, the throughput of the generator can be doubled at a low implementation cost by using a simple speed-up mechanism. This can be done with a circuit which computes two feedback bits for the LFSR, simultaneously, as described in [3]. This LFSR with doubled clock rate can be implemented within 192 flip-flops and 28 XORs. One additional copy of the filtering function is also required, and a 2-input ABSG mechanism must be used.

6   Decim-128

In this section, we describe DECIM-128 which is an adaptation of the design of DECIM^{v2} to get 128-bit security (we refer to [4] for more details).

DECIM-128 takes as input a 128-bit secret key and a 128-bit public initialization vector. The keystream generation mechanism is similar as the one described in Figure 1 and the Key/IV setup mechanism is similar as the one described in Figure 2 except that the LFSR has length 288.

6.1   The Filtered LFSR

The underlying LFSR is a maximum-length LFSR of length 288 (instead of 192) over $\mathbb{F}_2$. It is defined by the following primitive feedback polynomial:

$$P(X) = X^{288} + X^{285} + X^{284} + X^{247} + X^{204} + X^{185} + X^{154} + X^{125}$$
$$+ X^{124} + X^{123} + X^{82} + X^{35} + X^{18} + X^5 + 1$$

The filter function is the same as in DECIM^{v2}. The only difference between DECIM^{v2} and DECIM-128 is a different choice of tap positions[1]:

$$287, 276, 263, 244, 236, 203, 187, 159, 120, 73, 51, 39, 21, 1$$

The sequence **y** produced by the filter is of maximal nonlinear complexity, namely equal to $\frac{288 \times 289}{2} = 41616$.

6.2   The Buffer Mechanism

For DECIM-128, we choose a buffer of 64 bits instead of 32. Since the buffer outputs one bit exactly for every 4 bits that are input into the ABSG, the probability that the buffer is empty while it has to output one bit is less than 2^{-178} at each step.

6.3   Key/IV Setup

The secret key K is a 128-bit key denoted by $K = K_0, \ldots, K_{127}$ and the initialization vector IV is a 128-bit IV denoted by $IV = IV_0, \ldots, IV_{127}$. The initial filling of the LFSR is done as follows.

$$x_i = \begin{cases} K_i & 0 \leq i \leq 127 \\ K_{i-128} \oplus IV_{i-128} & 128 \leq i \leq 255 \end{cases}$$

We complete the register with $x_{256} \ldots x_{287} = \text{0x55555555}$. The number of possible initial values of the LFSR is 2^{256}.

This step slightly differs from the injection in DECIM^{v2}. Namely, it is simpler, partly due to the fact that the key and the IV have the same size.

The update of the LFSR is done in the same way as for DECIM^{v2}. The number of clocks performed is also four times the length of the LFSR, so here $4 \times 288 = 1152$ times. After this step, the buffer has to be filled in the same way like for DECIM^{v2}, i.e. by performing the same steps as for keystream generation without shifting the buffer and outputting bits, until the buffer is full. Nevertheless, the buffer is filled with probability bigger than $1 - 2^{-128}$ after 432 steps, which can be used if a constant initialization time is required.

7   Conclusion

We have presented the stream cipher DECIM^{v2} selected in the Phase 3 of the eSTREAM call for stream cipher Profile 2, and the 128-bit security version of DECIM^{v2} called DECIM-128.

---

[1] In the original version of DECIM-128 [4], the choice of taps for the filtering function does not fulfil the claim that "each difference between two positions of bits that are input to f should appear only once". The difference between the original version of DECIM-128 and the latest version presented in this paper is that tap 227 has been replaced by tap 236, and then the claim above is fulfilled.

DECIM^{v2} and DECIM-128 are especially suitable for hardware applications with restricted resources such as limited storage or gate count. Design choices influence the miniaturization of the cipher system:

- the ABSG mechanism has low-cost hardware implementation,
- the filtering function f only depends on the Hamming weight of its input in order to reduce the cost in hardware implementation,
- the IV injection/key schedule re-uses the main components of the keystream generation mechanism.

For applications requiring higher throughputs, speed-up mechanisms can be used to accelerate DECIM^{v2} and DECIM-128 at the expense of a higher hardware complexity. Finally, the security of DECIM^{v2} and DECIM-128 mainly relies on the security of the ABSG, and there is no identified attack better than exhaustive search.

Acknowledgement

This work was partially supported by the French Ministry of Research RNRT Project X-CRYPT and by the European Commission via the ECRYPT Network of Excellence IST-2002-507932. Note that this work was done while the 4th author was affiliated to Axalto/Gemalto (France), the 8th and the 13th authors were affiliated to France Télécom R&D/Orange Labs (France), the 9th author was affiliated to the École Normale Supérieure (France), the 11th author was affiliated to INRIA Rocquencourt (France).

References

1. eStream, Stream cipher project of the European Network of Excellence in Cryptology ECRYPT, http://www.ecrypt.eu.org/stream/
2. Batina, L., Lano, J., Örs, S.B., Preneel, B., Verbauwhede, I.: Energy, perfomance, area versus security trade-offs for stream ciphers. In: The State of the Art of Stream Ciphers: Workshop Record, Brugge, Belgium, October 2004, pp. 302–310 (2004)
3. Berbain, C., Billet, O., Canteaut, A., Courtois, N., Debraize, B., Gilbert, H., Goubin, L., Gouget, A., Granboulan, L., Lauradoux, C., Minier, M., Pornin, T., Sibert, H.: Decim– A new Stream Cipher for Hardware applications. In: ECRYPT Stream Cipher Workshop SKEW 2005 (2005), http://www.ecrypt.eu.org/stream/
4. Berbain, C., Billet, O., Canteaut, A., Courtois, N., Debraize, B., Gilbert, H., Goubin, L., Gouget, A., Granboulan, L., Lauradoux, C., Minier, M., Pornin, T., Sibert, H.: Decim-128 (2007), http://www.ecrypt.eu.org/stream/
5. Berbain, C., Billet, O., Canteaut, A., Courtois, N., Debraize, B., Gilbert, H., Goubin, L., Gouget, A., Granboulan, L., Lauradoux, C., Minier, M., Pornin, T., Sibert, H.: DECIM^{v2}. In: ECRYPT Stream Cipher Workshop SASC (2007), http://www.ecrypt.eu.org/stream/
6. De Cannière, C., Lano, J., Preneel, B.: Comments on the rediscovery of Time Memory Data Tradeoffs (2005), http://www.ecrypt.eu.org/stream/TMD.pdf

7. Coppersmith, D., Krawczyk, H., Mansour, Y.: The shrinking generator. In: Stinson, D.R. (ed.) CRYPTO 1993. LNCS, vol. 773, pp. 22–39. Springer, Heidelberg (1994)

8. Ekdahl, P., Johansson, T., Meier, W.: Predicting the shrinking generator with fixed connections. In: Biham, E. (ed.) EUROCRYPT 2003. LNCS, vol. 2656, pp. 345–359. Springer, Heidelberg (2003)

9. Gouget, A., Sibert, H.: The Bit-Search Generator. In: The State of the Art of Stream Ciphers: Workshop Record, Brugge, Belgium, October 2004, pp. 60–68 (2004)

10. Gouget, A., Sibert, H.: How to strengthen pseudo-random generators by using compression. In: Vaudenay, S. (ed.) EUROCRYPT 2006. LNCS, vol. 4004, pp. 129–146. Springer, Heidelberg (2006)

11. Gouget, A., Sibert, H.: Revisiting correlation-immunity in filter generators. In: Adams, C., Miri, A., Wiener, M. (eds.) SAC 2007. LNCS, vol. 4876. Springer, Heidelberg (2007)

12. Gouget, A., Sibert, H., Berbain, C., Courtois, N., Debraize, B., Mitchell, C.: Analysis of the Bit-Search Generator and sequence compression techniques. In: Gilbert, H., Handschuh, H. (eds.) FSE 2005. LNCS, vol. 3557, pp. 196–214. Springer, Heidelberg (2005)

13. Hong, J., Sarkar, P.: Rediscovery of Time Memory Tradeoffs (2005), http://eprint.iacr.org/2005/090.ps

14. Meier, W., Staffelbach, O.: The self-shrinking generator. In: De Santis, A. (ed.) EUROCRYPT 1994. LNCS, vol. 950, pp. 205–214. Springer, Heidelberg (1995)

15. Wu, H., Preneel, B.: Cryptanalysis of the stream cipher decim. In: Robshaw, M.J.B. (ed.) FSE 2006. LNCS, vol. 4047, pp. 30–40. Springer, Heidelberg (2006)

The Stream Cipher Edon80

Danilo Gligoroski[1], Smile Markovski[2], and Svein Johan Knapskog[1]

[1] Centre for Quantifiable Quality of Service in Communication Systems,
Norwegian University of Science and Technology,
O.S. Bragstads plass 2E, N-7491 Trondheim, Norway
{Danilo.Gligoroski,Svein.J.Knapskog}@q2s.ntnu.no
[2] "Ss Cyril and Methodius" University
Faculty of Natural Sciences and Mathematics, Institute of Informatics
P.O. Box 162, 1000 Skopje, Macedonia
smile@ii.edu.mk

Abstract. Edon80 is a hardware binary additive synchronous stream
cipher. It's properties are: 1.) The internal structure is highly pipelined;
2.) It is highly parallelizable, making it scalable from the speed of processing point of view; 3.) Its design principles offer possibilities to achieve
significant speed asymmetry — it belongs to a family of stream ciphers
that in hardware can have a constant speed of one bit per clock cycle, but
in software implementation on popular modern CPUs can be made as
slow as needed. Since its first description in 2005, it has been analyzed by
several cryptographers, have been implemented in a more compact way
and a MAC functionality have been added. We give a full description of
Edon80 including latest developments and updates.

Keywords: hardware, synchronous stream cipher, Latin square, quasigroup, quasigroup string transformations.

1 Introduction

Edon80 was submitted to the eSTREAM project [1] as a hardware stream cipher
under the Profile 2. It was designed by Gligoroski, Markovski, Kocarev, and
Gusev and its original description is given in [2]. It has a unique design among
known stream cipher designs: it concatenates 80 basic building blocks derived
from four small quasigroups of order 4.

Since its first publication it has been analyzed by several cryptographers and
a new knowledge has been gained that deepened the understanding of Edon80.
First Hong [3,4] observed that there is a small probability, for the period of the
keystream sequence to be quite short. That provoked the designers to investigate
further the issue of the periodicity of the keystream sequences in [5] and later
also in the paper [6]. The result of that was a decision that Edon80 will stay unchanged entering the Phase 2 of eSTREAM project, but the keystream sequence
was restricted to 2^{48} bits [7]. Vojvoda et. al [8] have investigated algebraic properties of quasigroups used in Edon80 and showed that they are isotopic with the
quasigroup of modular subtraction of order 4. Bjørstad [9] have examined the

M. Robshaw and O. Billet (Eds.): New Stream Cipher Designs, LNCS 4986, pp. 152–169, 2008.
© Springer-Verlag Berlin Heidelberg 2008

structure of Edon80 quasigroup permutation, viewed as an S-box or a pair of Boolean functions. He found some interesting relations but has not been able to apply these relations to attack the full cipher. So far, the best attack on Edon80 have been done by Hell and Johansson [10] that have used the analysis of the periods of the keystream sequences of Edon80 in [6] to mount an attack that can recover the key after using 2^{72} so called "simple operations". We will give additional comments about the total computational cost of that attack further in this text.

From the implementation point of view Kasper et. al have shown in [11] that Edon80 can be implemented using less than 3000 gates. On top of that work, Gligoroski and Knapskog [12] have introduced "MAC Edon80" — the stream cipher that is using the internal structure of Edon80 thus producing keystream same as Edon80 but that can compute also a 160 bit Message Authentication Code for the encrypted/decrypted messages.

Our work. This is an extended version of the initial paper [2] updated with the latest analysis of Edon80, latest information about the hardware implementations and information about the possibility to have a MAC functionality in Edon80.

The paper is organized as follows: In Section 2 we discuss the initial design goals for Edon80, in Section 3 we give the mathematical definition and preliminaries, then in Section 4 we describe Edon80 from algorithmic point of view, next in Section 5 we describe Edon80 from functional perspective (hardware point of view), in Section 6 we discuss the security of the cipher, in Section 7 we discuss Edon80 hardware implementations, and we conclude the paper with conclusions.

2   Design Goals for Edon80

Edon80 is a binary additive synchronous stream cipher. The designers of Edon80 set several goals that are common for a design of a modern hardware stream cipher:

1. To have small number of gates (and thus to have small power consumption);
2. To be fast;
3. To be secure (with as much as possible mathematical analytical ground for its security);
4. To be easily scalable i.e. parallelizable.

An additional goal of Edon80 design was Edon80 to have significant *Speed Asymmetry*: Superior performances when implemented in hardware (from both speed and cost perspective), and in the same time to have very pour performances when realized in software on modern CPUs. Moreover, the goal was to have a design that can be easily extensible, with possibilities to stretch the Speed Asymmetry as much as is needed, but not on the cost of reducing the security or introducing new uninvestigated design parts. The reasons for this design goal were that having a solid, strong and very fast stream cipher in hardware, while in the same time to be inappropriate to simulate it efficiently on modern CPUs, can be useful for industrial applications. One possible application would be for example in the entertainment industry where protection and reproduction of multimedia content is always challenged by pirate users which "rip" and then reproduce qualitatively the multimedia materials on modern computer systems with fast CPUs. As a support for this standing we can mention the very well known fiasco of DVD hardware (and software) protection as well as the latest stories of the cracking of AACS encryption scheme used by both HD-DVD and Blu-Ray video discs.

3   Preliminaries: Basic Mathematical Terms, Definitions, and Theorems Used for Edon80

We will briefly mention the definition of the synchronous stream ciphers as it is defined in [13], pp.193–194. A synchronous stream cipher is one in which the keystream is generated independently of the plaintext message and of the ciphertext. The encryption process of a synchronous stream cipher can be described by the equations:

$$\sigma_{i+1} = f(\sigma_i, k), \ z_i = g(\sigma_i, k), \ c_i = h(z_i, m_i),$$

where σ_0 is the initial state and may be determined from the key k, f is the next-state function, g is the function which produces the keystream z_i, and h is the output function which combines the keystream and plaintext m_i to produce ciphertext c_i. A binary additive stream cipher is a synchronous stream cipher in which the keystream, the plaintext and the ciphertext digits are binary digits, and the output function h is the XOR function.

By the definition of Edon80, we conclude that it is a binary additive synchronous stream cipher. It is defined by using quasigroup operations and quasigroup string transformations and here we give a brief overview of these notions (more detailed explanation the reader can find in [14,15]).

A quasigroup $(Q, *)$ is a groupoid satisfying the law

$$(\forall u, v \in Q)(\exists! \ x, y \in Q) \quad u * x = v \ \& \ y * u = v. \tag{1}$$

We use only finite quasigroups, i.e Q is a finite set. Closely related combinatorial structures to finite quasigroups are the so called Latin squares: A Latin square L on a finite set Q of cardinality $|Q| = n$ is an $n \times n$-matrix with elements from Q such that each row and each column of the matrix is a permutation of Q.

To any finite quasigroup $(Q, *)$ given by its multiplication table it is associated a Latin square L, consisting of the matrix formed by the main body of the table, and each Latin square L on a set Q define a quasigroup $(Q, *)$. The set of Latin squares of order n can be lexicographically ordered by concatenating the rows: $first \ row|| \ second \ row|| \ldots || \ n - th \ row$. Thus, for the quasigroups Nr. 61 and Nr. 241 from Table 2 we have:

$$0213||2130||1302||3021 < 1302||0123||2031||3210$$

There are 576 quasigroups of order 4, and for Edon80 designs, by our experiments, most suitable are the following 64 (given by their lexicographic numbers): 12, 19, 23, 30, 32, 58, 59, 61, 74, 76, 85, 90, 115, 117, 134, 136, 143, 149, 155, 158, 162, 167, 173, 177, 188, 190, 204, 205, 226, 231, 241, 255, 265, 286, 319, 320, 339, 350, 358, 362, 366, 384, 386, 391, 394, 404, 413, 419, 424, 428, 446, 459, 487, 493, 496, 503, 512, 513, 519, 530, 541, 558, 562, 564.

Next we define the method of quasigroup string transformations. Consider an alphabet (i.e. a finite set) Q, and denote by Q^+ the set of all nonempty words (i.e. finite strings) formed by the elements of Q. The elements of Q^+ will be rather denoted by $a_1 a_2 \ldots a_n$ than $(a_1, a_2, \ldots, a_n)$, where $a_i \in Q$. Let $*$ be a quasigroup operation on the set Q, i.e. consider a quasigroup $(Q, *)$. For each $a \in Q$ we define the function $e_{a,*} : Q^+ \longrightarrow Q^+$ as follows. Let $a_i \in Q$, $\alpha = a_1 a_2 \ldots a_n$. Then

$$e_{a,*}(\alpha) = b_1 b_2 \ldots b_n \iff b_1 = a * a_1, \ b_2 = b_1 * a_2, \ldots, \ b_n = b_{n-1} * a_n,$$

i.e. $b_{i+1} = b_i * a_{i+1}$ for each $i = 0, 1, \ldots, n-1$, where $b_0 = a$. The function $e_{a,*}$ is called an e-transformation of Q^+ based on the operation $*$ with leader a, and their graphical representation is shown on Figure 1.

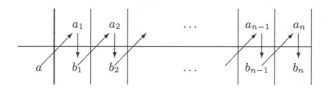

Fig. 1. Graphical representation of the transformation $e_{a,*}$

Several quasigroup operations can be defined on the set Q and let $*_1$, $*_2$, $\ldots$, $*_k$ be a sequence of (not necessarily distinct) such operations. We choose also leaders l_1, l_2, $\ldots$, $l_k \in Q$ (not necessarily distinct either), and then the composition of functions

$$E_k = E_{l_1 \ldots l_k} = e_{l_1,*_1} \circ e_{l_2,*_2} \circ \cdots \circ e_{l_k,*_k},$$

is said to be an E-transformation of Q^+. The function E_k has many interesting properties, and for our purposes the most important ones are the following:

Theorem 1. ([15]) *The transformations E_k are permutation of Q^+.*

Theorem 2. ([15]) *Consider an arbitrary string $\alpha = a_1 a_2 \ldots a_n \in Q^+$, where $a_i \in Q$, and let $\beta = E_k(\alpha)$. If n is large enough integer then, for each $l : 1 \leq l \leq k$, the distribution of substrings of β of length l is uniform. (We note that for $l > k$ the distribution of substrings of β of length l may not be uniform.)*

We say that a string $\alpha = a_1 a_2 \ldots a_n \in Q^+$, where $a_i \in Q$, has a period p if p is the smallest positive integer such that $a_{i+1} a_{i+2} \ldots a_{i+p} = a_{i+p+1} a_{i+p+2} \ldots \ldots a_{i+2p}$ for each $i \geq 0$. The following property holds:

Theorem 3. ([15]) *Let* $\alpha = a_1 a_2 \ldots a_n \in Q^+$, $a_i \in Q$, *and let* $\beta = E_k(\alpha)$, *where* $E_k = E_{aa\ldots a}$, $a \in A$ *and* $a * a \neq a$. *Then the periods of the string* β *is increasing at least linearly by* k.

We should note that the increasing of the periods depends of the number of quasigroup transformations k, and for some of them it is exponential, i.e. if α has a period p, then $\beta = E_k(\alpha)$ may have period greater than $p \, 2^{ck}$, where c is some constant. (Concerning Theorem 3, we notice that there are quasigroups $(Q, *)$ with $a * a = a$, $a \in Q$, that produce string $\beta = E_k(\alpha)$ with large period, if $\alpha = a_1 a_2 \ldots a_n \in Q^+$ is such that $a_1 \neq a$.)

4   Algorithmic Description of Edon80

4.1   *Keystream* Mode

We will start the description of Edon80 by description of the *Keystream* mode that is presented at the Table 1. In the first row of that table we place a periodic (potentially infinite) string that has shape: $01230123\cdots0123\cdots$. The next 80 rows in the table describe 80 e-transformations of that string by using the values a_i (obtained from *IVSetup* mode) and by the quasigroups $*_i$ (determined in *KeySetup* mode). The recurrence equations for these transformations are:

$$
\begin{cases}
a_{0,0} = a_0 *_0 0 & \\
a_{0,j} = a_{0,j-1} *_0 (j \bmod 4) & 1 \leq j \\
a_{i,0} = a_i *_i a_{i-1,0} & 1 \leq i \leq 79 \\
a_{i,j} = a_{i,j-1} *_i a_{i-1,j} & 1 \leq i \leq 79, \ 1 \leq j
\end{cases}
\tag{2}
$$

The output of the stream cipher is every second value of the last e-transformation i.e. the *Keystream* can be described as:

$$
Keystream = a_{79,1} \, a_{79,3} \, a_{79,5} \ \cdots \ a_{79,2k-1} \cdots, \quad k = 1, 2, \ldots
$$

Table 1. Representation of quasigroup string e-transformations of Edon80 during *Keystream* mode

$*_i$		0	1	2	3	0	1	2	3	0 . .
$*_0$	a_0	$a_{0,0}$	$a_{0,1}$	$a_{0,2}$	$a_{0,3}$	$a_{0,4}$	$a_{0,5}$	$a_{0,6}$	$a_{0,7}$	$a_{0,8}$ . .
$*_1$	a_1	$a_{1,0}$	$a_{1,1}$	$a_{1,2}$	$a_{1,3}$	$a_{1,4}$	$a_{1,5}$	$a_{1,6}$	$a_{1,7}$	$a_{1,8}$ . .
.	.	.		.		.		.		. . .
$*_{79}$	a_{79}	$a_{79,0}$	$a_{79,1}$	$a_{79,2}$	$a_{79,3}$	$a_{79,4}$	$a_{79,5}$	$a_{79,6}$	$a_{79,7}$	$a_{79,8}$ . .

4.2   *KeySetup* Mode

According to the values of the bits in the key in this mode we will make assignments of four predefined quasigroups of order 4 to the working 80 quasigroups. The working quasigroups will perform the e-transformations in the i-th row both

Table 2. Quasigroups used for our design of Edon80

Nr. 61 $(q = 2.66^{80})$ Nr. 241 $(q = 2.48^{80})$ Nr. 350 $(q = 2.43^{80})$ Nr. 564 $(q = 2.37^{80})$

$\bullet_0$	0 1 2 3		$\bullet_1$	0 1 2 3		$\bullet_2$	0 1 2 3		$\bullet_3$	0 1 2 3
0	0 2 1 3		0	1 3 0 2		0	2 1 0 3		0	3 2 1 0
1	2 1 3 0		1	0 1 2 3		1	1 2 3 0		1	1 0 3 2
2	1 3 0 2		2	2 0 3 1		2	3 0 2 1		2	0 3 2 1
3	3 0 2 1		3	3 2 1 0		3	0 3 1 2		3	2 1 0 3

Table 3. Representation of quasigroup string e-transformations of Edon80 during *IVSetup* mode

$*_i$		K_0	K_1	$\cdots$	K_{39}	v_0	v_1	$\cdots$	v_{39}
$*_0$	v_{39}	$t_{0,0}$	$t_{0,1}$	$\cdots$	$t_{0,39}$	$t_{0,40}$	$t_{0,41}$	$\cdots$	$t_{0,79}$
$*_1$	v_{38}	$t_{1,0}$	$t_{1,1}$	$\cdots$	$t_{1,39}$	$t_{1,40}$	$t_{1,41}$	$\cdots$	$t_{1,79}$
.	.			.		.	.	.	
$*_{38}$	v_1	$t_{38,0}$	$t_{38,1}$	$\cdots$	$t_{38,39}$	$t_{38,40}$	$t_{38,41}$	$\cdots$	$t_{38,79}$
$*_{39}$	v_0	$t_{39,0}$	$t_{39,1}$	$\cdots$	$t_{39,39}$	$t_{39,40}$	$t_{39,41}$	$\cdots$	$t_{39,79}$
$*_{40}$	K_{39}	$t_{40,0}$	$t_{40,1}$	$\cdots$	$t_{40,39}$	$t_{40,40}$	$t_{40,41}$	$\cdots$	$t_{40,79}$
$*_{41}$	K_{38}	$t_{41,0}$	$t_{41,1}$	$\cdots$	$t_{41,39}$	$t_{41,40}$	$t_{41,41}$	$\cdots$	$t_{41,79}$
.	.			.		.	.	.	
$*_{78}$	K_1	$t_{78,0}$	$t_{78,1}$	$\cdots$	$t_{78,39}$	$t_{78,40}$	$t_{78,41}$	$\cdots$	$t_{78,79}$
$*_{79}$	K_0	$t_{79,0}$	$t_{79,1}$	$\cdots$	$t_{79,39}$	$t_{79,40}$	$t_{79,41}$	$\cdots$	$t_{79,79}$

in *IVSetup* and in *Keystream* mode, as described in Table 3 and Table 1. Those four predefined quasigroups are described in Table 2.

It is known that there are 576 quasigroups of order 4. By our investigations 384 of them are suitable, and 64 of them are very suitable for our purposes. The list of those 64 quasigroups and the reasons why they are suitable for construction of Edon80 stream cipher are given in Section 3. In Table 2, Nr. denotes the lexicographic number of the quasigroup, and q denotes the projected period of the string 012301230123... after 80 e-transformations with that quasigroup.

The assignment of the working quasigroups is done by the following formula:

$$(Q, *_i) \leftarrow \begin{cases} (Q, \bullet_{K_i}) & 0 \le i \le 39 \\ (Q, \bullet_{K_{i-40}}) & 40 \le i \le 79 \end{cases} \tag{3}$$

where Key as a vector of 80 bits is represented as a concatenation of 40 2-bit variables K_i i.e. $Key = K_0 K_1 \cdots K_{39}$.

4.3 *IVSetup* Mode

IVSetup mode in fact defines the initial values of the internal states $a_0, \ldots, a_{79}$, from the values of initial vector IV. The initial vector IV of length 64 bits is padded by 16 constant bits 1110010000011011, represented as the string 32100123 of 2-bits. Thus, the padded initial vector IV is a concatenation of

40 2-bit variables $IV = v_0 v_1 \cdots v_{31} 3\ 2\ 1\ 0\ 0\ 1\ 2\ 3 = v_0 v_1 \cdots v_{39}$. Then we perform 80 e-transformations on IV as described in the Table 3. All of those transformations can be described by the following recurrence equations:

$$
\begin{cases}
t_{0,0} = v_{39} *_0 K_0 \\
t_{0,j} = t_{0,j-1} *_0 K_j & 1 \le j \le 39 \\
t_{0,j} = t_{0,j-1} *_0 v_{j-40} & 40 \le j \le 79 \\
t_{i,0} = v_{39-i} *_i t_{i-1,0} & 1 \le i \le 39 \\
t_{i,0} = K_{79-i} *_i t_{i-1,0} & 40 \le i \le 79 \\
t_{i,j} = t_{i,j-1} *_i t_{i-1,j} & 1 \le i \le 79,\ 1 \le j \le 79
\end{cases}
\tag{4}
$$

After all 80 e-transformations are performed, the values of $a_0, \ldots, a_{79}$ are initialized by the following assignments:

$$
a_i \leftarrow t_{79,i}\ ,\ i = 0, \ldots, 79.
\tag{5}
$$

5   Functional Description of Edon80

Edon80 is a binary additive stream cipher. On Figure 2 we give a global schematic presentation of Edon80 as a binary additive stream cipher.

Schematic and behavioral description of Edon80 is given on Figure 3. Edon80 works in three possible modes: 1) *KeySetup*, 2) *IVSetup* and 3) *Keystream* mode. For its proper work Edon80 beside the core (that will be described later) has the following additional resources:

1. One register *Key* of 80 bits to store the actual secret key;
2. One register *IV* of 80 bits to store padded initialization vector;
3. One internal 2-bit counter *Counter* as a feeder of Edon80 Core in *Keystream* mode;
4. One 7 bit *SetupCounter* that is used in *IVSetup* mode;
5. One $4 \times 4 = 16$ bytes ROM bank where 4 quasigroups (i.e. Latin squares) of order 4, indexed from $(Q, \bullet_0)$ to $(Q, \bullet_3)$, are stored.

The structure of the Edon80 Core is described in the next two figures. The internal structure of Edon80 can be seen as pipelined architecture of 80 simple 2-bit transformers called e-transformers. The schematic view of a single e-transformer is shown on Figure 4.

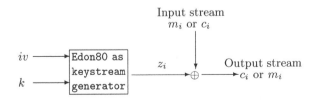

Fig. 2. Graphical representation of Edon80 as binary additive stream cipher

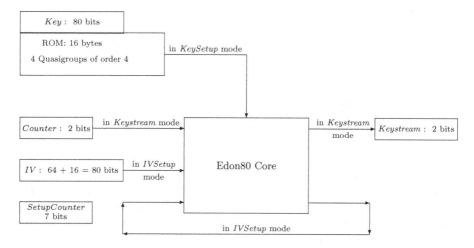

Fig. 3. Edon80 components and their relations

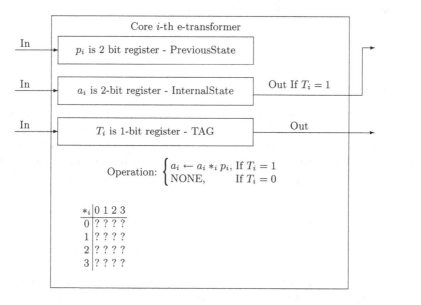

Fig. 4. Schematic representation of a single e-transformer of Edon80

The structure that performs the operation $*_i$ in e-transformers is a quasigroup operation of order 4. We refer an e-transformer by its quasigroup operation $*_i$. For the definition of quasigroup string transformations and some of their properties see Appendix A. So, in Edon80 we have 80 of this e-transformers (the index i varies from 0 to 79), cascaded in a pipeline, one feeding another. The two 2-bit registers inside every e-transformer (p_i and a_i) are used as two operands by which the new value of a_i is determined according to the defined quasigroup operation

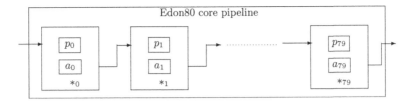

Fig. 5. Edon80 core of 80 pipelined e-transformers

$*_i$ for that e-transformer. For different e-transformers there is possibility different quasigroup operations to be defined, out of a set of 4 predefined quasigroups of order 4. More on the principles of choosing quasigroups for Edon80 is written in Section 2. Every e-transformer has one tag-bit T_i which controls whether the e-transformer will compute the next value of a_i or do nothing. All of this 80 e-transformers work in parallel to calculate their new value of a_i (if the tag permits that) and then pass that new value a_i to the right neighboring register p_{i+1}. If the tag forbids the calculation of a_i, the only value that is transferred to the neighboring element is the value of the tag T_i. Figure 5 shows the pipelined core of Edon80.

Next, we give a description how Edon80 parts works in the three different modes.

5.1 *KeySetup* Mode

When working in *KeySetup* mode, after transferring 80 bits in the register *Key*, the key is virtually divided into 40 2-bit consecutive values. That means we represent *Key* as $Key = K_0 K_1 \cdots K_{39}$, where each K_i consists of 2 bits, and thus it can have a value from 0 to 3. According to this values, in the *KeySetup* mode every working quasigroup operation $*_i$, $i = 0, 1, 2, \ldots, 79$, is assigned by the Equation 3.

5.2 *IVSetup* Mode

In *IVSetup* mode, after transferring 64 bits in the register *IV*, we pad the *IV* with 16 constant bits 1110010000011011, whose interpretation as a concatenation of 2-bit variables gives the string: 32100123. We represent the padded *IV* as concatenation of 40 2-bit variables v_i i.e. $IV = v_0 v_1 \cdots v_{31}\ 3\ 2\ 1\ 0\ 0\ 1\ 2\ 3$, where $v_0 v_1 \cdots v_{31}$ are the transferred 2-bits. *IVSetup* has the following steps:

- *Initialization:* Make the following assignments:

$$\begin{cases} T_i \leftarrow 0 & i = 0, ..., 79 \\ a_{39-i} \leftarrow v_i & i = 0, ..., 39 \\ a_{79-i} \leftarrow K_i & i = 0, ..., 39 \end{cases}$$

- *Cycle 0:* Set the tag T_0 to 1 and feed the register p_0 by the value of K_0. Recall that the value of a_0 is assigned to v_0 by the initialization, so the new value of a_0 will be $v_0 *_0 K_0$.

- *Cycle 1:* The new values of a_0 and T_0 are then send to the second e-transformer $*_1$ and the register p_0 is feeded by K_1. In such a way we have the assignments $p_0 \leftarrow K_1$, $p_1 \leftarrow a_0$, $T_1 \leftarrow T_0$.
- *Cycles 2–79:* In the next 78 cycles we feed the register p_0 of Edon80 Core in order by the following values: K_2, K_3, ..., K_{39} and after that by v_0, v_1, ..., v_{39}. Thus consecutively each of the e-transformers $*_2$, ..., $*_{79}$ will start working.
- *Cycle 80:* Set the tag T_0 to 0, and feed the content of the register a_{79} into the register a_0. Notice that after this cycle the e-transformer $*_0$ will stop and the value of the register a_0 will be preserved. (That value is in fact the starting internal state of the register a_0 for the *Keystream* mode.)
- *Cycle 81–159:* In the next 79 cycles all of the e-transformers $*_1, \ldots, *_{79}$ will stop consecutively. When the register $*_i$ stops, the content of the register a_{79} will be feeded into the register a_i. (Notice that the values of the registers $a_0, a_1, \ldots, a_{79}$ are starting internal states for the *Keystream* mode.)

For concrete realization of all cycles in *IVSetup* mode we use the internal 7 bit register *SetupCounter* and a related logic that will control its values (when it reaches the value 80, to set it again to 0).

5.3 *Keystream* Mode

To start the *Keystream* mode we just reset the value of *Counter* to 0 and set the value of T_0 to 1.

In the *Keystream* mode we feed the Edon80 Core by the values in the register *Counter* which increases its value every cycle. After a latency of 80 cycles, keystream starts to flow from the last e-transformer i.e. from the 2-bit register a_{79}. We have to stress here that the most important part for the security of the stream cipher is that the keystream consist of every second value that comes out from a_{79}.

5.4 Reference C Code Implementation and Test Vectors

The Reference C code implementation and test vectors are given at eSTREAM web pages [1].

6 Security of Edon80

The internal state of Edon80 has two parts:

1. Assign working quasigroups $*_i$, $i = 0, \ldots, 39$, which can be done in 4^{40} ways;
2. Actual values of a_i, $i = 0, \ldots, 79$, which has a space of 4^{80} possibilities.

So, it follows that the total internal space of Edon80 is $4^{40} \times 4^{80} = 2^{240}$. Thus we can conclude that a simple attack by searching the state space is much more worst then the exhaustive search attack on the key, which is 2^{80}. We will show that an exhaustive search attack on the key is the best attack on Edon80.

6.1   Security on Related Key Attack

Related key attack is attempt to find two different keys that will produce the same keystream. Edon80 uses initial values for $a_0, \ldots, a_{79}$ obtained by *IVSetup* where every bit of the key is involved in highly correlated and nonlinear way. Additionally, since computation of the initial values for $a_0, \ldots, a_{79}$ is done by involvement of 64 bit vector of IV, the search for keys that will produce a same keystream (related or unrelated) should be done in the space of proportions $2^{80} \times 2^{64} = 2^{144}$. From the last estimation, it is expected that by birthday paradox, finding a combination of Key and IV that would give the same keystream would take 2^{72} attempts. However, it is possible only under the assumption that collisions exist and they are easy to find. We have designed the *IVSetup* procedure to act as a one-way and collision resistant function, and that is the basis of the resistance of Edon80 on related key attack.

6.2   Security of *IVSetup* Mode

We would consider that the adversary would jeopardize the security of the system if, by knowing the initialization vector IV, she/he can gain some knowledge about the internal states of the cipher. The internal states are loaded into the registers $a_0, \ldots, a_{79}$ from the last e-transformer in Edon80 core (i.e. from the corresponding values of $t_{79,j}$, $j = 0, \ldots, 79$, given in Table 3). Thus, the adversary should obtain the values from $t_{79,j}$, $j = 0, \ldots, 79$, and for this aim she/he can use the recursively defined equation (4) or the Table 3. By supposing that the IV, i.e. the values $v_0, \ldots, v_{39}$, are known to the adversary it is clear that $t_{79,j}$, $j = 0, \ldots, 39$, depends of 40 unknown variables $K_0, \ldots, K_{39}$, in a highly nonlinear way determined by the 4 quasigroups of order 4. From algebraic point of view those 4 quasigroups has very small number of algebraic properties: they are not groups, not semigroups, and they are not commutative. In the current development of the algebraic theory of quasigroups, there is not known methodology to solve such huge and complex systems of quasigroup equations, except the simple combinatorial approach by examining all the possibilities. There are $4^{40} = 2^{80}$ possible choices of the key, and $4^{80} = 2^{160}$ possible assignments of the registers $a_0, \ldots, a_{79}$. Thus, the best choice for an adversary is to guess the key.

If Edon80 is used in combination with a protocols that will transmit IV secretely, then the adversary has $2^{64} \times 2^{80} \times 2^{160} = 2^{304}$ cases to examine and to find internal state of the cipher.

From algebraic point of view, we can see the *IVSetup* mode as a function that maps $\{0,1\}^{64} \rightarrow \{0,1\}^{160}$. To be more specific, given the key $K_0, \ldots, K_{39}$, a function $ivs : \{0,1\}^{64} \rightarrow \{0,1\}^{160}$ can be defined by the equation (4) or the Table 3, such that ivs maps $(v_0 \ldots v_{31})$ into $(a_0 \ldots a_{79})$. The function ivs act as a one-way function, since it is computationally infeasible to find the value $(v_0 \ldots v_{31})$, given $(a_0 \ldots a_{79})$. We can make a fairly assumption that the distribution of the images $ivs(v_0 \ldots v_{31})$ in the space 2^{160} is uniform, having in mind the Theorems 1 and 2 in Section 3. Thus, we can take that the probability of obtaining a collision $ivs(v_0 \ldots v_{31}) = ivs(v'_0 \ldots v'_{31})$ for some $(v_0 \ldots v_{31}) \neq (v_0 \ldots v_{31})$

is very small, about $2^{64}/2^{160} = 2^{-96}$. So, the adversary cannot apply a chosen initial vector attack.

6.3   Guess-and-Verify Attack

In this attack, the attacker will guess a part of the internal states of the cipher, and then will try to predict the outcome of the next bits.

The nature of the design of Edon80 is such that according to the values of the *Key*, appropriate quasigroups are chosen to perform e-transformations. So, in order to try to predict the outcome of the cipher, she/he has to have at least the assumption about the last quasigroup operation $*_{79}$ and the last actual value of the internal variable a_{79}. The total number of guesses for this situation is in fact not very big. Only 16 possible situations can be guessed for $*_{79}$ and a_{79}. However, for predicting the next output value from the stream cipher, important part is the input that comes from 78-th e-transformer. By the Theorems 1 and 2 (in Section 3) it follows that the probability for every 4 values $\{0, 1, 2, 3\}$ to come from the 78-th e-transformer is $\frac{1}{4}$. Since the 79-th e-transformation is done by a quasigroup, it follows that the outcome from the last 79-th e-transformation would have the probability of $\frac{1}{4}$ again for every value $\{0, 1, 2, 3\}$. Thus, the attacker has to have a knowledge about the actual value of a_{78} as well as the type of $*_{78}$ e-transformation in order to achieve better prediction of the outcome of the stream cipher. That implies that additional 16 guesses have to be made.

The above reasoning can be repeated at least 80 times, implying that the total number of guesses to make in order to have significant success of the guesses is rapidly increasing to the value of $16^{80} = 2^{320}$. So, again, the exhaustive attack on the key is better then this attack.

6.4   Projected Period of the *Keystream*

In the initial submission of Edon80 it was projected that the period of the *Keystream* after applying 80 e-transformation is $\approx 2^{103}$ bits.

However, after Hong's attack [4] the designers did a much detailed analysis in [5,6] and posted a note [7] to eSTREAM before entering the Phase 2. The result is that now Edon80 as a stream cipher has one of the best understood and elaborated mathematical models that describe the distribution of the periods of its produced keystream. We present here some parts of [7].

The attack presented in [3] is based on analyzing *(key, state)* pairs (concrete assignment of working quasigroups $*_i$ and initial values for a_i) that give small periods. Hong experimentally counted all possible *(key, state)* pairs for periods 4, 8, and 16, with the number d of rows from 5 to 18 and summarized the results in Table 1 of [3]. These numbers were then extrapolated for the value $d = 40$ in Table 2 of [3]. Then, by repeating the sequence of obtained working quasigroups $*_i$ from the first 40 e-transformations to the last 40 e-transformations (as it is done in Edon80) and by giving a freedom of 80 bits for choosing the leaders for those transformations a_i, $i = 39, 40, \ldots, 79$ he computed that the probabilities of obtaining periods with the lengths in the range $2^{53} - 2^{55}$ are in the range

Table 4. Summary table from [3] with the projections of the probabilities for obtaining streams with the lengths shorter then indicated in the first column

Stream length less than	Probability
2^{20}	?
2^{53}	2^{-88}
2^{54}	2^{-78}
2^{55}	2^{-71}
2^{61}	2^{-75}
2^{62}	2^{-66}
2^{63}	2^{-60}

from $2^{-88} - 2^{-71}$. By reducing the initial extrapolation not to the 40-th row, but to the 34-th row, he computed the probabilities of obtaining periods in the range $2^{61} - 2^{63}$ with even much higher values in the range $2^{-75} - 2^{-60}$. He even mentioned the possibility of the existence of a (*key, state*) pair that will give a very short period of only 2^{20} but does not give the projection of the probability for obtaining that period. The summary of his findings are given in Table 4.

In [6] we treated the situation of finding (*key, state*) pairs that will produce short keystreams as a *weak key attack* on Edon80. Further on, we derived a precise formula for the distribution of the lengths of Edon80 keystreams as well as for the whole family Edon-$(2m, 2k)$ of stream ciphers with different key lengths

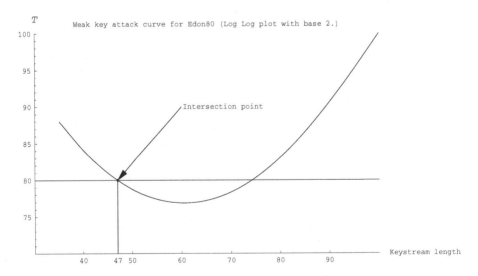

Fig. 6. Log-Log plot of the weak key curve for Edon80. The intersection with the security limit of 2^{80} is for the keystreams with length slightly larger than 2^{47} 2-bit letters i.e. of length 2^{48} bits.

of $2k$ bits and internal pipelines of length $2m$. The distribution is given by the following expression:

$$F_{Y_{2m}}(y) = \frac{1}{2}\left(1 + \text{erf}\left(\frac{1.00777\,(\ln(2y) - 1.535086\,m)}{\sqrt{m}}\right)\right), \quad 0 < y < \infty, \quad (6)$$

and from there for the Edon80 stream cipher (which renamed would be Edon-(80,80)) the concrete distribution is:

$$F_{Y_{80}}(y) = \frac{1}{2}\left(1 + \text{erf}\left(\frac{1.00777\,(\ln(2y) - 61.4034)}{\sqrt{40}}\right)\right), \quad 0 < y < \infty. \quad (7)$$

In the same paper [6] (in Lemma 2) a criterion for the weak keys attack have been given and can be expressed by the following expression:

$$\min_{m}\left(\frac{y}{F_{Y_{2m}}(y)} \geq 2^{2m}, \ \forall y > 0\right).$$

If we put $T(y) = \frac{y}{F_{Y_{2m}}(y)}$ then one possible way for achieving $T(y) \geq 2^{2m}$ is by increasing the length of internal pipeline $2m$. That possible tweak for Edon80 was mentioned in [6]. Namely, simple increasing of the internal pipeline from 80 to 84 elements eliminates the weak key attack and meets the criterion of Lemma 2. However, there is another possible tweak that would need not intervention in the original submission of Edon80. That is the tweak in which the mode of operation of Edon80 is such that it needs reinitialization with new IV after every 2^{48} produced bits of the keystream. From the equation (7) we can compute that the probability a period of a keystream to be less than 2^{48} bits is $2^{-33.01}$.

According to our analysis in [5,6] and the remarks given in [7] it was decided for entering Phase 2 of eSTREAM: The original design, source code and test vectors for Edon80 to remain unchanged; Edon80 should be reinitialized after maximum 2^{48} produced keystream bits.

6.5   Key Recovery Attack of Hell and Johansson

Recently Hell and Johansson [10] have used the analysis of the periods of the keystream sequences of Edon80 in [6] to mount an attack that can recover the key after using 2^{72} so called "simple operations". Their attack is based on exploiting the periodicity inside the generator. Using the fact that some elements will repeat with larger probability, than the others, they built a test for finding the correct values of the key bits. This leads to a key recovery attack, where by varying some parameters as a trade-off between required length of the received key stream and the computational complexity, they constructed an attack that is performing 2^{72} simple operations for recovering the key with the probability $\frac{1}{2}$. We think that so far, this is the most advanced attack on Edon80, with a concrete setup that shows how to recover the secret key. Further advancement in this line of research will deepen our knowledge for the number of rounds in

Edon80. However, is the attack in its latest status better than the brute force attack? Being a hardware stream cipher, we know how to build "efficient" hardware for brute force attack on Edon80. It will consist of a pipelined set of 80 simple e-transformers (full hardware implementation) that will need: 160 cycles for the *IVSetup* and additional 80 cycles for obtaining the first 80 keystream bits, i.e. in total around 2^8 cycles to obtain the first 80 keystream bits (per key). So by checking 2^{79} keys $\times$ 2^8 cycles i.e. after approximately 2^{87} circuit cycles, we will find the secret key with the probability $\frac{1}{2}$.

Now, what is the cost of Hell-Johansson attack? What is the cost of those 2^{72} simple operations expressed as number of cycles? Is the attack faster than brute force attack? Our opinion is that it is not faster! Here are the arguments: As described in the paper [10] one simple operation consists of even simpler operations (on the sets X_1 and X_2 described in the paper) — seen as assembly instructions:

1. Retrieving elements of X_1;
2. Sorting elements of X_1;
3. Retrieving elements of X_2;
4. Sorting elements of X_2;
5. Preparation for intersection;
6. Operations of intersection;
7. Retrieving the results from the intersection;
8. Storing the results in temp memory.

All these operations can take more than 2^{15} cycles. Now, the cost of the attack expressed as number of basic circuit cycles is bigger than $2^{72} \times 2^{15} = 2^{87}$ cycles. This analysis naturally points out to the following idea: How efficient (and costly) would be to implement Hell-Johansson attack in a hardware circuit?

7   Hardware Implementation, Simulations and Performances

We have programmed Edon80 in VHDL language using free web edition of Xilinx ISE 7.1i application and then mapped the algorithm in several Xilinx FPGAs. Our VHDL implementation is far from optimal, but here we give several quantities that we achieved by our VHDL implementation. An equivalent encoding of the above algorithm programmed in VHDL gives total amount of equivalent gates count around 7500.

On simulated mapping on several Xilinx FPGA platforms (from Spartan 2 to Virtex 4) the projected speed of Edon80, and achieved total equivalent gate count are given in Table 5.

The speed of processing of Edon80 is obtained from the speed of the FPGA chip, since the output of the cipher is every second cycle, and in every second cycle Edon80 produces 2 keystream bits. In the last column we give potential full usage of the capacities of the mentioned FPGA platforms, when Edon80 is parallelized several times.

Table 5. Projected characteristics of Edon80 on different FPGA platforms

FPGA type	MHz	Speed	Gates	Logic Utilization	Max Speed / Gates
Spartan 2 Target Device : xc2s50 Target Package : fg256 Target Speed : -5	92.30	92.3 Mbps	7,562	Slice Flip Flops: 472/1,536 4 input LUTs: 592/1,536	277 Mbps / 23K
Spartan 3 Target Device : xc3s200 Target Package : fg256 Target Speed : -5	157.37	157.37 Mbps	7,169	Slice Flip Flops: 472/3,840 4 input LUTs: 584/3,840	944 Mbps / 43K
Virtex 2 Target Device : xc2v250 Target Package : fg256 Target Speed : -6	220.75	220.75 Mbps	7,149	Slice Flip Flops: 426/3,072 4 input LUTs: 586/3,072	1.1 Gbps / 35K
Virtex 4 Target Device : xc4vlx25 Target Package : sf363 Target Speed : -12	318.07	318.07 Mbps	7,160	Slice Flip Flops: 427/21,504 4 input LUTs: 585/21,504	9.54 Gbps / 215K

We have to mention the following remark about the way of parallelizing of Edon80. Parallelizing of Edon80 can be done in two ways:

1. The first one is the standard way of sending different IV to parallel instances of Edon80. In this way we can share one ROM of 16 bytes where we can store four initial quasigroups.
2. The second one is a little more costly: Every instance of Edon80 to have different and disjoint sets of four appropriate quasigroups of order 4.

In 2007, Kasper et. al [11] realized Edon80 in ASIC, with an area of 2922 equivalent gates (which is less than the area of the smallest AES implementation) and with throughput of 2.18 Mbit/s at 175 MHz. They have concluded that the hardware resources required for the implementation of Edon80 can be further reduced to less than 1850 equivalent gates if a micro-controller is available to input the initialization sequence.

7.1 Adding MAC Functionality to Edon80

In 2007, Gligoroski and Knapskog [12] inspired by the work of Kasper et. al [11] have introduced "MAC Edon80". That stream cipher is using the internal structure of Edon80 (thus producing keystream same as Edon80) but it can compute also a 160 bit Message Authentication Code for the encrypted/decrypted messages. The way how they achieved the MAC upgrade of Edon80 was by adding two-bit registers into the e-transformers of Edon80 core, an additional 160-bit shift register and by putting additional communication logic between neighboring e-transformers of the Edon80 pipeline core. The upgrade does not change the produced keystream from Edon80 and they projected that in total it will need not more then 1500 gates.

7.2 Stretching the Speed Asymmetry of Edon80

As we mentioned in the Section 2, one of the design goals for Edon80 was the stream cipher to manifest significant speed asymmetry when realized in hardware and software, and that asymmetry to be extensible and flexible. We have prepared a summary table of the averaged speed of all 7 synchronous hardware stream ciphers that are finalists in the eSTREAM project [16], as well as their hardware speeds and the asymmetry coefficient expressed as

$$\text{speed asymmetry} = \frac{\text{software speed}}{\text{hardware speed}}.$$

From Table 6 we can see that Edon80 has the biggest speed asymmetry. Moreover, the analysis performed on the family of stream ciphers Edon-$(2m, 2k)$ in [6] and the flexibility and extensibility that has been concluded by Kasper et. al in [11] gives opportunities to define stream ciphers from the same family that can have asymmetry coefficient as big as needed.

Table 6. Speed asymmetry of seven synchronous hardware stream ciphers of the eSTREAM project

Name	SW cycles/byte	HW cycles/byte	Asymmetry
Edon80	5806.99	8.000	725.87
DECIM v2	12070.04	32.000	502.92
Pomaranch v3	2222.16	8.000	277.77
Grain v1	1078.66	8.000	134.83
MICKEY 2.0	724.98	8.000	90.62
F-FCSR-H v2	54.13	1.000	54.13
Trivium	4.48	0.125	35.86

8   Conclusions

Edon80 is a binary additive synchronous stream cipher characterized by its flexibility and mathematical provability of many of its components. It offers 80 bits cryptographic primitive and can be implemented with hardware resources from 3000 to 7,500 electronic gates. If the needs for security bits have to be increased to arbitrary value, or the speed asymmetry have to be increased, than it can be done with a simple addition of a basic components called e-transformers. In that case, the speed of the cipher in the hardware would not be affected at all (except initialization phases), but its speed in software would be significantly decreased. The size of IV can be also easily changed, without affecting the speed of the cipher. It is easily parallelizable. It can be easily and cheaply upgraded to become a stream cipher with authentication.

References

1. eSTREAM: ECRYPT Stream Cipher Project,
   http://www.ecrypt.eu.org/stream
2. Gligoroski, D., Markovski, S., Kocarev, L., Gusev, M.: Edon80, eSTREAM [1], Report 2005/007 (2005)

3. Hong, J.: Remarks on the Period of Edon80, eSTREAM [1], Report 2005/041 (June 18, 2005)

4. Hong, J.: Period of Stream Cipher Edon80. In: Maitra, S., Veni Madhavan, C.E., Venkatesan, R. (eds.) INDOCRYPT 2005. LNCS, vol. 3797, pp. 23–34. Springer, Heidelberg (2005)

5. Gligoroski, D., Markovski, S., Kocarev, L., Gusev, M.: Understanding periods in Edon80, eSTREAM [1], Report 2005/054 (2005)

6. Gligoroski, D., Markovski, S., Knapskog, S.J.: On periods of Edon-$(2m, 2k)$ family of stream ciphers. In: State of the Art of Stream Ciphers, Workshop Record, SASC 2006, Leuven, Belgium (2006)

7. Gligoroski, D., Markovski, S., Kocarev, L., Gusev, M.: Status of Edon80 in the second phase of eSTREAM, eSTREAM [1] (2006),
   http://www.ecrypt.eu.org/stream/p2ciphers/edon80/edon80_p2note.pdf

8. Vojvoda, M., Sýs, M., Jókay, M.: A note on algebraic properties of quasigroups in Edon80, eSTREAM [1], Report 2007/032 (2007)

9. Bjørstad, T.E.: A note on the Edon80 S-box, eSTREAM [1], Report 2007/043 (2007)

10. Johansson, T., Hell, M.: A Key Recovery Attack on Edon80. In: Kurosawa, K. (ed.) ASIACRYPT 2007. LNCS, vol. 4833, pp. 568–581. Springer, Heidelberg (in print, 2007)

11. Kasper, M., Kumar, S., Lemke-Rust, K., Paar, C.: A Compact Implementation of Edon80, eSTREAM [1], Report 2006/057 (2006)

12. Gligoroski, D., Knapskog, S.J.: Adding MAC functionality to Edon80, Report 2007/031, [1] (2007)

13. Menezes, A., van Oorschot, P., Vanstone, S.: Handbook of Applied Cryptography. CRC Press, Inc., Boca Raton (1997)

14. Dénes, J., Keedwell, A.D.: Latin Squares and their Applications. English Univer. Press Ltd. (1974)

15. Markovski, S., Gligoroski, D., Bakeva, V.: Quasigroup String Processing: Part 1. Maced. Acad. of Sci. and Arts, Sc. Math. Tech. Scien. XX 1-2, 13–28 (1999)

16. eSTREAM Pase 3, Software Performance Figures,
    http://www.ecrypt.eu.org/stream/phase3perf.html

F-FCSR Stream Ciphers

François Arnault[1], Thierry Berger[1], and Cédric Lauradoux[2]

[1] XLIM DMI, Université de Limoges, France
{arnault,thierry.berger}@unilim.fr
[2] INRIA Rocquencourt, France
cedric.lauradoux@inria.fr

1   Introduction

Feedback with Carry Shift Registers (FCSRs) are a promising alternative to Linear Feedback Shift Registers (LFSRs) for the design of stream ciphers. The main difference between these two automata lies in the computation of the feedback. While LFSRs use simple bitwise addition, FCSRs use addition with carries. Hence, the transition function of an FCSR is non-linear, more precisely quadratic. Since FCSRs were introduced by Goresky and Klapper [11], the properties of the sequences generated by an FCSR are now considered well mastered from a mathematical point of view.

FCSR can help to solve the problem which is always raised when using LFSR. In LFSR-based stream ciphers, a filtering or combining Boolean function must be used to break the linearity of LFSR. With FCSR-based stream ciphers, this issue is directly solved by the intrinsic non-linearity of the FCSR. Thus, a linear filter can be used to extract the keystream from the internal state. Moreover, sequences obtained from an FCSR have the same suitable statistical properties of LFSR sequences: known period, balancedness, equal distribution of patterns...

We present in this chapter two designs based on filtered FCSR (F-FCSR) which are dedicated to hardware applications. F-FCSR-H is our first proposition which fulfill the requirement of eSTREAM profile 2: 80 bits of key and 80 bits of IV. A second proposition, F-FCSR-16, is similar to F-FCSR-H, but uses larger keys and IVs (128 bits for the key and 128 bits for the IV).

2   Background on FCSR Automata

2.1   FCSR vs LFSR

The underlying mathematical model for LFSRs is rational series in the ring $GF(2)[[x]]$. For FCSRs, the model is provided by rational 2-adic numbers (cf. [7,13]). In practice, those two theories lead to very similar analysis. However, the transition function of an LFSR is linear while it is quadratic for an FCSR. The main advantage of this quadratic transition function is the intrinsic resistance to algebraic attacks and to correlation attacks, which are the main weaknesses of LFSR-based stream ciphers. However, it has a drawback: the implementation

M. Robshaw and O. Billet (Eds.): New Stream Cipher Designs, LNCS 4986, pp. 170–178, 2008.
© Springer-Verlag Berlin Heidelberg 2008

Table 1. Comparison between LFSRs and FCSR for equivalent parameters

	LFSR	FCSR
Register Flip-Flops	n	n
Carry Flip-Flops	0	$k-1$
xor Gates	$k-1$	$4(k-1)$
and Gates	0	$k-1$

of an FCSR costs more than the one of an LFSR. Table 1 compares the implementation of LFSR and FCSR for equivalent size of parameters, *i.e.* a feedback polynomial $Q(X)$ of degree n and Hamming weight k for the LFSR, and a connection integer q of bitlength $n+1$ and weight k for the FCSR. We assume here that the addition with carries propagation is computed using full-adders which consists in four XOR gates and one AND gate.

As for LFSRs, FCSR sequences are predictable and therefore not suitable for a direct use in cryptography. An attacker can synthesize the FCSR given a small amount of keystream using the algorithms described in [1, 12]. This is why we need to filter the internal state of a FCSR to generate the keystream.

2.2 FCSR in Galois Mode

There exists two forms of LFSR circuits: the Galois setup and Fibonacci setup. These two forms also exist for FCSR [7]. In the Fibonacci setup of an FCSR, the feedback bit obtained by combining some bit of the internal state and the content of a k-bit memory using a parallel count (Hamming weight) and a k-bit adder. In the Galois setup of an FCSR, the feedback is combined with some bits of the internal state using a full-adder with a forward carry. Then, it appears that the Galois setup is more suitable for hardware applications than the Fibonacci setup since it offers more parallelism.

The Galois setup of an FCSR is an automaton which computes the binary expansion of the quotient of an integer p by a fixed odd integer q following the ascending order of the powers of 2. The integer q is called the connection integer of the FCSR, while the integer p depends on the initial state of the FCSR. To avoid non purely periodic sequences, we choose q to be a negative odd integer and p satisfying $0 < p < |q|$. We suppose that the size of the binary representation of $|q|$ requires $n+1$ bits, i.e. $2^n < -q < 2^{n+1}$. Let be $d = (1-q)/2$ and put $d = \sum_{i=0}^{n-1} d_i 2^i$, with $d_i \in \{0, 1\}$ (and $d_{n-1} = 1$). For a fixed q, the 2-adic rational number p/q can be computed by a FCSR automaton for any p, $0 \le p < |q|$.

An FCSR automaton is composed of a main register M and of a carry register C. The main register M is composed of n binary cells where each bit is denoted by $m_i(t)$ $(0 \le i \le n-1)$. The integer $m(t) = \sum_{i=0}^{n-1} m_i(t) 2^i$ represents the content of M. The carry register C consists in ℓ cells where $\ell + 1$ is the Hamming weight of the binary expansion of d. We denote $c_i(t)$ the content of each carry cell. A carry cell c_i is present only if $d_i = 1$ and $i < n-1$. Otherwise, we put $c_i(t) = 0$ for all t. The integer $c(t) = \sum_{i=0}^{n-2} c_i(t) 2^i$ is called the content of C. The Hamming weight of the binary expansion of $c(t)$ is at most ℓ. We say that an FCSR automaton is in state (m, c) when the integers m and c are respectively the contents of M and C.

Let consider a state (m, c) at time $t = t_0$ of the automaton, i.e. $m = m(t_0)$ and $c = c(t_0)$, then the observed sequence in the last cell $(m_0(t_0 + i))_{i \in \mathbb{N}}$ is the 2-adic expansion of p/q, with $p = m + 2c$. Moreover, for every cell of the main register, there exists an integer $p^{(j)}$ such that the observed sequence $(m_j(t_0 + i))_{i \in \mathbb{N}}$ is the 2-adic expansion of $p^{(j)}/q$. This number $p^{(j)}$ can be explicitly computed from the knowledge of m and c. The reader can refer to [4, 5] for more details. The following circuit represents the Galois setup of an FCSR for $q = -347$, and so $d = 174 = (10101110)_2$.

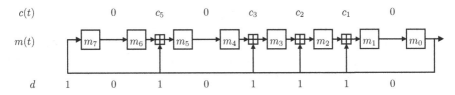

Fig. 1. A Galois FCSR for $q = -347$, $d = 174 = (10101110)_2$, $n = 8$ and $\ell = 4$

Here the symbol $\boxplus$ represents addition with carry. More precisely it consists of a full adder with a carry cell, as represented below. The carry part of the output is delayed and given back in input at the next transition:

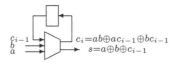

2.3   Choice of the Connection Integer q

The connection integer q determines the period of the sequences generated by an FCSR [11, 13]. We usually choose the connection integer according to the following criterions:

1. q is a (negative) prime of bitsize $n + 1$.
2. The order of 2 modulo q is $|q| - 1$.
3. $T = (|q| - 1)/2$ is also prime.
4. Set $d = (1 + |q|)/2$. The Hamming weight $W(d)$ of the binary expansion of d is not too small. Typically, $W(d)$ is about $n/2$ or slighty greater.

Condition 1 was already discussed (n is the size of the main register). Condition 2 is similar to the choice of a primitive polynomial in the case of LFSR. Here, it ensures that the period of the sequences output by the FCSR automaton equals $|q| - 1$. Such sequences of maximal period are called ℓ-sequences [11, 13]. Condition 3 is used for filtered sequences (see below) : when xoring several sequences of period $|q| - 1$ we get a sequence of period T or $2T$ except in degenerated cases. The last condition ensures that the transition function has a large nonlinear part and that the feedback bit has a good diffusion.

3   Filtering and IV Setup Procedure

3.1   Filtering

The choice of a filter function is critical in LFSR-based stream ciphers. The filter must achieve a high non-linearity, a high resiliency and a high resistance to algebraic attacks. In the case of the filtered FCSR, the situation is different since the transition provides the non-linearity and the resistance to algebraic attacks. It is well-known that linear functions achieve the best resiliency. This is why our designs are based on linear filters. A bit-filter function is defined by a mask of n bits $(f_0, \ldots, f_{n-1})$. One bit k of keystream is obtained in the following way:

$$k = \bigoplus_{i=0}^{n-1} f_i m_i.$$

In our designs, we extract more than one bit from the main register of the FCSR. In the case of F-FCSR-H, we extract one byte while we extract two bytes in the case of F-FCSR-16. For that we need word-filter functions which consists respectively of eight and sixteen bit-filters.

When there is no feedback bit between two consecutive cells m_i and m_{i+1} (i.e. $d_i = 0$), the two observed sequences in these cells are derived each other by just a shift of one step. When there is a feedback the two sequences are much different. They are derived each other by a large shift, depending on the initial state of the FCSR. So we use, in each filter, only cells that are separated each other by at least one feedback.

An n bit word can define a filter which outputs a word of bitsize s as follows:

$$\text{bit } j \text{ of output word} = \bigoplus_{i=0}^{n/s-1} d_{si+j} m_{si+j}.$$

3.2   IV Setup

The design of the IV setup procedure is a difficult task in view of chosen IV attacks. Some previous propositions of F-FCSR stream ciphers [5, 3] suffered from a slow diffusion of changes in the initial state of a FCSR. This has been exploited in a resynchronization attack by Jaulmes and Muller [9, 10]. Taking in account the lessons learned from our previous mistakes, we initialize the internal state of F-FCSR-H and F-FCSR-128 using the following procedure:

1. the main register M is initialized with the concatenation of the IV and the secret key K *i.e.* $M = (IV\|K)$, and all the carries are set to zero.
2. The device is clocked 20 times for F-FCSR-H and 16 times for F-FCSR-16. Using the filter, we obtain respectively $20 \times 8 = 160$ bits for F-FCSR-H and $16 \times 16 = 256$ bits for F-FCSR-16. These bits are used to re-initialize the main register of F-FCSR-H and F-FCSR-16 (also the carries are reset to zero).
3. The automaton is clocked $n + 2$ times before using the keystream to ensure a good diffusion of all bits in the main register.

4   Description of F-FCSR Stream Ciphers

4.1   F-FCSR-H

According to the Profile 2 requirements, the size of the secret key is 80 bits and the size of the IV is 80 bits (after padding if needed). In order to resist to TMD attacks, we have choosen a FCSR of length $n = 160$. Its connection integer is:

$$q = -1993524591318275015328041611344215036460140087963.$$

The carry register contains $\ell = 82$ cells, which are present at the positions matching the ones (except of the leading one) in the binary expansion of $d = (|q|+1)/2$. This binary expansion is the following 160 bits string (it has Hamming weight 83):

$$d = (\text{AE985DFF } 26619\text{FC5 } 8623\text{DC8A } \text{AF46D590 } 3\text{DD4254E})_{16}.$$

As described in Section 3.1, at each iteration of the FCSR automaton, the output $S(t)$ is the byte $(s_0(t), \dots, s_7(t))$ which is defined by $s_j(t) = \sum_{i=0}^{19} d_{8i+j} m_{8i+j}(t)$ where $m_i(t)$ is the content of the cell m_i at time t.

The Key+IV setup procedure is:

- Input a key K of length $k = 80$ and an IV of length $v \le 80$
- Initialize the main and carry registers:

$$M := (0^{80-v}\|IV\|K) \qquad C := 0.$$

- Clock the FCSR 20 times and compute $S(t)$ for $t := 1$ to 20.
- $M := (S(20), \dots, S(1))$.
- Clock the FCSR 162 times (output is discarded in this step).

Then, to obtain N pseudo-random bytes, repeat N times the following operations:

- Clock the FCSR;
- Use the byte-filter to extract one byte $S(t)$.

4.2   F-FCSR-16

F-FCSR-16 differs from F-FCSR-H by the size of the key which is 128 bits the size of the IV which is also 128 (after padding if needed). It differs also by its length which is $n = 256$ and by the filter which extracts a 16 bits word. The connection integer is

$$q = -18397144084561947112986916180934413\_$$
$$16582983176559231357530171284621556187150 19$$

and the positions of the $\ell = 130$ carry cells are given by the binary expansion of $d = (|q| + 1)/2$ which as weight 131:

$$d = (\text{CB5E129F AD4F7E66 780CAA2E C8C9CEDB}\_$$
$$\text{2102F996 BAF08F39 EFB55A6E 390002C6})_{16}.$$

At each iteration of the FCSR automaton, the output $S(t)$ is the 16-bits word $(s_0(t), \ldots, s_{15}(t))$ defined by $s_j(t) = \sum_{i=0}^{16} d_{16i+j} m_{s16i+j}(t)$.
   The key+IV setup procedure is:

- Input a key K of length $k = 128$ and an IV of length $v \le 128$
- Initialize the main and carry registers:

$$M := (0^{128-v} \| \text{IV} \| K) \qquad C := 0.$$

- Clock the FCSR 16 times and compute $S(t)$ for t from 1 to 16.
- $M := (S(16), \ldots, S(1))$.
- Clock the FCSR 258 times (output is discarded in this step).

Then, to obtain $2N$ pseudo-random bytes, repeat N times the following steps:

- Clock the FCSR.
- Use the word-filter to get two bytes $S(t)$.

5   Security Analysis

in this section, we give a security analysis of F-FCSR schemes. First, we establish the resistance of F-FCSRs against the state of the art of cryptanalysis. Then, we describe some dedicated attacks.

5.1   Resistance to Generic Attacks

Statistical properties. There is not any known statistical bias on the pseudo-random sequences output by our filtered FCSR. We have check that they pass the Statistical Test Suite of the NIST.

Linear complexity. Since the FCSR automaton has a quadratic transition function and has a 2-adic structure, we can expect that the linear complexity of the generated pseudo-random sequences satisfies the same distribution law as the one observed for a random sequence of period $|q| - 1 > 2^n$. Experiments we have done support this assumption.

2-adic complexity. The 2-adic structure is broken by the linear filter function. Hence, we can expect that the 2-adic complexity of the generated pseudo-random sequences is high, as it is the case for random sequences of period $|q| - 1 > 2^n$. We have also done experiments which support this assumption.

Algebraic cryptanalysis. The transition function of a FCSR automaton is quadratic and the filter function F_ℓ is linear. The algebraic equations the attacker has to solve are of the form $F_\ell(T_q^i(x)) = s_i$. At each iteration the degree of the equations is increasing. It becomes computationally infeasible to obtain these equations for $i \geq 12$. To solve this system, we need at least n iterations.

Correlation attack. There are two major obstacles to the adaptation of this attack on a filtered FCSR:

-   the filtering function is linear with ℓ inputs. Then, such a function is $\ell - 1$ resilient, *i.e.* balanced and without correlation between its output and any sum of at most $\ell - 1$ of its inputs. In that situation, the attack is more difficult than an exhaustive research.
-   the dependencies between the cells of an FCSR are nonlinear, since the transition function is quadratic. Thus, it seems difficult to obtain linear dependencies.

Time-Memory-Data tradeoff attacks. The size of the registers has been chosen in order the stream cipher to be resistant to these attacks.

Distinguishing attacks. Distinguishing attacks can be based on the existence of linear relations between some internal states of the automaton which occur with a biased probability. Due to the presence of carry cells, the existence of such relations seems unlikely. We did not find any of them and we think that there are none.

5.2   Dedicated Attacks

Some dedicated attacks against older versions of F-FCSR have been proposed in [2, 3, 5, 6, 9, 10]. Most of them use the fact that the diffusion of a difference between two states remains local as soon as this difference does not affect the feedback bit. For an FCSR of length n, we need in the worst case n iterations of the automaton before a full diffusion. Jaulmes and Muller [9, 10] used this property to mount some distinguishing and resynchronization attacks. In [6], T. Berger and M. Minier used a very small number of iterations in the IV setup procedure of an older version of F-FCSR to design an algebraic attack. All these attacks are avoided if the FCSR is clocked n times after a change of IV.

A more specific attack on weak filters was presented in [2]. It worked only when the number ℓ of inputs of the filter is less than 3 or when all of them are located in a small part of the register. We have chosen the filter in F-FCSR schemes to avoid this weakness.

5.3 Weak Keys

A null key must not be used. Using it with a null IV produces a null keystream. There are no other weak keys. If the key is non null, an FCSR is initialized to a non zero state. In this case, the FCSR does not return to its initial state before $|q| - 1$ transitions.

6   Conclusion

We described FCSRs in Galois mode and how it is possible to filter them to obtain a keystream. We discussed the choice of the connection prime and the design of IV-setup. Then we presented the F-FCSR-H and F-FCSR-16 stream ciphers which have been selected to enter in Phase 3 of the eSTREAM project with Profile 2. We considered different kinds of attacks that could be effective on stream ciphers. According to the current knowledge, none of them breaks any of these two stream ciphers.

7   Future Directions

Some further work has to be done in some directions. First, we need to complete the study of transition graphs of FCSR automata to obtain stronger assurance for the security of F-FCSR. Secondly, we would like to design a fast software FCSR based stream cipher, especially suited for constrained environment. At the moment, known software filtered FCSRs suffer from a relative slowness. Also, while the presence of carry cells makes the parallelization of FCSR not so easy, we think it should be possible and we expect to obtain a speed up in hardware.

References

1. Arnault, F., Berger, T.P., Necer, A.: Feedback with Carry Shift Registers synthesis with the Euclidean Algorithm. IEEE Trans. Inform. Theory 50(5), 910–917 (2004)
2. Arnault, F., Berger, T.P.: Design of new pseudo random generators based on a filtered FCSR automaton. In: SASC, State of the Art of Stream Ciphers Workshop, Bruges, Belgium, October 2004, pp. 109–120 (2004)
3. Arnault, F., Berger, T.P.: F-FCSR: design of a new class of stream ciphers. In: Gilbert, H., Handschuh, H. (eds.) FSE 2005. LNCS, vol. 3557, pp. 83–97. Springer, Heidelberg (2005)
4. Arnault, F., Berger, T.P., Minier, M.: On the security of FCSR-based pseudorandom generators. In: ECRYPT Network of Excellence - SASC Workshop (2007), http://sasc.crypto.rub.de/files/sasc2007_179.pdf

5. Arnault, F., Berger, T.P.: Design and properties of a new pseudorandom generator based on a filtered FCSR automaton. IEEE Trans. Computers 54(11), 1374–1383 (2005)
6. Berger, T.P., Minier, M.: Two algebraic attacks against the F-FCSRs using the IV mode. In: Maitra, S., Veni Madhavan, C.E., Venkatesan, R. (eds.) INDOCRYPT 2005. LNCS, vol. 3797, pp. 143–154. Springer, Heidelberg (2005)
7. Goresky, M., Klapper, A.: Fibonacci and Galois representation of feedback with carry shift registers. IEEE Trans. Inform. Theory 48, 2826–2836 (2002)
8. Goresky, M., Klapper, A.: Periodicity and distribution properties of combined FCSR sequences. In: Gong, G., Helleseth, T., Song, H.-Y., Yang, K. (eds.) SETA 2006. LNCS, vol. 4086, pp. 334–341. Springer, Heidelberg (2006)
9. Jaulmes, E., Muller, F.: Cryptanalysis of ecrypt candidates F-FCSR-8 and F-FCSR-H. ECRYPT Stream Cipher Project Report 2005/046 (2005), http://www.ecrypt.eu.org/stream
10. Jaulmes, E., Muller, F.: Cryptanalysis of the F-FCSR stream cipher family. In: Preneel, B., Tavares, S.E. (eds.) SAC 2005. LNCS, vol. 3897, pp. 20–35. Springer, Heidelberg (2006)
11. Klapper, A., Goresky, M.: 2-adic shift registers. In: Anderson, R. (ed.) FSE 1993. LNCS, vol. 809, pp. 174–178. Springer, Heidelberg (1994)
12. Klapper, A., Goresky, M.: Cryptanalysis based on 2-adic rational approximation. In: Coppersmith, D. (ed.) CRYPTO 1995. LNCS, vol. 963, pp. 262–273. Springer, Heidelberg (1995)
13. Klapper, A., Goresky, M.: Feedback Shift Registers, 2-Adic Span, and Combiners with Memory. Journal of Cryptology 10, 111–147 (1997)

The Grain Family of Stream Ciphers

Martin Hell[1], Thomas Johansson[1], Alexander Maximov[2], and Willi Meier[3],[*]

[1] Dept. of Electrical and Information Technology, Lund University,
P.O. Box 118, 221 00 Lund, Sweden
{martin,thomas}@eit.lth.se
[2] Ericsson AB, Lund, Sweden
alexander.maximov@ericsson.com
[3] FHNW, CH-5210 Windisch, Switzerland
willi.meier@fhnw.ch

Abstract. A new family of stream ciphers, Grain, is proposed. Two
variants, a 80-bit and a 128-bit variant are specified, denoted Grain and
Grain-128 respectively. The designs target hardware environments where
gate count, power consumption and memory are very limited. Both variants are based on two shift registers and a nonlinear output function.
The ciphers also have the additional feature that the speed can be easily
increased at the expense of extra hardware.

When designing a cryptographic primitive there are many different properties
that have to be addressed. These include e.g., speed and security. Comparing
several ciphers, it is likely that one is faster on a 32-bit processor, another is faster
on an 8 bit processor and yet another one is faster in hardware. The simplicity of
the design is another factor that has to be taken into account. While the software
implementation can be very simple, the hardware implementation might be quite
complex.

There is a need for cryptographic primitives that have very low hardware
complexity. A radio-frequency identification (RFID) tag is a typical example of
a product where the amount of memory and power is very limited. These are
microchips capable of transmitting an identifying sequence upon a request from
a reader. Forging an RFID tag can have devastating consequences if the tag is
used e.g., in electronic payments and hence, there is a need for cryptographic
primitives implemented in these tags. Today, a hardware implementation of e.g.,
AES on an RFID tag is not feasible due to the large number of gates needed.
The Grain family of stream ciphers is designed to be very easy and small to
implement in hardware.

Several recent LFSR based stream cipher proposals, see e.g., [1,2] and their
predecessors, are based on word oriented LFSRs. This allows them to be efficiently
implemented in software but it also allows them to increase the throughput since
words instead of bits are output. In hardware, a word oriented cipher is likely to be
more complex than a bit oriented one. In the Grain ciphers, this issue has been

---

[*] Supported by Hasler Foundation http://www.haslerfoundation.ch under project
number 2005.

M. Robshaw and O. Billet (Eds.): New Stream Cipher Designs, LNCS 4986, pp. 179–190, 2008.

addressed by basing the design on bit oriented shift registers with the extra feature of allowing an increase in speed at the expense of more hardware. The user can decide the speed of the cipher depending on the amount of hardware available. This property is not explicitly found in most other stream ciphers.

The proposed designs, denoted Grain (or more formally Grain Version 1 or Grain V1) and Grain-128, are bit oriented synchronous stream ciphers. The designs are based on two shift registers, one with linear feedback (LFSR) and one with nonlinear feedback (NFSR). The LFSR guarantees a minimum period for the keystream and it also provides balancedness in the output. The NFSR, together with a nonlinear output function introduces nonlinearity to the cipher. The input to the NFSR is masked with the output of the LFSR so that the state of the NFSR is balanced. Hence, we use the notation NFSR even though this is actually a filter. What is known about cycle structures of nonlinear feedback shift registers cannot immediately be applied here.

The first, unpublished, version of the cipher is denoted version 0. This version was cryptanalyzed in [3,4,5]. The design of version 0 will not be given in this paper but the attack will be discussed in Section 3.1.

The paper is organized as follows. Section 1 provides a detailed description of the Grain and Grain-128 designs. The possibility to easily increase the throughput is discussed in Section 2. The security of Grain is discussed in Section 3 together with a motivation for the different design parameters. Section 4 concludes the paper.

1   Design Specifications

This section specifies the details of the designs of both Grain and Grain-128. Both ciphers follow the same design principle. They consist of three main building blocks, namely an LFSR, an NFSR and an output function. The contents of the two shift registers represent the state of the cipher and their sizes are $|K|$ bits each, where K is the key. In the following, the content of the LFSR is denoted $S_t = s_t, s_{t+1}, \ldots, s_{t+|K|-1}$ and the content of the NFSR is denoted $B_t = b_t, b_{t+1}, \ldots, b_{t+|K|-1}$. The output function, denoted $H(B_t, S_t)$ consists of two parts. A nonlinear Boolean function $h(x)$ and a set of linear terms added to $h(x)$. The output of $H(B_t, S_t)$ is the keystream bit z_t. A general overview of the design is given in Fig. 1.

1.1   Grain - Design Parameters

The keysize of Grain is $|K| = 80$ bits and the cipher supports an IV of size $|IV| = 64$ bits. The feedback polynomial of the LFSR, denoted $f(x)$ is a primitive polynomial of degree 80. It is defined as

$$f(x) = 1 + x^{18} + x^{29} + x^{42} + x^{57} + x^{67} + x^{80}. \tag{1}$$

To remove any possible ambiguity we also define the update function of the LFSR as

$$s_{t+80} = s_{t+62} \oplus s_{t+51} \oplus s_{t+38} \oplus s_{t+23} \oplus s_{t+13} \oplus s_t. \tag{2}$$

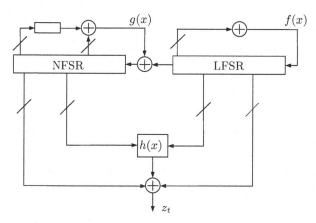

Fig. 1. Overview of the different design blocks in the Grain family of stream ciphers

The feedback polynomial of the NFSR, $g(x)$, is defined as

$$
\begin{aligned}
g(x) = &\; 1 + x^{18} + x^{20} + x^{28} + x^{35} + x^{43} + x^{47} + x^{52} + x^{59} + x^{66} + \\
&+ x^{71} + x^{80} + x^{17}x^{20} + x^{43}x^{47} + x^{65}x^{71} + x^{20}x^{28}x^{35} + \\
&+ x^{47}x^{52}x^{59} + x^{17}x^{35}x^{52}x^{71} + x^{20}x^{28}x^{43}x^{47} + x^{17}x^{20}x^{59}x^{65} + \\
&+ x^{17}x^{20}x^{28}x^{35}x^{43} + x^{47}x^{52}x^{59}x^{65}x^{71} + x^{28}x^{35}x^{43}x^{47}x^{52}x^{59}.
\end{aligned}
\tag{3}
$$

Again, to remove any possible ambiguity we also write the update function of the NFSR. Note that the bit s_t which is masked with the input is included in the update function below.

$$
\begin{aligned}
b_{t+80} = &\; s_t \oplus b_{t+62} \oplus b_{t+60} \oplus b_{t+52} \oplus b_{t+45} \oplus b_{t+37} \oplus b_{t+33} \oplus b_{t+28} \oplus \\
&\oplus b_{t+21} \oplus b_{t+14} \oplus b_{t+9} \oplus b_t \oplus b_{t+63}b_{t+60} \oplus b_{t+37}b_{t+33} \oplus \\
&\oplus b_{t+15}b_{t+9} \oplus b_{t+60}b_{t+52}b_{t+45} \oplus b_{t+33}b_{t+28}b_{t+21} \oplus \\
&\oplus b_{t+63}b_{t+45}b_{t+28}b_{t+9} \oplus b_{t+60}b_{t+52}b_{t+37}b_{t+33} \oplus \\
&\oplus b_{t+63}b_{t+60}b_{t+21}b_{t+15} \oplus b_{t+63}b_{t+60}b_{t+52}b_{t+45}b_{t+37} \oplus \\
&\oplus b_{t+33}b_{t+28}b_{t+21}b_{t+15}b_{t+9} \oplus b_{t+52}b_{t+45}b_{t+37}b_{t+33}b_{t+28}b_{t+21}.
\end{aligned}
\tag{4}
$$

From the two registers, 5 variables are taken as input to a Boolean function, $h(x)$. This filter function is chosen to be balanced, correlation immune of the first order and has algebraic degree 3. The nonlinearity is the highest possible for these functions, namely 12. The function is defined as

$$
h(x) = h(x_0, x_1, \ldots, x_4) =
$$

$$
= x_1 \oplus x_4 \oplus x_0x_3 \oplus x_2x_3 \oplus x_3x_4 \oplus x_0x_1x_2 \oplus x_0x_2x_3 \oplus x_0x_2x_4 \oplus x_1x_2x_4 \oplus x_2x_3x_4
\tag{5}
$$

where the variables x_0, x_1, x_2, x_3 and x_4 correspond to the tap positions s_{t+3}, s_{t+25}, s_{t+46}, s_{t+64} and b_{t+63} respectively. The output function $H(B_t, S_t)$ is given by

$$
z_t = H(B_t, S_t) = \bigoplus_{j \in \mathcal{A}} b_{t+j} \oplus h(s_{t+3}, s_{t+25}, s_{t+46}, s_{t+64}, b_{t+63})
\tag{6}
$$

where $\mathcal{A} = \{1, 2, 4, 10, 31, 43, 56\}$.

Cipher Initialization: Before any keystream is generated the cipher must be initialized with the key and the IV. Let the bits of the key, K, be denoted k_i, $0 \leq i \leq 79$ and the bits of the IV be denoted IV_i, $0 \leq i \leq 63$. The initialization of the key is done as follows. First the NFSR and LFSR are loaded with key and IV bits as

$$\begin{cases} b_i = k_i, & 0 \leq i \leq 79, \\ s_i = IV_i, & 0 \leq i \leq 63. \end{cases} \tag{7}$$

The remaining bits of the LFSR are filled with ones, $s_i = 1$, $64 \leq i \leq 79$. Then the cipher is clocked 160 times without producing any keystream. Instead the output function is fed back and xored with the input, both to the LFSR and to the NFSR, see Fig. 2.

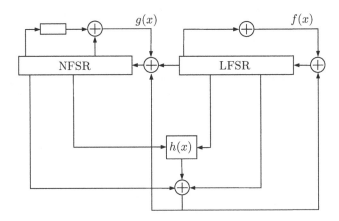

Fig. 2. Overview of the key initialization

1.2   Grain-128 — Design Parameters

Grain-128 supports a keysize of $|K| = 128$ bits, as suggested by the name. The size of the IV is specified to be $|IV| = 96$ bits. The feedback polynomial of the LFSR, $f(x)$, is a primitive polynomial of degree 128. It is defined as

$$f(x) = 1 + x^{32} + x^{47} + x^{58} + x^{90} + x^{121} + x^{128}. \tag{8}$$

To remove any possible ambiguity we also give the corresponding update function of the LFSR as

$$s_{t+128} = s_t \oplus s_{t+7} \oplus s_{t+38} \oplus s_{t+70} \oplus s_{t+81} \oplus s_{t+96}. \tag{9}$$

The nonlinear feedback polynomial of the NFSR, $g(x)$, is the sum of one linear and one bent function. It is defined as

$$\begin{aligned} g(x) = 1 &+ x^{32} + x^{37} + x^{72} + x^{102} + x^{128} + x^{44}x^{60} + x^{61}x^{125} + x^{63}x^{67} + \\ &+ x^{69}x^{101} + x^{80}x^{88} + x^{110}x^{111} + x^{115}x^{117}. \end{aligned} \tag{10}$$

Again, we also write the corresponding update function of the NFSR. In the update function below, note that the bit s_t which is masked with the input to the NFSR is included, while omitted in the feedback polynomial.

$$
\begin{aligned}
b_{t+128} = {} & s_t \oplus b_t \oplus b_{t+26} \oplus b_{t+56} \oplus b_{t+91} \oplus b_{t+96} \oplus b_{t+3}b_{t+67}\oplus \\
& \oplus b_{t+11}b_{t+13} \oplus b_{t+17}b_{t+18} \oplus b_{t+27}b_{t+59}\oplus \\
& \oplus b_{t+40}b_{t+48} \oplus b_{t+61}b_{t+65} \oplus b_{t+68}b_{t+84}.
\end{aligned}
\tag{11}
$$

From the state, nine variables are taken as input to a Boolean function, $h(x)$. Two inputs to $h(x)$ are taken from the NFSR and seven are taken from the LFSR. This function is of degree $\deg(h(x)) = 3$ and very simple. It is defined as

$$
h(x) = h(x_0, x_1, \ldots, x_8) = x_0x_1 \oplus x_2x_3 \oplus x_4x_5 \oplus x_6x_7 \oplus x_0x_4x_8
\tag{12}
$$

where the variables x_0, x_1, x_2, x_3, x_4, x_5, x_6, x_7 and x_8 correspond to the tap positions b_{t+12}, s_{t+8}, s_{t+13}, s_{t+20}, b_{t+95}, s_{t+42}, s_{t+60}, s_{t+79} and s_{t+95} respectively. The output function $H(B_t, S_t)$ is defined as

$$
z_t = H(B_t, S_t) = \bigoplus_{j \in \mathcal{A}} b_{t+j} \oplus h(x) \oplus s_{t+93},
\tag{13}
$$

where $\mathcal{A} = \{2, 15, 36, 45, 64, 73, 89\}$.

Cipher Initialization: The initialization is very similar to the initialization of the 80-bit variant of the cipher. The bits of the key K, denoted k_i, $0 \le i \le 127$, and the bits of the IV, denoted IV_i, $0 \le i \le 95$, are loaded into the NFSR and LFSR respectively as

$$
\begin{cases}
b_i = k_i, & 0 \le i \le 127, \\
s_i = IV_i, 0 \le i \le 95.
\end{cases}
\tag{14}
$$

The last 32 bits of the LFSR are filled with ones, $s_i = 1$, $96 \le i \le 127$. After loading key and IV bits, the cipher is clocked 256 times without producing any keystream. The output function is fed back and xored with the input, both to the LFSR and to the NFSR.

2   Throughput Rate

It is possible to increase the throughput rate of the Grain ciphers by adding some additional hardware. This is an important feature of the Grain family of stream ciphers compared to many other stream ciphers. Increasing the speed can very easily be done by just implementing the feedback functions, $f(x)$ and $g(x)$, and the output function several times. In order to simplify this implementation, the last 15 bits in Grain and the last 31 bits in Grain-128 of the shift registers are not used in the feedback functions or in the input to the output function. I.e., s_i, $65 \le i \le 79$ and b_i, $65 \le i \le 79$ in Grain and s_i, $97 \le i \le 127$ and b_i, $97 \le i \le 127$ in Grain-128 are not used in the three functions. This allows the speed to be easily multiplied by up to 16 for Grain and 32 for Grain-128 if

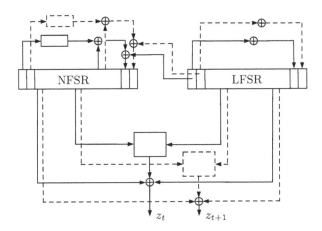

Fig. 3. Implementation of Grain which outputs 2 bits/clock

a sufficient amount of hardware is available. An overview of the implementation when the speed is doubled can be seen in Fig. 3. Naturally, the shift registers also need to be implemented such that each bit is shifted δ steps instead of one when the speed is increased by a factor δ. Since, in the key initialization, the cipher is clocked 160 times (Grain) or 256 times (Grain-128), the possibilities to increase the speed is limited to factors that are divisors of 160 or 256 respectively. The number of clockings needed in the key initialization phase is then $160/\delta$ or $256/\delta$. Since the output and feedback functions are small, it is quite feasible to increase the throughput in this way.

3   Security and Design Choices

In this section we give a security analysis of the construction and motivate the different design choices.

3.1   Linear Approximations

Attacking Grain using linear approximations of the two nonlinear functions turned out to be successful on the first version of Grain, (version 0). This attack was discovered by several independent researchers and the details can be found in [3,4,5]. Some design choices in the current versions are influenced by this attack. In this subsection, we temporarily switch to the notation $s(t)$ instead of s_t as previously used to denote a value at time t. We also use the notation $x \overset{p}{=} y$ meaning that $\Pr(x = y) = p$.

With a slight abuse of notation, let us rewrite the update function of the NFSR as

$$0 = g(B_t) \oplus s(t). \tag{15}$$

Let the weight of a binary linear function ℓ, denoted $w(\ell)$, be the number of terms in the function. I.e., if $\ell = \bigoplus_{i=0}^{n} c_i x_i$, then

$$w(\ell) = |\{i \in 0..n : c_i = 1\}|. \tag{16}$$

Assume that we have found a linear approximation $\ell_g(t)$ of $g(B_t)$ i.e.,

$$\ell_g(t) = \bigoplus_{i=0}^{w(\ell_g)-1} b(t + \phi_i), \tag{17}$$

where $\phi_0, \phi_1, \ldots, \phi_{w(\ell_g)-1}$ denote the positions in the NFSR that are present in the linear approximation. The bias of $\ell_g(t)$ is denoted ε_g, i.e.,

$$\Pr(\ell_g(t) = g(B_t)) = \Pr(\ell_g(t) = s(t)) = \frac{1}{2}(1 + \varepsilon_g), \quad 0 < |\varepsilon_g| \leq 1. \tag{18}$$

Similarly, a linear approximation $\ell_H(t)$ of the output function $H(B_t, S_t)$ can be found. Let $w_N(\ell)$ and $w_L(\ell)$ be the number of terms from the NFSR and from the LFSR respectively. Then $\ell_H(t)$ can be written as

$$\ell_H(t) = \bigoplus_{i=0}^{w_N(\ell_H)-1} b(t + \xi_i) \oplus \bigoplus_{i=0}^{w_L(\ell_H)-1} s(t + \psi_i), \tag{19}$$

where $\xi_0, \xi_1, \ldots, \xi_{w_N(\ell_H)-1}$ and $\psi_0, \psi_1, \ldots, \psi_{w_L(\ell_H)-1}$ determine the location of the taps in the NFSR and LSFR used in the linear approximation. The bias of (19) is denoted ε_H, i.e.,

$$\Pr(\ell_H(t) = z(t)) = \frac{1}{2}(1 + \varepsilon_H), \quad 0 < |\varepsilon_H| \leq 1. \tag{20}$$

Now, sum up the keystream bits determined by ϕ_i in (17),

$$z(t + \phi_0) \oplus z(t + \phi_1) \oplus \ldots \oplus z(t + \phi_{w(\ell_g)-1}) \stackrel{p}{=}$$
$$\ell_H(t + \phi_0) \oplus \ell_H(t + \phi_1) \oplus \ldots \oplus \ell_H(t + \phi_{w(\ell_g)-1}). \tag{21}$$

Using the piling-up lemma, the relation (21) holds with probability $p = 1/2(1 + \varepsilon_H^{w(\ell_g)})$. The terms on the right hand side of (21) will consist of $w_N(\ell_H) \cdot w(\ell_g)$ terms from the NFSR and $w_L(\ell_H) \cdot w(\ell_g)$ terms from the LFSR. All terms from the NFSR can now be approximated using (17) resulting in a relation involving only keystream bits and LFSR bits as

$$\bigoplus_{i=0}^{w(\ell_g)-1} z(t + \phi_i) \stackrel{p'}{=} \bigoplus_{i=0}^{w(\ell_g)-1} \bigoplus_{j=0}^{w_L(\ell_H)-1} s(t + \phi_i + \psi_j) \oplus \bigoplus_{i=0}^{w_N(\ell_H)-1} s(t + \xi_i), \tag{22}$$

which holds with probability $p' = 1/2(1 + \varepsilon_{tot})$ with

$$\varepsilon_{tot} = \varepsilon_g^{w_N(\ell_H)} \cdot \varepsilon_H^{w(\ell_g)}. \tag{23}$$

From this point there are several possibilities for attacks. By finding a multiple of the LFSR feedback polynomial of weight 3, a distinguishing attack can be mounted. The expected degree of this multiple would be around $2^{|K|/2}$ (see e.g., [6]). Combining the keystream bits given by the multiple and using the approximation that $1/\varepsilon^2$ samples are needed in the distinguisher, about

$$N = 2^{|K|/2} + \frac{1}{\varepsilon_{tot}^6} \tag{24}$$

keystream bits are required in the attack.

Another approach is to try to recover the state of the LFSR. An obvious way of doing this is to exhaustively search the state and determine which state gives the bias in (23). In this case, only about

$$N = \frac{|K| \cdot 2 \ln 2}{\varepsilon_{tot}^2} \tag{25}$$

keystream bits are needed. This expression can be derived from the capacity of a binary symmetric channel, see e.g. [7]. Since the size of the LFSR is the same as the key size, this method is obviously more expensive than exhaustive key search. A faster algorithm was given in [4], where they generate more equations of the form (22). By only using equations of a certain form, and by using the Fast Walsh Transform, the attack complexity could be made significantly lower. We refer to [4] for more details on this attack.

Due to this attack, the parameters of the original version of Grain were changed. A higher resiliency was added to the NFSR feedback function, increasing $w(\ell_g)$ and several linear terms from the NFSR were added to the output function, increasing $w_N(\ell_H)$.

The design of Grain-128 is inspired by the analysis in this section. Thus, the NFSR feedback function should satisfy the following three criteria

- *High resiliency*, implying many terms in the linear approximation (high $w(\ell_g)$). This can be achieved by adding several linear terms to the function. Each linear term will increase the resiliency by one.
- *High nonlinearity*, implying small bias of the linear approximations (small ε_g). This can be achieved by using a bent function, i.e., a function with maximum nonlinearity.
- *Small hardware implementation*, implying that the design is attractive in low-cost implementations.

A well-known n-variable bent function is the function $x_1 x_2 \oplus x_3 x_4 \oplus \ldots \oplus x_{n-1} x_n$. This function is also very small in hardware. Using $n = 14$ and adding 5 linear terms gives a 4-resilient Boolean function with nonlinearity 260096. The best linear approximations have bias $\varepsilon_g = 2^{-7}$ and $w(\ell_g) \geq 5$.

The output function has the same design criteria as the NFSR feedback function. However, to increase the algebraic degree it has a term of degree 3. It has nonlinearity 61440 and resiliency 7. The best linear approximations have bias $\varepsilon_H = 2^{-4}$ and $w_N(\ell_H) \geq 7$.

3.2   Time-Memory Tradeoff Attacks

It is well known that the state of a stream cipher must be at least twice the key size in order to prevent time-memory tradeoff attacks [8,9,10]. Both the LFSR and NFSR are of size $|K|$ bits, and thus the state is exactly twice the key size. Since Grain is designed to be as small as possible in hardware, no extra state bits are added to the design. The state is relatively expensive to implement in hardware and it is important to keep it as small as possible. In [11] it was noted that the initialization process of a stream cipher could be seen as a one-way function i.e., the function taking the key K and the IV IV as input and outputs the first $|K|+|IV|$ bits of the keystream. In this case the search space is $2^{|K|+|IV|}$ and new data is generated by repeated initializations of the cipher. If we allow a preprocessing time P that is higher than exhaustive key search $2^{|K|}$, then it is possible to have an attack with real time complexity lower than exhaustive key search. Table 1 gives attack complexities for Grain and Grain-128 in the time-memory tradeoff setting of [11] i.e., $N^2 = TM^2D^2$ and $P = N/D$, where N is the search space, T the computational complexity in the realtime phase, D the number of initializations, M the amount of memory and P the computational complexity in the preprocessing phase. If $|IV| < \frac{1}{2}|K|$ then it is possible to have the preprocessing time also smaller than exhaustive key search. In this case we need to initialize with several different keys and we will only retrieve one of these keys in the real time phase. In the Grain ciphers $|IV| > \frac{1}{2}|K|$ so this is not applicable here.

Table 1. Time-Memory tradeoff attack with real time complexity T, D initializations, M memory words and preprocessing time P

Attack Complexities			
	T	D	M	P
Grain	2^{80} 2^{40} 2^{64} 2^{104}		
	2^{72} 2^{36} 2^{72} 2^{108}		
Grain-128	2^{128} 2^{64} 2^{96} 2^{160}		
	2^{112} 2^{56} 2^{112} 2^{168}		

3.3   Algebraic Attacks

Algebraic attacks can be very successful on nonlinear filter generators. Especially if the output function is of very low degree. Grain is very similar to a nonlinear filter. However, the introduction of the NFSR in the design will defeat all algebraic attacks known today. Since the update function of the NFSR is nonlinear, the later state bits of the NFSR as a function of the initial state bits will have varying but large algebraic degree. As the output function has several inputs from the NFSR, the algebraic degree of the keystream bits expressed as functions of key bits will be large in general. This will defeat known algebraic attacks.

3.4   Chosen-IV Attacks

A necessary condition for defeating differential-like or statistical chosen-IV attacks is that the initial states for any two chosen IV's (or sets of IV's) are
algebraically and statistically unrelated. The number of cycles in key initialization has been chosen so that the Hamming weight of the differences in the
full initial 160-bit state for two IV's after initialization is close to random. This
should prevent chosen-IV attacks.

It may be tempting to improve the efficiency of the key initialization by just
decreasing the number of initial clockings. Considering the 80-bit variant of
Grain, after only 80 clocks, all bits in the state will depend on both the key and
the IV. However, in a chosen-IV attack it is possible to reinitialize the cipher
with the same key but with an IV that differs in only one position from the
previous IV. Consider the case when the number of initial clockings is 80 and
the last bit of the IV is flipped i.e., s_{63} is flipped. This is the event that occurs
if the IV is chosen as a sequence number. Looking at the difference of the states
after initialization it is clear that several positions will be predictable. The bit
s_{63} is not used in the feedback or in the filter function, hence, the first register
update will be the same in both cases. Consequently, the bit s_0 will be the same
in both initializations. In the next update, the flipped bit will be in position s_{62}.
This position is used in the linear feedback of the LFSR, and consequently the
bit s_1 will always be different for the two initializations. Similar arguments can
be used to show that the difference in the state will be deterministic in more
than half of the 160 state bits. This deterministic difference in the state can be
exploited in a distinguishing attack. Let $\mathbf{x}$ be the input variables to the output
function, H, after the first initialization and let $\mathbf{x}_\Delta$ be the input variables to the
output function after the second initialization. Now, compute the distribution
of $\Pr(\mathbf{x}, \mathbf{x}_\Delta)$. If this distribution is biased, it is possible[1] that the distribution of
the difference in the first output bit,

$$\Pr(H(\mathbf{x}) \oplus H(\mathbf{x}_\Delta)), \qquad (26)$$

is biased. Assume that

$$\Pr(H(\mathbf{x}) \oplus H(\mathbf{x}_\Delta) = 0) = 1/2(1 + \varepsilon), \quad 0 < |\varepsilon| \leq 1. \qquad (27)$$

then the number of initializations we need will be in the order of $1/\varepsilon^2$. This
attack can be optimized by calculating which output bit will give the highest
bias since it is not necessarily the bits in the registers corresponding to the
input bits of $H(\mathbf{x})$ that have deterministic difference after the initializations.
This attack shows that it is preferred that the probability that any state bit is
the same after initialization with two different IVs should be close to 0.5. As
with the case of 80 initialization clocks, it is easy to show that after 96, 112 and
128 there are also state bits that will always be the same or that will always
differ.

---

[1] It is possible, but maybe not very likely. One unbiased linear variable is enough to
make the output unbiased.

It is possible to reduce the required number of initial clockings by loading the NFSR and LFSR differently. If each entry of the registers is loaded with the xor of a few key and IV bits and each key and IV bit influences the loading of several entries, differences in the IV will propagate faster. The reason for not doing this is mainly that all the extra xors needed would make the cipher larger in hardware.

3.5   Fault Attacks

Amongst the strongest attacks conceivable on any cipher, are fault attacks. Fault attacks against stream ciphers have been initiated in [12], and have shown to be efficient against many known constructions of stream ciphers. This suggests that it is hard to completely defeat fault attacks on stream ciphers. In the scenario in [12] it is assumed that the attacker can apply some bit flipping faults to one of the two feedback registers at his will. However he has only partial control over their number, location, and exact timing, and similarly on what concerns his knowledge. A stronger assumption one can make, is that he is able to flip a single bit (at a time instance, and thus at a location, he does not know exactly). In addition, he can reset the device to its original state and then apply another randomly chosen fault to the device. We adapt the methods in [12] to the present cipher. Thereby, we make the strongest possible assumption (which may not be realistic) that an attacker can induce a single bit fault in the LFSR, and that he is somehow able to determine the exact position of the fault. The aim is to study input-output properties for $H(B_t, S_t)$, and to derive information on the inputs. As long as the difference induced by the fault in the LFSR does not propagate to position b_{t+63} in Grain or b_{t+95} in Grain-128, the difference observed in the output of the cipher is coming from inputs of $H(B_t, S_t)$ from the LFSR alone. If an attacker is able to reset the device and to induce a single bit fault many times and at different positions that he can correctly guess from the output difference, we cannot preclude that he will get information about a subset of the state bits in the LFSR. Such an attack seems more difficult under the (more realistic) assumption that the fault induced affects several state bits at (partially) unknown positions, since in this case it is more difficult to determine the induced difference from output differences.

Likewise, one can consider faults induced in the NFSR alone. These faults do not influence the contents of the LFSR. However, faults in the NFSR propagate nonlinearly and their evolution will be harder to predict. Thus, a fault attack on the NFSR seems more difficult.

4   Conclusions

In this paper we introduced the Grain family of stream ciphers. Two different versions, denoted Grain and Grain-128, have been specified. The designs target hardware environments where small area is of high importance. The basic implementation is very small but outputs only one bit/clock. An important feature in the Grain ciphers is the possibility to easily increase the throughput by adding some extra hardware. This is done by simply implementing the relatively small feedback and output functions several times. This flexibility makes the Grain ciphers attractive for a wide range of applications spanning from the most demanding in terms of small hardware area to applications requiring a very high throughput.

References

1. Ekdahl, P., Johansson, T.: A new version of the stream cipher SNOW. In: Nyberg, K., Heys, H.M. (eds.) SAC 2002. LNCS, vol. 2595, pp. 47–61. Springer, Heidelberg (2003)
2. Hawkes, P., Rose, G.: Primitive specification for SOBER-128. Cryptology ePrint Archive, Report 2003/081 (2003), `http://eprint.iacr.org/`
3. Maximov, A.: Cryptanalysis of the Grain family of stream ciphers. In: Lin, F., Lee, D., Lin, B., Shieh, S., Jajodia, S. (eds.) ACM Symposium on Information, Computer and Communications Security (ASIACCS 2006), pp. 283–288. ACM, New York (2006)
4. Berbain, C., Gilbert, H., Maximov, A.: Cryptanalysis of Grain. In: Robshaw, M.J.B. (ed.) FSE 2006. LNCS, vol. 4047, pp. 15–29. Springer, Heidelberg (2006)
5. Khazaei, S., Hassanzadeh, M., Kiaei, M.: Distinguishing attack on Grain. eS-TREAM, ECRYPT Stream Cipher Project, Report2005/071 (2005), `http://www.ecrypt.eu.org/stream`
6. Golić, J.: Computation of low-weight parity-check polynomials. Electronic Letters 32(21), 1981–1982 (1996)
7. Hell, M.: On the design and analysis of stream ciphers. PhD thesis, Lund University (2007)
8. Babbage, S.: A space/time tradeoff in exhaustive search attacks on stream ciphers. In: European Convention on Security and Detection. IEE Conference Publication, vol. 408 (1995)
9. Golić, J.: Cryptanalysis of alleged A5 stream cipher. In: Fumy, W. (ed.) EURO-CRYPT 1997. LNCS, vol. 1233, pp. 239–255. Springer, Heidelberg (1997)
10. Biryukov, A., Shamir, A.: Cryptanalytic time/memory/data tradeoffs for stream ciphers. In: Okamoto, T. (ed.) ASIACRYPT 2000. LNCS, vol. 1976, pp. 1–13. Springer, Heidelberg (2000)
11. Hong, J., Sarkar, P.: New applications of time memory data tradeoffs. In: Roy, B. (ed.) ASIACRYPT 2005. LNCS, vol. 3788, pp. 353–372. Springer, Heidelberg (2005)
12. Hoch, J., Shamir, A.: Fault analysis of stream ciphers. In: Joye, M., Quisquater, J.-J. (eds.) CHES 2004. LNCS, vol. 3156, pp. 240–253. Springer, Heidelberg (2004)

The MICKEY Stream Ciphers

Steve Babbage[1] and Matthew Dodd[2]

[1] Vodafone Group R&D, Newbury, UK
steve.babbage@vodafone.com
[2] Independent consultant
matthew@mdodd.net

Abstract. The family of stream ciphers MICKEY (which stands for Mutual Irregular Clocking KEYstream generator) is aimed at resource-constrained hardware platforms. It is intended to have low complexity in hardware, while providing a high level of security. It uses irregular clocking of shift registers, with some novel techniques to balance the need for guarantees on period and pseudorandomness against the need to avoid certain cryptanalytic attacks.

1 Introduction and Overview

The MICKEY family of algorithms was designed in response to the ECRYPT 'Call for Stream Cipher Primitives' in 2005, and directed at 'Profile 2' — stream ciphers intended for use on resource-constrained hardware platforms. Specifically, it is intended to have low complexity in hardware, while providing a high level of security. In fact, two variants of the algorithm have been defined: MICKEY, with an 80-bit key, and MICKEY-128, with a 128-bit key.

'MICKEY' is an abbreviation of 'Mutual Irregular Clocking KEYstream generator', and this encapsulates the original design concept, illustrated in Figure 1. The algorithm is based around two registers R and S, each of which has two modes of clocking selected by a control bit. With this as a starting point, we were lead to design a clocking rule for the ensemble (R, S), in which the control bit for each register is formed from combination of bits dependent on both registers.

It was also intended from the outset that R should clock as a Galois-stepping feedback shift register either 1 or J times, given that J steps can be implemented efficiently in a single clock cycle by taking advantage of an idea introduced by Jansen [14]. This is discussed in detail in section 2.1 below.

The register S, on the other hand, was intended to clock non-linearly, in two different ways. Successive bits of keystream are formed by combining bits from the registers R and S. Broadly speaking, the idea was that the linearity of R would ensure good statistical properties and guarantees about period, whilst the non-linearity of S would protect against attacks that might be mounted against a linear system.

M. Robshaw and O. Billet (Eds.): New Stream Cipher Designs, LNCS 4986, pp. 191–209, 2008.
© Springer-Verlag Berlin Heidelberg 2008

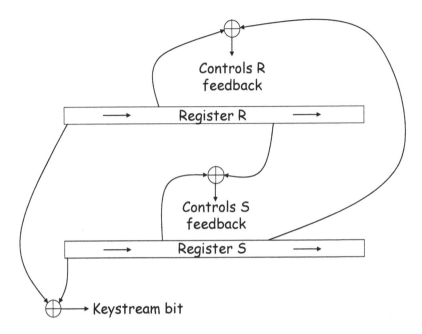

Fig. 1. MICKEY algorithm structure

2   Design Principles

In this section we describe the design, and the choices behind it, in further detail. Note that complete formal specifications of MICKEY and MICKEY-128 are provided in appendices A and B.

This section applies equally to both variants of the cipher, and we introduce the parameter n so that we can discuss both at the same time; $n = 100$ for MICKEY and $n = 160$ for MICKEY-128. Thus n is the length of register R, and, equally, the length of register S. As stipulated in sections A.2 and B.2, keystream sequences are limited to $2^{|K|/2}$ bits, and at most $2^{|K|/2}$ sequences may be produced from different IV values with a single key; here $|K|$ denotes the key length.

When used in accordance with the rules set out in sections A.2 and B.2, both MICKEY variants are intended to resist any attack faster than exhaustive key search. The designers have not deliberately inserted any hidden weaknesses in the algorithms.

The designers of MICKEY family of algorithms do not claim any IPR over it, and make it freely available for any purpose. To the best of our knowledge no one else has any relevant IPR either.

2.1   The Variable Clocking of R: What It Does

Register R has a set of feedback taps $RTAPS$, and clocks in one of two ways according to the value of a control bit $CONTROL\_BIT\_R$. When the value of

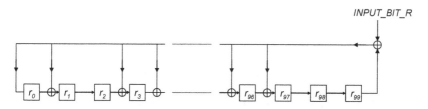

Fig. 2. Clocking the R register with $CONTROL\_BIT\_R = 0$

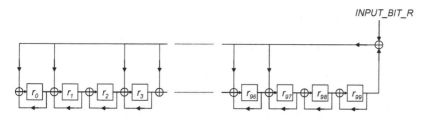

Fig. 3. Clocking the R register with $CONTROL\_BIT\_R = 1$

$CONTROL\_BIT\_R = 0$, the clocking of R is a standard linear feedback shift register clocking operation (with Galois-style feedback, according to the primitive characteristic polynomial $C_R(x) = x^n + \sum_{i \in RTAPS} x^i$, with $INPUT\_BIT\_R$ XORed into the feedback). This is shown in Figure 2 for the case $n = 100$.

If we represent elements of the field $GF(2^n)$ as polynomials $\sum_{i=0}^{n-1} r_i x^i$, modulo $C_R(x)$, then shifting the register corresponds to multiplication by x in the field.

When $CONTROL\_BIT = 1$, as well as shifting each bit in the register to the right, we also XOR it back into the current stage, as shown in Figure 3. This corresponds to multiplication by $x + 1$ in the same field.

The characteristic polynomial $C_R(x)$ has been chosen so that $C_R(x) \mid x^J + x + 1$ where $J = 2^{50} - 157$ for MICKEY and $J = 2^{80} - 255$ for MICKEY-128 . Thus, clocking the register with $CONTROL\_BIT\_R = 1$ is equivalent to clocking the register J times.

This technique — a simple operation, related to the standard linear register clocking operation but equivalent to making the register 'jump' by clocking it J times — is due to Cees Jansen [14]. In [14], Jansen presents the technique applied to LFSRs with Fibonacci-style clocking, but it is clear that the same approach is valid with Galois-style clocking.

This observation is elaborated in [6], where we describe a technique, reproduced below, for finding suitable characteristic polynomials. Suppose first that $C(x)$ is a polynomial of even degree n over GF(2) that divides $x^J + x + 1$, where $J = 2^{n/2} - \delta$ for a small positive integer δ. Since $C(x) \mid x^J + x + 1$,

$$C(x) \mid x^{2^{n/2}} + x^{\delta+1} + x^\delta$$

Hence, if we denote congruence mod $C(x)$ by $\equiv$,

$$x^{2^n} + x = \left(x^{2^{n/2}}\right)^{2^{n/2}} + x$$

$$\equiv \left(x^{\delta+1} + x^{\delta}\right)^{2^{n/2}} + x$$

$$= \left(x^{2^{n/2}}\right)^{\delta+1} + \left(x^{2^{n/2}}\right)^{\delta} + x$$

$$\equiv \left(x^{\delta+1} + x^{\delta}\right)^{\delta+1} + \left(x^{\delta+1} + x^{\delta}\right)^{\delta} + x$$

If moreover $C(x)$ is primitive, then $x^{2^n} + x \equiv 0$, so the polynomial

$$G_\delta(x) = \left(x^{\delta+1} + x^{\delta}\right)^{\delta+1} + \left(x^{\delta+1} + x^{\delta}\right)^{\delta} + x$$

of degree $(\delta + 1)^2$ must have $C(x)$ as a factor.

To find suitable characteristic polynomials for the MICKEY family of algorithms, we can therefore apply the following algorithm, starting at $\delta = \lceil\sqrt{n}\rceil - 1$:

- Construct $G_\delta(x)$, and see if it has any factor $F(x)$ of degree n
- If it does, check whether $F(x)$ is primitive
- If it is, then check whether $F(x)$ really does divide $x^{2^{n/2}-\delta} + x + 1$
- If it does, set $C(x) = F(x)$ and stop
- Otherwise, increment δ and start again

The following variant may be slightly more efficient:

- Compute $\gcd(G_\delta(x), x^{2^{n/2}-\delta} + x + 1)$ and factorise it
- If there is any factor $F(x)$ of degree n, check whether $F(x)$ is primitive
- If a primitive factor $F(x)$ is found, set $C(x) = F(x)$ and stop
- Otherwise, increment δ and start again

Notice, from the considerations above, that any factor of $\gcd(G_\delta(x), x^{2^{n/2}-\delta} + x + 1)$ is also a factor of $x^{2^n} + x$.

2.2 Motivation for the Variable Clocking

Stream ciphers making use of variable clocking often lend themselves to statistical attacks, in which the attacker guesses how many times the register has been clocked at a particular time. There are a number of characteristics of a cipher design that may make such attacks possible.

To illustrate these possible characteristics, let us consider the stream cipher LILI-128 [9]. LILI-128 uses two LFSRs, of length 39 and 89; the 89-stage register is clocked 1, 2, 3 or 4 times at each clock of the overall generator, based on two control bits from the 39-stage register. Attacks based on guessing a likely number of clocks of the 89-stage register may be possible because:

1. Clocking the 89-stage register r times and then s times gives the same result as clocking s times and then r times. For instance, clocking twice and then

three times gives the same result as clocking three times and then twice. The different possible clocking operations commute. So for instance the attacker may guess that, after ten clocks of the overall generator, the 89-stage register has had two single-clocks, three double-clocks, three triple-clocks and two quadruple-clocks; she doesn't need to guess the order in which the different clockings occurred.

2. Furthermore, clocking once and then four times gives the same end result as clocking twice and then three times. There are lots of combinations that give, for example, 25 clocks of the register after 10 clocks of the overall generator; the attacker can assign a single overall probability to this event, without having to distinguish between the many different clocking combinations that could have led to it. This further improves the efficiency of a statistical attack.

3. Finally, 25 clocks of the 89-stage register may have occurred after ten genera-tor clocks, or after nine generator clocks, or after eleven generator clocks, ... Again, this can be used to make attacks more efficient — see [10,15] for an example.

The principles behind the design of the MICKEY algorithms are:

− to take all of the benefits of variable clocking, in protecting against many forms of attack;
− to guarantee period and local randomness;
− subject to those, to reduce the susceptibility to statistical attacks as far as possible.

Specifically, taking points 1 to 3 in turn:

1. does apply to register R (because $\text{clock}^J \circ \text{clock}^1 = \text{clock}^1 \circ \text{clock}^J$), but does not apply to register S, whose different clocking operations do not commute.
2. does not apply to either register. In the case of R, for any given values $t \leq 2^{|K|/2}$ and u, there is at most one possible pair of values n_1 and n_J such that $0 \leq n_1, n_J \leq t$; $n_1 + n_J = t$; and $n_1 + n_J J = u$. (n_1 and n_J represent the number of times that R is clocked once and J times respectively.)
3. does not apply to either register. In the case of R, since $J > 2^{|K|/2}$ (for either MICKEY variant), it is true that for any given value u, there is as most one triple of values t, n_1 and n_J such that $t \leq 2^{|K|/2}$; $0 \leq n_1, n_J \leq t$; $n_1 + n_J = t$; and $n_1 + n_J J = u$.

In the MICKEY family of stream ciphers, the register R acts as the 'engine', ensuring that the state of the generator does not repeat within the generation of a single keystream sequence, and ensuring good local statistical properties. The influence of R on the clocking of S also prevents S from becoming stuck in a short cycle. If the 'jump index' $J < 2^{n-|K|/2}$, then the state of R will not repeat during the generation of a maximum length $\left(2^{|K|/2}\right)$-bit keystream sequence; and if $J > 2^{|K|/2}$, then property 3 above is satisfied. We chose the 'jump index' J to have the largest possible value subject to $J < 2^{n/2}$; then indeed both $J < 2^{n-|K|/2}$ and $J > 2^{|K|/2}$.

2.3   Selection of Clock Control Bits

We deliberately chose the clock control bits for each register to be derived from both registers, in such a way that knowledge of either register state is not sufficient to tell the attacker how either register will subsequently be clocked. This helps to guard against 'guess and determine' or 'divide and conquer' attacks.

2.4   The S Register Feedback Function

The clocking rule for register S is specified in sections A.3 and B.3. Figure 4 illustrates the principle by showing the updating of the particular cell s_{56} in MICKEY. In general, the new value of a cell s_i is formed from the exclusive-or of the following:

- s_{i-1}, if $1 \leq i \leq n-1$;
- the product of $s_i \oplus COMP0_i$ and $s_{i+1} \oplus COMP1_i$, if $1 \leq i \leq n-2$, for predefined bit values $COMP0_i$ and $COMP1_i$;
- $s_{n-1} \oplus INPUT\_BIT\_S$, for certain predefined values of i which depend also on the value of the clock control bit.

For any fixed value of $CONTROL\_BIT\_S$, the clocking function of S is invertible (so that the space of possible register values is not reduced by clocking S).

Our design goal for the clocking function of S can be stated as follows. Assume that the initial state of S is randomly selected, and that the sequence of values of $CONTROL\_BIT\_S$ applied to the clocking of S are also randomly selected. Then consider the sequence $(s_0(i))_{i=0,1,2,\ldots}$. (By $s_0(i)$ we mean the contents of s_0 after the generator has been clocked i times.) We want to avoid any strong affine relations in that sequence — that is, we do not want there to exist a set I such that the value $p = \sum_{i \in I} s_0(i)$ is especially likely to be equal to 0 (or to 1) as the initial state and $CONTROL\_BIT\_S$ range over all possible values.

The reason for this design goal is to avoid attacks based on establishing a probabilistic linear model (i.e. a set I as described above) that would allow a

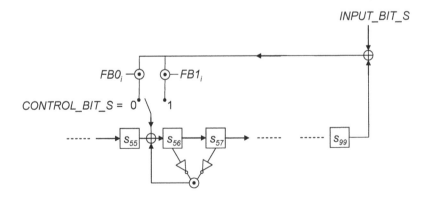

Fig. 4. Clocking the S register

linear combination of keystream bits to be strongly correlated to a combination of bits only from the ('linear', 'weaker') R register. We are thinking here especially of distinguishing attacks.

It is not straightforward to meet this design goal in an optimum sense (even if we defined it more precisely than we have done), but we do have some reason to believe that we have met it pretty well. At least, earlier proposals we considered for S were weaker in this regard. We modelled a number of constructions on a scaled down version of S, and looked for the strongest linear relations holding over relatively short sequences $(s_0(i))$, and we found that the construction we have chosen performed well.

In particular, our construction preserves local randomness, in the sense that, if the initial state is uniformly random, then a sequence of n successive bits $s_0(i)$ will also be uniformly random. So no sum of fewer than $n + 1$ successive bits $s_0(i)$ will be equal to 0 with probability distinct from $1/2$. From our empirical analysis, we believe that the strongest bias will come from a combination selected from precisely $n + 1$ successive bits $s_0(i)$.

We should be honest, though, and say that we would ideally have liked more time to analyse possible constructions. There is probably some scope for further improvement.

2.5   Key Loading

We use a non-linear loading mechanism to protect against resynchronisation attacks.

2.6   Algebraic Attacks

Algebraic attacks usually become possible when the keystream is correlated to one or more linearly clocking registers, whose clocking is either entirely predictable or can be guessed.

We have taken care that the attacker cannot eliminate the uncertainty about the clocking of either register by guessing a small set of values. (By illustrative contrast, some attacks on LILI-128 [9] were possible because the state of the 39-stage register could be guessed, and then the clocking of the 89-stage register became known.)

Furthermore, each keystream bit produced by MICKEY is not correlated to the contents of either one register (so in particular not to the 'linear register' R).

2.7   Output Function

MICKEY uses a very simple output function $(r_0 \oplus s_0)$ to compute keystream bits from the register states.

We considered more complex alternatives, e.g. of the form $r_0 \oplus g(r_1 \ldots r_{79}) \oplus s_0 \oplus h(s_1 \ldots s_{79})$ for some Boolean functions g and h. Although these might increase the security margin against some types of attack, we preferred to keep the output function simple and elegant, and rely instead on the mutual irregular clocking of the registers.

3   Register Sizes

In this section we consider the choice of the parameter n.

Initially, n was chosen to be the same as the key length, and this choice was retained in the first, version 1, proposals for MICKEY and MICKEY-128 to ECRYPT [2,3]. Subsequently this decision was revised [4,5] in the current (version 2.0) MICKEY algorithms, so that n became 1.25 times the key length.

This change was made in response to the work of Jin Hong and Woo-Hwan Kim [12]. They considered three areas of (arguable) vulnerability, which are all addressed by this new choice for the parameter n. We explain the details in the following sections.

3.1   Time-Memory-Data (TMD) Tradeoff, with or without BSW Sampling

Let N be the size of the keystream generator state space (so 2^{160} for MICKEY version 1). Let X be the set of all possible keystream generator states. Let $f : X \rightarrow Y$ be the function that maps a generator state to the first $\log_2 N$ bits of keystream produced. Suppose the attacker has harvested a large number of $\log_2 N$-bit keystream sequences $y_i \in Y$, and wants to identify a keystream generator state $x \in X$ such that $f(x) = y_i$ for some i.

BS tradeoff. The Biryukov-Shamir TMD [7] algorithm succeeds with high probability if the following conditions are satisfied:

$$TM^2D^2 = N^2 \quad \text{and} \quad 1 \leq D^2 \leq T$$

where T is the online time complexity, M is the memory requirement, and D is the number of keystream sequences available to the attacker. The offline time complexity is $P = N/D$.

BSW sampling. When we say that we can perform BSW sampling [8] with a sampling factor W, we mean that:

- there is a subset $X' \subseteq X$ with cardinality N/W, and it is easy to generate elements of X'; and
- if Y' is the image of X' under f, then it is easy to recognise elements of Y'.

Our attacker may consider only those keystream sequences that are elements of Y', and apply the BS tradeoff to the problem of inverting the restricted function $f' : X' \rightarrow Y'$. If the total number of keystream sequences available to the attacker is D, only roughly D/W of these will fall in Y' and so be usable; on the other hand, the size of the set of preimages is now N/W instead of N. The conditions for success become

$$TM^2 \left(\frac{D}{W}\right)^2 = \left(\frac{N}{W}\right)^2 \quad \text{and} \quad 1 \leq \left(\frac{D}{W}\right)^2 \leq T$$

i.e.

$$TM^2D^2 = N^2 \quad \text{and} \quad W^2 \leq D^2 \leq TW^2$$

and the offline time complexity remains $P = \frac{(N/W)}{(D/W)} = N/D$. Also, very importantly, the number of table lookups in the online attack is reduced by a factor W, which greatly reduces the actual time it takes.

TMD tradeoff against MICKEY version 1. Hong and Kim [12] show that BSW sampling can be performed on MICKEY version 1 with a sampling factor $W = 2^{27}$. This allows a TMD tradeoff attack to be performed with the following complexity, for instance:

- unfiltered data complexity $D = 2^{60}$, e.g. 2^{20} keystream sequences each of length roughly 2^{40} bits; filtering these by BSW sampling means that the attack is performed against a reduced set of $D/W = 2^{33}$ keystream sequences;
- search space of reduced size $N/W = 2^{133}$;
- time complexity $T = 2^{66}$;
- memory complexity $M = 2^{67}$;
- offline time complexity $P = 2^{100}$.

So we have an attack whose online time, data and memory complexities are all less than the key size of 2^{80}. However, the one-off precomputation time complexity is greater than 2^{80}. Other parameter values are possible, but the precomputation time is always greater than 2^{80}.

There is no consensus as to whether this constitutes a successful attack. Some authors seem to ignore precomputation time completely, and consider only online complexity to matter; others would say that an attack requiring overall complexity greater than exhaustive search is of no practical significance. Although we incline more towards the second view, we recognise that some will deem the cipher less than fully secure if such attacks exist.

MICKEY 2.0. In MICKEY 2.0, the state size $N = 2^{200}$. Thus, for any BS tradeoff attack, with or without BSW sampling, if $TM^2D^2 = N^2$ then at least one of T, M or D must be at least 2^{80}. So no attack is possible with online complexity faster than exhaustive key search.

Earlier papers (e.g. [1]) have recommended that the state size of a keystream generator should be at least twice the key size, to protect against what is now usually called the Babbage-Golić TMD attack. By making the state size at least 2.5 times the key size, we also provide robust protection against the Biryukov-Shamir TMD attack, with or without BSW sampling[1]. This rather simple observation has not appeared in previous literature, as far as we have been able to discover.

---

[1] We refer here only to TMD attacks to invert the function mapping keystream generator state to keystream. We are not talking about the function mapping key and IV to keystream, as discussed by Hong and Sarkar in [13].

BSW sampling of MICKEY 2.0. It is still possible to perform BSW sampling on MICKEY 2.0. We have made no attempt to prevent this — we see no reason to do so that would justify an additional complication to the cipher design.

3.2   State Entropy Loss and Keystream Convergence

It is fundamental to the design of the MICKEY algorithm family that the keystream generator is subject to variable clocking under control of bits from within the generator. This results in a reduction of the entropy of the overall generator state: some generator states after clocking have two or more possible preimages, and some states have no possible preimages. The fact that the control bit for each register is derived by XORing bits from both registers, and hence is uncorrelated to the state of the register it controls, is crucial: it means that clocking the overall generator does not reduce the entropy of either one register state.

However, for MICKEY version 1, Hong and Kim [12] show that the overall entropy loss can result in the convergence of distinct keystream sequences within the parameters of legitimate use of the cipher. For example, if V keystream sequences of length 2^{40} are generated from different (K, IV) pairs, then for large enough V there will be state collisions — and of course, once identical states are reached, subsequent keystream sequences are identical. An exact analysis seems difficult, but it appears that V may not have to be much larger than 2^{22} before collisions will begin to occur.

This uncomfortable property holds because, after the generator has been run for long enough to produce a 2^{40}-bit sequence, the state entropy will have reduced by nearly 40 bits, from the initial 2^{160} to only just over 2^{120}. Because 120 is less than twice the key size, we begin to see collisions within an amount of data less than the key size.

In MICKEY 2.0, the state size is 200 bits, and the maximum permitted length of a single keystream sequence is 2^{40} bits. After the generator has been run for long enough to produce a 2^{40}-bit sequence, the entropy will still be just over 160 bits. This is twice the key size, and so we no longer have a problem.

3.3   Weak Keys

There is an obvious 'lock-up' state for the register R: if the key and IV loading and initialisation leaves R in the all zeroes state, then it will remain permanently in that state. For MICKEY version 1 we reasoned as follows:

> It is clear that, if an attacker assumes that this is the case, she can readily confirm her assumption and deduce the remainder of the generator state by analysing a short sequence of keystream. But, because this can be assumed to occur with probability roughly 2^{-80} — the same probability for any guessed secret key to be correct — we do not think it necessary to prevent it (and so in the interests of efficiency we do not do so).

Hong and Kim [12] point out that, for MICKEY version 1, there is also a lock-up state for the register S. If the key and IV loading and initialisation leaves S in this particular state, then it will remain permanently in that state, irrespective of the values of the clock control bits. The probability of a 'weak state' in MICKEY version 1 is thus roughly 2^{-79}. And 2^{-79} is greater than 2^{-80} ....

It is undoubtedly much easier to try two candidate secret keys, with a success probability of 2^{-79}, than to mount an attack based on these possible weak states. So we would still argue that it is not necessary to guard against their occurrence. But anyway, with MICKEY 2.0 the increased register lengths mean that the probability of a weak state goes down to roughly 2^{-99}, which is clearly too small to concern us.

4   Performance of the Algorithm

The MICKEY cipher family is not designed for notably high speeds in software, although it is straightforward to implement it reasonably efficiently. Our own reasonably efficient (but not turbo-charged) implementations generated 10^8 bits of keystream in 3.81 seconds for MICKEY, and in 4.81 seconds for MICKEY-128, using a PC with a 3.4GHz Pentium 4 processor. There may be scope for more efficient software implementations that produce several bits of keystream at a time, making use of look-up tables to implement the register clocking and keystream derivation.

Further information on the performance of MICKEY and MICKEY-128 in software — on various platforms — and hardware can be found via [11].

5   Afterthoughts

So how is MICKEY looking now, compared to the other eSTREAM candidates?

5.1   Security Against Classical Cryptanalysis

In terms of security against classical cryptanalysis, we believe that MICKEY is standing up very well. The observations of Hong and Kim [12] on the MICKEY version 1 ciphers are all fully addressed in the current versions. No other threatening analysis has emerged, despite the efforts of some very good cryptanalysts.

5.2   Security Against Side Channel Attacks

If security against side channel attacks is required, then MICKEY is perhaps not optimal. The main area of susceptibility is the variable clocking of the linear register R. When $CONTROL\_BIT\_R = 1$, the additional XORs will consume more power in a naïve implementation.

By contrast, the eSTREAM submission Pomaranch also uses the "jumping" idea, but in such a way that half of the cells in a register have an XOR when the control bit takes one value, and the other half do when the control bit takes the other value. So the overall power consumption is likely to be the same. A similar approach could have been taken with MICKEY, and would give readier protection against power analysis attacks.

Having said that, we think that side channel attacks are largely irrelevant in the great majority of real world stream cipher applications. The legitimate user of an encrypting device has no motivation to extract their own encryption key (whereas they may, for instance, be motivated to clone their own SIM card or Pay-TV card). And if an outsider has close enough access to the encrypting device to carry out attacks of this kind, then there are more obvious bad things that she can do. It is possible to think up use cases in which side channel attacks on a stream cipher might matter, but they are not typical.

5.3   Performance

MICKEY's main performance goal is to run at very low power, or with very few logic gates, in resource-constrained hardware. As such, it compares very well with other eSTREAM submissions; it is indeed one of the very smallest.

Some other submissions have been designed to allow faster operation than MICKEY, by allowing a much greater degree of pipelining. Trivium is the most extreme example. The variable clocking approach taken in MICKEY does not lend itself well to pipelining.

So overall we think that MICKEY is a good choice where power or gate count are the prime performance considerations; less so where the highest speeds are required.

6   Conclusion

The evidence so far from the eSTREAM process is that MICKEY is a high security cipher, well suited to stream cipher applications where very low power or gate count are required.

References

1. Babbage, S.: Improved Exhaustive Search Attacks on Stream Ciphers. In: European Convention on Security and Detection, IEE Conference Publication, vol. 408, pp. 161–166. IEE (1995)
2. Babbage, S.H., Dodd, M.W.: The stream cipher MICKEY (version 1), Algorithm specification Issue 1.0. In: ECRYPT stream cipher submission, in the proceedings of the SKEW Workshop, Århus (May 2005),
   http://www.ecrypt.eu.org/stream/ciphers/mickey/mickey.pdf
3. Babbage, S.H., Dodd, M.W.: The stream cipher MICKEY-128 (version 1), Algorithm specification Issue 1.0. In: ECRYPT stream cipher submission, in the proceedings of the SKEW Workshop, Århus (May 2005),
   http://www.ecrypt.eu.org/stream/ciphers/mickey128/mickey128.pdf

4. Babbage, S.H., Dodd, M.W.: The stream cipher MICKEY 2.0, revised ECRYPT stream cipher submission,
   http://www.ecrypt.eu.org/stream/p3ciphers/mickey/mickeyp3.pdf
5. Babbage, S.H., Dodd, M.W.: The stream cipher MICKEY-128 2.0, revised ECRYPT stream cipher submission,
   http://www.ecrypt.eu.org/stream/p3ciphers/mickey/mickey128_p3.pdf
6. Babbage, S.H., Dodd, M.W.: Finding Characteristic Polynomials with Jump Indices, http://eprint.iacr.org/2006/010
7. Biryukov, A., Shamir, A.: Cryptanalytic Time/Memory/Data Tradeoffs for Stream Ciphers. In: Okamoto, T. (ed.) ASIACRYPT 2000. LNCS, vol. 1976, pp. 1–13. Springer, Heidelberg (2000)
8. Biryukov, A., Shamir, A., Wagner, D.: Real time cryptanalysis of A5/1 on a PC. In: Schneier, B. (ed.) FSE 2000. LNCS, vol. 1978, pp. 1–18. Springer, Heidelberg (2001)
9. Dawson, E., Clark, A., Golić, J., Millan, W., Penna, L., Simpson, L.: The LILI-128 Keystream Generator, NESSIE submission. In: proceedings of the First Open NESSIE Workshop, Leuven (November 2000), http://www.cryptonessie.org
10. Ekdahl, P., Johansson, T.: Another attack on A5/1. IEEE Transactions on Information Theory 49(1), 284–289 (2003)
11. Algorithm performance pages on the eStream web site:
    http://www.ecrypt.eu.org/stream/sw.html
    http://www.ecrypt.eu.org/stream/hw.html
12. Hong, J., Kim, W.: TMD-Tradeoff and State Entropy Loss Considerations of Streamcipher MICKEY. In: Maitra, S., Veni Madhavan, C.E., Venkatesan, R. (eds.) INDOCRYPT 2005. LNCS, vol. 3797, pp. 169–182. Springer, Heidelberg (2005), http://eprint.iacr.org/2005/257
13. Hong, J., Sarkar, P.: Rediscovery of Time Memory Tradeoffs, http://eprint.iacr.org/2005/090
14. Jansen, C.J.A.: Streamcipher Design: Make your LFSRs jump!, presented at the ECRYPT SASC (State of the Art in Stream Ciphers) workshop. In: the workshop record, Bruges (October 2004), http://www.isg.rhul.ac.uk/research/projects/ecrypt/stvl/sasc-record.zip
15. Maximov, A., Johansson, T., Babbage, S.: An Improved Correlation Attack on A5/1. In: Handschuh, H., Hasan, M.A. (eds.) SAC 2004. LNCS, vol. 3357, pp. 1–18. Springer, Heidelberg (2004)

A   Specification of the Cipher MICKEY

In this appendix, we provide a full specification of the stream cipher MICKEY (version 2.0).

A.1   Input and Output Parameters

MICKEY takes two input parameters:

- an 80-bit secret key K, whose bits are labelled $k_0 \ldots k_{79}$;
- an initialisation variable IV, anywhere between 0 and 80 bits in length, whose bits are labelled $iv_0 \ldots iv_{IVLENGTH-1}$.

The keystream bits output by MICKEY are labelled $z_0, z_1, \ldots$. Ciphertext is produced from plaintext by bitwise XOR with keystream bits, as in most stream ciphers.

A.2 Acceptable Use

The maximum length of keystream sequence that may be generated with a single (K, IV) pair is 2^{40} bits. It is acceptable to generate 2^{40} such sequences, all from the same K but with different values of IV. It is not acceptable to use two initialisation variables of different lengths with the same K. And it is not, of course, acceptable to reuse the same value of IV with the same K.

A.3 Components of the Keystream Generator

The registers. The generator is built from two registers R and S. Each register is 100 stages long, each stage containing one bit. We label the bits in the registers $r_0 \ldots r_{99}$ and $s_0 \ldots s_{99}$ respectively.

Broadly speaking, we think of R as 'the linear register' and S as 'the non-linear register'.

Clocking the register R. Define a set of feedback tap positions for R:

$$RTAPS = \{0, 1, 3, 4, 5, 6, 9, 12, 13, 16, 19, 20, 21, 22, 25, 28, 37, 38,$$
$$41, 42, 45, 46, 50, 52, 54, 56, 58, 60, 61, 63, 64, 65, 66, 67,$$
$$71, 72, 79, 80, 81, 82, 87, 88, 89, 90, 91, 92, 94, 95, 96, 97\}$$

We define an operation CLOCK_R $(R, INPUT\_BIT\_R, CONTROL\_BIT\_R)$ as follows:

- Let $r_0 \ldots r_{99}$ be the state of the register R before clocking, and let $r'_0 \ldots r'_{99}$ be the state of the register R after clocking.
- $FEEDBACK\_BIT = r_{99} \oplus INPUT\_BIT\_R$
- For $1 \leq i \leq 99$, $r'_i = r_{i-1}$; $r'_0 = 0$
- For $0 \leq i \leq 99$, if $i \in RTAPS$, $r'_i = r'_i \oplus FEEDBACK\_BIT$
- If $CONTROL\_BIT\_R = 1$:
  - For $0 \leq i \leq 99$, $r'_i = r'_i \oplus r_i$

Clocking the register S. Define four sequences $(COMP0_i)_{i=1}^{98}$, $(COMP1_i)_{i=1}^{98}$, $(FB0_i)_{i=0}^{99}$ and $(FB1_i)_{i=0}^{99}$ according to Table 1.

We define an operation CLOCK_S $(S, INPUT\_BIT\_S, CONTROL\_BIT\_S)$ as follows:

- Let $s_0 \ldots s_{99}$ be the state of the register S before clocking, and $s'_0 \ldots s'_{99}$ be the state of the register after clocking. We will also use $\hat{s}_0 \ldots \hat{s}_{99}$ as intermediate variables to simplify the specification.
- $FEEDBACK\_BIT = s_{99} \oplus INPUT\_BIT\_S$

Table 1. S register tables for MICKEY

i	0	1	2	3	4	5	6	7	8	9	10	11	12	13	14	15	16	17	18	19
$COMP0_i$		0	0	0	1	1	0	0	0	1	0	1	1	1	1	0	1	0	0	1
$COMP1_i$		1	0	1	1	0	0	1	0	1	1	1	1	0	0	1	0	1	0	0
$FB0_i$	1	1	1	1	0	1	0	1	1	1	1	1	1	1	1	0	0	1	0	1
$FB1_i$	1	1	1	0	1	1	1	0	0	0	0	1	1	1	0	1	0	0	1	1

i	20	21	22	23	24	25	26	27	28	29	30	31	32	33	34	35	36	37	38	39
$COMP0_i$	0	1	0	1	0	1	0	1	0	1	1	0	1	0	0	1	0	0	0	0
$COMP1_i$	0	1	1	0	1	0	1	1	1	0	1	1	1	1	0	0	0	1	1	0
$FB0_i$	1	1	1	1	1	1	1	1	1	0	0	1	1	0	0	0	0	0	0	1
$FB1_i$	0	0	0	1	0	0	1	1	0	0	1	0	1	1	0	0	0	1	1	0

i	40	41	42	43	44	45	46	47	48	49	50	51	52	53	54	55	56	57	58	59
$COMP0_i$	0	0	0	1	0	1	0	1	0	1	0	0	0	0	0	1	0	1	0	0
$COMP1_i$	1	0	1	1	1	0	0	0	0	1	0	0	0	1	0	1	1	1	0	0
$FB0_i$	1	1	0	0	1	0	0	1	0	1	0	1	0	0	1	0	1	1	1	1
$FB1_i$	0	0	0	0	1	1	0	1	1	0	0	0	1	0	0	0	1	0	0	1

i	60	61	62	63	64	65	66	67	68	69	70	71	72	73	74	75	76	77	78	79
$COMP0_i$	1	1	1	0	0	1	0	1	0	1	1	1	1	1	1	1	1	1	0	1
$COMP1_i$	0	1	1	1	1	1	1	0	1	0	1	1	1	0	1	1	1	1	0	0
$FB0_i$	0	1	0	1	0	1	0	0	0	0	0	0	0	0	0	1	1	0	1	0
$FB1_i$	0	0	1	0	1	1	0	1	0	1	0	0	1	0	1	0	0	0	0	1

i	80	81	82	83	84	85	86	87	88	89	90	91	92	93	94	95	96	97	98	99
$COMP0_i$	0	1	1	1	1	1	1	0	1	0	1	0	0	0	0	0	0	1	1	
$COMP1_i$	0	1	0	0	0	0	1	1	1	0	0	0	1	0	0	1	1	0	0	
$FB0_i$	0	0	1	1	0	1	1	1	0	0	1	1	1	0	0	1	1	0	0	0
$FB1_i$	1	1	0	1	1	1	1	1	0	0	0	0	0	0	1	0	0	0	0	1

- For $1 \le i \le 98$, $\hat{s}_i = s_{i-1} \oplus ((s_i \oplus COMP0_i) \cdot (s_{i+1} \oplus COMP1_i))$; $\hat{s}_0 = 0$; $\hat{s}_{99} = s_{98}$.
- If $CONTROL\_BIT\_S = 0$:
  - For $0 \le i \le 99$, $s'_i = \hat{s}_i \oplus (FB0_i \cdot FEEDBACK\_BIT)$
- If instead $CONTROL\_BIT\_S = 1$:
  - For $0 \le i \le 99$, $s'_i = \hat{s}_i \oplus (FB1_i \cdot FEEDBACK\_BIT)$

Clocking the overall generator. We define an operation CLOCK_KG $(R, S, MIXING, INPUT\_BIT)$ as follows:

- If $MIXING = TRUE$,
  - CLOCK_R $(R, INPUT\_BIT\_R = INPUT\_BIT \oplus s_{50}, CONTROL\_BIT\_R = s_{34} \oplus r_{67})$
- If instead $MIXING = FALSE$,
  - CLOCK_R $(R, INPUT\_BIT\_R = INPUT\_BIT, CONTROL\_BIT\_R = s_{34} \oplus r_{67})$
- CLOCK_S $(S, INPUT\_BIT\_S = INPUT\_BIT, CONTROL\_BIT\_S = s_{67} \oplus r_{33})$

A.4   Key Loading and Initialisation

The registers are initialised from the input variables as follows:

- Initialise the registers R and S with all zeros.
- (Load in IV.) For $0 \leq i \leq IVLENGTH - 1$:
  - CLOCK_KG (R, S, $MIXING = TRUE$, $INPUT\_BIT = iv_i$)
- (Load in K.) For $0 \leq i \leq 79$:
  - CLOCK_KG (R, S, $MIXING = TRUE$, $INPUT\_BIT = k_i$)
- (Preclock.) For $0 \leq i \leq 99$:
  - CLOCK_KG (R, S, $MIXING = TRUE$, $INPUT\_BIT = 0$)

A.5   Generating Keystream

Having loaded and initialised the registers, we generate keystream bits $z_0 \ldots z_{L-1}$ as follows:

- For $0 \leq i \leq L - 1$:
  - $z_i = r_0 \oplus s_0$
  - CLOCK_KG (R, S, $MIXING = FALSE$, $INPUT\_BIT = 0$)

B   Specification of the Cipher MICKEY-128

In this appendix, we provide a full specification of the stream cipher MICKEY-128 (version 2.0).

B.1   Input and Output Parameters

MICKEY-128 takes two input parameters:

- a 128-bit secret key K, whose bits are labelled $k_0 \ldots k_{127}$;
- an initialisation variable IV, anywhere between 0 and 128 bits in length, whose bits are labelled $iv_0 \ldots iv_{IVLENGTH-1}$.

The keystream bits output by MICKEY-128 are labelled $z_0, z_1, \ldots$. Ciphertext is produced from plaintext by bitwise XOR with keystream bits, as in most stream ciphers.

B.2   Acceptable Use

The maximum length of keystream sequence that may be generated with a single (K, IV) pair is 2^{64} bits. It is acceptable to generate 2^{64} such sequences (time permitting!), all from the same K but with different values of IV. It is not acceptable to use two initialisation variables of different lengths with the same K. And it is not, of course, acceptable to reuse the same value of IV with the same K.

B.3   Components of the Keystream Generator

The registers. The generator is built from two registers R and S. Each register is 160 stages long, each stage containing one bit. We label the bits in the registers $r_0 \ldots r_{159}$ and $s_0 \ldots s_{159}$ respectively.

Broadly speaking, we think of R as 'the linear register' and S as 'the non-linear register'.

Clocking the register R. Define a set of feedback tap positions for R:

$$RTAPS = \{0, 4, 5, 8, 10, 11, 14, 16, 20, 25, 30, 32, 35, 36, 38, 42, 43, 46, 50,$$
$$51, 53, 54, 55, 56, 57, 60, 61, 62, 63, 65, 66, 69, 73, 74, 76, 79, 80,$$
$$81, 82, 85, 86, 90, 91, 92, 95, 97, 100, 101, 105, 106, 107, 108,$$
$$109, 111, 112, 113, 115, 116, 117, 127, 128, 129, 130, 131, 133,$$
$$135, 136, 137, 140, 142, 145, 148, 150, 152, 153, 154, 156, 157\}$$

We define an operation CLOCK_R (R, $INPUT\_BIT\_R$, $CONTROL\_BIT\_R$) as follows:

- Let $r_0 \ldots r_{159}$ be the state of the register R before clocking, and let $r'_0 \ldots r'_{159}$ be the state of the register R after clocking.
- $FEEDBACK\_BIT = r_{159} \oplus INPUT\_BIT\_R$
- For $1 \le i \le 159$, $r'_i = r_{i-1}$; $r'_0 = 0$
- For $0 \le i \le 159$, if $i \in RTAPS$, $r'_i = r'_i \oplus FEEDBACK\_BIT$
- If $CONTROL\_BIT\_R = 1$:

  • For $0 \le i \le 159$, $r'_i = r'_i \oplus r_i$

Clocking the register S. Define four sequences $(COMP0_i)_{i=1}^{158}$, $(COMP1_i)_{i=1}^{158}$, $(FB0_i)_{i=0}^{159}$ and $(FB1_i)_{i=0}^{159}$ according to Table 2.

We define an operation CLOCK_S (S, $INPUT\_BIT\_S$, $CONTROL\_BIT$) as follows:

- Let $s_0 \ldots s_{159}$ be the state of the register S before clocking, and $s'_0 \ldots s'_{159}$ be the state of the register after clocking. We will also use $\hat{s}_0 \ldots \hat{s}_{159}$ as intermediate variables to simplify the specification.
- $FEEDBACK\_BIT = s_{159} \oplus INPUT\_BIT\_S$
- For $1 \le i \le 158$, $\hat{s}_i = s_{i-1} \oplus ((s_i \oplus COMP0_i) \,.\, (s_{i+1} \oplus COMP1_i))$; $\hat{s}_0 = 0$; $\hat{s}_{159} = s_{158}$.
- If $CONTROL\_BIT\_S = 0$:

  • For $0 \le i \le 159$, $s'_i = \hat{s}_i \oplus (FB0_i \,.\, FEEDBACK\_BIT)$

- If instead $CONTROL\_BIT\_S = 1$:

  • For $0 \le i \le 159$, $s'_i = \hat{s}_i \oplus (FB1_i \,.\, FEEDBACK\_BIT)$

Table 2. S register tables for MICKEY-128

i	0	1	2	3	4	5	6	7	8	9	10	11	12	13	14	15	16	17	18	19
$COMP0_i$		1	1	1	1	0	1	0	0	1	0	0	1	1	1	1	0	1	1	0
$COMP1_i$		0	0	0	1	1	0	0	1	1	1	1	1	0	0	0	1	0	0	1
$FB0_i$	1	1	1	1	0	1	0	1	1	1	1	1	1	0	0	0	0	0	1	1
$FB1_i$	1	1	0	1	0	1	0	1	1	1	1	0	1	1	1	0	0	0	1	0

i	20	21	22	23	24	25	26	27	28	29	30	31	32	33	34	35	36	37	38	39
$COMP0_i$	1	0	1	1	1	0	1	1	1	0	1	0	1	0	1	0	1	0	1	0
$COMP1_i$	1	0	0	0	1	0	1	1	1	1	1	0	0	0	0	1	1	0	0	1
$FB0_i$	1	1	0	0	0	0	1	0	0	0	1	1	0	1	0	0	0	1	0	0
$FB1_i$	1	1	1	1	1	1	0	1	1	0	0	1	0	0	0	0	1	0	0	1

i	40	41	42	43	44	45	46	47	48	49	50	51	52	53	54	55	56	57	58	59
$COMP0_i$	1	0	0	1	0	0	0	0	0	1	1	0	0	1	0	0	1	0	0	1
$COMP1_i$	0	0	1	1	1	1	0	0	0	1	1	0	1	1	0	1	0	1	1	1
$FB0_i$	1	1	0	0	0	1	0	1	1	1	1	1	0	1	0	0	0	1	1	1
$FB1_i$	0	0	1	1	0	0	0	1	1	0	0	1	1	1	1	0	0	0	0	0

i	60	61	62	63	64	65	66	67	68	69	70	71	72	73	74	75	76	77	78	79
$COMP0_i$	1	1	1	0	0	1	0	0	0	1	1	0	0	0	0	0	0	1	1	0
$COMP1_i$	1	1	1	1	0	0	0	0	0	0	1	1	1	1	1	0	0	0	1	1
$FB0_i$	0	0	0	0	1	0	0	0	0	0	0	0	1	1	0	1	1	0	0	1
$FB1_i$	1	1	1	0	0	1	1	0	1	1	0	1	0	0	0	0	1	1	0	0

i	80	81	82	83	84	85	86	87	88	89	90	91	92	93	94	95	96	97	98	99
$COMP0_i$	0	0	0	0	0	0	0	0	1	0	0	1	1	1	1	0	1	0	0	0
$COMP1_i$	0	0	0	0	0	0	0	0	0	0	1	1	1	1	1	0	1	0	1	0
$FB0_i$	1	0	1	0	0	1	1	1	0	1	1	0	0	1	1	0	1	0	0	0
$FB1_i$	0	1	0	1	1	0	0	1	1	1	1	1	0	1	1	0	1	1	1	0

i	100	101	102	103	104	105	106	107	108	109	110	111	112	113	114	115	116	117	118	119
$COMP0_i$	1	1	0	0	1	0	0	1	1	0	1	1	1	1	1	1	0	1	0	1
$COMP1_i$	0	0	1	0	1	1	0	0	0	1	1	1	0	0	0	0	0	1	1	0
$FB0_i$	1	0	0	1	1	1	0	1	0	0	1	0	0	0	1	0	1	0	1	0
$FB1_i$	0	1	1	1	0	1	1	1	1	1	1	1	0	1	1	0	1	0	0	1

i	120	121	122	123	124	125	126	127	128	129	130	131	132	133	134	135	136	137	138	139
$COMP0_i$	1	1	1	0	1	1	0	0	0	1	1	1	1	1	0	1	0	1	1	0
$COMP1_i$	0	1	1	0	0	1	1	0	1	0	1	0	1	1	0	1	1	1	0	1
$FB0_i$	0	0	1	0	1	0	1	1	1	0	0	0	0	0	1	1	1	1	0	1
$FB1_i$	0	0	1	1	0	1	1	0	1	1	1	1	0	1	1	1	0	0	0	0

i	140	141	142	143	144	145	146	147	148	149	150	151	152	153	154	155	156	157	158	159
$COMP0_i$	0	0	0	0	0	1	1	1	1	1	0	1	1	1	1	1	0	0	0	
$COMP1_i$	1	0	1	0	0	0	1	0	1	1	1	1	1	1	1	1	1	1	1	
$FB0_i$	0	0	0	0	1	1	0	0	0	1	1	0	1	1	0	0	0	0	0	1
$FB1_i$	0	0	0	1	1	1	1	0	0	1	0	1	1	0	0	0	1	0	0	0

Clocking the overall generator. We define an operation CLOCK_KG $(R, S, MIXING, INPUT\_BIT)$ as follows:

- If $MIXING = TRUE$,
  - CLOCK_R $(R, INPUT\_BIT\_R = INPUT\_BIT \oplus s_{80}, CONTROL\_BIT\_R = s_{54} \oplus r_{106})$
- If instead $MIXING = FALSE$,
  - CLOCK_R $(R, INPUT\_BIT\_R = INPUT\_BIT, CONTROL\_BIT\_R = s_{54} \oplus r_{106})$
- CLOCK_S $(S, INPUT\_BIT\_S = INPUT\_BIT, CONTROL\_BIT\_S = s_{106} \oplus r_{53})$

B.4   Key Loading and Initialisation

The registers are initialised from the input variables as follows:

- Initialise the registers R and S with all zeros.
- (Load in IV.) For $0 \le i \le IVLENGTH - 1$:
  - CLOCK_KG $(R, S, MIXING = TRUE, INPUT\_BIT = iv_i)$
- (Load in K.) For $0 \le i \le 127$:
  - CLOCK_KG $(R, S, MIXING = TRUE, INPUT\_BIT = k_i)$
- (Preclock.) For $0 \le i \le 159$:
  - CLOCK_KG $(R, S, MIXING = TRUE, INPUT\_BIT = 0)$

B.5   Generating Keystream

Having loaded and initialised the registers, we generate keystream bits $z_0 \ldots z_{L-1}$ as follows:

- For $0 \le i \le L - 1$:
  - $z_i = r_0 \oplus s_0$
  - CLOCK_KG $(R, S, MIXING = FALSE, INPUT\_BIT = 0)$

The Self-synchronizing Stream Cipher
MOUSTIQUE

Joan Daemen[1] and Paris Kitsos[2]

[1] STMicroelectronics Belgium
joan.daemen@st.com
[2] Hellenic Open University, Patras, Greece and Dept. of Computer Science and
Technology, University of the Peloponnese, Tripoli, Greece
pkitsos@eap.gr

Abstract. We present a design approach for hardware-oriented self-synchronizing stream ciphers and illustrate it with a concrete design called MOUSTIQUE. The latter is intended as a research cipher: it proves that the design approach can lead to concrete results and will serve as a target for cryptanalysis where new attacks may lead to improvements in the design approach such as new criteria for the cipher building blocks.

1 Introduction

This chapter is an abridged version of the two documents [6] and [8], both submitted to eSTREAM as documentation material for the ciphers MOSQUITO and its tweaked version MOUSTIQUE. Most of the ideas were already presented in [3] and some of them even earlier in [2] as an alternative to the design approach as proposed by Ueli Maurer in [1]. We refer to [6] for a discussion on the latter design approach and alternative modes of operation of MOSQUITO (and similarly MOUSTIQUE), such as using it as a MAC function or for authenticated encryption and synchronous stream encryption.

Single-bit self-synchronizing stream encryption has a unique advantage: in providing an existing communication system with encryption, it can be applied without the need for additional synchronization or segmentation. Actually, single-bit self-synchronizing stream encryption can be performed by using a block cipher in (single-bit) CFB mode. Still, we see two reasons for designing dedicated single-bit self-synchronizing stream ciphers.

First, the attainable encryption speed is a factor n_b slower than the encryption speed of the underlying block cipher implementation, with n_b the block length. For high-speed applications they may not be fast enough and a dedicated self-synchronizing stream cipher is required.

Second, a dedicated self-synchronizing stream cipher is a primitive different from both synchronous stream ciphers and block ciphers and is therefore theoretically interesting. Up to date, only a handful of dedicated self-synchronizing stream ciphers have been published and all except one (being the recent proposal MOUSTIQUE) have been broken. In our opinion, only the availability of

M. Robshaw and O. Billet (Eds.): New Stream Cipher Designs, LNCS 4986, pp. 210–223, 2008.

concrete targets for cryptanalysis may lead to a better insight in the design of self-synchronizing stream ciphers.

The following of this document is structured as follows. After introducing self-synchronizing stream encryption and its security properties in Section 2, we present the architecture underlying the design of MOUSTIQUE in Section 3. In Section 4 we specify MOUSTIQUE and we motivate the design choices in Section 5. Finally, Section 6 discusses the performance and resource usage of field programmable gate array implementations of MOUSTIQUE.

2   Self-synchronizing Stream Encryption

In this section we define self-synchronizing stream encryption, propose a pair of security claims and deduce from that some criteria for the cipher function that stem from differential and linear cryptanalysis.

2.1   Definition

In stream encryption operating at the bit level, each plaintext bit m^t is encrypted by adding a keystream bit z^t modulo two resulting in a ciphertext symbol c^t:

$$c^t = m^t \oplus z^t . \tag{1}$$

Decryption is:

$$m^t = c^t \oplus z^t . \tag{2}$$

In single-bit self-synchronizing stream encryption, the keystream symbol z^t is the result of applying a *cipher function* f_c to a window of the ciphertext stream with index range $[t - n_m, t - (b_s + 1)]$ and a *cipher key* K of n_k bits:

$$z^t = f_c[K](c^{t-n_m} \ldots c^{t-(b_s+1)}) . \tag{3}$$

n_m is called the *input memory* and we call b_s the *cipher function delay*. A block diagram of self-synchronizing stream encryption is given in Fig. 1.

For the encryption of the first n_m bits of the plaintext, there are no ciphertext bits available. The place of these bits are taken by an initialization vector that must be shared between sender and receiver and that may be public:

$$c^{-n_m} \ldots c^0 = \text{initialization vector (IV)} . \tag{4}$$

In general, encrypting a plaintext with a key using different IV values results in different ciphertexts. However, one should be careful. If the IV values only differ in the first ℓ bits, the probability that the two ciphertexts are equal is $2^{-\ell}$. Additionally, if the IV values only differ in the last $b_s - \ell$ bits, the ℓ first bits of the ciphertext will be the same with certainty.

Despite their name, self-synchronizing stream ciphers are more similar to block ciphers than to synchronous stream ciphers, where the keyed cipher function takes the place of the keyed permutation in a block cipher. An attacker can query the output of the cipher function (keystream symbols) for chosen values of its input: a series of n_m ciphertext symbols. We call the latter an *input vector*.

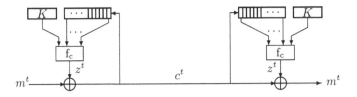

Fig. 1. Self-synchronizing stream encryption

2.2 Security Claims

The claimed security properties of a self-synchronizing stream cipher may be expressed in terms of its cipher function. In our opinion, the following two security claims are reasonable.

Claim 1. *The probability of success of an attack not involving key recovery, that guesses the output of the cipher function corresponding to ℓ input vectors C_i while given the cipher function output corresponding to any set of (adaptively) chosen input vectors not containing any of the C_i, is $2^{-\ell}$.*

Claim 2. *There are no key recovery attacks faster than exhaustive key search, i.e. with an expected complexity less than 2^{n_k} cipher function executions.*

Note that these claims do not include resistance against so-called related-key attacks. One may extend the claims to include related-key attacks. In our attack model, the attacker has no knowledge about the key whatsoever. It is the responsibility of the application developer to employ key management functions ensuring the adversary has no knowledge about the key. If the same key is used for encrypting different sequences and if one fears ciphertext collisions leaking information on the plaintext, one should use unique IV values to diversify the ciphertexts.

Additionally, these claims do not cover resistance against attackers that have access to (part of) the internal state or that can disrupt the proper operation of an implementation of the cipher function. While such attack scenarios may be realistic in the context of side-channel attacks, we do not consider that these problems should be tackled in the cipher design but rather in its implementation. For a discussion on how a hardware implementation of MOSQUITO (and likewise MOUSTIQUE) can be made with a high resistance against side channel attacks, we refer to [6].

2.3 Differential Cryptanalysis

A class of attacks that can be very powerful when applied to self-synchronizing stream ciphers is differential cryptanalysis.

For every pair of n_m-bit (ciphertext) input vectors with a specific difference a', f_c returns a pair of keystream bits. The probability that the keystream bits are different is denoted by $DP(a', 1)$. The usability in differential cryptanalysis of $DP(a', 1)$ is determined by its bias from $1/2$. If this probability is $(1 \pm \ell^{-1})/2$, the number of input pairs needed to detect this bias is approximately ℓ^2.

Consequently, a cipher function should not have differentials with probabilities that deviate significantly more than $2^{-(n_m - b_s)/2}$ from $1/2$. The input differences a' with the highest biases should depend in a complex way on the cipher key.

Differential attacks can be generalized in several ways. One generalization that proved to be powerful in the cryptanalysis of some weak proprietary designs can be labeled as *second order* differential cryptanalysis. Here the inputs to the cipher function are applied in 4-tuples. The 4 inputs denoted by a_0, a_1, a_2 and a_3 have differences $a' = a_0 + a_1 = a_2 + a_3$ and $a'' = a_0 + a_2 = a_1 + a_3$. By examining the 4 corresponding output bits it can be observed whether complementing certain input bits (a'') affects the propagation of a difference (a'). This can be used to determine useful internal state bits or even key bits. Typically these attacks exploit properties very specific to the design under analysis. This can be generalized to even higher order DC in a straightforward way.

2.4 Linear Cryptanalysis

The number of inputs needed to detect a correlation C of the keystream bit with a linear combination of input bits is C^{-2}. It follows that a cipher function should not have input-output correlations significantly larger than $2^{-(n_m - b_s)/2}$. The selection vectors v_a with the highest correlations should depend in a complex way on the cipher key. By imposing a number ℓ of affine relations on the input bits, the cipher function is effectively converted to a Boolean function in $n_m - b_s - \ell$ variables. These functions should have no correlations significantly larger than $2^{-(n_m - b_s - \ell)/2}$ for any set of affine relations.

A special case of a selection vector is the zero vector. An output function that is correlated to the constant function is unbalanced. A correlation of C to the constant function gives rise to an information leakage of approximately $C^2/\ln 2$ bits per encrypted bit for $C < 2^{-2}$.

3 Cipher Function Architecture

We address the problem of realizing a cipher function providing high resistance against cryptanalysis and high speed in dedicated hardware by combining two structures: *pipelining* and *conditional complementing shift registers*.

3.1 Pipelining

We can realize a cipher function as a number of b_s *stages* G_i. In hardware, every stage can be implemented by a combinatorial circuit and a register storing the intermediate result. This pipelined approach is illustrated in Figure 2. As the encryption speed is limited by the critical path (largest occurring gate delay), the stages should have small gate delay and hence be relatively simple. This approach impacts the general dependency relations of the self-synchronizing stream cipher: the implementation of the cipher function in b_s stages causes the keystream bit

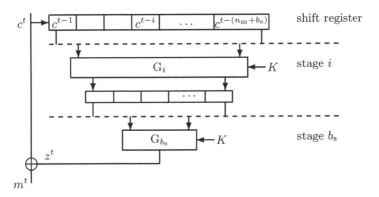

Fig. 2. Self-synchronizing stream cipher with a cipher function consisting of stages

z^t to depend on the contents of the shift register b_s time steps ago. The pipelining increases the input memory n_m of the cipher by b_s symbols. However, the number of input symbols in the cipher function remains the same, as a keystream symbol z^t is independent of the ciphertext symbols c^{t-b_s} to c^{t-1}. Therefore we call the quantity b_s the *cipher function delay*.

3.2   Machines with Finite Input Memory

The input to the first stage of the pipelined structure consists of the last $n_m - b_s$ ciphertext bits, contained in a shift register. This construction guarantees that the keystream bit z^t only depends on the cipher key K and ciphertext bits c^{t-n_m} to $c^{t-(b_s+1)}$.

Replacing the shift register by a finite state machine with finite input memory n_m *can* improve the propagation properties without violating this dependence restriction. If the gate delay of this finite state machine is not larger than the critical path, the maximum encryption speed of a hardware implementation is not impacted.

A finite state machine with finite input memory has specific propagation properties. Let q be the internal state and G the state-updating transformation. Then

$$q^{t+1} = G(q^t, c^t) , \qquad (5)$$

with c^t the ciphertext bit at time t.

One can associate with every component of the internal state q an input memory, i.e., the number of past ciphertext bits that it depends on. The internal state, confined to the components with input memory j is denoted by q^j, with q_i^j its ith component. While not a part of the internal state, c can be considered as the component with input memory zero: q^0. The input memory of the finite state machine is equal to the largest occurring component input memory.

Clearly, q_i^j at time $t + 1$ must be independent of all q^ℓ with $\ell \geq j$ at time t and *must* depend on q^{j-1} at time t. From this, it follows that the input memory partitions the components of the internal state into non-empty subsets with input memory 1 to $n_m - b_s$. The components of the state-updating transformation are of the form:

$$q_i^{j^{t+1}} = G[K]_i^j(c^t, q^{1^t}, \ldots, q^{j-1^t}) , \tag{6}$$

for $0 < j \le n_m - b_s$.

3.3 Conditional Complementing Shift Registers

An important potential problem in a finite state machine with finite memory is the existence of high-probability extinguishing differentials. An extinguishing differential is a difference in the (ciphertext) input vector leading to a zero difference in the internal state. This may lead to exploitable differentials in the cipher function. Assume that for the function corresponding with the stages $DP(q', 0) = 1/2$ for all nonzero difference patterns q'. In that case if the CCSR has an extinguishing differential $(a, 0)$ with high probability $DP(a, 0) = p$, the differential $(a, 0)$ in the cipher function will have a high bias from $1/2$: $DP(a, 0) \approx (1 + p)/2$. The existence of extinguishing differentials can be prevented by imposing (partial) linearity on the components of the state-updating transformation. For simplicity we impose the preliminary restriction that all q^j have only one component, i.e., that there is only one bit for every input memory value. The components of the state-updating transformations are of the form

$$q^{j^{t+1}} = q^{j-1^t} + E[K]^j(q^{j-2^t}, \ldots, q^{1^t}, c^t) . \tag{7}$$

Since the new value of q^j is equal to the bitwise sum of the old value of q^{j-1} and some Boolean function, we call this type of finite state machine a *conditional complementing shift register* (CCSR).

A finite state machine with finite input memory ℓ realizes a mapping from a length-ℓ sequence of ciphertext bits $c^{t-\ell}, \ldots, c^{t-1}$ to an internal state q^t. For a CCSR we have the following result.

Proposition 1. *The mapping from $c^{t-\ell}, \ldots, c^{t-1}$ to the internal state q^t of a CCSR is an injection.*

Proof: We show how to reconstruct $c^t q^{1^t} \ldots q^{j-1^t}$ from $q^{1^{t+1}} \ldots q^{j^{t+1}}$. The components are reconstructed starting from c and finishing with q^{j-1}. For q^1 Equation (7) becomes

$$q^{1^{t+1}} = q^{0^t} + E[K]^1 = c^t + E[K]^1 ,$$

since $E[K]^1()$ depends only on K. From this we can calculate c^t. The values of q^{k-1^t} for k from 2 to j can be calculated iteratively from the previously found values by

$$q^{k-1^t} = q^{k^{t+1}} + E[K]^j(q^{k-2^t}, \ldots, q^{1^t}, c^t) .$$

$c^{t-\ell} \ldots c^{t-1}$ can be calculated uniquely from $q^{1^t} \ldots q^{\ell^t}$ by iteratively applying the described algorithm.   □

It follows that a nonzero difference in $c^{t-\ell} \ldots c^{t-1}$ must give rise to a nonzero difference in q^t. Therefore in a CCSR there are no extinguishing differentials between the input vector and its state.

The CCSR has the undesired property that a difference in $c^{-\ell-t}$ propagates to q^{ℓ^t} with a probability of 1. This can be avoided by "expanding" the high input memory end of the CCSR, i.e., taking more than a single state bit per input memory value near memory value ℓ.

3.4 The Pipelined Stages Revisited

In our architecture, the cipher function consists of a CCSR followed by a number of pipelined stages. The stages are similar to the rounds in a block cipher but are less restricted.

A round of an iterated block cipher must be a permutation, and its inverse must be easily implementable. The stages do not have this restriction and the length of their outputs can be different from that of their inputs. The output of the last stage is a Boolean function of the components of the state q some cycles ago. An imbalance in this function leads to an imbalance in the cipher function. This Boolean function can be forced to be balanced by imposing that all the stage functions are *semi-invertible*. We call an n-bit to m-bit mapping $b = f(a)$ semi-invertible if there exists an n-bit to $(n-m)$-bit mapping $b' = f'(a)$ so that a is uniquely determined by the couple (b, b'). In that case the output bit may have figured as a component of the output of an invertible function of the state q.

The last round of an iterated block cipher must be followed by a key application or include a key dependence. This is necessary for preventing the cryptanalyst calculating an intermediate encryption state thereby making the last round useless. For the cipher function the calculation of intermediate values is impossible since only a single output bit z^t is given per input. Therefore, key dependence is not a strict requirement for the stage functions.

4 The MOUSTIQUE Cipher Function

MOUSTIQUE is a single-bit self-synchronizing stream cipher with:

- : Key size n_k: 96
- : Input memory n_m: 105
- : cipher function delay b_s: 9

4.1 The MOUSTIQUE Internal State

MOUSTIQUE consists of a conditional complementing shift register (CCSR) and a number of pipelined stages. The MOUSTIQUE CCSR has 128 bits that are

Table 1. Number of bits per cell

Range of j	n_j
$1 - 88$	1
$89 - 92$	2
$93 - 94$	4
95	8
96	16

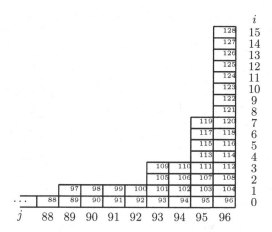

Fig. 3. Expansion of the CCSR in the high memory region. q indexing at the right and bottom, a^0 indexing inside the boxes.

partitioned in 96 *cells* denoted by q^j. The index j ranges from 1 to 96. The number of bit per cells depends on the value of j and is denoted by n_j. The values of n_j are specified in Table 1.

The bits within a cell q^j are denoted by q_i^j with $0 \leq i < n_j$. We index the bits of the CCSR in two ways: we use q_i^j in the specification of the updating function of the CCSR itself, and a_i^0 in the specification of of the updating function of the first stage. Figure 3 shows the expansion of the CCSR at the high input memory end and the two ways of indexing.

The MOUSTIQUE internal state has 8 stage registers denoted by a^i, including the CCSR:

- a^0 is the CCSR and has a length of 128.
- a^1 to a^5 have length 53.
- a^6 has length 12.
- a^7 has length 3.

The bits of the registers a^1 to a^7 are indexed starting from 0, those of a^0 start from 1. The cipher key k consists of 96 bits: $k_0 \ldots k_{95}$.

4.2 The MOUSTIQUE State Updating Function

For all bits in the internal state, the value of a bit at time t is a simple function of bits of the internal state, possibly a key bit and possibly the ciphertext bit at time $t - 1$. We distinguish three Boolean functions, defined in terms of addition and multiplication in the field GF(2):

$$g_0(a, b, c, d) = a + b + c + d \tag{8}$$
$$g_1(a, b, c, d) = a + b + c(d + 1) + 1 \tag{9}$$
$$g_2(a, b, c, d) = a(b + 1) + c(d + 1) . \tag{10}$$

Figure 4 gives combinatorial circuits of these functions.

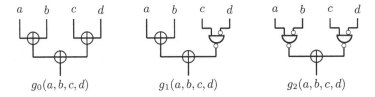

Fig. 4. The three functions used in the state-updating transformation

For the bits of the CCSR we have:

$$q_i^j \Leftarrow g_x(q_{i \bmod n_{j-1}}^{j-1}, k_{j-1}, q_{i \bmod n_v}^v, q_{i \bmod n_w}^w) , \tag{11}$$

with $0 \le v, w < j - 1$. The values of x, v and w for all combinations (i, j) are specified in Table 2, except those for $j \le 2$ and those with $j = 96$ and $i > 1$. In this table a 0 in columns v or w denotes the bit at the input to the CCSR.

Table 2. Function and v and w values for equation 11

Index	Function	v	w
$(j - i) \bmod 3 = 1$	g_0	$2(j - i - 1)/3$	$j - 2$
$(j - i) \bmod 3 = 2$	g_1	$j - 4$	$j - 2$
$(j - i) \bmod 6 = 3$	g_1	0	$j - 2$
$(j - i) \bmod 6 = 0$	g_1	$j - 5$	0

For $j \le 2$, the q^v and q^w entries are taken to be 0. The 15 bits q_i^{96} with $i > 0$ are specified by:

$$q_i^{96} \Leftarrow g_2(q_{i \bmod 8}^{95}, q_0^{95-i}, q_{i \bmod 4}^{94}, q_{1 \bmod n_{94-i}}^{94-i}) . \tag{12}$$

The bit updating functions for the stages are specified in Table 3. In this table, if a lower index in the right-hand side of the equations is out of the specified range, the corresponding bit is taken to be 0, e.g., $a_{53}^3 = 0$.

Table 3. Bit updating function for the stages

Output	Equation	Input
$a_i^1, 0 \le i < 53$ $a_{4i \bmod 53} \Leftarrow g_1(a_{128-i}, a_{i+18}, a_{113-i}, a_{i+1})$		$a_i^0, 1 \le i < 128$
$a_i^2, 0 \le i < 53$ $a_{4i \bmod 53} \Leftarrow g_1(a_i, a_{i+3}, a_{i+1}, a_{i+2})$		$a_i^1, 0 \le i < 53$
$a_i^3, 0 \le i < 53$ $a_{4i \bmod 53} \Leftarrow g_1(a_i, a_{i+3}, a_{i+1}, a_{i+2})$		$a_i^2, 0 \le i < 53$
$a_i^4, 0 \le i < 53$ $a_{4i \bmod 53} \Leftarrow g_1(a_i, a_{i+3}, a_{i+1}, a_{i+2})$		$a_i^3, 0 \le i < 53$
$a_i^5, 0 \le i < 53$ $a_{4i \bmod 53} \Leftarrow g_1(a_i, a_{i+3}, a_{i+1}, a_{i+2})$		$a_i^4, 0 \le i < 53$
$a_i^6, 0 \le i < 12$ $a_i \quad \Leftarrow g_1(a_{4i}, a_{4i+3}, a_{4i+1}, a_{4i+2})$		$a_i^5, 0 \le i < 53$
$a_i^7, 0 \le i < 3 \quad a_i \quad \Leftarrow g_0(a_{4i}, a_{4i+1}, a_{4i+2}, a_{4i+3})$		$a_i^6, 0 \le i < 12$

The keystream bit is given by

$$z = a_0^7 + a_1^7 + a_2^7 . \tag{13}$$

This yields:

$$p \Leftarrow g_0(c, a_0^7, a_1^7, a_2^7) . \tag{14}$$

and

$$c \Leftarrow g_0(p, a_0^7, a_1^7, a_2^7) . \tag{15}$$

4.3 Putting It Together

Figure 5 shows the MOUSTIQUE self-synchronizing stream cipher. Its critical path delay is 2 XOR gates, equal to the gate delay of the state-updating transformation. Building a circuit that can perform both encryption and decryption while maintaining this path delay necessitates the introduction of extra intermediate storage cells, denoted in Figure 5 by boxes containing a **d**. In the encryptor this cell is located between the encryption and the input of the CCSR. For correct decryption this necessitates a double delay at the input of the CCSR.

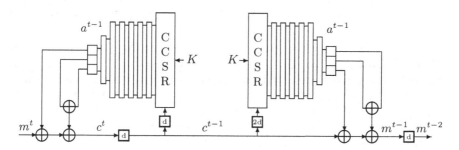

Fig. 5. Encryption and decryption with MOUSTIQUE

5   Design Rationale

In this section we discuss the structure of the components in MOUSTIQUE. Actually, the design of MOUSTIQUE goes back to KNOT [2], that was improved to become $\Upsilon\Gamma$ [3]. We submitted $\Upsilon\Gamma$ to eSTREAM [5] under the name MOSQUITO[6]. $\Upsilon\Gamma$ and MOSQUITO have the same cipher function but the cipher function delay b_s has increased from 8 in $\Upsilon\Gamma$ to 9 in MOSQUITO. After MOSQUITO was broken in [7], we tweaked it and called the new version MOUSTIQUE.

5.1   The CCSR

The CCSR of MOUSTIQUE is a tweaked version of the one in MOSQUITO to address the attack in [7] that in turn is a tweaked version of the one in KNOT due to our discovery of extinguishing differentials.

The CCSR is designed to prevent differentials from $c^{t-96}\ldots c^{t-1}$ to Q^t with a probability larger than 2^{-15}, while keeping the gate delay very small and the description simple. Observe that the 15 components G_i^{96} with $i > 0$ are unbalanced functions resulting in a bias in the corresponding components q_i^{96}.

In KNOT, the component G_0^{96} was also an imbalanced function, resulting in extinguishing differentials from the input vector to the CCSR state. For this reason, we replaced this component function from KNOT to $\Upsilon\Gamma$ by a balanced function. The extinguishing differentials in the CCSR of KNOT were later exploited to break it in [4].

In all versions of the CCSR, an input difference diffuses immediately to components all over q. This is a consequence of the fact that c^t is not only injected in q^1, but in many components at once. These are represented by the zero v and w entries in Table 2 (keep in mind that $q^0 = c$). For $j - i$ a multiple of 3, depending on the value of q_0^{j-2}, a difference in c propagates to either q_0^j or q_0^{j+3}. Since there are more than 15 of these "double injections", the probabilities are below 2^{-15}. In subsequent iterations this pattern is subject to the nonlinearity of the CCSR state-updating transformation.

In the CCSR of MOUSTIQUE, the components q_i^j with $j - i - 1$ a multiple of 3 are updated according to the linear function g_0 while for the CCSR of MOSQUITO and KNOT, all components q_i^j with $j < 96$ used the nonlinear function g_1. This modification was due to the attack on MOSQUITO in [7] shortly described hereafter.

If the first ℓ bits of the key are (assumed to be) known, the propagation of a difference applied at the input can be controlled up to q^ℓ. The attacker can apply a difference in the ciphertext that leads at time $t = 1$ to a difference equal to 1 in cell q^1 and 0 in cells q^2 to q^ℓ. He then iterates the CCSR ℓ times, while ensuring that the difference in q^1 at time $t = 1$ propagates to a difference in only q^i at time $t = i$, and nowhere else in the complete CCSR. Due to the fact that the worst-case diffusion inside the CCSR is very small, the attacker can easily enforce this by choosing the appropriate ciphertext bits. At time $t = \ell$, the difference in the cells q^1 to q^ℓ is a single 1 in q^ℓ and zero elsewhere.

Consider now the cells $q^{\ell+1}$ and higher. At time $t = 1$, the attacker has no knowledge of the difference in this section. However, at time $t = i$, the difference in cells $q^{\ell+1}$ up to $q^{\ell+i-1}$ is zero. If the input memory of the SSSC is 2ℓ or smaller, at time $t = \ell$ the difference in the CCSR is 1 in cell q^{ℓ} and zero elsewhere. The stages realise some confusion in the mapping from the CCSR state to the output bit, but clearly not sufficient to such a powerful differential. They have been designed assuming that an attacker cannot construct high probability differentials in the CCSR. The authors of [7] proved this assumption to be wrong and showed that guessing about half of the key and decrypting some chosen ciphertext pairs suffices to find the remaining part of the key, thereby breaking the cipher.

In the design of the CCSR of MOSQUITO care was taken to have high diffusion from its input bit to the cells by injecting the input bit in at least 15 positions. However, the attack exploits the low worst-case diffusion *within* the CCSR. Actually, the attack exploits this low diffusion in combination with two other properties of MOSQUITO: the insufficient confusion realised by the stages and the fact that guessing part of the cipher key gives access to the first part of the CCSR. A tweak should therefore address at least one of these three properties. In our choice of the tweak, we also considered that the efficiency of the cipher in dedicated hardware should not degrade too much: the area and the critical path delay should not change significantly with respect to MOSQUITO. This rules out the introduction of a key schedule, the augmentation of the number of stages or their width or an increase of the width of cells of the CCSR. Only the CCSR updating function remains.

The worst-case diffusion in the CCSR is dramatically improved by using for about one third of the bits the function g_0 instead of g_1. The indexing ensures that differences in the low-end part of the CCSR propagate much faster to differences in the high-end part of the CCSR. This makes containment of single-bit differences in the first cells of the CCSR to a small number of cells during a significant number of iterations infeasible. Therefore, we believe chosen-ciphertext key-guessing attacks as in [7] cannot be mounted for MOUSTIQUE. Clearly, replacing the nonlinear function g_1 by the linear function g_0 for one third of the bits of the CCSR may introduce new weaknesses and possibly lead to new attacks. It remains to be seen whether there will appear attacks that manage to exploit this.

5.2   The Pipelined Stages

The input to the first stage consists of the state bits of the CCSR. Special care has been taken with respect to difference patterns restricted to the high-memory region and those resulting from a difference in the most recent cipher bit. The purpose of stages $\langle 1 \rangle$ to $\langle 6 \rangle$ is the elimination of low-weight linear and differential trails. The components of these stage functions combine diffusion, nonlinearity and dispersion respectively in the linear term, in the quadratic term and in the arrangement of inputs and outputs. Their effectiveness is reinforced by the diffusion in stage $\langle 7 \rangle$ and the output function that computes the keystream bit as the bitwise addition of all 12 bits of $a^{\langle 6 \rangle}$ to the output. During the writing of [3], we discovered that the output function of KNOT had a detectable imbalance. This problem was solved in $\Upsilon\Gamma$ by modifying the stages to be semi-invertible.

6 Hardware Performance and Implementation Aspects

MOUSTIQUE has been designed with dedicated hardware implementations in mind and does not lend itself to software implementations at all. Therefore we only give performance results for dedicated hardware implementations.

We have implemented a MOUSTIQUE encryption/decryption circuit with gate delay of 2 XOR gates as described in [6] using Field Programmable Gate Array (FPGA). We designed and coded the hardware implementation in VHSIC Hardware Description Language (VHDL) with structural description logic and verified the resulting implementation using the Mentor Graphics ModelSim simulation environment, with test vectors returned by the software implementation. We synthesized the circuit using Mentor Graphics LeonardoSpectrum tool in both XILINX [9] and ALTERA [10] FPGAs.

The synthesis results and performance analysis are shown in Table 4 indicating the number of D Flip-Flops (DFFs), Configurable Logic Blocks (CLBs) and Function Generators (FGs) for XILINX FPGAs and the number of D Flip-Flops (DFFs) and Logic Cells (LCs) in cases of ALTERA FPGAs. The indicated throughput is that for encryption/decryption, after the initialization phase.

Table 4. MOUSTIQUE synthesis results and performance numbers

FPGA Device	# DFF		# FG/LC		# CLB		Speed
	total	used	total	used	total	used	Mb/sec
XILINX VIRTEX (V50BG256)	1536	503	1536	405	768	252	228
XILINX VIRTEX-E (V50EPQ240)	2010	503	1536	405	768	252	263
XILINX VIRTEX-II (2V80FG256)	1384	503	1024	405	512	252	369
ALTERA APEX (EP20K200RC208)	-	-	8320	503	-	-	336
ALTERA FLEX (EPF10K70RC240)	4096	503	3744	503	-	-	146
ALTERA MAX (EPM3512AQC208)	512	503	512	503	-	-	167

Almost in all the cases, both for XILINX and ALTERA, we used the smallest FPGA devices with low hardware resources utilization for each FPGA family. A circuit with fully parallel key loading has 103 I/Os, one with single-bit serial key loading has only 8 I/Os.

The experimental delay measurements (critical path delay, 1/Freq.) are very close to the expected values produced by the theoretical expression (critical path delay $= 2 * t_{XOR}$). The slight differences between the experimental and the theoretical values are due to the fact that in the theoretical values the FPGA internal interconnection wires delays, D flip flop or buffer transfer delays are not calculated. All in all the cipher achieves a low level of FPGA utilization and is suitable for hardware implementation. In [6] we have compared our implementations of MOSQUITO with that of block ciphers operating in single-bit CFB mode and show that they are an order of magnitude faster and more efficient.

Acknowledgements

We would like to thank Joe Lano for stimulating us to submit MOSQUITO to eSTREAM and Sanand Sule, Ralf-Philipp Weinmann and Sean O'Neal for reporting problems with the reference implementation in MOSQUITO and draft versions of MOUSTIQUE. Finally we would like to thank Frédéric Muller and Antoine Joux for doing the effort to cryptanalyze KNOT and MOSQUITO, which have led to MOUSTIQUE.

References

1. Maurer, U.M.: New Approaches to the Design of Self-Synchronizing Stream Ciphers. In: Davies, D.W. (ed.) EUROCRYPT 1991. LNCS, vol. 547, pp. 458–471. Springer, Heidelberg (1991)
2. Daemen, J., Govaerts, R., Vandewalle, J.: On the Design of High Speed Self-Synchronizing Stream Ciphers. In: Kam, P.Y., Hirota, O. (eds.) Singapore ICCS/ISITA 1992 Conference Proceedings, pp. 279–283. IEEE, Los Alamitos (1992)
3. Daemen, J.: Cipher and hash function design strategies based on linear and differential cryptanalysis. Doctoral Dissertation, K.U.Leuven (March 1995)
4. Joux, A., Muller, F.: Loosening the KNOT. In: Johansson, T. (ed.) FSE 2003. LNCS, vol. 2887, pp. 87–99. Springer, Heidelberg (2003)
5. http://www.ecrypt.eu.org/stream/
6. Daemen, J., Kitsos, P.: Submission to ECRYPT call for stream ciphers: the self-synchronizing stream cipher Mosquito: eSTREAM documentation, version 2 (December 8, 2005), http://www.ecrypt.eu.org/stream/
7. Joux, A., Muller, F.: Chosen-Ciphertext Attacks against MOSQUITO. In: Robshaw, M.J.B. (ed.) FSE 2006. LNCS, vol. 4047, pp. 390–404. Springer, Heidelberg (2006)
8. Daemen, J., Kitsos, P.: Submission to ECRYPT call for stream ciphers: the self-synchronizing stream cipher Moustique (June 30, 2006), http://www.ecrypt.eu.org/stream/
9. Xilinx Virtex FPGA Data Sheets (2005), URL: http://www.xilinx.com
10. Altera FPGA Data Sheets (2005), URL: http://www.altera.com

Cascade Jump Controlled Sequence Generator and Pomaranch Stream Cipher

Cees J.A. Jansen[1], Tor Helleseth[2], and Alexander Kholosha[2]

[1] DeltaCrypto BV
Jv. Riebeeckstr. 10
5684 EJ Best, The Netherlands
[2] The Selmer Center
Department of Informatics, University of Bergen
P.O. Box 7800, N-5020 Bergen, Norway
cja@iae.nl, {Tor.Helleseth,Alexander.Kholosha}@uib.no

Abstract. Jump registers have been proposed as building blocks for stream ciphers. In this paper, a construction based on these principles is described. The proposed encryption primitive is a synchronous stream cipher accommodating a key of 128 bits and an IV of 64 up to 162 bits, or an 80-bit key and 32 to 108 bit IV. The stream cipher is particularly designed to resist side-channel attacks and can be efficiently implemented in hardware for a wide range of target processes and platforms.

Keywords: stream cipher, Pomaranch, jump register.

1 Introduction

Linear feedback shift registers (LFSR's) are known to allow fast implementation and produce sequences with a large period and good statistical properties (if the feedback polynomial is chosen appropriately). But the inherent linearity of these sequences results in susceptibility to algebraic attacks. That is the prime reason why LFSR's are not used directly for key-stream generation. A well-known method for increasing the linear complexity, preserving at the same time a large period and good statistical properties is to apply clock control, i.e., to irregularly step an LFSR through successive states. Key-stream generators based on regularly clocked LFSR's are susceptible to basic and fast correlation attacks. Use of irregular clocking limits the possibilities for mounting classical correlation attacks.

Due to the multiple clocking, key-stream generators that use clock-controlled LFSR's have decreased rates of sequence generation since such generators are usually stepped a few times to produce just one bit of the key-stream. The efficient way to let an LFSR move to a state that is more than one step further but without having to step though all the intermediate states (so called, jumping) was suggested in [1]. Further, in Section 2 we give a brief description of the this technique.

M. Robshaw and O. Billet (Eds.): New Stream Cipher Designs, LNCS 4986, pp. 224–243, 2008.

The extremely serious weakness found in key-stream generators that use irregular clocking is their vulnerability to timing, power and other side-channel attacks. This was one of the reasons why stream ciphers such as SOBER-t16 and SOBER-t32 did not pass the security evaluation and were not included into the NESSIE [2] portfolio of strong cryptographic primitives. Using jump registers instead of the traditional clock-controlled ones allows to build efficient countermeasures against the side-channel attacks while preserving all the advantages of irregular clocking.

Pomaranch is a stream cipher that follows a classical design of synchronous bit-oriented stream ciphers and consists of a key-stream generator producing a secure sequence of bits that is further XORed with the plain text previously converted into bits. The key-stream generator of Pomaranch is called Cascade Jump Controlled Sequence Generator (CJCSG) and is primarily intended for hardware implementation. Along with providing an appropriate security level it can be used in a wide range of hardware platforms included those having very limited computing and memory resources (see Section 4). However, our current generator can hardly reach the bit generation rate achieved by word-oriented algorithms especially designed for software implementation. Therefore, the software use of the bit-oriented CJCSG is mostly interesting from the academic point of view. Word-oriented stream cipher designs based on the ideas of jump control have been investigated. The theoretical basis for such an arrangement, referred to as "jumping in extension fields", has been developed (see [3,4]). This will be implemented in future versions of the CJCSG.

The original version of Pomaranch turned out to be vulnerable to correlation attacks which will be discussed in Section 6. Because of that, the cipher has undergone two stages of tweaking and the latest version that is presented in this paper is often referred to as Version 3.

2   Jumping Technique

The ideas presented in this section are well described in [1,5,6,3] and were presented at SASC 2004, the Benelux Information Theory Symposium 2005 and earlier at RECSI 2002 and EIDMA Cryptography Working Group meeting in February 2003.

Consider an autonomous Linear Finite State Machine (LFSM), not necessarily an LFSR, defined by the transition matrix A of size L over $\mathrm{GF}(2)$ with a primitive characteristic polynomial $f(x) = \det(xI + A)$, where I is the identity matrix. It is well known that A is similar to the companion matrix $S(f)$ of $f(x)$, i.e., there exists a nonsingular matrix M such that $M^{-1}AM = S(f)$. Let z_t $(t = 0, 1, 2, \ldots)$ denote the inner state of the LFSM at time t. Then $z_t = z_0 A^t = z_0 M S(f)^t M^{-1}$ and $z_t M = (z_0 M) S(f)^t$. Thus, LFSMs defined by A and $S(f)$ are equivalent up to a linear coordinate transformation.

Take a matrix representation of the elements of the finite field $\mathrm{GF}(2^L)$. Since $f(S(f)) = 0$ and $f(x)$ is primitive, $S(f)$ can play the role of a root of f that is a primitive element in $\mathrm{GF}(2^L)$. Then $S(f) + I$ being an element of $\mathrm{GF}(2^L)$ is equal to $S(f)^J$ for some power J and, thus, $A^J = MS(f)^J M^{-1} = MS(f)M^{-1} + I = A + I$. Note that identity $S(f)^J = S(f) + I$ is equivalent to $x^J \equiv x + 1 \pmod{f(x)}$ and, therefore, such a value of J is called the *jump index* of f. It is important to observe here that changing the transition matrix of the LFSM from A to $A + I$ results in making J steps through the state space of the original LFSM.

Let $f^\perp(x)$ denote the characteristic polynomial of the modified transition matrix $A + I$ that is equal to $f^\perp(x) = \det(xI + A + I) = f(x + 1)$. The polynomial $f^\perp(x)$ is called the *dual* of $f(x)$. It is easy to see that $f(x)$ is irreducible if and only if $f^\perp(x)$ is irreducible (however, this equivalence does not hold for being primitive). It can also be shown (see [6, Theorem 2]) that if the dual polynomial $f^\perp$ is primitive (the jump index of $f^\perp$, naturally, exists) then the jump index of f is coprime with $\lambda = 2^L - 1$ and $J^\perp \equiv J^{-1} \pmod{\lambda}$.

The transition matrix A that defines the LFSM used in the CJCSG has a very special form, namely,

$$
A = \begin{pmatrix}
d_L & 0 & 0 & \cdots & 0 & 1 \\
1 & d_{L-1} & 0 & \cdots & 0 & t_{L-1} \\
0 & 1 & d_{L-2} & \ddots & \vdots & \vdots \\
0 & 0 & \ddots & \ddots & 0 & \vdots \\
\vdots & \vdots & \ddots & 1 & d_2 & t_2 \\
0 & 0 & \cdots & 0 & 1 & d_1 + t_1
\end{pmatrix}
\tag{1}
$$

This is the companion matrix of a polynomial of degree L (L is even) with some corrections made on the main diagonal, where half of the d_i's are equal to 0 and another half are equal to 1. The characteristic polynomial of A can be determined directly as

$$
C(x) = 1 + \sum_{i=0}^{L-1} t_i \prod_{j=i+1}^{L} (d_j + x) ,
$$

where $t_0 = 1$ is introduced for simplicity of the formula. Taking the aforementioned restrictions on the d_i's into account and assuming only t_{n_1}, t_{n_2} and t_{n_3} for $n_3 > n_2 > n_1$ are nonzero with k_1 nonzero d_i in the range $i = \{1, \ldots, n_1\}$, k_2 nonzero d_i in the range $i = \{n_1 + 1, \ldots, n_2\}$ and k_3 nonzero d_i in the range $i = \{n_2 + 1, \ldots, n_3\}$ one arrives at

$$
C(x) = 1 + x^{\frac{L}{2} + k_1 + k_2 + k_3 - n_3}(x + 1)^{\frac{L}{2} - k_1 - k_2 - k_3} + x^{\frac{L}{2} + k_1 + k_2 - n_2}(x + 1)^{\frac{L}{2} - k_1 - k_2}
$$
$$
+ x^{\frac{L}{2} + k_1 - n_1}(x + 1)^{\frac{L}{2} - k_1} + x^{\frac{L}{2}}(x + 1)^{\frac{L}{2}}.
\tag{2}
$$

The parameters are chosen in such a way that the characteristic polynomial $C(x)$ is primitive and is neither self-reciprocal nor self-dual nor dual-reciprocal, i.e., belongs to a primitive S_6 set, that is a set of six primitive polynomials which are each others reciprocals and duals (for the details, see [6]). Jump indices of the polynomials in S_6 are coprime with the period λ. In particular, this means that the jump index of the characteristic polynomial satisfies $\gcd(J-1, \lambda) = 1$. The latter property is required to guarantee the maximal period of the output sequence as will be discussed further in Section 5. Choosing A to be of such a form implies that the same number of XOR's is used in the LFSM irrespective of the value of the jump control signal that defines whether the LFSM is stepped once or makes a jump.

3   Description of the CJCSG

The CJCSG is a generic binary one clock pulse cascade clock control sequence generator that operates in the Initialization Value (IV) accommodation mode comprising N jump registers. It is intended for hardware implementation and comes as Pomaranch in two versions, i.e., with 128-bit or 80-bit keys. These versions differ only in the number of jump register sections used, the number of shift mode steps during the IV setup, and the key-stream output function. In the 128-bit version, the IV length is allowed arbitrary in the range from 64 to 162 bits. The 80-bit version accommodates the IV of 32 to 108 bits long. Hereafter, take $N = 9$ for the 128-bit and $N = 6$ for the 80-bit version. Also denote the key length as κ that can be equal to 128 or 80. The κ-bit key K is split into $N-1$ 16-bit *subkeys* k_1 to k_{N-1}. The most significant bit (msb) of K is the msb of k_1, and so on, the least significant bit (lsb) of K is the lsb of k_{N-1}.

The generator consists of $N-1$ complete sections plus the last, Nth section that consists of the jump register only. The sections are numbered from 1 to N and every odd numbered section is of type 1 (Fig. 2 (a)) and every even numbered section is of type 2 (Fig. 2 (b)). All sections are combined in a cascade construction in which registers jump depends on all previous jump registers.

3.1   Jump Register Section

Jump Registers (JR) implement an autonomous LFSM and are built on 18 memory cells, each of them acting either as a simple delay shift cell (S-cell) or feedback cell (F-cell), depending on the value of the Jump Control (JC) bit (see Fig. 1).

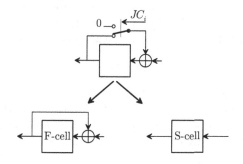

Fig. 1. Jump Register Cell

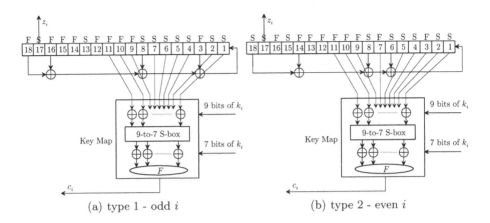

(a) type 1 - odd i (b) type 2 - even i

Fig. 2. Jump Register Section

At any moment, half of the cells in each register are S-cells, while the others are F-cells which is seen as an important feature against power and side-channel attacks. The LFSM implemented by every JR is defined by the binary transition matrix A shown in (1) with $L = 18$, where $t_1, \ldots, t_{L-1}$ correspond to the positions of feedback taps and nonzero $d_1, \ldots, d_L$ – to the positions of F-cells in the register. Transition matrix A is applied if the JC value is zero, otherwise, all cells are switched to the opposite mode which is equivalent to changing the transition matrix to $A + I$ with I being the identity matrix.

There are two different types of JR sections that differ by their cell configurations and feedback taps. Fig. 2 (a) and (b) shows the configuration of cells that corresponds to the zero value of the JC-bit for the odd and even numbered sections respectively. When JC is one then all the cells are switched to the opposite mode. The JR of the odd numbered sections is a feedback shift register with the tap positions located at cells 3, 8, 16 and 18 that gives $n_1 = 3$, $n_2 = 8$ and $n_3 = 16$. For this configuration and choosing $k_1 = 1$, $k_2 = 0$, $k_3 = 7$, the characteristic polynomial of the LFSM (see (2)) is primitive with a jump index of 84074. The JR of the even numbered sections is a feedback shift register with the tap positions located at cells 6, 8, 14 and 18 that gives $n_1 = 6$, $n_2 = 8$ and $n_3 = 14$. For this configuration and choosing $k_1 = 1$, $k_2 = 1$, $k_3 = 6$, the characteristic polynomial of the LFSM (see (2)) is primitive with a jump index of 27044. Let R_i^t denote the state of the register R_i in section i at time $t \geq 0$. Then

$$R_i^{t+1} = R_i^t(A_i + JC_i^t \cdot I) \qquad (i = 1, \ldots, N) ,$$

where JC_i^t denotes the jump control bit for R_i at time t and A_i is the transition matrix (1) which concrete form is defined by whether i is even or odd.

The current state of the registers R_1 to R_{N-1} is nonlinearly filtered using a function (Key Map) that involves the corresponding subkey k_i $(i = 1, \ldots, N-1)$. These functions together provide an output of $N - 1$ bits c_1^t to c_{N-1}^t which are used to produce the bits JC_2^t to JC_N^t controlling the registers R_2 to R_N at time t as follows

$$JC_i^t = c_1^t \oplus \ldots \oplus c_{i-1}^t \quad (i = 2, \ldots, N) .$$

In the key-stream generation mode, the jump control bit JC_1 of register R_1 is permanently set to zero. The two complete jump register sections are shown in Fig. 2. Section N consists of the JR only and does not have the Key Map.

The 9-bit input vectors for the *Key Map* are composed of the cells numbered 1, 2, 4, 5, 6, 7, 9, 10, 11 of the type 1 jump register and 1, 2, 3, 4, 5, 7, 9, 10, 11 of the type 2 jump register. These 9-bit vectors are considered as the numbers (denoted as v) in the range from 0 to $2^9 - 1$ with the bit from cell 1 being the least significant and from cell 11 the most significant in v. Next, the 9 least significant bits of the subkey are bitwise XORed to v with the lsb of v XORed with the lsb of the subkey. The sum (considered as a 9-bit number) is substituted by the 9-to-7 bit S-box, for which a lookup table is provided in Appendix A. The result (denoted as w) is taken as a 7-bit vector and is bitwise XORed to the 7 most significant bits of the subkey with the msb of w XORed with the msb of the subkey. The resulting 7-bit sum is fed into the Boolean function F, for which a lookup table is also provided in Appendix A. The output of F obtained from section $i = \{1, \ldots, N - 1\}$ at time t is denoted c_i^t.

3.2   Modes of Operation

Key-stream generation mode is shown in Fig. 3. The key-stream bit r^t generated at time t is obtained by applying Boolean function H of N variables to the bits tapped from the register states R_1^t to R_N^t, so $r^t = H(z_1^t, \ldots, z_N^t)$ and

$$H(z_1^t, \ldots, z_9^t) = z_1^t \oplus \ldots \oplus z_9^t \qquad \text{in the 128-bit version} ,$$
$$H(z_1^t, \ldots, z_6^t) = G(z_1^t, \ldots, z_5^t) \oplus z_6^t \quad \text{in the 80-bit version} ,$$

where G is a Boolean function with the lookup table provided in Appendix A. z_1^t becomes the msb bit in the integer indexing the table for G. All the taps are taken from the cell 17 of the jump registers.

Shift mode is shown in Fig. 4 This mode is used during the initialization and IV setup of the CJCSG. In this mode, the bit c_i^t (the Key Map output) of section i $(i = 1, \ldots, N - 1)$ is added to the feedback of the R_{i+1}. The tap from cell 1 in the R_N is added to the feedback of the R_1 and this closes "the big loop". The configuration of the jump registers does not change in the shift mode, they all operate as if the JC bit was constantly zero.

The shift mode is used to make the register contents depend on all initial content bits and all key bits. This mode defines a key dependent one-to-one mapping of the set of all $(18 \cdot N)$-bit states onto itself. Indeed, if $R_i^t = (r_{i,18}^t, \ldots, r_{i,1}^t)$ then the following equations define the shift mode:

$$R_1^{t+1} = R_1^t A_1 \oplus (0, \ldots, 0, r_{N,1}^t)$$
$$R_i^{t+1} = R_i^t A_i \oplus (0, \ldots, 0, c_{i-1}^t) \qquad (i = 2, \ldots, N) .$$

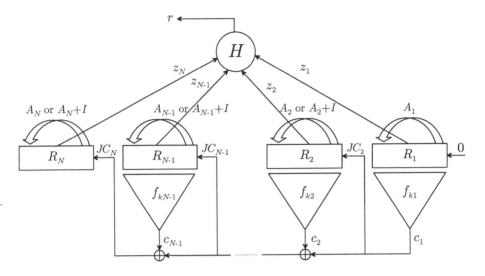

Fig. 3. Key-Stream Generation Mode

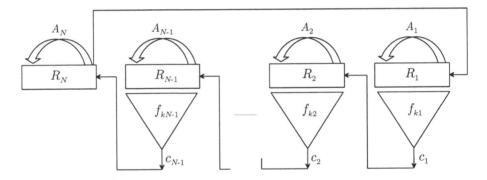

Fig. 4. Shift Mode

From the concrete form of matrices A_i applied in the shift mode it is clear that $r_{i,2}^{t+1} = r_{i,1}^t$ $(1 \leq i \leq N)$. So the inverse of the above equations can be written as

$$R_1^t = \left(R_1^{t+1} \oplus (0, \ldots, 0, r_{N,2}^{t+1})\right) A_1^{-1}$$
$$R_i^t = \left(R_i^{t+1} \oplus (0, \ldots, 0, c_{i-1}^t)\right) A_i^{-1} \qquad (i = 2, \ldots, N)$$

and R_i^t can be found one after another starting from $i = 1$. This shows that shift mode defines an invertible onto mapping which needs to be a bijection.

Also note that in shift mode, the worst case diffusion of all IV bits is achieved after $N + 23 + 2 \cdot (N \bmod 2)$ steps, the respective number for IV-plus-key bits diffusion is $2N + 23 + 2 \cdot (N \bmod 2)$ steps.

3.3   Initialization

The initialization combines key setup, IV setup and the run-up. In the *key setup*, firstly preset the state of the jump register i $(i = 1, \ldots, N)$ to the value of pi[i] (see Appendix A) with the lsb of pi[i] coming in cell 1 of the register. Then run the generator for 128 steps in the shift mode. Finally, save the 18-bit states of all N jump registers (call it the Initialization Vector) for later use during the IV setup.

The sequence of steps for the *IV setup* is the following:

1. The IV can have an arbitrary length in the range from 64 for the 128-bit version (32 in the 80-bit) to $18 \cdot N = Q$ bits. If the IV length is less than Q then extend the IV to the maximal length by cyclically repeating its bits.
2. XOR the Q-bit (extended) IV with the Initialization Vector saved after the key setup and load the result into the N jump registers. The 18 most significant bits of the IV modify R_1 (msb of the IV modifies the msb of R_1), the next 18 bits of the IV similarly modify R_2 and so on.
3. Run the generator in the shift mode for $S = 108$ steps if $N = 9$ (128 key bits) or for $S = 88$ steps if $N = 6$ (80 key bits).
4. If any of the N registers has the all-zero state then set its least significant bit to 1.
5. Perform a run-up of 64 steps in the key-stream generation mode discarding the output bits.

After the run-up, the CJCSG starts generating the key-stream in the key-stream generation mode. Initialization of the CJCSG is done only once for a given key. Therefore, using the Initialization Vector allows to achieve fast start of a new IV session and re-synchronization. Since the shift mode defines a bijection, the suggested IV setup procedure not only guarantees a key dependent diffusion of the IV bits but also provides a different internal state before Step 4 for different IV's.

4   Lightweight Implementation of the S-Box

The CJCSG is ideally suited for hardware implementation since it requires standard components and has no complex circuits causing timing bottlenecks. The 80-bit version of the CJCSG consists of 6 sections with 5 of them containing the Key Map. The linear shift register part (jump registers) uses 18 memory cells, each with an XOR and a switch. Typically, this takes about 225 gates (two-input equivalent). The 9-to-7 bit S-box in the Key Map is the most expensive real-estate, followed by the 7-to-1 Boolean function and 16 XOR's. Implementation of these components by direct synthesis of the Boolean circuitry is estimated at 1000 gates. No attempts have been made to optimize the footprint of these circuits by means of a silicon compiler. For the complete design a total primary estimate is obtained of $5 \cdot 1000 + 6 \cdot 225 \approx 6300$ gates. Reduction of the gate-complexity of the S-box can lower this number substantially as can be seen from the following.

First note that the 9-to-7 bit S-box presented in Appendix A is defined by the inversion operation in the multiplicative group of $GF(2^9)$ when the finite field is defined by the irreducible polynomial $f(x) = x^9 + x + 1$ of period 73. Further, the most and the least significant bits (msb and lsb) of the result are truncated to obtain a 7-bit value.

For an implementation in software, it suffices to define a table of 512 entries of 7 bits. However, for hardware implementations such a table is not suitable, as multiple copies (8 copies for the 128-bit version of Pomaranch) of the S-box are needed. Moreover, straightforward hardware implementations, based on electronic circuit design programs, typically use input-output relations and therefore result in too complex solutions, i.e., requiring a large number of Boolean gates. In this section, we define a more efficient (having lower gate-complexity) implementation of the inverse modulo $f(x)$ as the inverse in the composite field $GF((2^3)^3)$, i.e., modulo $x^3 + c_1x^2 + c_2x + c_3 \in GF(2^3)[x]$.

This section is organized as follows. First, an optimal composite field representation is derived. Further, the equations are produced that are involved in taking the direct inverse and their solution is found. Finally, the resulting hardware complexity is discussed and some detailed numerical examples to support hardware implementation are provided.

4.1   The Composite Field Representation

The finite field $GF(2^9)$ is commonly represented by the elements which are degree eight polynomials. These polynomials are given by their nine binary constants as 9-bit vectors. Addition and multiplication of elements are the component-wise addition modulo 2 (the XOR), and the multiplication of degree-8 polynomials modulo some degree-9 irreducible polynomial $p_1(x)$. The elements are said to be represented in the polynomial basis $B_1 = (\alpha^8, \alpha^7, \ldots, \alpha, 1)$, where α is a root of $p_1(x)$, so $p_1(\alpha) = 0$. Note that changing to a different basis $B_2 = (\beta^8, \beta^7, \ldots, \beta, 1)$, with $\beta = \alpha^e$ and $1 < e < 511$, merely results in a linear transformation of basis, if the minimum polynomial of β has degree nine as well. Consequently, changing the irreducible polynomial $p_1(x)$ into $p_2(x)$ of the same degree, to do the modular multiplications, is realized by a linear transformation.

The field $GF(2^9)$ can also be represented as $GF((2^3)^3)$, where the elements are given as polynomials of degree at most 2 with coefficients from $GF(2^3)$. These field elements can be seen as comprising three times three bits. Addition is again the bitwise modulo 2 addition, but multiplication now becomes the multiplication of two polynomials of degree 2 modulo an irreducible polynomial $q(x)$ of degree three over $GF(2^3)$.

Let α be a primitive element of $GF(2^9)$ with $p(\alpha) = 0$, then it is easy to see $(511 = 7 \cdot 73)$ that powers of α^{73} comprise the subfield $GF(2^3)$. Let $\gamma = \alpha^{73}$, then the minimal polynomial of γ over $GF(2)$ is given by

$$r(x) = (x + \gamma)(x + \gamma^2)(x + \gamma^4) = x^3 + (\gamma + \gamma^2 + \gamma^4)x^2 + (\gamma^3 + \gamma^5 + \gamma^6)x + 1 \ .$$

Since there are only two irreducible polynomials of degree 3 over $GF(2)$, $r(x)$ is either $x^3 + x^2 + 1$ or $x^3 + x + 1$, depending on $p(x)$. Similarly, the minimal polynomial of α over $GF(2^3)$ if given by

$$q(x) = (x+\alpha)(x+\alpha^8)(x+\alpha^{64}) = x^3 + (\alpha+\alpha^8+\alpha^{64})x^2 + (\alpha^9+\alpha^{65}+\alpha^{72})x + \alpha^{73} .$$

The coefficients of x^2 and x in $q(x)$ are elements of $GF(2^3)$ and, hence, if being non-zero, can be expressed as powers of γ. The values of the coefficients depend on the primitive polynomial $p(x)$ chosen to define $GF(2^9)$.

In the composite field representation, there are two bases involved in representing elements of $GF(2^9)$. That is the basis $(\alpha^2, \alpha, 1)$ used to represent the elements of $GF(2^9)$ as vectors of three elements belonging to $GF(2^3)$, and also the basis $(\gamma^2, \gamma, 1)$, with $\gamma = \alpha^{73}$, to represent the elements of the subfield $GF(2^3)$ as vectors of three bits. This can be seen as a combined equivalent basis $B_c = (\alpha^{148}, \alpha^{75}, \alpha^2, \alpha^{147}, \alpha^{74}, \alpha, \alpha^{146}, \alpha^{73}, 1)$ for $GF(2^9)$. Again, a simple linear transformation relates B_c to a polynomial basis B, once $p(x)$ is known.

In general, for calculations involved in determining the inverse modulo some irreducible polynomial it is advantageous to have as many *binary* values as possible for the coefficients of the polynomial. A simple search through the set of primitive polynomials of degree nine over $GF(2)$ identified the polynomial $x^9 + x^7 + x^5 + x + 1$ as suitable. For if we take $p(x) = x^9 + x^7 + x^5 + x + 1$, then $q(x) = x^3 + x + \gamma$ and $r(x) = x^3 + x + 1$. In this case, $(\alpha^7)^9 + \alpha^7 + 1 = 0$, so that $\alpha^7 \mapsto \alpha$ determines the linear transformation mapping polynomials modulo $x^9 + x + 1$ to polynomials modulo $p(x)$. Suffice to give the resulting transform matrix M_{pom} and its inverse, mapping vectors in $GF(2^9)$ defined by $x^9 + x + 1$ to vectors in $GF((2^3)^3)$ defined by $p(x)$ and $\gamma = \alpha^{73}$. "Row vector times matrix" notation is used.

$$M_{\mathrm{pom}} = \begin{pmatrix} 1 & 1 & 1 & 0 & 0 & 1 & 0 & 1 & 0 \\ 1 & 0 & 1 & 1 & 1 & 1 & 1 & 1 & 0 \\ 0 & 0 & 1 & 1 & 0 & 1 & 1 & 1 & 0 \\ 1 & 0 & 1 & 0 & 0 & 0 & 1 & 0 & 0 \\ 0 & 1 & 1 & 1 & 1 & 0 & 1 & 1 & 0 \\ 1 & 0 & 1 & 1 & 0 & 0 & 1 & 0 & 0 \\ 1 & 1 & 1 & 0 & 0 & 0 & 1 & 0 & 0 \\ 0 & 0 & 0 & 1 & 0 & 1 & 0 & 1 & 0 \\ 0 & 0 & 0 & 0 & 0 & 0 & 0 & 0 & 1 \end{pmatrix} \qquad M_{\mathrm{pom}}^{-1} = \begin{pmatrix} 0 & 0 & 1 & 1 & 0 & 0 & 0 & 1 & 0 \\ 0 & 0 & 0 & 1 & 0 & 0 & 1 & 0 & 0 \\ 1 & 0 & 1 & 1 & 0 & 1 & 1 & 0 & 0 \\ 0 & 0 & 0 & 1 & 0 & 1 & 0 & 0 & 0 \\ 0 & 1 & 0 & 1 & 0 & 0 & 0 & 1 & 0 \\ 0 & 1 & 1 & 0 & 1 & 0 & 1 & 1 & 0 \\ 1 & 0 & 0 & 1 & 0 & 1 & 1 & 1 & 0 \\ 0 & 1 & 1 & 1 & 1 & 1 & 1 & 0 & 0 \\ 0 & 0 & 0 & 0 & 0 & 0 & 0 & 0 & 1 \end{pmatrix}$$

4.2   Calculating the Inverse

Let $a(x)$ and $b(x)$ be polynomials of degree at most 2 with coefficients from $GF(2^3)$, and let $b(x) = a(x)^{-1} \bmod (x^3 + x + \gamma)$. Given any $a(x)$, it is a straightforward exercise to calculate its inverse $b(x)$: multiply $a(x)$ and $b(x)$ symbolically and reduce the powers x^4 and x^3 modulo the irreducible polynomial. The resulting polynomial must be equal to 1 and thus gives rise to a set of three linear equations in three unknowns, that can be solved using Cramer's rule.

$$1 = (a_2x^2 + a_1x + a_0)(b_2x^2 + b_1x + b_0) \bmod (x^3 + x + \gamma)$$
$$= (a_0b_2 + a_2b_0 + a_1b_1 + a_2b_2)x^2 + (a_0b_1 + a_1b_0 + a_1b_2 + a_2b_1 + a_2b_2\gamma)x +$$
$$+ a_0b_0 + (a_1b_2 + a_2b_1)\gamma$$

This yields:

$$\begin{pmatrix} a_2 + a_0 & a_1 & a_2 \\ a_2\gamma + a_1 & a_2 + a_0 & a_1 \\ a_1\gamma & a_2\gamma & a_0 \end{pmatrix} \cdot \begin{pmatrix} b_2 \\ b_1 \\ b_0 \end{pmatrix} = \begin{pmatrix} 0 \\ 0 \\ 1 \end{pmatrix} .$$

Finally, we obtain:

$$D = (a_2^2\gamma + a_1a_0)(a_2\gamma + a_1) + a_0(a_2 + a_0)^2 + a_1^3\gamma ,$$
$$b_2 = (a_1^2 + a_2(a_2 + a_0))D^{-1} ,$$
$$b_1 = (a_2^2\gamma + a_1a_0)D^{-1} ,$$
$$b_0 = ((a_2 + a_0)^2 + a_1(a_2\gamma + a_1))D^{-1} .$$

The above results have been written in a form that allows reuse of calculated intermediate values. The calculations are carried out in $GF(2^3)$, with γ being a primitive element, satisfying $\gamma^3 + \gamma + 1 = 0$.

4.3   Hardware Implementation

All calculations are done in $GF(2^3)$, where the elements are represented in the polynomial basis $(\gamma^2, \gamma, 1)$. Hence, the field elements are $(0, 1, \gamma, \gamma^2, \ldots, \gamma^6)$, corresponding to the vectors $(000, 001, 010, 100, 011, 110, 111, 101)$. This means that all operations on single field elements are implemented as three Boolean functions of three binary variables. The multiplication is realized with three Boolean functions of six binary variables. Clearly, addition is realized with three XORs. The following table shows the functions that are realized and their (2-input Boolean) gate complexities (rightmost column).

$y = x^{-1}$	$y_0 = x_0 + (x_1 \vee x_2)$ $y_1 = x_0x_1 + x_2$ $y_2 = x_1 + \overline{x_0}x_2$	6
$y = x \cdot \gamma$	$y_0 = x_2$ $y_1 = x_0 + x_2$ $y_2 = x_1$	1
$y = x^2$	$y_0 = x_0$ $y_1 = x_2$ $y_2 = x_1 + x_2$	1
$y = x^3 \cdot \gamma$	$y_0 = x_0x_1 + x_2$ $y_1 = (x_0 \vee x_1) + x_1x_2$ $y_2 = (x_0 \vee x_1) + x_0\overline{x_2}$	7
$z = x \cdot y$	$z_0 = x_0y_0 + x_1y_2 + x_2y_1$ $z_1 = x_0y_1 + x_1y_0 + x_1y_2 + x_2y_1 + x_2y_2$ $z_2 = x_0y_2 + x_2y_0 + x_1y_1 + x_2y_2$	17

To calculate D, we need three multiplications, two squares, five additions, two multiplications by γ and one $x^3 \cdot \gamma$ operation, for a total of 77 Boolean gates. Calculation of D^{-1} requires six gates. To calculate b_2, b_1, b_0, another $38 + 17 + 37 = 92$ gates are required, bringing the total number of gates to 175.

The linear transformation M_{pom} and its inverse also require XOR-gates. Their complexity is small, however, if they are implemented by using partial sums, as illustrated below:

$$
M_{\mathrm{pom}} : \begin{cases}
p_1 = x_8 + x_2 \\
p_2 = x_6 + x_4 \\
y_8 = p_1 + x_7 + x_5 + x_3 \\
y_7 = p_1 + x_4 \\
y_6 = y_8 + p_2 \\
y_5 = y_1 + x_8 + x_3 \\
y_4 = x_7 + x_4 \\
y_3 = x_8 + x_7 + x_6 + x_1 \\
y_2 = y_6 + x_8 \\
y_1 = y_3 + x_4 \\
y_0 = x_0
\end{cases}
\qquad
M_{\mathrm{pom}}^{-1} : \begin{cases}
p = y_8 + y_4 \\
x_8 = y_6 + y_2 \\
x_7 = x_4 + y_4 \\
x_6 = x_4 + y_8 + y_6 \\
x_5 = x_3 + p + y_7 \\
x_4 = y_3 + y_1 \\
x_3 = x_8 + y_5 + y_1 \\
x_2 = x_8 + x_4 + y_7 \\
x_1 = p + y_3 + y_2 \\
x_0 = y_0
\end{cases}.
$$

The total number of gates for the linear transformations equals 29 when using the illustrated implementation.

The fact that the msb and lsb of the output are not needed, reduces the gate count by one XOR in the inverse linear transformation and four gates in the final multiplication of b_0. This brings the total number of gates for this implementation of the Pomaranch S-box to 199 gates.

4.4 Numerical Examples

To facilitate implementation, two numerical examples are given.
First example.

$$
x \,\hat{=}\, (000000010) \xrightarrow{M_{\mathrm{pom}}} (000101010) \,\hat{=}\, \gamma^6 x + \gamma
$$

$$
a_2 = (000), \ a_1 = (101), \ a_0 = (010)
$$

$$
\begin{aligned}
h_1 &= a_2^2 \gamma + a_1 a_0 = 1 \quad (001) \\
h_2 &= a_2 \gamma + a_1 \quad = \gamma^6 \ (101) \\
h_3 &= a_2 + a_0 \quad = \gamma \ (010)
\end{aligned}
$$

$$
D = h_1 h_2 + a_0 h_3^2 + a_1^3 \gamma = \gamma^6 + \gamma^3 + \gamma^5 = 1 \quad (001) \longrightarrow D^{-1} = 1 \quad (001)
$$

$$
\begin{aligned}
b_2 &= (a_1^2 + a_2 h_3) D^{-1} = \gamma^5 \ (111) \\
b_1 &= h_1 D^{-1} \quad = 1 \ (001) \\
b_0 &= (h_3^2 + a_1 h_2) D^{-1} = \gamma^3 \ (011)
\end{aligned}
$$

$$
\gamma^5 x^2 + x + \gamma^3 \,\hat{=}\, (111001011) \xrightarrow{M_{\mathrm{pom}}^{-1}} (100000001) \,\hat{=}\, x^8 + 1
$$

Second example.

$$x^8 + x^6 + x^4 + x^2 + 1 \hat{=} (101010101) \xrightarrow{M_{\text{pom}}} (010010111) \hat{=} \gamma x^2 + \gamma x + \gamma^5$$

$$a_2 = (010), \ a_1 = (010), \ a_0 = (111)$$

$$
\begin{aligned}
h_1 &= a_2^2 \gamma + a_1 a_0 = \gamma^4 \ (110) \\
h_2 &= a_2 \gamma + a_1 \ \ = \gamma^4 \ (110) \\
h_3 &= a_2 + a_0 \ \ \ \ = \gamma^6 \ (101)
\end{aligned}
$$

$$D = h_1 h_2 + a_0 h_3^2 + a_1^3 \gamma = \gamma + \gamma^3 + \gamma^4 = \gamma^5 \ (111) \longrightarrow D^{-1} = \gamma^2 \ (100)$$

$$
\begin{aligned}
b_2 &= (a_1^2 + a_2 h_3) D^{-1} = \gamma \ \ (010) \\
b_1 &= h_1 D^{-1} \ \ \ \ \ \ \ \ = \gamma^6 \ (101) \\
b_0 &= (h_3^2 + a_1 h_2) D^{-1} = 0 \ \ \ (000)
\end{aligned}
$$

$$\gamma x^2 + \gamma^6 x \hat{=} (010101000) \xrightarrow{M_{\text{pom}}^{-1}} (011011010) \hat{=} x^7 + x^6 + x^4 + x^3 + x$$

In the above examples, the leftmost and the rightmost bits of the results must be discarded in order to obtain the corresponding Pomaranch S-box outputs. Indeed, entry 2 of the S-box table contains the value 0 and entry 341 contains the value 109.

To conclude this section, we again emphasize that the Pomaranch S-box can be implemented with as few as 200 Boolean 2-input gates by applying the composite field representation of the field GF(512). It should be noted that this complexity might even be reduced by using normal basis representations. These results should facilitate the hardware implementation of Pomaranch Version 3. One section of this stream cipher can be realized with some 500 gates (225 for the last section which has no S-box), bringing the total gate count to 4200 gates for the 128-bit version and 2700 gates for the 80-bit version.

It should also be noted that this complexity has been determined analytically, without the use of hardware design tools, and therefore we lack accurate data about footprint and equivalent NAND-gate complexity. Such hardware synthesis tools might be able to optimize the circuits, thereby further reducing the gate count. Some information about the hardware design of Pomaranch for FPGA and standard cell CMOS can be found in [20,21].

5   Period and Linear Complexity

The CJCSG consists of N sections. We will number the sections from 1 to N starting with the rightmost section that is clocked regularly. Consider section number $i > 1$ of the CJCSG. It consists of the LFSR of length L which clocking is controlled by the binary Jump Control (JC) signal. A zero value in the JC signal makes the LFSR shift c_0 times and a one makes it shift c_1 times. Assume that the JC sequence cycles periodically with the period $\pi_i = \lambda^{i-1}$ where $\lambda = 2^L - 1$ and there are N_i^0 zeroes and N_i^1 ones in the period. Obviously, $N_i^0 + N_i^1 = \lambda^{i-1}$. Denote $S_i = c_0 N_i^0 + c_1 N_i^1$ that is equal to the total number of shifts the LFSR makes when the JC sequence runs over its full period. Assume also that the characteristic polynomial of the LFSR is primitive of degree L and order λ.

Consider the sequence of LFSR states obtained when the clocking is controlled by the JC sequence and denote this sequence of states as u that is further called the output. We assume that the initial LFSR state is nonzero which means that the zero state will never be found in the output sequence. It is known (see, for instance, [7, Chapter 3] and [8]) that the period of the output sequence divides $\frac{\pi_i \lambda}{\gcd(S_i, \lambda)}$ and from [9, Lemma 1] it also follows that this period is a multiple of $\frac{\pi_i' \lambda}{\gcd(S_i, \lambda)}$ where π_i' is the product of all prime factors of π_i, not necessarily distinct, which are also factors of $\frac{\lambda}{\gcd(S_i, \lambda)}$. In particular, if every prime factor of π_i also divides $\frac{\lambda}{\gcd(S_i, \lambda)}$ then the period of u reaches the maximal value $\frac{\pi_i \lambda}{\gcd(S_i, \lambda)}$. This will be the case if we provide $\gcd(S_i, \lambda) = 1$.

Now for $i > 1$ consider the $\gcd(S_i, \lambda)$ with

$$S_i = c_0 N_i^0 + c_1 N_i^1 = c_0(N_i^0 + N_i^1) + (c_1 - c_0)N_i^1 = c_0 \lambda^{i-1} + (c_1 - c_0)N_i^1 \ .$$

By the appropriate selection of the jump indices we guarantee that $\gcd(c_1 - c_0, \lambda) = 1$ (in our case one of the c_i is 1 and the other is J or $J^\perp$). Then $\gcd(S_i, \lambda) = \gcd((c_1 - c_0)N_i^1, \lambda) = \gcd(N_i^1, \lambda)$. Recall that the JC sequence is obtained as a sum of the Key Map output from the previous section and the JC signal for the previous section. Exception is the second section where the JC sequence is just the Key Map output from the first section.

Further we apply induction on $i > 1$ to prove that $\gcd(S_i, \lambda) = 1$. For $i = 2$ (the induction base) the JC sequence of the second section is the Key Map output from the first section that is a filtered m-sequence of period λ. Since the filter function (the Key Map) is balanced, then N_2^1 is either equal to 2^{L-1} or $2^{L-1} - 1$ depending on the value the filter function takes on the all-zero input vector. Thus, $\gcd(S_2, \lambda) = \gcd(N_2^1, \lambda) = 1$. Now assume that $\gcd(S_i, \lambda) = \gcd(N_i^1, \lambda) = 1$.

It is easy to see that any uniform π_i-decimation of the output sequence u is a uniform S_i-decimation of the original LFSR sequence of states. If $\gcd(S_i, \lambda) = 1$ then the latter decimation has period λ and contains all the nonzero states of the LFSR. We can write down the sequence u row-by-row in a matrix with π_i columns and λ rows that will contain the full period of u. Each column of the matrix contains all the nonzero states of the LFSR. Let ν denote the number of nonzero states of the LFSR producing a one when fed into the Key Map of section number i. Since the Key Map is a balanced Boolean function, then ν is either equal to 2^{L-1} or $2^{L-1} - 1$ depending on the value the filter function takes on the all-zero input vector. We can write down the JC sequence of period π_i that controls the section number i in another matrix of the same size. This matrix will consist of N_i^1 columns containing only ones and $N_i^0 = \pi_i - N_i^1$ columns containing only zeros. Adding the matrices we get the full period of the JC sequence for the next section with

$$N_{i+1}^1 = (\lambda - \nu)N_i^1 + \nu(\pi_i - N_i^1) = \lambda N_i^1 + \nu \lambda^{i-1} - 2\nu N_i^1$$

and
$$\gcd(S_{i+1}, \lambda) = \gcd(N_{i+1}^1, \lambda) = \gcd(2\nu N_i^1, \lambda) = \gcd(N_i^1, \lambda) = 1$$

by the induction hypothesis.

Therefore, provided primitive characteristic polynomials for all the sections of the CJCSG, section number i generates the output sequence of the maximal period λ^i. Note that if just the Key Map output from the previous section was used to control the clocking then we would have

$$\gcd(S_{i+1}, \lambda) = \gcd(N_{i+1}^1, \lambda) = \gcd(\nu \lambda^{i-1}, \lambda) = \lambda \neq 1$$

for $i > 1$.

On the other hand, using [10, Theorem 2] we can evaluate the linear complexity of the component sequences of the output u. In particular, if the LFSR characteristic polynomial is primitive and $\gcd(S_i, \lambda) = 1$ then any component sequence taken from the output of the section number i is a linear recurring sequence with irreducible characteristic polynomial of degree $\lambda^{i-1}L$ giving the maximal linear complexity. In the 128-bit version, $N = 9$ component sequences taken from the output of each section are XORed to produce the key-stream. Characteristic polynomials of these component sequences are irreducible and have different degrees $\lambda^{i-1}L$ for $i = 1, \ldots, N$ which means that they are pairwise coprime. Thus, by [11, Theorem 8.57], the linear complexity of the key-stream sequence is equal to $L(1 + \lambda + \lambda^2 + \ldots + \lambda^{N-1})$ and, by [11, Theorem 8.59], the period is equal to λ^N. In the 80-bit version, the maximal period is guaranteed by the XOR of the output from section $N = 6$ having period λ^N to the output from function G. The linear complexity is lower bounded by $\lambda^{N-1}L$.

Note that every component sequence taken from the output of the section number i contains $\lambda^{i-1}(2^{L-1} - 1)$ zeros and $\lambda^{i-1}2^{L-1}$ ones in the period. The XOR (with nonlinear balanced function G for the 80-bit version) of output sequences allows to compensate for this imbalance.

6   Security Analysis of the Cipher

The most important aspect of a cipher security is its resistance to different attacks. The goal is to make any attack at least as difficult as the exhaustive search. Consider some general attacks on stream ciphers. We always assume the known plain text scenario when the attacker knows the key-stream. No weak keys have been identified.

Exhaustive Key Search. This is the most efficient key recovery attack against the CJCSG. Searching through the whole key space gives the complexity of 2^κ with $\kappa = 128$ and $\kappa = 80$ for the two versions and corresponding key length.

Algebraic Attacks. The algebraic analysis of Pomaranch was undertaken in [12]. The authors found annihilators and low degree multiples for both filter functions F and G. More careful investigation is needed for finding out if an algebraic approach can lead to any weaknesses.

Time-Memory Trade-off. Assume that the attacker knows the state of the jump registers right before the generator starts producing the key-stream. Then the kind of meet in the middle attack can be launched. The procedure is as follows. Take all possible 2^{16} keys that define the Key Map of section $N - 1$ (denote it K) and take all 2^n binary sequences of length n as the jump control for section $N - 1$ (denote this a). For each combination generate the sequence of length n that is the key-stream contribution from section N (denote it $F(K, a)$). Put the vector $(F(K, a), a, K)$ in a list sorted along $(F(K, a), a)$. The value of n is chosen to be minimal with the property that the multi-set

$$\{(F(K, a), a) \mid K \in V_{2^{16}}, a \in V_{2^n}\}$$

consists of different vectors. Then obviously, $n \geq 16$ and assuming the randomness of the F mapping we can take $n = 16$.

Run the exhaustive search on the remaining $\kappa - 16$ bits of the key. Calculate the sum of the key-stream contributions from sections 1 to $N - 1$, add it to the key-stream (get n bits like that) and also calculate n bits of the jump control sequence for section $N - 1$. If n is taken to be equal 16 then for each choice of the remaining $\kappa - 16$ bits of the key we will find one match in the pre-computed list. The final elimination of wrong keys is done by generating and matching more bits in the jump control sequence for section $N - 1$ and the key-stream contribution from section N.

The total computational complexity consists of $O(2^{16+n})$ in pre-computation plus $O(2^{\kappa-16})$ in the main phase. If $\kappa = 128$ then the lowest time complexity of the attack is achieved if we start with trying 32 bits of the key (take the last 2 sections and not just one). Then we need $O(2^{32+n})$ bits of memory and the computational complexity is $O(2^{32+n})$ in pre-computation plus $O(2^{96})$ in the main phase. If n is equal 32 then the total complexity will have the order of $O(2^{96})$. It can be concluded that if the internal state of the generator just before it starts producing the key-stream is made secret then security against this type of the attacks is achieved.

Correlation Attacks. A key-recovery attack [13,14] on the original Pomaranch was built due to the spotted biases in the distribution of certain linear relations of length $L + 1$ in the output sequence of a jump register section. The suggested attack on the 128-bit version has the complexity $O(2^{87})$ and requires less than 2^{72} bits of the key-stream. That became a primary reason for changing the configuration of jump registers in Version 2 of the cipher where it was guaranteed that no relation of length $L + 1$ has a large enough bias. However, the updated configuration was also found to be insecure due to the new biased linear relation of a larger length found in [15]. Using this relation, a feasible key-recovery attack has the complexity $O(2^{94})$ requiring 2^{74} bits of the key-stream for the 128-bit key version and $O(2^{65})$ with 2^{45} bits for the 80-bit key version. Distinguishing attacks would have the same complexity but require less key-stream bits. By increasing the length of the registers to 18 and choosing new configuration, we bring the bias of the best linear relation (that we were able to compute which is up to $L + 11 = 29$ bits long) for a separate register down to a level that brings the complexity of the attack up to the level exceeding the one of the exhaustive key search. Additionally, having jump register section of two different types and adding their outputs also decreases the resulting bias.

Distinguishing Attacks. The distinguishing attack is assumed to succeed if the attacker can distinguish the key-stream from the purely random sequence. It is reasonable to assume that the needed key-stream length does not exceed the total number of keys for the generator since the distinguishing attack should not run longer than the exhaustive key search. The key-stream produced by the CJCSG is obtained as a sum of linear recurring sequences and this makes any statistical weaknesses in the key-stream unlikely. The alternative is to look for the regularities during the initialization phase but we were not able to find any of this kind. The distinguishing attack on Version 2 found in [15] was to be countered by a new configuration of the jump registers. However, using the same approach as in the best key-recovery attack [15], a new distinguisher for the latest version of Pomaranch was built in [16]. It has the computational complexity $O(2^{126})$ for the 128-bit key version and $O(2^{71})$ for the 80-bit key version and requires the amount of the key-stream bits that is equal to the corresponding complexity.

Recall that the key-stream in Pomaranch is obtained by applying Boolean function to the bits tapped from the register states. For the 128-bit key version, this function is an XOR. On the contrary, the nonlinear function is used in the 80-bit key version and this fact was essentially used in the attack. Replacing the function with XOR will increase the complexity of the distinguishing attack to $O(2^{84})$ and will simplify the design at the same time.

The distinguisher's complexity of $O(2^{126})$ for the 128-bit key version is a consequence of our construction where we use nine 18-bit registers. A safety margin can only be obtained by increasing the length and the number of registers which will come at the cost of extra implementation complexity (gates or software) or performance. However, $O(2^{126})$ seems to be close enough to the exhaustive key search complexity.

Another approach would be to consider a set of key-stream sequences generated with the same key but for different IV values trying to find some dependencies between them that can not be found in the set of random independent sequences. This is also related to differential attack considered next.

Differential Chosen IV Attacks. This type of attacks, that was initially introduced for block ciphers, can also be applied to stream ciphers (see [17]). For synchronous stream ciphers differential attacks can use the known difference in the IV value. Moreover, usually it is assumed that the attacker can choose the IV. Two chosen IV key-recovery attacks on the original 128-bit Pomaranch were found in [18,19] and they exploit the weakness in the original IV setup procedure. The attack in [18] allows to recover the 128-bit key with the complexity $O(2^{65})$ or even faster, with $O(2^{52})$ if the escape from all-zero state feature in the initialization is used. The attack in [19] has a higher complexity of $O(2^{73.5})$ and is an extension of the correlation attack from [13]. This became the reason for introducing a new IV setup procedure in Version 2 of the cipher that provides good diffusion of IV bits. The updated versions are believed to be secure against this type of attacks.

Square Root IV Attack. This new attack suggested in [16] can be applied to any key-stream generator with the key size larger than half of the state size, when the part of the state only affected by the key (like subkeys in Pomaranch) is not considered. For Pomaranch, this means that the key is longer than half of the total register length. In the attack scenario, the key is fixed and one assumes to have a long key-stream section (2^{62} bits for 80-bit and 2^{88} bits for 128-bit Pomaranch) stored in a table. Given short key-stream samples from many other IVs (about 2^{54} for 80-bit and 2^{81} for 128-bit Pomaranch), one will find a collision with the stored stream. When a collision is found, future key-stream bits can be predicted. The key will not be recovered but this attack is still more powerful than a distinguisher.

To protect against this attack, a reasonable limit on the number of IVs that are allowed to be used with the same key has to be imposed. In our understanding, this is a worthy limitation which allows to keep the internal state size in Pomaranch small enough to result in a compact hardware implementation.

Timing, Power, and Side-Channel Attacks. Resistance against timing attacks is inherent of the CJCSG and is achieved due to the use of jump control instead of the traditional clock control. Power and side-channel attacks are additionally countered by the important feature that the same number of XOR's are used in each section of the generator irrespective of the jump control signal.

Fault Analysis Attacks. These attacks are countered due to the nonlinear functions in conditional jumping, accumulation of JC signals and accumulation of key-stream outputs from individual LFSM's.

References

1. Jansen, C.J.A.: Modern stream cipher design: A new view on multiple clocking and irreducible polynomials. In: González, S., Martínez, C. (eds.) Actas de la VII Reunión Española sobre Criptología y Seguridad de la Información. Volume Tomo I. Servicio de Publicaciones de la Universidad de Oviedo, pp. 11–29 (2002)
2. NESSIE: New European Schemes for Signatures, Integrity, and Encryption (2000–2003), https://www.cosic.esat.kuleuven.be/nessie/
3. Jansen, C.J.A.: Partitions of polynomials: Stream ciphers based on jumping shift registers. In: Cardinal, J., Cerf, N., Delgrange, O., Markowitch, O. (eds.) 26th Symposium on Information Theory in the Benelux, Enschede, Werkgemeenschap voor Informatie- en Communicatietheorie, pp. 277–284 (2005)
4. Jansen, C.J.A.: Stream cipher constructions over binary extension fields. In: Lagendijk, I., Weber, J.H. (eds.) 27th Symposium on Information Theory in the Benelux, Enschede, Werkgemeenschap voor Informatie- en Communicatietheorie, pp. 213–218 (2006)
5. Jansen, C.J.A.: Streamcipher design: Make your LFSRs jump! In: The State of the Art of Stream Ciphers, Workshop Record, ECRYPT Network of Excellence in Cryptology, pp. 94–108 (2004),
http://www.ecrypt.eu.org/stvl/sasc/sasc-record.zip

6. Jansen, C.J.A.: Stream cipher design based on jumping finite state machines. Cryptology ePrint Archive, Report 2005/267 (2005), http://eprint.iacr.org/2005/267/.

7. Kholosha, A.: Investigations in the Design and Analysis of Key-Stream Generators. PhD thesis, Technische Universiteit Eindhoven (2003), http://alexandria.tue.nl/extra2/200410591.pdf

8. Kholosha, A.: Clock-controlled shift registers and generalized Geffe key-stream generator. In: Pandu Rangan, C., Ding, C. (eds.) INDOCRYPT 2001. LNCS, vol. 2247, pp. 287–296. Springer, Heidelberg (2001)

9. Golić, J.D.: Periods of interleaved and nonuniformly decimated sequences. IEEE Trans. Inf. Theory 44(3), 1257–1260 (1998)

10. Chambers, W.G.: Clock-controlled shift registers in binary sequence generators. IEE Proceedings - Computers and Digital Techniques 135(1), 17–24 (1988)

11. Lidl, R., Niederreiter, H.: Finite Fields. Encyclopedia of Mathematics and its Applications, vol. 20. Cambridge University Press, Cambridge (1997)

12. Wong, K.K.H., Colbert, B.D., Batten, L.M., Al-Hinai, S.: Algebraic attacks on clock-controlled cascade ciphers. In: Barua, R., Lange, T. (eds.) INDOCRYPT 2006. LNCS, vol. 4329, pp. 32–47. Springer, Heidelberg (2006)

13. Khazaei, S.: Cryptanalysis of Pomaranch (CJCSG). eSTREAM, ECRYPT Stream Cipher Project, Report 2005/065 (2005), http://www.ecrypt.eu.org/stream/papersdir/065.pdf

14. Helleseth, T., Jansen, C.J.A., Khazaei, S., Kholosha, A.: Security of jump controlled sequence generators for stream ciphers. In: Gong, G., Helleseth, T., Song, H.-Y., Yang, K. (eds.) SETA 2006. LNCS, vol. 4086, pp. 141–152. Springer, Heidelberg (2006)

15. Hell, M., Johansson, T.: On the problem of finding linear approximations and cryptanalysis of Pomaranch version 2. In: Biham, E., Youssef, A.M. (eds.) SAC 2006. LNCS, vol. 4356, pp. 220–233. Springer, Heidelberg (2007)

16. Englund, H., Hell, M., Johansson, T.: Two general attacks on Pomaranch-like keystream generators. In: Biryukov, A. (ed.) FSE 2007. LNCS, vol. 4593, pp. 274–289. Springer, Heidelberg (2007)

17. Muller, F.: Differential attacks and stream ciphers. In: The State of the Art of Stream Ciphers, Workshop Record, ECRYPT Network of Excellence in Cryptology, pp. 133–146 (2004), http://www.ecrypt.eu.org/stvl/sasc/sasc-record.zip

18. Cid, C., Gilbert, H., Johansson, T.: Cryptanalysis of Pomaranch. IEE Proceedings Information Security 153(2), 51–53 (2006)

19. Hasanzadeh, M.M., Khazaei, S., Kholosha, A.: On IV setup of Pomaranch. In: SASC 2006, Stream Ciphers Revisited, Workshop Record, ECRYPT Network of Excellence in Cryptology, pp. 7–12 (2006), http://www.ecrypt.eu.org/stream/papersdir/082.pdf

20. Hwang, D., Chaney, M., Karanam, S., Ton, N., Gaj, K.: Comparison of FPGA-targeted hardware implementations of eSTREAM stream cipher candidates. In: SASC 2008, The State of the Art of Stream Ciphers, Workshop Record, ECRYPT Network of Excellence in Cryptology, pp. 151–162 (2008), http://www.ecrypt.eu.org/stvl/sasc2008/SASCRecord.zip

21. Good, T., Benaissa, M.: Hardware performance of eStream phase-III stream cipher candidates. In: SASC 2008, The State of the Art of Stream Ciphers, Workshop Record, ECRYPT Network of Excellence in Cryptology, pp. 163–173 (2008), http://www.ecrypt.eu.org/stvl/sasc2008/SASCRecord.zip

A   Functions and Constants

S-box is defined by the inversion operation in the multiplicative group of $\mathrm{GF}(2^9)$ when the finite field is defined by the irreducible polynomial $f(x) = x^9 + x + 1$.

```
unsigned char S[512] = {
0,0,0,127,64,85,127,54,96,18,42,57,63,83,91,51,112,17,73,38,21,
103,92,49,95,122,105,113,45,104,25,61,120,107,8,112,100,89,19,39,
74,102,115,41,110,80,88,119,47,62,61,15,52,29,56,88,22,16,52,26,
12,125,94,93,124,75,53,14,4,77,120,84,114,2,44,112,73,9,19,19,
101,121,115,21,57,5,20,115,55,72,104,14,108,63,59,116,87,121,31,
89,94,80,7,91,90,98,14,33,92,84,44,72,75,82,72,82,90,85,13,48,70,
97,62,34,47,24,46,108,126,91,101,76,26,69,71,119,66,30,38,95,60,
97,106,117,57,82,65,78,86,78,56,82,100,111,4,34,73,65,9,51,50,94,
124,87,57,72,10,77,92,54,2,64,74,78,121,48,27,56,100,18,52,98,7,
51,54,84,31,94,93,31,122,12,43,29,60,70,79,5,108,110,111,76,40,
121,3,39,45,68,45,14,113,13,71,117,16,120,46,63,42,1,22,80,100,
76,37,44,105,13,36,2,41,21,109,125,106,71,70,122,88,23,35,84,48,
87,95,12,81,7,87,81,12,30,23,105,54,3,127,1,109,42,114,36,102,39,
77,34,98,79,99,117,123,81,97,86,79,51,83,77,111,33,30,125,48,59,
53,33,58,123,28,22,41,27,96,4,39,19,43,115,103,10,28,16,105,126,
50,114,55,32,66,69,17,41,36,37,96,43,68,66,89,49,25,55,111,11,62,
61,107,67,28,37,36,28,69,95,102,3,46,60,27,17,1,109,96,29,37,112,
103,68,60,40,24,62,13,59,92,11,114,24,9,79,26,29,113,106,3,127,25,
32,27,88,42,5,15,123,47,116,46,40,15,25,61,34,6,83,85,2,78,73,30,
68,35,107,103,45,66,26,118,122,119,67,55,44,38,9,20,102,124,32,65,
101,83,10,86,74,98,5,22,110,7,123,56,75,6,63,35,120,58,90,8,97,
124,81,23,119,31,49,85,58,64,126,11,49,104,118,50,80,38,69,18,4,
86,8,52,90,6,117,18,89,65,76,20,74,10,21,118,93,126,23,53,113,35,
67,99,110,125,116,108,99,11,33,17,8,106,53,24,50,43,20,47,59,6,99,
104,93,67,71,107,16,40,101,70,118,15,58,75,32,116,109,91,64,1,0};
```

Boolean function F of 7 variables is 2-resilient of degree 4 and nonlinearity 56.

```
unsigned char F[128] = {
0,1,1,1,1,0,0,1,0,1,1,0,1,0,0,1,1,0,0,0,0,0,0,1,0,1,1,1,1,1,0,0,
1,1,0,0,0,1,0,1,1,0,0,0,1,0,0,1,0,0,1,1,1,0,1,1,1,0,1,0,0,1,1,0,
1,0,1,0,1,1,0,0,0,0,1,1,0,0,1,0,0,1,1,0,1,1,1,0,0,1,0,0,0,1,1,1,
0,1,1,0,0,0,0,1,1,0,0,1,1,1,1,1,0,1,0,1,1,0,1,0,1,1,0,1,0,0,0,0};
```

Boolean function G of 5 variables is 1-resilient of degree 3 and nonlinearity 12.

```
unsigned char G[32] =
{0,1,0,1,0,1,0,0,1,0,0,1,1,0,1,1,1,0,1,0,0,1,1,1,0,1,1,0,1,0,0,0};
```

Initial state of the jump registers.

```
unsigned long pi[9] = {
0x090FD, 0x2A888, 0x168C2, 0x0D313, 0x06628,
0x2E037, 0x01CD1, 0x0A409, 0x0E088};
```

TRIVIUM[*]

Christophe De Cannière[1,2] and Bart Preneel[1]

[1] Katholieke Universiteit Leuven, Dept. ESAT/SCD-COSIC and IBBT,
Kasteelpark Arenberg 10, B–3001 Heverlee, Belgium
[2] Département d'Informatique École Normale Supérieure,
45, rue d'Ulm, F-75230 Paris cedex 05
christophe.decanniere@{esat.kuleuven.be,ens.fr}

Abstract. In this chapter, we propose a new stream cipher construction based on block cipher design principles. The main idea is to replace the building blocks used in block ciphers by equivalent stream cipher components. In order to illustrate this approach, we construct a very simple synchronous stream cipher which provides a lot of flexibility for hardware implementations, and seems to have a number of desirable cryptographic properties.

1 Introduction

In the last few years, widely used stream ciphers have started to be systematically replaced by block ciphers. An example is the A5/1 stream cipher used in the GSM standard. Its successor, A5/3, is a block cipher. A similar shift took place with wireless network standards. The security mechanism specified in the original IEEE 802.11 standard (called 'wired equivalent privacy' or WEP) was based on the stream cipher RC4; the newest standard, IEEE 802.11i, makes use of the block cipher AES.

The declining popularity of stream ciphers can be explained by different factors. The first is the fact that the security of block ciphers seems to be better understood. Over the last decades, cryptographers have developed a rather clear vision of what the internal structure of a secure block cipher should look like. This is much less the case for stream ciphers. Stream ciphers proposed in the past have been based on very different principles, and many of them have shown weaknesses. A second explanation is that efficiency, which has been the traditional motivation for choosing a stream cipher over a block cipher, has ceased to be a decisive factor in many applications: not only is the cost of computing power rapidly decreasing, today's block ciphers are also significantly more efficient than their predecessors.

Still, as pointed out by the eSTREAM Stream Cipher Project, it seems that stream ciphers could continue to play an important role in those applications

---

[*] The work described in this chapter has been partly supported by the European Commission under contract IST-2002-507932 (ECRYPT), by the Fund for Scientific Research – Flanders (FWO), and the Chaire France Telecom pour la sécurité des réseaux de télécommunications.

M. Robshaw and O. Billet (Eds.): New Stream Cipher Designs, LNCS 4986, pp. 244–266, 2008.
© Springer-Verlag Berlin Heidelberg 2008

where high throughput remains critical and/or where resources are very restricted. This poses two challenges for the cryptographic community: first, restoring the confidence in stream ciphers, e.g., by developing simple and reliable design criteria; secondly, increasing the efficiency advantage of stream ciphers compared to block ciphers.

In this chapter, we try to explore both problems. The first part of this chapter reviews some concepts which lie at the base of today's block ciphers (Sect. 3), and studies how these could be mapped to stream ciphers (Sects. 4–5). The design criteria derived this way are then used as a guideline to construct a simple and flexible hardware-oriented stream cipher in the second part (Sect. 6).

2   Security and Efficiency Considerations

Before devising a design strategy for a stream cipher, it is useful to first clearly specify what we expect from it. Our aim in this chapter is to design hardware-oriented binary additive stream ciphers which are both efficient and secure. The following sections briefly discuss what this implies.

2.1   Security

The additive stream cipher which we intend to construct takes as input a k-bit secret key K and a v-bit IV. The cipher is then requested to generate up to 2^d bits of key stream $z_t = S_K(IV, t)$, $0 \leq t < 2^d$, and a bitwise exclusive OR of this key stream with the plaintext produces the ciphertext. The security of this additive stream cipher is determined by the extent to which it mimics a one-time pad, i.e., it should be hard for an adversary, who does not know the key, to distinguish the key stream generated by the cipher from a truly random sequence. In fact, we would like this to be as hard as we can possibly ask from a cipher with given parameters k, v, and d. This leads to a criterion called K-security [1], which can be formulated as follows:

Definition 1. *An additive stream cipher is called K-secure if any attack against this scheme would not have been significantly more difficult if the cipher had been replaced by a set of 2^k functions $S_K \colon \{0,1\}^v \times \{0, \ldots, 2^d - 1\} \to \{0,1\}$, uniformly selected from the set of all possible functions.*

The definition assumes that the adversary has access to arbitrary amounts of key stream, that he knows or can choose the a priory distribution of the secret key, that he can impose relations between different secret keys, etc.

Attacks against stream ciphers can be classified into two categories, depending on what they intend to achieve:

- *Key recovery attacks*, which try to deduce information about the secret key by observing the key stream.
- *Distinguishing attacks*, the goal of which is merely to detect that the key stream bits are not completely unpredictable.

Owing to their weaker objective, distinguishing attacks are often much easier to apply, and consequently harder to protect against. Features of the key stream that can be exploited by such attacks include periodicity, dependencies between bits at different positions, non-uniformity of distributions of bits or words, etc. In this chapter we will focus in particular on linear correlations, as it appeared to be the weakest aspect in a number of recent stream cipher proposals such as SOBER-tw [2] and SNOW 1.0 [3]. Our first design objective will be to keep the largest correlations below safe bounds. Other important properties, such as a sufficiently long period, are only considered afterwards. Note that this approach differs from the way LFSR or T-function based schemes are constructed. The latter are typically designed by maximizing the period first, and only then imposing additional requirements.

2.2   Efficiency

In order for a stream cipher to be an attractive alternative to block ciphers, it must be efficient. In this chapter, we will be targeting hardware applications, and a good measure for the efficiency of a stream cipher in this environment is the number of key stream bits generated per cycle per gate.

There are two ways to obtain an efficient scheme according to this measure. The first approach is illustrated by A5/1, and consists in minimizing the number of gates. A5/1 is extremely compact in hardware, but it cannot generate more than one bit per cycle. The other approach, which was chosen by the designers of PANAMA [4], is to dramatically increase the number of bits per cycle. This allows to reduce the clock frequency (and potentially also the power consumption) at the cost of an increased gate count. As a result, PANAMA is not suited for environments with very tight area constraints. Similarly, designs such as A5/1 will not perform very well in systems which require fast encryption at a low clock frequency. One of the objectives of this chapter is to design a flexible scheme which performs reasonably well in both situations.

3   How Block Ciphers Are Designed

As explained above, the first requirement we impose on the construction is that it generates key streams without exploitable linear correlations. This problem is very similar to the one faced by block cipher designers. Hence, it is natural to attempt to borrow some of the techniques used in the block cipher world. The ideas relevant to stream ciphers are briefly recapitulated in the following sections.

3.1   Block Ciphers and Linear Characteristics

An important problem in the case of block ciphers is that of restricting linear correlations between input and output bits in order to thwart linear cryptanalysis.

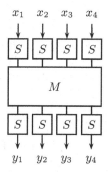

Fig. 1. Three layers of a block cipher

More precisely, let P be any plaintext block and C the corresponding ciphertext under a fixed secret key, then any linear combination of bits

$$\Gamma_P^\mathsf{T} \cdot P + \Gamma_C^\mathsf{T} \cdot C,$$

where the column vectors Γ_P and Γ_C are called linear masks, should be as balanced as possible. That is, the correlation (or imbalance)

$$c = 2 \cdot \frac{|\{P \mid \Gamma_P^\mathsf{T} \cdot P = \Gamma_C^\mathsf{T} \cdot C\}|}{|\{P\}|} - 1$$

has to be close to 0 for any Γ_P and Γ_C. The well-established way to achieve this consists in alternating two operations. The first splits blocks into smaller words which are independently fed into nonlinear substitution boxes (S-boxes); the second step recombines the outputs of the S-boxes in a linear way in order to 'diffuse' the nonlinearity. The result, called a substitution-permutation network, is depicted again in Fig. 1.

In order to estimate the strength of a block cipher against linear cryptanalysis, one will typically compute bounds on the correlation of linear characteristics. A linear characteristic describes a possible path over which a correlation might propagate through the block cipher. It is a chain of linear masks, starting with a plaintext mask and ending with a ciphertext mask, such that every two successive masks correspond to a nonzero correlation between consecutive intermediate values in the cipher. The total correlation of the characteristic is then estimated by multiplying the correlations of all separate steps (as dictated by the Piling-up Lemma).

3.2   Branch Number

Linear diffusion layers, which can be represented by a matrix multiplication $Y = M \cdot X$, do not by themselves contribute in reducing the correlation of a characteristic. Clearly, it suffices to choose $\Gamma_X = M^\mathsf{T} \cdot \Gamma_Y$, where M^T denotes the transpose of M, in order to obtain perfectly correlating linear combinations of X and Y:

$$\Gamma_Y^\mathsf{T} \cdot Y = \Gamma_Y^\mathsf{T} \cdot MX = (M^\mathsf{T}\Gamma_Y)^\mathsf{T} \cdot X = \Gamma_X^\mathsf{T} \cdot X \,.$$

However, diffusion layers play an important indirect role by forcing characteristics to take into account a large number of nonlinear S-boxes in the neighboring layers (called active S-boxes). A useful metric in this context is the *branch number* of M.

Definition 2. *The branch number of a linear transformation M is defined as*

$$\mathcal{B} = \min_{\Gamma_Y \neq 0} [\mathrm{w_h}(\Gamma_Y) + \mathrm{w_h}(M^\mathsf{T}\Gamma_Y)] \,,$$

where $\mathrm{w_h}(\Gamma)$ represents the number of nonzero words in the linear mask Γ.

The definition above implies that any linear characteristic traversing the structure shown in Fig. 1 activates at least $\mathcal{B}$ S-boxes. The total number of active S-boxes throughout the cipher multiplied by the maximal correlation over a single S-box gives an upper bound for the correlation of the characteristic.

The straightforward way to minimize this upper bound is to maximize the branch number $\mathcal{B}$. It is easy to see that $\mathcal{B}$ cannot exceed $m + 1$, with m the number of words per block. Matrices M that satisfy this bound (known as the Singleton bound) can be derived from the generator matrices of maximum distance separable (MDS) block codes.

Large MDS matrices are expensive to implement, though. Therefore, it is often more efficient to use smaller matrices, with a relatively low branch number, and to connect them in such a way that linear patterns with a small number of active S-boxes cannot be chained together to cover the complete cipher. This was the approach taken by the designers of RIJNDAEL [5].

4   From Blocks to Streams

In this section, we try to adapt the concepts described above to a system where the data is not processed in blocks, but rather as a stream.

Since the data stream enters the system one word at a time, each layer of S-boxes in Fig. 1 can be replaced by a single S-box which substitutes individual words as they arrive. A general mth-order linear filter can take over the task of the diffusion matrix. The new system is represented in Fig. 2, where D denotes the delay operator (usually written as z^{-1} in signal processing literature), and f and g are linear functions.

4.1   Polynomial Notation

Before analyzing the properties of this construction, we introduce some notations. First, we adopt the common convention to represent streams of words $x_0, x_1, x_2, \ldots$ as polynomials with coefficients in the finite field:

$$x(D) = x_0 + x_1 D + x_2 D^2 + \ldots \,.$$

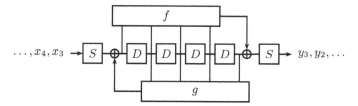

Fig. 2. Stream equivalent of Fig. 1

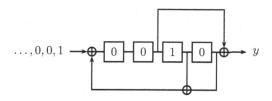

Fig. 3. A 4th-order linear filter

The rationale for this representation is that it simplifies the expression for the input/output relation of the linear filter, as shown in the following equation:

$$y(D) = \frac{f(D)}{g(D)} \cdot \left[x(D) + x^0(D) \right] + y^0(D) . \tag{1}$$

The polynomials f and g describe the feedforward and feedback connections of the filter. They can be written as

$$f(D) = D^m \cdot \left(f_m D^{-m} + \cdots + f_1 D^{-1} + 1 \right) ,$$
$$g(D) = 1 + g_1 D + g_2 D^2 + \cdots + g_m D^m .$$

The Laurent polynomials x^0 and y^0 represent the influence of the initial state s^0, and are given by $x^0 = D^{-m} \cdot \left(s^0 \cdot g \bmod D^m \right)$ and $y^0 = D^{-m} \cdot \left(s^0 \cdot f \bmod D^m \right)$.

Example 1. The 4th-order linear filter depicted in Fig. 3 is specified by the polynomials $f(D) = D^4 \cdot (D^{-2} + 1)$ and $g(D) = 1 + D^3 + D^4$. Suppose that the delay elements are initialized as shown in the figure, i.e., $s^0(D) = D$. Knowing s^0, we can compute $x^0(D) = D^{-3}$ and $y^0(D) = D^{-1}$. Finally, using (1), we find the output stream corresponding to an input consisting, for example, of a single 1 followed by 0's (i.e., $x(D) = 1$):

$$y(D) = \frac{D^{-1} + D + D^2 + D^4}{1 + D^3 + D^4} + D^{-1}$$
$$= D + D^3 + D^5 + D^6 + D^7 + D^8 + D^{12} + D^{15} + D^{16} + D^{18} + \ldots$$

4.2 Linear Correlations

In order to study correlations in a stream-oriented system we need a suitable way to manipulate linear combinations of bits in a stream. It will prove convenient to represent them as follows:

$$\mathrm{Tr}\left[[\gamma_x(D^{-1}) \cdot x(D)]_0\right].$$

The operator $[\cdot]_0$ returns the constant term of a polynomial, and $\mathrm{Tr}(\cdot)$ denotes the trace to GF(2).[1] The coefficients of γ_x, called *selection polynomial*, specify which words of x are involved in the linear combination. In order to simplify expressions later on we also introduce the notation $\gamma^*(D) = \gamma(D^{-1})$. The polynomial γ^* is called the *reciprocal* polynomial of γ.

As before, the correlation between x and y for a given pair of selection polynomials is defined as

$$c = 2 \cdot \frac{|\{(x, s^0) \mid \mathrm{Tr}[[\gamma_x^* \cdot x]_0] = \mathrm{Tr}[[\gamma_y^* \cdot y]_0]\}|}{|\{(x, s^0)\}|} - 1,$$

where $\deg x \le \max(\deg \gamma_x, \deg \gamma_y)$.

4.3 Propagation of Selection Polynomials

Let us now analyze how correlations propagate through the linear filter. For each selection polynomial γ_x at the input, we would like to determine a polynomial γ_y at the output (if it exists) such that the corresponding linear combinations are perfectly correlated, i.e.,

$$\mathrm{Tr}[[\gamma_x^* \cdot x]_0] = \mathrm{Tr}[[\gamma_y^* \cdot y]_0], \quad \forall x, s^0.$$

If this equation is satisfied, then this will still be the case after replacing x by $x' = x + x^0$ and y by $y' = y + y^0$, since x^0 and y^0 only consist of negative powers, none of which can be selected by γ_x or γ_y. Substituting (1), we find

$$\mathrm{Tr}[[\gamma_x^* \cdot x']_0] = \mathrm{Tr}[[\gamma_y^* \cdot f/g \cdot x']_0], \quad \forall x, s^0,$$

which implies that $\gamma_x^* = \gamma_y^* \cdot f/g$. In order to get rid of negative powers, we define $f^* = D^m \cdot f^*$ and $g^* = D^m \cdot g^*$ (note the subtle difference between both stars), and obtain the equivalent relation

$$\gamma_y = g^*/f^* \cdot \gamma_x. \tag{2}$$

Note that neither of the selection polynomials γ_x and γ_y can have an infinite number of nonzero coefficients (if it were the case, the linear combinations would be undefined). Hence, they have to be of the form

$$\gamma_x = q \cdot f^*/\gcd(f^*, g^*) \quad \text{and} \quad \gamma_y = q \cdot g^*/\gcd(f^*, g^*), \tag{3}$$

with $q(D)$ an arbitrary polynomial.

---

[1] The trace from $GF(2^n)$ to $GF(2)$ is defined as $\mathrm{Tr}(a) = a + a^2 + a^4 + \cdots + a^{2^{n-1}}$.

Example 2. For the linear filter in Fig. 3, we have that $f^\star(D) = 1 + D^2$ and $g^\star(D) = D^4 \cdot (D^{-4} + D^{-3} + 1)$. In this case, $f^\star$ and $g^\star$ are coprime, i.e., $\gcd(f^\star, g^\star) = 1$. If we arbitrarily choose $q(D) = 1 + D$, we obtain a pair of selection polynomials

$$\gamma_x(D) = 1 + D + D^2 + D^3 \quad \text{and} \quad \gamma_y(D) = 1 + D^2 + D^4 + D^5 \,.$$

By construction, the corresponding linear combinations of input and output bits satisfy the relation

$$\text{Tr}(x_0 + x_1 + x_2 + x_3) = \text{Tr}(y_0 + y_2 + y_4 + y_5), \quad \forall x, s^0 \,.$$

4.4   Branch Number

The purpose of the linear filter, just as the diffusion layer of a block cipher, will be to force linear characteristics to pass through as many active S-boxes as possible. Hence, it makes sense to define a branch number here as well.

Definition 3. *The branch number of a linear filter specified by the polynomials f and g is defined as*

$$\mathcal{B} = \min_{\gamma_x \neq 0} [w_h(\gamma_x) + w_h(g^\star/f^\star \cdot \gamma_x)]$$
$$= \min_{q \neq 0} [w_h(q \cdot f^\star / \gcd(f^\star, g^\star)) + w_h(q \cdot g^\star / \gcd(f^\star, g^\star))] \,,$$

where $w_h(\gamma)$ represents the number of nonzero coefficients in the selection polynomial γ.

From this definition we immediately obtain the following upper bound on the branch number

$$\mathcal{B} \leq w_h(f^\star) + w_h(g^\star) \leq 2 \cdot (m + 1) \,. \tag{4}$$

Filters for which this bound is attained can be derived from MDS convolutional $(2, 1, m)$-codes [6]. For example, one can verify that the 4th-order linear filter over $\text{GF}(2^8)$ with

$$f(D) = D^4 \cdot \left(02_x D^{-4} + D^{-3} + D^{-2} + 02_x D^{-1} + 1\right) \,,$$
$$g(D) = 1 + 03_x D + 03_x D^2 + D^3 + D^4 \,,$$

has a branch number of 10. The example uses the same field polynomial as RIJNDAEL, i.e., $x^8 + x^4 + x^3 + x + 1$. Note that in the next sections, we will not try to maximize the branch number, but use much sparser linear filters instead.

5   Constructing a Key Stream Generator

In the previous section, we introduced S-boxes and linear filters as building blocks, and presented some tools to analyze how they interact. Our next task is to determine how these components can be combined into a key stream generator. Again, block ciphers will serve as a source of inspiration.

5.1   Basic Construction

A well-known way to construct a key stream generator from a block cipher is to use the cipher in output feedback (OFB) mode. This mode of operation takes as input an initial data block (called initial value or IV), passes it through the block cipher, and feeds the result back to the input. This process is iterated and the consecutive values of the data block are used as key stream. We recall that the block cipher itself typically consists of a sequence of rounds, each comprising a layer of S-boxes and a linear diffusion transformation.

By taking the very same approach, but this time using the stream cipher components presented in Sect. 4, we obtain a construction which, in its simplest form, might look like Fig. 4(a). The figure represents a key stream generator consisting of two 'rounds', where each round consists of an S-box followed by a very simple linear filter. Data words traverse the structure in clockwise direction, and the output of the second round, which also serves as key stream, is fed back to the input of the first round.

While the scheme proposed above has some interesting structural similarities with a block cipher in OFB mode, there are important differences as well. The most fundamental difference comes from the fact that linear filters, as opposed to diffusion matrices, have an internal state. Hence if the algorithm manages to keep this state (or at least parts of it) secret, then this eliminates the need for a separate key addition layer (another important block cipher component, which we have tacitly ignored so far).

5.2   Analysis of Linear Characteristics

As stated before, the primary goal in this chapter is to construct a scheme which generates a stream of seemingly uncorrelated bits. More specifically, we would

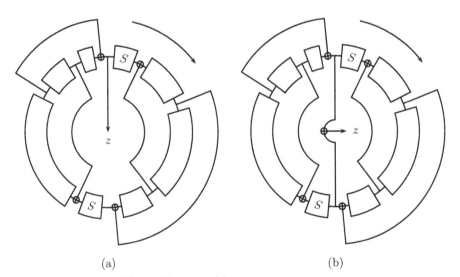

(a)   (b)

Fig. 4. Two-round key stream generators

like the adversary to be unable to detect any correlation between linear combinations of bits at different positions in the key stream. In the following sections, we will see that the study of linear characteristics provides some guidance on how to design the components of our scheme in order to reduce the magnitude of these correlations.

Applying the tools from Sect. 4 to the construction in Fig. 4(a), we can easily derive some results on the existence of low-weight linear characteristics. The term 'low-weight' in this context refers to a small number of active S-boxes. Since we are interested in correlations which can be detected by an adversary, we need both ends of the characteristic to be accessible from the key stream. In order to construct such characteristics, we start with a selection polynomial γ_u at the input of the first round, and analyze how it might propagate through the cipher.

First, the characteristic needs to cross an S-box. The S-box preserves the positions of the non-zero coefficients of γ_u, but might modify their values. For now, however, let us only consider characteristics for which the values are preserved as well. Under this assumption and using (2), we can compute the selection polynomials γ_v and γ_w at the input and the output of the second round:

$$\gamma_v = g_1^\star / f_1^\star \cdot \gamma_u \quad \text{and} \quad \gamma_w = g_2^\star / f_2^\star \cdot \gamma_v \, .$$

Since all three polynomials γ_u, γ_v, and γ_w need to be finite, we have that

$$\gamma_u = q \cdot f_1^\star f_2^\star / d, \quad \gamma_v = q \cdot g_1^\star f_2^\star / d, \quad \text{and} \quad \gamma_w = q \cdot g_1^\star g_2^\star / d \, ,$$

with $d = \gcd(f_1^\star f_2^\star, g_1^\star f_2^\star, g_1^\star g_2^\star)$ and q an arbitrary polynomial. Note that since both γ_u and γ_w select bits from the key stream z, they can be combined into a single polynomial $\gamma_z = \gamma_u + \gamma_w$.

The number of S-boxes activated by a characteristic of this form is given by $\mathcal{W} = \mathrm{w_h}(\gamma_u) + \mathrm{w_h}(\gamma_v)$. The minimum number of active S-boxes over this set of characteristics can be computed with the formula

$$\mathcal{W}_{\min} = \min_{q \neq 0} [\mathrm{w_h}(q \cdot f_1^\star f_2^\star / d) + \mathrm{w_h}(q \cdot g_1^\star f_2^\star / d)] \, ,$$

from which we derive that

$$\mathcal{W}_{\min} \leq \mathrm{w_h}(f_1^\star f_2^\star) + \mathrm{w_h}(g_1^\star f_2^\star) \leq \mathrm{w_h}(f_1^\star) \cdot \mathrm{w_h}(f_2^\star) + \mathrm{w_h}(g_1^\star) \cdot \mathrm{w_h}(f_2^\star) \, .$$

Applying this bound to the specific example of Fig. 4(a), where $\mathrm{w_h}(f_i^\star) = \mathrm{w_h}(g_i^\star) = 2$, we conclude that there will always exist characteristics with at most 8 active S-boxes, no matter where the taps of the linear filters are positioned.

5.3   An Improvement

We will now show that this bound can potentially be doubled by making the small modification shown in Fig. 4(b). This time, each non-zero coefficient in the selection polynomial at the output of the key stream generator needs to propagate to both the upper and the lower part of the scheme. By constructing linear characteristics in the same way as before, we obtain the following selection polynomials:

$$\gamma_u = q \cdot \frac{f_1^\star f_2^\star + f_1^\star g_2^\star}{d}, \quad \gamma_v = q \cdot \frac{f_1^\star f_2^\star + g_1^\star f_2^\star}{d}, \quad \text{and} \quad \gamma_z = q \cdot \frac{f_1^\star f_2^\star + g_1^\star g_2^\star}{d},$$

with $d = \gcd(f_1^\star f_2^\star + f_1^\star g_2^\star, f_1^\star f_2^\star + g_1^\star f_2^\star, f_1^\star f_2^\star + g_1^\star g_2^\star)$. The new upper bounds on the minimum number of active S-boxes are given by

$$\begin{aligned} \mathcal{W}_{\min} &\leq \mathrm{w_h}(f_1^\star f_2^\star + f_1^\star g_2^\star) + \mathrm{w_h}(f_1^\star f_2^\star + g_1^\star f_2^\star) \\ &\leq 2 \cdot \mathrm{w_h}(f_1^\star) \cdot \mathrm{w_h}(f_2^\star) + \mathrm{w_h}(f_1^\star) \cdot \mathrm{w_h}(g_2^\star) + \mathrm{w_h}(g_1^\star) \cdot \mathrm{w_h}(f_2^\star), \end{aligned}$$

or, in the case of Fig. 4(b), $\mathcal{W}_{\min} \leq 16$. In general, if we consider extensions of this scheme with r rounds and $\mathrm{w_h}(f_i^\star) = \mathrm{w_h}(g_i^\star) = w$, then the bound takes the form:

$$\mathcal{W}_{\min} \leq r^2 \cdot w^r. \tag{5}$$

This result suggests that it might not be necessary to use a large number of rounds, or complicated linear filters, to ensure that the number of active S-boxes in all characteristics is sufficiently large. For example, if we take $w = 2$ as before, but add one more round, the bound jumps to 72.

Of course, since the bound we just derived is an upper bound, the minimal number of active S-boxes might as well be much smaller. First, some of the product terms in $f_1^\star f_2^\star + f_1^\star g_2^\star$ or $f_1^\star f_2^\star + g_1^\star f_2^\star$ might cancel out, or there might exist a $q \neq d$ for which $\mathrm{w_h}(\gamma_u) + \mathrm{w_h}(\gamma_v)$ suddenly drops. These cases are rather easy to detect, though, and can be avoided during the design. A more important problem is that, by fixing the behavior of S-boxes, we have limited ourselves to a special set of characteristics, which might not necessarily include the one with the minimal number of active S-boxes. However, if the feedback and feedforward functions are sparse, and the linear filters sufficiently large, then the bound is increasingly likely to be tight. On the other hand, if the state of the generator is sufficiently small, then we can perform an efficient search for the lowest-weight characteristic without making any additional assumption.

This last approach allows to show, for example, that the smallest instance of the scheme in Fig. 4(b) for which the bound of 16 is actually attained, consists of two 11th-order linear filters with

$$\begin{aligned} f_1^\star(D) &= 1 + D^{10}, & g_1^\star(D) &= D^{11} \cdot (D^{-3} + 1), \\ f_2^\star(D) &= 1 + D^9, & g_2^\star(D) &= D^{11} \cdot (D^{-8} + 1). \end{aligned}$$

5.4   Linear Characteristics and Correlations

In the sections above, we have tried to increase the number of active S-boxes of linear characteristics. We now briefly discuss how this number affects the correlation of key stream bits. This problem is treated in several papers in the context of block ciphers (see, e.g., [5]).

We start with the observation that the minimum number of active S-boxes $\mathcal{W}_{\min}$ imposes a bound on the correlation c_c of a linear characteristic:

$$c_c^2 \leq (c_s^2)^{\mathcal{W}_{\min}},$$

where c_s is the largest correlation (in absolute value) between the input and the output values of the S-box. The squares c_c^2 and c_s^2 are often referred to as *linear probability*, or also *correlation potential*. The inverse of this quantity is a good measure for the amount of data that the attacker needs to observe in order to detect a correlation.

What makes the analysis more complicated, however, is that many linear characteristics can contribute to the correlation of the same combination of key stream bits. This occurs in particular when the scheme operates on words, in which case there are typically many possible choices for the coefficients of the intermediate selection polynomials describing the characteristic (this effect is called *clustering*). The different contributions add up or cancel out, depending on the signs of c_c. If we now assume that these signs are randomly distributed, then we can use the approach of [5, Appendix B] to derive a bound on the expected correlation potential of the key stream bits:

$$E(c^2) \leq (c_s^2)^{\mathcal{W}_{\min}-n}. \tag{6}$$

The parameter n in this inequality represents the number of degrees of freedom for choosing the coefficients of the intermediate selection polynomials.

For the characteristics propagating through the construction presented in Sect. 5.3, one will find, in non-degenerate cases, that the values of $n = r \cdot (r-1) \cdot w^{r-1}$ non-zero coefficients can be chosen independently. Hence, for example, if we construct a scheme with $w = 2$ and $r = 3$, and if we assume that it attains the bound given in (5), then we expect the largest correlation potential to be at most $c_s^{2 \cdot 48}$. Note that this bound is orders of magnitude higher than the contribution of a single characteristic, which has a correlation potential of at most $c_s^{2 \cdot 72}$.

Remark 1. In order to derive (6), we replaced the signs of the contributing linear characteristics by random variables. This is a natural approach in the case of block ciphers, where the signs depend on the value of the secret key. In our case, however, the signs are fixed for a particular scheme, and hence they might, for some special designs, take on very peculiar values. This happens for example when $r = 2$, w is even, and all non-zero coefficients of f_i and g_i equal 1 (as in the example at the end of the previous section). In this case, all signs will be positive, and we obtain a significantly worse bound:

$$c^2 \leq (c_s^2)^{\mathcal{W}_{\min}-2 \cdot n}.$$

6   Trivium's Design

We now present an experimental 80-bit key stream cipher based on the approach outlined above. In this section, we concentrate on the basic design ideas behind the scheme. The complete specifications of the cipher, which was submitted to the eSTREAM Stream Cipher Project under the name TRIVIUM, can be found in Sect. 7.

6.1   A Bit-Oriented Design

The main idea of TRIVIUM's design is to turn the general scheme of Sect. 5.3 into a bit-oriented stream cipher. The first motivation is that bit-oriented schemes are typically more compact in hardware. A second reason is that, by reducing the word-size to a single bit, we may hope to get rid of the clustering phenomenon which, as seen in the previous section, has a significant effect on the correlation.

Of course, if we simply apply the previous scheme to bits instead of words, we run into the problem that the only two existing 1×1-bit S-boxes are both linear. In order to solve this problem, we replace the S-boxes by a component which, from the point of view of our correlation analysis, behaves in the same way: an exclusive OR with an external stream of unrelated but biased random bits (see Fig. 5). Assuming that these random bits equal 0 with probability $(1 + c_s)/2$, we will find as before that the output of this component correlates with the input with correlation coefficient c_s.

The introduction of this artificial 1×1-bit S-box greatly simplifies the correlation analysis, mainly because of the fact that the selection polynomial at the output of an S-box is now uniquely determined by the input. As a consequence, we neither need to make special assumptions about the values of the non-zero coefficients, nor to consider the effect of clustering: the maximum correlation in the key stream is simply given by the relation

$$c_{\max} = c_s^{\mathcal{W}_{\min}} . \tag{7}$$

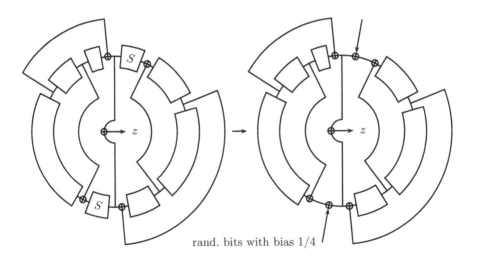

rand. bits with bias $1/4$

Fig. 5. How to design 1-bit S-boxes?

The obvious drawback, however, is that the construction now relies on external streams of random bits, which have to be generated somehow. TRIVIUM attempts to solve this problem by interleaving three identical key stream generators, where each generator obtains streams of biased bits (with $c_s = 1/2$) by ANDing together state bits of the two other generators.

6.2 Specifying the Parameters

Let us now specify suitable parameters for each of those three identical 'sub-generators'. Our goal is to keep all parameters as small and simple as possible, given a number of requirements.

1. The first requirement we impose is that the correlations in the key stream do not exceed 2^{-40}. Since each sub-generator will be fed with streams of bits having correlation coefficient $c_s = 1/2$, we can derive from (7) that a minimum weight $\mathcal{W}_{\min}$ of at least 40 is needed. The smallest values of w and r for which this requirement could be satisfied (with a fairly large margin, in fact) are $w = 2$ and $r = 3$.

2. Now that w and r are fixed, we raise our requirements and impose that the minimum weight actually reaches the upper bound of (5). In this case, this translates to the condition $\mathcal{W}_{\min} = 72$, which is fulfilled if $\mathrm{w_h}(\gamma_u) + \mathrm{w_h}(\gamma_v) + \mathrm{w_h}(\gamma_w) \geq 72$ for all $q \neq 0$, where

$$\gamma_u = q \cdot \frac{f_1^\star f_2^\star f_3^\star + f_1^\star f_2^\star g_3^\star + f_1^\star g_2^\star g_3^\star}{d} , \quad \gamma_v = \ldots , \quad \text{etc.}$$

3. Although the preceding sections have almost exclusively focused on linear correlations, other security properties such as periodicity remain important. Controlling the period of the scheme is difficult because of the non-linear interaction between the sub-generators, but we can try to decrease the probability of short cycles by maximizing the periods of the individual sub-generators after turning off the streams feeding their 1×1-bit S-boxes. The connection polynomial of these (completely linear) generators is given by $f_1^\star f_2^\star f_3^\star + g_1^\star g_2^\star g_3^\star$, and ideally, we would like this polynomial to be primitive. Our choice of w prevents this, though: for $w = 2$, the polynomial above is always divisible by $(D + 1)^3$. Therefore, we just require that the remaining factor is primitive, and rely on the initialization of the state bits to avoid the few short cycles corresponding to the factor $(D + 1)^3$ (see Sect. 8.2).

4. Finally, we also impose some efficiency requirements. The first is that state bits of the sub-generators should not be used for at least $64/3$ iterations, once they have been modified. This will provide the final scheme with the flexibility to generate up to 64 bits in parallel. Secondly, the length of the sub-generators should be as short as possible and a multiple of 32.

We can now exhaustively run over all possible polynomials $f_1^\star, \ldots, g_3^\star$ in order to find combinations for which all previous requirements are fulfilled simultaneously. Surprisingly enough, it turns out that the solution is unique:

$$f_1^\star(D) = 1 + D^9, \qquad\qquad g_1^\star(D) = D^{31} \cdot (D^{-23} + 1),$$
$$f_2^\star(D) = 1 + D^5, \qquad\qquad g_2^\star(D) = D^{28} \cdot (D^{-26} + 1),$$
$$f_3^\star(D) = 1 + D^{15}, \qquad\qquad g_3^\star(D) = D^{37} \cdot (D^{-29} + 1).$$

In order to construct the final cipher, we interleave three of these sub-generators and interconnect them through AND-gates. Since the reasoning above does not suggest which state bits to use as inputs of the AND-gates, we simply choose to minimize the length of the wires. The resulting scheme is shown in Fig. 6. The 96 state bits $s_1, s_4, s_7, \ldots, s_{286}$ belong to the first sub-generator, $s_2, s_5, s_8, \ldots, s_{287}$ to the second one, etc.

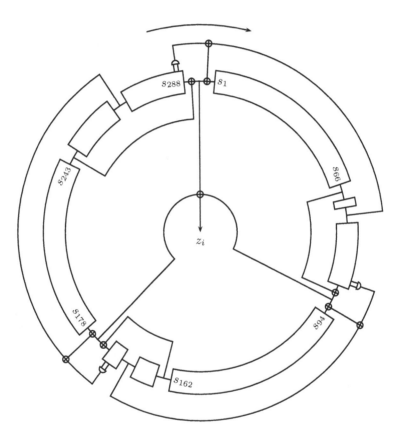

Fig. 6. Trivium

7   Specifications of Trivium

In this section, we give the complete specifications of Trivium. The synchronous stream cipher is designed to generate up to 2^{64} bits of key stream from an 80-bit secret key and an 80-bit initial value (IV). As for most stream ciphers, this

Table 1. Parameters of Trivium

Parameters	
Key size:	80 bit
IV size:	80 bit
Internal state:	288 bit

process consists of two phases: first the internal state of the cipher is initialized using the key and the IV, then the state is repeatedly updated and used to generate key stream bits. We first describe this second phase.

7.1 Key Stream Generation

The proposed design contains a 288-bit internal state denoted by $(s_1, \ldots, s_{288})$. The key stream generation consists of an iterative process which extracts the values of 15 specific state bits and uses them both to update 3 bits of the state and to compute 1 bit of key stream z_i. The state bits are then rotated and the process repeats itself until the requested $N \leq 2^{64}$ bits of key stream have been generated. A complete description is given by the following simple pseudo-code:

for $i = 1$ to N **do**
$\quad t_1 \leftarrow s_{66} + s_{93}$
$\quad t_2 \leftarrow s_{162} + s_{177}$
$\quad t_3 \leftarrow s_{243} + s_{288}$
$\quad z_i \leftarrow t_1 + t_2 + t_3$
$\quad t_1 \leftarrow t_1 + s_{91} \cdot s_{92} + s_{171}$
$\quad t_2 \leftarrow t_2 + s_{175} \cdot s_{176} + s_{264}$
$\quad t_3 \leftarrow t_3 + s_{286} \cdot s_{287} + s_{69}$
$\quad (s_1, s_2, \ldots, s_{93}) \leftarrow (t_3, s_1, \ldots, s_{92})$
$\quad (s_{94}, s_{95}, \ldots, s_{177}) \leftarrow (t_1, s_{94}, \ldots, s_{176})$
$\quad (s_{178}, s_{179}, \ldots, s_{288}) \leftarrow (t_2, s_{178}, \ldots, s_{287})$
end for

We remind the reader that here, as in the rest of this chapter, the '+' and '·' operations stand for addition and multiplication over GF(2) (i.e., XOR and AND), respectively. A graphical representation of the key stream generation process is given in Fig. 6.

7.2 Key and IV Setup

The algorithm is initialized by loading an 80-bit key and an 80-bit IV into the 288-bit initial state, and setting all remaining bits to 0, except for s_{286}, s_{287}, and s_{288}. Then, the state is rotated over 4 full cycles, in the same way as explained above, but without generating key stream bits. This is summarized in the pseudo-code below:

$$(s_1, s_2, \ldots, s_{93}) \leftarrow (K_{80}, \ldots, K_1, 0, \ldots, 0)$$
$$(s_{94}, s_{95}, \ldots, s_{177}) \leftarrow (IV_{80}, \ldots, IV_1, 0, \ldots, 0)$$
$$(s_{178}, s_{179}, \ldots, s_{288}) \leftarrow (0, \ldots, 0, 1, 1, 1)$$

for $i = 1$ to $4 \cdot 288$ **do**
$$t_1 \leftarrow s_{66} + s_{91} \cdot s_{92} + s_{93} + s_{171}$$
$$t_2 \leftarrow s_{162} + s_{175} \cdot s_{176} + s_{177} + s_{264}$$
$$t_3 \leftarrow s_{243} + s_{286} \cdot s_{287} + s_{288} + s_{69}$$

$$(s_1, s_2, \ldots, s_{93}) \leftarrow (t_3, s_1, \ldots, s_{92})$$
$$(s_{94}, s_{95}, \ldots, s_{177}) \leftarrow (t_1, s_{94}, \ldots, s_{176})$$
$$(s_{178}, s_{179}, \ldots, s_{288}) \leftarrow (t_2, s_{178}, \ldots, s_{287})$$
end for

7.3 Alternative Description

Alternatively, TRIVIUM's key stream generation algorithm can also be written in the following recursive way, proposed by Bernstein [7]:

for $i = 1$ to N **do**
$$a_i = c_{i-66} + c_{i-111} + c_{i-110} \cdot c_{i-109} + a_{i-69}$$
$$b_i = a_{i-66} + a_{i-93} + a_{i-92} \cdot a_{i-91} + b_{i-78}$$
$$c_i = b_{i-69} + b_{i-84} + b_{i-83} \cdot b_{i-82} + c_{i-87}$$
$$z_i = c_{i-66} + c_{i-111} + a_{i-66} + a_{i-93} + b_{i-69} + b_{i-84}$$
end for

This notation is often more convenient when describing attacks against the stream cipher.

8 Security

In this section we briefly discuss some of the cryptographic properties of TRIVIUM. The security requirement we would like to meet is that any type of cryptographic attack should not be significantly easier to apply to TRIVIUM than to any other imaginable stream cipher with the same external parameters (i.e., any cipher capable of generating up to 2^{64} bits of key stream from an 80-bit secret key and an 80-bit IV). Unfortunately, this requirement is not easy to verify, and the best we can do is to provide arguments why we believe that certain common types of attacks are not likely to affect the security of the cipher. A summary of the results discussed in the next sections is given in Table 2.

8.1 Correlations

When analyzing the security of a synchronous stream cipher, a cryptanalyst will typically consider two different types of correlations The first type are correlations between linear combinations of key stream bits and internal state bits, which can potentially lead to a complete recovery of the state. The second type,

Table 2. Cryptanalytical results

Attack	Time	Data	Reference
Linear distinguisher	2^{144}	2^{144}	Sect. 8.1
Guess-and-determine attack	2^{195}	288	Sect. 8.3
Guess-and-determine attack	2^{135}	288	[8]
Guess-and-determine attack	2^{90}	2^{61}	[9]
Solving system of equations	2^{164}	288	[10]
Exhaustive key search	2^{80}	80	

exploited by distinguishing attacks, are correlations between the key stream bits themselves.

Obviously, linear correlations between key stream bits and internal state bits are easy to find, since z_i is simply defined to be equal to $s_{66} + s_{93} + s_{162} + s_{177} + s_{243} + s_{288}$. However, as opposed to LFSR based ciphers, TRIVIUM's state evolves in a nonlinear way, and it is not clear how the attacker should combine these equations in order to efficiently recover the state.

An easy way to find correlations of the second type is to follow linear characteristics through the cipher and to approximate the outputs of all encountered AND gates by 0. However, as explained in the previous section, the positions of the taps in TRIVIUM have been chosen in such a way that any characteristic of this specific type is forced to approximate at least 72 AND gate outputs. An example of a correlated linear combination of key stream bits obtained this way is

$$z_1 + z_{16} + z_{28} + z_{43} + z_{46} + z_{55} + z_{61} + z_{73}$$
$$+ z_{88} + z_{124} + z_{133} + z_{142} + z_{202} + z_{211} + z_{220} + z_{289} .$$

If we assume that the correlation of this linear combination is completely explained by the specific characteristic we considered (i.e., the contributions of other characteristics to the correlation of this linear combination can be neglected), then it would have a correlation coefficient of 2^{-72}. Detecting such a correlation would require at least 2^{144} bits of key stream, which is well above the security requirement.

Other more complicated types of linear characteristics with larger correlations might exist in principle, but given the size of the state and the sparseness of the feedback and feedforward functions, the linear combination given above has a good chance to be optimal, and hence, it seems unlikely that the correlations of other characteristics will exceed 2^{-40}. The preliminary results given by Maximov and Biryukov [9] seem to confirm this.

8.2   Period

Because of the fact that the internal state of TRIVIUM evolves in a nonlinear way, its period is hard to determine. Still, a number of observations can be made. First, if the AND gates are omitted (resulting in a completely linear scheme), one can show that any key/IV pair would generate a stream with a period of at least $2^{96-3} - 1$. This has no immediate implications for TRIVIUM itself, but it might be seen as an indication that the taps have been chosen properly.

Secondly, TRIVIUM's state is updated in a reversible way, and the initialization of $(s_{178}, \ldots, s_{288})$ prevents the state from cycling in less than 111 iterations. If we believe that TRIVIUM behaves as a random permutation after a sufficient number of iterations, then all cycle lengths up to 2^{288} would be equiprobable, and hence the probability for a given key/IV pair to cause a cycle smaller than 2^{80} would be 2^{-208}.

8.3   Guess and Determine Attacks

In each iteration of TRIVIUM, only a few bits of the state are used, despite the general rule-of-thumb that sparse update functions should be avoided. As a result, guess and determine attacks are certainly a concern. A straightforward attack would guess $(s_{25}, \ldots, s_{93})$, $(s_{97}, \ldots, s_{177})$, and $(s_{244}, \ldots, s_{288})$, 195 bits in total, after which the rest of the bits can immediately be determined from the key stream.

More sophisticated attacks can significantly reduce this number, though. A first idea, proposed by Khazaei [8], is to guess a_{i-109}, b_{i-91}, and c_{i-82} for $i = 0, 2, \ldots, 88$ (we use here the alternative description of Sect. 7.3). Once these 135 bits are fixed, it can easily be verified that each key stream bit t_i with $0 \leq i \leq 90 + 66$ is reduced to a linear function in $288 - 135$ unknowns. By solving this linear system for all 2^{135} guesses, the attacker will eventually recover the complete internal state.

A considerably improved guess-and-determine attack is presented by Maximov and Biryukov [9]. Instead of guessing one out of two bits of a, b, and c over a certain interval, the authors propose to guess every third bit. In order to get a solvable linear system, they additionally assume that all three AND gates produce zero bits at every third step over a number of consecutive cycles. This assumption is only fulfilled with a small probability, and the attack will therefore have to be repeated for different positions in the stream. With some additional tricks, and given about 2^{61} bits of known key stream, the attack complexity can be reduced to an estimated 2^{90} key setups.

8.4   Algebraic Attacks

TRIVIUM seems to be a particularly attractive target for algebraic attacks. The complete scheme can easily be described with extremely sparse equations of low degree. However, its state does not evolve in a linear way, and hence the efficient linearization techniques [11] used to solve the systems of equations generated by LFSR based schemes will be hard to apply. Other techniques might be applicable, though, and their efficiency in solving this particular system of equations needs to be investigated.

Recently, some interesting research has been conducted on this topic by several cryptanalysts. In [10], Raddum presents a new technique to solve systems of equations associated with TRIVIUM. His attack has a very high complexity of $\mathcal{O}(2^{164})$ when applied to the full cipher, but breaks BIVIUM-A, a key stream generator similar to the one shown in Fig. 4(a), in a day. This same variant is also analyzed by McDonald et al. [12], who show that its state can be recovered in seconds using off-the-shelve satisfiability solvers. While these experiments are useful to test new techniques, it is important to note that the final remark of Sect. 5.2, combined with the use of 1-bit S-boxes, indeed implies a fundamental weakness of two-round ciphers such as BIVIUM-A.

Finally, Fischer and Meier [13] analyze TRIVIUM in the context of algebraic attacks based on augmented functions. They show that TRIVIUM's augmented function can easily be analyzed, and conclude that TRIVIUM seems to be resistant against this particular type of algebraic attacks.

8.5 Resynchronization Attacks

A last type of attacks are resynchronization attacks, in which the adversary is allowed to manipulate the value of the IV, and tries to extract information about the key by examining the corresponding key stream. TRIVIUM tries to preclude this type of attacks by cycling the state a sufficient number of times before producing any output. It can be shown that each state bit depends on each key and IV bit in a nonlinear way after two full cycles (i.e., $2 \cdot 288$ iterations). We expect that two more cycles will suffice to protect the cipher against resynchronization attacks. So far, this seems to be confirmed (or at least not contradicted) by the analysis of Turan and Kara [14], Vielhaber [15], and Fischer et al. [16].

9 Implementation Aspects

We conclude this chapter with a discussion of some implementation aspects of TRIVIUM.

9.1 Hardware

As stated in Sect. 2.2, our aim was to design a cipher which is compact in environments with restrictions on the gate count, power-efficient on platforms with limited power resources, and fast in applications that require high-speed encryption. In TRIVIUM, this flexibility is achieved by ensuring that state bits are not used for at least 64 iterations after they have been modified. This way, up to 64 iterations can be computed at once, provided that the 3 AND gates and 11 XOR gates in the original scheme are duplicated a corresponding number of times. This allows the clock frequency to be divided by a factor 64 without affecting the throughput.

Based on the figures stated in [18] (i.e., 12 NAND gates per Flip-flop, 2.5 gates per XOR, and 1.5 gates per AND), we can compute a first estimation of the gate count for different degrees of parallelization. The actual results found by Good and Benaissa [17] for 0.13 µm Standard Cell CMOS show that these estimations are rather pessimistic, however. Both figures are compared in Table. 3.

Table 3. Gate counts of 1-bit to 64-bit hardware implementations

Components	1-bit	8-bit	16-bit	32-bit	64-bit
Flip-flops:	288	288	288	288	288
AND gates:	3	24	48	96	192
XOR gates:	11	88	176	352	704
Estimated NAND gates:	3488	3712	3968	4480	5504
NAND gates, 0.13 µm CMOS [17]	2599	2801	3185	3787	4921

The hardware efficiency of TRIVIUM has been independently evaluated by several other research teams. Güerkanyak et al. [19] report a 64-bit implementation in 0.25 µm 5-metal CMOS technology with a throughput per area ratio of 129 Gbit/s · mm², three times higher than for any other eSTREAM candidate. Gaj et al. [20] come to similar conclusions, and also note that TRIVIUM is perceived to be the easiest eSTREAM candidate to implement amongst students following an introductory course on VHDL at the George Mason University. FPGA implementations of TRIVIUM are independently studied by Bulens et al. [21], Good et al. [22], and Rogawski [23]. The general conclusion, here as well, is that TRIVIUM offers a very good trade-off between throughput and area. Finally, Feldhofer [24] analyzes implementations of TRIVIUM for RFID tags, and shows that the power consumption is reduced to one fourth compared to a low-power AES implementation.

9.2 Software

Despite the fact that TRIVIUM does not target software applications, the cipher is still reasonably efficient on a standard PC. The measured performance of the reference C-code on a 1 700 MHz Pentium M processor can be found in Table 4.

Table 4. Measured performance on an Intel® Pentium™ M CPU 1 700 MHz

Operation	
Stream generation:	5.3 cycles/byte
Key setup:	51 cycles
IV setup:	774 cycles

10   Conclusion

In this chapter we have presented a simple synchronous stream cipher called TRIVIUM, which seems to be particularly well suited for applications requiring a flexible hardware implementation. The design is based on the study of the propagation of linear characteristics, and shows that the effect of a few small non-linear components can be amplified considerably by a carefully designed linear structure.

References

1. Daemen, J.: Cipher and hash function design. Strategies based on linear and differential cryptanalysis. PhD thesis, Katholieke Universiteit Leuven (1995)
2. Hawkes, P., Rose, G.G.: Primitive specification and supporting documentation for SOBER-tw submission to NESSIE. In: Proceedings of the First NESSIE Workshop, NESSIE (2000)
3. Ekdahl, P., Johansson, T.: SNOW – A new stream cipher. In: Proceedings of the First NESSIE Workshop, NESSIE (2000)
4. Daemen, J., Clapp, C.S.K.: Fast hashing and stream encryption with PANAMA. In: Vaudenay, S. (ed.) FSE 1998. LNCS, vol. 1372, pp. 60–74. Springer, Heidelberg (1998)
5. Daemen, J., Rijmen, V.: The Design of Rijndael: AES — The Advanced Encryption Standard. Springer, Heidelberg (2002)
6. Rosenthal, J., Smarandache, R.: Maximum distance separable convolutional codes. Applicable Algebra in Engineering, Communication and Computing 10(1), 15–32 (1999)
7. Bernstein, D.J.: Re: A reformulation of TRIVIUM. Posted on the eSTREAM Forum (2006), http://www.ecrypt.eu.org/stream/phorum/read.php?1,448
8. Khazaei, S.: Re: A reformulation of TRIVIUM. Posted on the eSTREAM Forum (2006), http://www.ecrypt.eu.org/stream/phorum/read.php?1,448
9. Maximov, A., Biryukov, A.: Two trivial attacks on Trivium. eSTREAM, ECRYPT Stream Cipher Project, Report 2007/003 (2007), http://www.ecrypt.eu.org/stream
10. Raddum, H.: Cryptanalytic results on TRIVIUM. eSTREAM, ECRYPT Stream Cipher Project, Report 2006/039 (2006), http://www.ecrypt.eu.org/stream
11. Courtois, N.T., Meier, W.: Algebraic attacks on stream ciphers with linear feedback. In: Biham, E. (ed.) EUROCRYPT 2003. LNCS, vol. 2656, pp. 345–359. Springer, Heidelberg (2003)
12. McDonald, C., Charnes, C., Pieprzyk, J.: Attacking Bivium with MiniSat. eSTREAM, ECRYPT Stream Cipher Project, Report 2007/040 (2007), http://www.ecrypt.eu.org/stream
13. Fischer, S., Meier, W.: Algebraic immunity of S-boxes and augmented functions. In: Biryukov, A. (ed.) FSE 2007. LNCS, vol. 4593, pp. 366–381. Springer, Heidelberg (2007)
14. Turan, M.S., Kara, O.: Linear approximations for 2-round Trivium. eSTREAM, ECRYPT Stream Cipher Project, Report 2007/008 (2007), http://www.ecrypt.eu.org/stream
15. Vielhaber, M.: Breaking ONE.FIVIUM by AIDA an algebraic IV differential attack. Cryptology ePrint Archive, Report 2007/413 (2007), http://eprint.iacr.org/
16. Fischer, S., Khazaei, S., Meier, W.: Key recovery with probabilistic neutral bits. Presented at the Echternach Symmetric Cryptography Seminar (2008)
17. Good, T., Benaissa, M.: Hardware results for selected stream cipher candidates. eSTREAM, ECRYPT Stream Cipher Project, Report 2007/023 (2007), http://www.ecrypt.eu.org/stream
18. Lano, J., Mentens, N., Preneel, B., Verbauwhede, I.: Power analysis of synchronous stream ciphers with resynchronization mechanism. In: ECRYPT Workshop, SASC – The State of the Art of Stream Ciphers, pp. 327–333 (2004)

19. Gürkaynak, F.K., Luethi, P., Bernold, N., Blattmann, R., Goode, V., Marghitola, M., Kaeslin, H., Felber, N., Fichtner, W.: Hardware evaluation of eSTREAM candidates: Achterbahn, Grain, MICKEY, MOSQUITO, SFINKS, TRIVIUM, VEST, ZK-Crypt. eSTREAM, ECRYPT Stream Cipher Project, Report 2006/015 (2006), http://www.ecrypt.eu.org/stream
20. Gaj, K., Southern, G., Bachimanchi, R.: Comparison of hardware performance of selected Phase II eSTREAM candidates. eSTREAM, ECRYPT Stream Cipher Project, Report 2007/027 (2007), http://www.ecrypt.eu.org/stream
21. Bulens, P., Kalach, K., Standaert, F.X., Quisquater, J.J.: FPGA implementations of eSTREAM Phase-2 focus candidates with hardware profile. eSTREAM, ECRYPT Stream Cipher Project, Report 2006/024 (2007), http://www.ecrypt.eu.org/stream
22. Good, T., Chelton, W., Benaissa, M.: Review of stream cipher candidates from a low resource hardware perspective. eSTREAM, ECRYPT Stream Cipher Project, Report 2006/016 (2006), http://www.ecrypt.eu.org/stream
23. Rogawski, M.: Hardware evaluation of eSTREAM candidates: Grain, Lex, Mickey128, Salsa20 and Trivium. eSTREAM, ECRYPT Stream Cipher Project, Report 2007/025 (2007), http://www.ecrypt.eu.org/stream
24. Feldhofer, M.: Comparison of low-power implementations of Trivium and Grain. eSTREAM, ECRYPT Stream Cipher Project, Report 2007/027 (2007), http://www.ecrypt.eu.org/stream

ASIC Hardware Performance

Tim Good and Mohammed Benaissa

Department of Electronic and Electrical Engineering,
University of Sheffield, Mappin Street, Sheffield, S1 3JD, UK
{t.good,m.benaissa}@sheffield.ac.uk

Abstract. This chapter presents detailed hardware implementation results and performance metrics for the eSTREAM candidate stream ciphers remaining in the Phase 3 hardware profile. Performance assessment has been made in accordance with the eSTREAM hardware testing
framework in terms of power, area and speed. An attempt has been made
to quantify the flexibility and scalability dimensions of performance. The
results are presented in tabular and graphical format together with sum-
marising the utility of the candidates against two notional applications:
one for 10Mbps wireless network and a second for 100kHz RFID. Where
applicable to a particular cipher, guidance on any limitations on the
choice of key or IV is given. The chapter concludes with a summary of
the performance of each of the candidates and some general guidance for
future low resource hardware stream cipher development.

1 Introduction

In 2004, a project under the Information Societies Technology (IST) Programme
of the European Commission ECRYPT Network of Excellence called eSTREAM
was started [1] tasked with seeking a strong stream cipher. Thirty-four candidate
ciphers were submitted to either a software or hardware profile. From initial
evaluations at SASC 2006 and SASC 2007, the commencement of Phase 3 saw
the eSTREAM candidates reduced to eight in the software profile and eight in
the hardware profile. There is no single cipher listed in both profiles. The aim of
this chapter is to document the hardware performance aspects of those ciphers
short-listed in the hardware profile.

A stream cipher, formally, is a symmetric cipher which generates a sequence
of cryptographically secure bits called the key stream which is then combined
with either the plaintext or ciphertext, at the bit level, using the exclusive-or
operation. The basic topology (Fig. 1) of a stream cipher consists of a register
to store the key and an initialisation vector (IV) together with a function for its
update (typically some sort of feedback shift register). This register forms the
current state of the cipher and is clocked for successive bits of the keystream.
The next component is a non-linear reduction function which takes part or all of
this state and combines the bits in a non-linear fashion normally to yield a single
bit of the keystream. This bit is then exclusive-or'ed with the plain / cipher text.
In a second form, the plain or cipher text may be incorporated into the state
update feedback function to effectively create a cipher-feedback mode.

M. Robshaw and O. Billet (Eds.): New Stream Cipher Designs, LNCS 4986, pp. 267–293, 2008.
© Springer-Verlag Berlin Heidelberg 2008

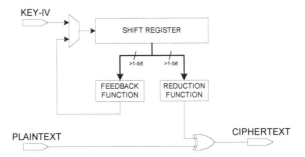

Fig. 1. Generic stream cipher

A vital function, in terms of security, is the period of the initial key and IV mixing to prevent key recovery attacks. In this period, a cryptographically strong feedback function is needed to operate upon the state for a number of iterations (basically hashing). The reduction function used to output the keystream can be somewhat weaker.

The same XOR per-bit property which does not change (permute) the cipher-text/plain-text order and provides stream ciphers with their simplicity also leads to an attack on all basic stream ciphers. This is the bit-flip attack where an active attacker may change the state of bit of plaintext at any positions within the ciphertext. The effectiveness of this attack depends on application and may be prevented using a message authentication code.

The original eSTREAM call for cipher primitives [1] made provision for two profiles, one for software, requiring equivalent security of 2^{128}, and one for hard-ware, requiring 80-bit (2^{80}) security. An extension to the basic cipher was also defined for those wishing to supply a message authentication code (MAC). The call recognised the importance of resource utilisation for both profiles in that the deployed environments for stream ciphers often have very restricted resources (eg smart cards). Subsequently, many of the hardware candidates have provided 128-bit key versions which have also been considered in this treatment.

Security analysis remains the overriding concern compared to hardware or software performance analyses; however, performance is both a technical re-quirement and economic imperative for any design including a cipher primitive. Put at its simplest, in the context of hardware design, it is the cost for each primitive in attaining the security. The aim of this chapter is to provide an in-dependent set of hardware results for the promising candidates to further the understanding of their relative merits and to focus cryptanalysis efforts on the low resource candidates.

Hardware performance is multi-dimensional and the importance of the various quantities such as area, throughput and power depends on the specific application. The eSTREAM hardware testing framework [2] defines five dimensions: compactness, throughput, power/energy consumption, flexibility and simplicity. It was also stated that the Advanced Encryption Standard (AES) is to be used as the benchmark for comparison and candidates should be *smaller* and *faster* than the AES.

Economics plays a crucial role in contemporary consumer electronics, this leads designers to be concerned about design efficiency. Low-resource design is an increasingly important area due to customer appetite for feature-rich hand-held battery operated ICT devices. Typically, a system will have specified requirements in terms of timeliness or throughput which the designer must meet. The cost of achieving the required specification is measured broadly in terms of design costs, device cost (proportional to area occupied by the design) and energy consumption (battery life).

For any digital design the fundamental performance metrics are power, area and time. From these many other metrics are derived (eg throughput versus area ratio) the applicability of which depends on application. For this treatment two representative applications are selected, a wireless LAN operating at 10Mbps and a Radio Frequency Identification Device (RFID) operating at 100kHz clock.

2   Measuring Hardware Performance

For any digital design there is a small set of metrics which can be obtained from the design flow together with some simulations. It is this primary set of metrics which is used to calculate the other derived metrics which designers use as a convenient method for comparing different designs. The definitions used in this paper are given below:

Process: The fabrication technology used. The name normally indicates the smallest feature size, library usage and gate construction (e.g. $0.13\mu m$ standard cell CMOS).

Interface: Designs are invariably part of a larger system and thus require connections (on or off chip) with other designs. All the designs in this paper use a synchronous interface with handshaking and on-chip communication is assumed. In this paper, the interfaces differ by their bus widths. Thus the bus width in bits for I/O is included in the results.

Area: Amount of silicon used for the core design (excluding power rings and I/O cells). This result is typically expressed in μm^2 for a specified process. However, the more usable process independent method of expressing the area is to calculate the Gate Equivalence (GE) of the total area by dividing by the lowest power two-input NAND gate's area.

Load/Initialisation Cycles: The definition used here was from RESET going inactive, through loading key and IV, until the validity of the first output bit is signalled. Many would quote just the key/IV mixing cycles however this would fail to account for the impact on interfacing decisions on the latency.

Bits per cycle (running): For the simplest stream ciphers this is the number of bits of output keystream per clock cycle. However, many operate in a way that produces batches of output (e.g. a block cipher in output feedback mode) thus the definition has to include a second clause on sustainable output rate. Thus the better definition is number of bits of output for all subsequent batches/blocks of keystream divided by the number of cycles per batch/block.

Design frequency: This is the clock rate selected by the designer and applied as a constraint to the design tools. The tools will make decisions on driver strengths to meet this requirement. Thus the higher the constraint the more area will be consumed. For low resource design a modest rate must be selected.

Max. Clock frequency: Designs have many connections between inputs outputs and registers, each of these form a timing path (or arc). Simplistically, the slowest arc in the design is the critical path and sets an upper bound on the clock frequency. The design may be clocked at a significantly lower rate.

Power consumption: Ideally a chip would be manufactured and measurements made for a large set of operations, however, this would be both time-consuming and costly. The alternative is to use specialist tools which operate using estimations of parasitic parameters (resistance and capacitance) from the physical layout of a design together with switching activity from a set of random test vectors. For CMOS there are two components to the power: the static power (roughly proportional to area) and a second dynamic component proportional to the switching activity (probability of a switching event occurring and frequency of operation). Both components also depend on supply voltage. The typical core voltage for the process should be used. At low frequency the static power is significant whilst at the other extreme may be neglected. Power results can be scaled with an acceptable margin of error to other frequencies if the static and dynamic components are treated separately.

The primary metrics may be used to wholly describe a designs performance, however, as can be seen there are many dimensions to performance so engineers often use derived metrics to provide a single dimension for comparison. There is no universal agreement on which metric is the best. The true requirement is to meet all the application driven design constraints. The commonly used derived metrics are given below:

Throughput: The rate at which new output is produced with respect to time, typically expressed in bits-per-second. This definition is further clarified to be the sustainable rate once initialisation is completed at a given operating clock frequency. It is thus simply bits-per-cycle multiplied by the clock-frequency. The maximum throughput will occur at the maximum clock frequency, however, remember that the design tools were given a slack timing constraint to favour area so this metric must be used with care when considering low resource design performance.

Area-Time product: The product of the time taken to produce each new output bit and the area of the design. The reciprocal metric is presented as the **throughput-to-area ratio** (TPAR). Either representation is frequently used as a measure of design efficiency. However, once again, note that the metrics are at their best at the maximum clock frequency.

Energy-per-bit: This is calculated by dividing the total power consumption by the throughput. Care must be taken to ensure that the power and throughput figures used are for the same clock frequency. At first this measure may appear to be frequency independent, however, if modelled at a low frequency (eg 100kHz) the static power will have a significant impact thus larger area designs will be *less efficient*. Conversely, at higher frequencies designs with large amounts of switching activity (including that from switching hazards to do path differences in the large fields of XOR gates present in most crypto-primitives) dominates the power.

Power-area-time product: This is the triple product formed from area-time product and the power consumption. As with energy per bit, this is maximised at the highest operating frequency due to the diminishing effect of the static power.

Power-Time product: Specifically, the product of power and latency (total time taken including initialisation and loading key and IV). This metric is particularly useful for measuring utility of a candidate in application such as RFID where both the power consumption and timeliness of response are important.

As has been frequently stated hardware performance analysis is multidimensional and application specific. Thus to resolve the impasse on which figures to quote the decision is made here to quote the following:

1. The primary design results for designs prepared with a slack timing constraint of 10MHz clock.
2. 'Best' metrics: Performance metrics for the designs operating at their maximum frequency given the 10MHz constraint.
3. High-end wireless: Performance metrics for an output rate of 10Mbps, taken as a typical estimate for future wireless LAN (proposed standards range between 1-100Mbps).
4. Low-end wireless: Performance metrics for a clock rate of 100kHz, as the low end of RFID/WSN tags which may be powered / clocked directly from the interrogating RF field.

The first three performance dimensions: compactness, throughput and power consumption may be readily compared quantitatively however the remaining two of flexibility and simplicity are much more subjective. There is little quantitative guidance in the testing framework so some definitions are offered here; admittedly the choice of metric is arbitrary but any *scale* is better than none.

Flexibility: It is assumed that a measure of the design space performance trade-offs is required. Herein defined as the (dimensionless) ratio of the throughput-to-area ratio for the maximum performance design variant ($TPAR_{max}$) divided by the corresponding ratio for a low-resource design operating at 100kHz ($TPAR_{100kHz}$)

Simplicity: It is assumed that the desired metric here is a measure of the design time (unfortunately the design work had to be fitted around existing work load thus this could not be reliably accounted for). There are a number of software-engineering metrics which are generally used to describe the complexity / simplicity of a source file. Metrics vary in sophistication and applicability to hardware design; one of the simplest, used here is the number of lines excluding blank lines and comments for all the design source (VHDL) files.

3   Candidate Ciphers

This section describes implementation specifics for the hardware design of the candidate ciphers in alphabetical order. All the designs are complete in that they contain a suitable finite state machine as controller and support usable handshaking. Further, for candidate ciphers requiring any padding of key/IV or specific initialisation constants these are performed within the architecture thus included in the stated results. However, for brevity only the critical aspects of the datapath are described.

3.1   Decim^{v2} and Decim-128

Decim has two variants for 80-bit and 128-bit key lengths. The datapath comprises four principle modules, a linear feedback shift register (LFSR), non-linear filter (NLF), an irregular decimation mechanism $ABSG$ and a first-in first out (FIFO) buffer. The LFSR stores the internal state of the cipher, a total of 192 bits. The NLF combines 14 taps from the LFSR using the reduction XOR and conventional addition to yield a single bit output. This output is fed back to the LFSR during the mixing phase to produce non-linear feedback and in the running phase feeds the ABSG. The ABSG produces bits in an irregular pattern of clock cycles, thus the output and its control is feed to a FIFO which is read monotonically to restore a regular clocking pattern for the output keystream. The design of Decim permits up to ×4 parallelism by replicating the filter function at the expense of an ABSG of exponentially increasing complexity, the simplest solution being to use a lookup table for the ×4-ABSG. A compact circuit for the ×1 ABSG is shown in Fig. 2.

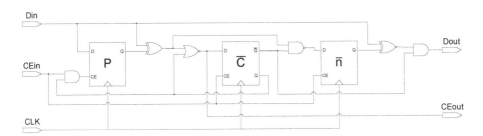

Fig. 2. Compact implementation of the Decim ABSG function

The initial internal state derived using arithmetic operations from the key (80-bit) and IV (64-bit), initially appears complex, however may be implemented using only a few conditionally applied XOR gates. The padding sequence required for Decim-128 may be conveniently generated using a toggle-flip-flop. The required circuit for the LFSR for both the 80-bit and 128-bit versions of Decim are shown in Fig. 3 and Fig. 4.

The initial phase of mixing (4×192 cycles) is followed by a second phase, of variable period, performed in multiples of 4 cycles, until the FIFO is full.

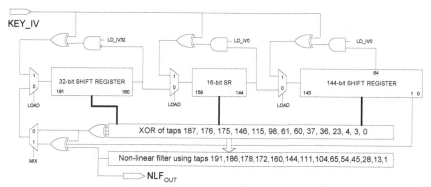

Fig. 3. Decim-80 LFSR supporting loading key, IV, padding, mixing and running phases

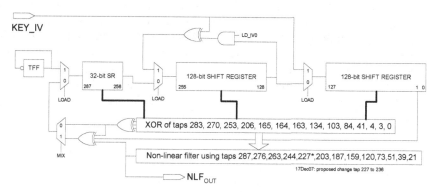

Fig. 4. Decim-128 LFSR supporting loading key, IV, padding, mixing and running phases

The FIFO is 32-bits for Decim-80 and 64-bits for Decim-128. Its implementation must support simultaneous or individual read/write operations inclusive of both buffer empty and buffer full conditions. The Decim specification requires a buffer refill mechanism, this halts the keystream output and refills the FIFO, however such an event is highly improbable (would be a distinguisher for the cipher) and would require the NLF to output a sequence buffer-length long of all zeros or all ones. From a hardware perspective, this presents a practical verification problem (finding a suitable test vector to test the buffer refill condition is improbable). In normal operation, the FIFO drops excess bits from the ABSG once full, incorrect implementation will appear as a single cycle misalignment of portions of the keystream from known test vectors.

3.2   Edon80

Edon80 by design was intended as an 80-element pipeline. However, the simple software definition for the initial mixing and running phases belies relatively high hardware complexity for its implementation. The nature and direction of shifting between loading key, IV and padding, mixing phase and running phase changes resulting in a significant number of additional multiplexers and a need to duplicate the key register. The implementation (Fig. 6) requires an additional 80 cycles at the end of the initialisation phase to avoid requiring additional pipelining of control lines (saves 160 FF). Edon80 (pipelined) is the largest design in the hardware profile so a more iterative and lower area version was also designed (Edon80×4). This comprises only four *e-transformers* rather than the more usual 80, however, has relatively poor performance, thus only the pipelined version is described in further detail.

The datapath is area is dominated by the 80 pipeline processing elements each of which comprises several multiplexers and an *e-transformer* and two bits of internal state storage. For clarity, it should be noted that the majority of the values used in Edon80 comprise two bits. Due to correlative nature of the initial mixing phase a second temporary copy of the internal state (160 bits), the temporary register, is required. To meet the required different bit ordering for load, mixing and running both the pipeline and temporary registers require multiplexers to support shifting in either direction. The temporary register is also used to provide key storage using suitable feedback, however, the key bits are required to be cycled in both forward and reverse orders during mixing so a second key register is also required. The key is 40×2-bit elements and used consecutively to drive the 80 processing elements; this results in a conceptual

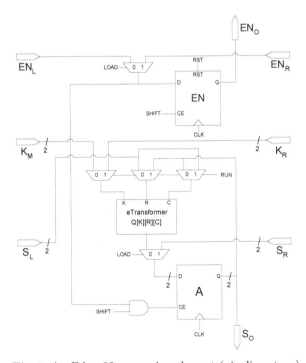

Fig. 5. An Edon-80 processing element (pipeline stage)

floorplan for the pipeline elements to be laid out around two revolutions of the
perimeter of a circle.

The datapath used accepts the loading of a key (80-bits) followed by an IV
(64-bits) and performs the necessary padding and bit-order reversal needed for
the mixing phase. A suitable design for each pipeline element is shown in Fig. 5.
A controller is used to generate the various control lines. For clarity, it should
be noted that when the load and run multiplexer select lines are both low then
mixing should be assumed.

The Edon80 reference code is written from a software efficiency perspective
and the stored state for each clock cycle, during mixing, for a pipelined architecture is not readily available. The following fragment of C provides a suitable
reference model for debugging such a hardware design:

```
#define mod80(x) (((x)+800)%80)
for (j=0;j<160; j++)
{
    Enable[0] = (j<80) ? TRUE : FALSE;
    NextState[0] = (Enable[0]==TRUE)
        ? ctx->Q[j%80][Temp[mod80(80-1-j)]][State[0]] : State[0];
    for (k=1; k<80; k++)
        NextState[k] = (Enable[k]==TRUE)
        ? ctx->Q[mod80(j-k)][State[k-1]][State[k]] : State[k];
    PrintInternalState(j,State);
    for (k=i-1; k>=0; k--) State[k]  = NextState[k];
    for (k=i-1; k> 0; k--) Enable[k] = Enable[k-1];
}
```

3.3   F-FCSR-16 and F-FCSR-H

There are two variants of the core F-FCSR design: F-FCSR-H supports an 80-bit
key and F-FCSR-16 a 128-bit key. Both are conveniently implemented using shift
registers for state storage. In comparison to many of the other designs, F-FCSR
has a non-linear shift register and a linear reduction filter. The state register
is updated according to a fixed polynomial, poly, which defines the inclusion of
non-linear carry units which act on the feedback term to modify the state update.
The key followed by the IV may be directly loaded into the state register with the
feedback suppressed. As part of the mixing process, the original initial state is
needed thus has to be stored in a second temporary shift register. This effectively
doubles the size of the internal state. A side effect is that in order to minimise the
cycles taken for mixing, the cipher needs to operate at the word level (8-bits for
F-FCSR-H and 16-bits for F-FCSR-16) during the second phase of mixing (often
convenient for key/IV loading too). However, due to the non-linear nature of the
feedback operates using single-bit shifts during both the first phase of mixing and
the running phase. This is performed in hardware using multiplexers between
the state register elements. A suitable datapath is shown in Fig. 7, the design for
F-FCSR-16 is similar except operates on 16-bit words and has a 256-bit internal
state. An additional shift register may be used to convert the key/IV input and
keystream output to/from serial format.

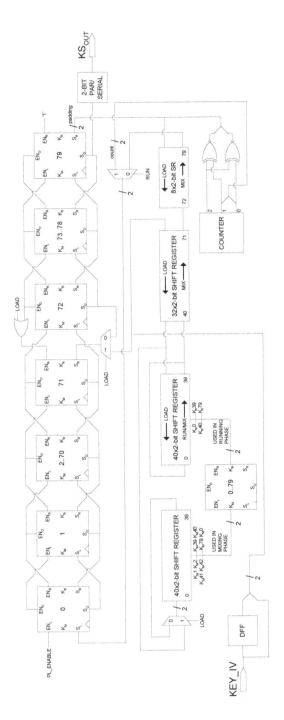

Fig. 6. A possible datapath architecture for pipelined Edon-80

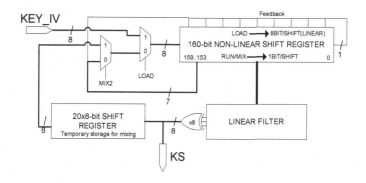

Fig. 7. Datapath for core of F-FCSR-H

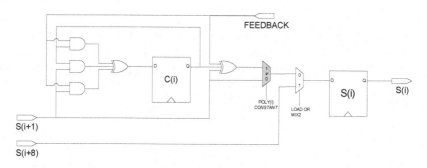

Fig. 8. Schematic of F-FCSR-H non-linear shift register element including *carry bit*

Fig. 8 shows a construction for the elements of the non-linear shift register, a virtual multiplexer (shaded and marked v) is shown to depict the presence of the cell according to the specified (constant) polynomial.

The cautious implementer should detect the all zero internal state (will be entered when both key and IV are all zero). If this state is entered it will persist (keystream all zeros) and result in the unencrypted output of plaintext! One low-resource solution is to detect the all zero IV and set the final bit to one. Without such a test the cipher's implementation would fail to demonstrate plaintext-ciphertext segregation to an assessor. This can be done with a single flip-flop and few combinatorial gates attached to the KEY/IV input.

3.4 Grain and Grain-128

Grain comes in two versions Grain-v1 for 80-bit key and Grain-128 for 128-bit key. For clarity these are referred to in this chapter as Grain-80 and Grain-128. Both support extensive parallelism at a cost of only replicating the filter functions, ×16 is possible for Grain-80 and ×32 for Grain-128. This feature, in common with Trivium, affords Grain a large and advantageous design space for trading between speed, area and power.

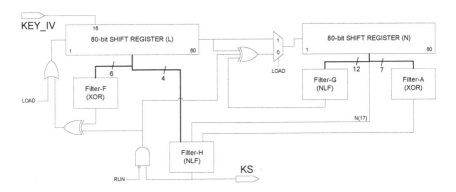

Fig. 9. Block diagram of Grain-80 datapath

During initialisation, the shift registers for Grain-80 are loaded with key (80-bits) and IV (64-bits) then padded with 16 ones. This padding may be done at the same time the key & IV are loaded. The mixing phase is then carried out for 160-bits of shifting before the cipher enters its running mode. The typical architecture for Grain-80 is shown in Fig. 9.

3.5 Mickey

Mickey is based on a pair of shift registers and has versions for 80-bit and 128-bit key and IV. One feature of the cipher is that the shift registers conditionally *jump* this is typically implemented by including the previous state bit in the feedback XOR sum and maintaining monotonic clocking. The two shift registers are each 100-bits for Mickey-80 and 160-bits for Mickey-128. Prior to key loading the state is initialised to zero, this is required as the feedback remains operative during key and IV loading. A number of constant polynomials are used in the description of Mickey to define the required feedback taps. In a hardware description language, conventional logic operations are used to define the required functionality however these are essentially virtual-gates as being constant will be removed during optimisation. Fig. 10 depicts a suitable datapath for Mickey-80 with the detailed composition of the shift registers in Fig. 11 in which virtual gates are shaded and marked by the letter-v and those which conditionally form inverters are marked *inv*. Mickey-128 is very similar except for the longer registers and different tap combinations used to form the *control-bits*. In the circuit shown it is necessary to load the IV first followed by the key.

The cautious hardware designer may additionally wish to detect the all-zero states in either the R or S registers. If either occurs it would be prudent to disable the ciphertext output and signal an error state (this would result in a distinguisher, but *not* of low complexity).

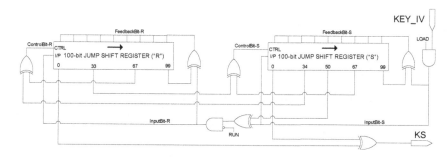

Fig. 10. Datapath for Mickey-80

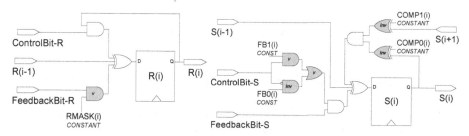

Fig. 11. Schematic detail for performing jump control functions within Mickey's shift registers

3.6   Moustique

Moustique is a self-synchronising stream cipher, which for some communications systems, is an advantageous property. The datapath compromises a 96-bit key register, a 128-bit non-linear shift register (CCSR) and a seven stage pipelined non-linear reduction filter. Three simple functions, g0, g1, g2, are used throughout the CCSR and filter, g1 & g2 providing the non-linearity.

It has a small design space in that a number of the *stages* may be performed iteratively to save area at the expense of latency. The key is contained in a static register thus could support the use of a one-time-programmable memory for key storage directly.

Once the 96-bit key has been entered, sequentially in this design, the 128-bit IV may loaded into the CCSR or in its self-synchronising mode, prefixed by a '0' and applied to the data-input along with ciphertext for decipherment. None of the flip-flops in the key or CCSR require resetting. The only exception is the flip-flop feeding the CCSR for encryption if the IV is not prefixed with a zero.

A suitable datapath is given in Fig. 12 which supports both enciphering and self-synchronising deciphering operations. Although the design in terms of gates would appear relatively simple, the permutative wiring within the stages results in hardware architectures which are dominated by the routing.

In a typical application, a self-synchronising stream cipher operates on the entire data stream, including synchonisation, header and framing bits. This is the principal advantage which can be gained by having the self-synchronising

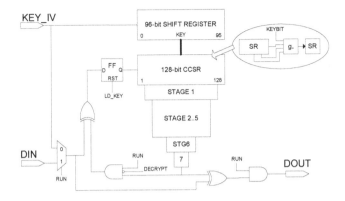

Fig. 12. Combined Moustique encipher/decipher datapath

property. There are a couple of circumstances that the cautious implementer should prevent from occurring.

The use of the all-zero IV for encryption followed by a sequence of plaintext zeros will result in all zero ciphertext irrespective of key. This may allow a potential attacker to gain some limited information and distinguish Moustique from other ciphers. The all-zero IV also results in the first byte of ciphertext being unencrypted. The all-one IV has similar undesirable properties. It is recommended that the cautious implementer prevent the use of IVs containing repeating sequences of low period.

The response of the decipher operation to an all-zero ciphertext, of N bits in length, is to output a portion of constant plaintext N-104 bits long.

3.7 Pomaranch

Pomaranch has 80-bit and 128-bit versions and consist of 6 or 9 sections each being an 18-bit jump-controlled linear feedback shift register (CJCSG), two different types defined, connected by non-linear function (Fig. 13). A jump-control term is derived using a complex key-dependant non-linear function and passed between the stages. This function is formed by the modulo-2 addition of 9 key bits followed by inversion in $GF(2^9)$, further mod-2 addition of another 7 key bits to the middle 7-bits of the inversion result and finally a 7-bit reduction filter (PNLBF) to yield a single jump-control output bit. The final stage does not require the JCout term this is depicted (Fig. 14) by a shaded (virtual) multiplexer marked with the letter-v.

The ciphers authors provide the necessary field constructions for a composite field equivalent in $GF((2^3)^3)$. Such construction is typically much more efficient than a conventional ROM look-up table or typical optimisers *random* logic implementation. However, only the middle 7-bits of the 9-bit inversions output are required thus the ROM is approx. $\times 4$ smaller than that needed to describe the $GF(2^9)$ inversion so the advantage of using composite field arithmetic in this

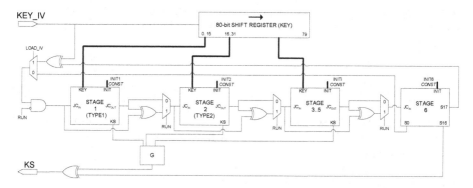

Fig. 13. Pomaranch-80 datapath architecture

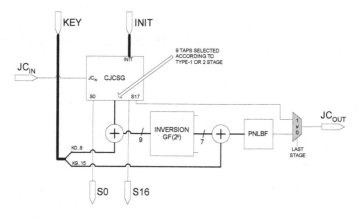

Fig. 14. Generic stage processing element for Pomaranch

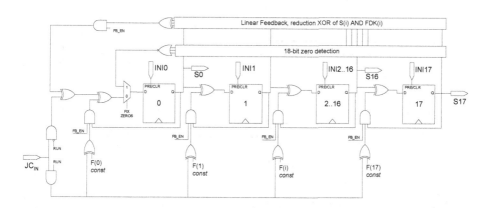

Fig. 15. Pomaranch CJCSG detail

instance is more marginal. The jump-control feedback between the sections frustrates attempts to roll the design into a single configurable stage supported by a suitable memory.

The state contained in CJCSG's must be initialised to a set of constants and the feedback terms being defined by constant polynomials for each type of CJCSG (Fig. 15). During IV loading the feedback must be disabled. To avoid the all-zero state in any CJCSG a step is required during initialisation to conditionally set the LSB. A second output from the CJCSG is one bit of the internal state from each which are combined by a function, G, to yield a single bit of keystream per cycle.

3.8   Trivium

The key feature of Trivium is its simplicity, it supports parallelism by replicating the filter functions from ×1 to ×64 which gives a large design space for trading between throughput, area and power. The internal state is 288-bits giving Grain the edge in terms of lowest area, however, its superior parallelism and simplicity give Trivium the edge in terms of throughput.

The datapath (Fig. 16) may be readily arranged with a few additional gates to perform the required padding during the key/IV loading phase without resorting to additional cycles. Many implementers will favour the ×8 design giving 8-bit I/O, however even if serial output is desired working at say ×4 or ×8 and adding an SR for serialising the I/O to give superior power-area-time performance and reduce the initial mixing time. As an alternative the parallel input/output may be used directly. For ×32 and ×64 variants, the padding between the key and IV is most naturally input as part of the wider key/IV words.

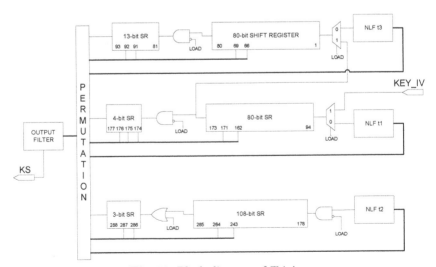

Fig. 16. Block diagram of Trivium

4   Results

This section summarises the ASIC performance results for the authors' hardware designs for the various stream cipher candidates submitted to the State-of-the-art stream ciphers conferences, SASC 2006 [3], SASC 2007 [4] and SASC 2008 [5]. The results include the complete set of Phase 3 candidates submitted to the hardware profile including any clarfications.

All the designs have been implemented using the *same design flow*. The natural bus-width for interfacing to each design was selected rather than forcing all designs to use the same bus-width in order to avoid skewing the results. Cadence tools were used together with ModelSim. The process selected was the same $0.13\mu m$ CMOS and standard cell library. Best-case worst-case timing analysis was carried out for a desired clock rate of 10MHz. The designs were taken through to physical layout (including clock tree synthesis, placement and routing). The final core area was converted to gate-equivalents. The resulting parasitic values were extracted and the netlist back annotated and simulated with known test vectors to validate the design. To estimate the power consumption, random test vectors were applied to the back annotated netlist and simulated to collect switching activity for a set of 100 different 1 kilobit keystream generations. The power modelling was done using the foundry typical values for the process ($1.2V_{core}$ $25°C$), the total power and static component are quoted in the results to permit scaling. The results (Tables 2, 3, 4 & 5) incorporate both initialisation and operational phases of the design under test.

For the notional future wireless network application, battery life, meeting throughput requirements and area are important to the designer. A good

Table 1. Flexibility and simplicity

Design	Flexibility $TPAR_{max} \div TPAR_{100k}$	VHDL (bytes)	Simplicity[a] Comment lines	Empty lines	VHDL code lines
Grain80 ($\times 1 - 16$)	39,472	5,415	31	10	158
Trivium ($\times 1 - 64$)	116,913	5.916	45	26	159
F-FCSR-H	3,922	4,923	22	33	152
Grain128 ($\times 1 - 32$)	58,224	4,703	21	29	138
Mickey128	4,132	6,399	41	34	127
F-FCSR-16	3,175	5,668	20	38	177
Mickey2(80)	4,545	5,645	20	37	149
Pomaranch80	1,245	23,378	71	156	578
Pomaranch128	1,049	23,378	71	156	578
Moustique	4,762	16,960	44	77	496
Decim80[b]	4,274	16,210	79	103	421
Decim128[b]	3,096	16,560	95	117	396
Edon80 ($\times 4 - 80_{PL}$)	19,632	20,704	95	149	618

[a] Figures quoted for designer's first validated draft.

[b] Decim with $\times 4$ versions are possible but not implemented by these authors. However, the estimated 'best-case' flexibility result will be less than 4 times the stated value.

measure for comparing designs is to consider the trade off between the Energy per bit and Throughput/Area metrics.

RFID applications place limits on power, area and latency directly, excesses in any would make a candidate unsuitable for the application. RFID tags must be fundamentally low cost thus low area. A good metric for performance would be power-latency product versus area.

These results are presented graphically in Figures 17, 18, 19 & 20.

Table 2. Our design results for $0.13\mu m$ Standard Cell CMOS

Design	Key bits	Interface bits	Load/Ini cycles	Bits/Cycle (running)	Max. clock freq. MHz	Area NAND GE, gates	Leakage power, μW	Total Power @10MHz, μW
Grain80	80	1	321	1	724.6	1294	2.224	109.4
Grain80×4	80	4	81	4	694.4	1678	3.243	126.6
Grain80×8	80	8	41	8	632.9	2191	4.634	150.7
Grain80×16	80	16	21	16	617.3	3239	7.399	200.5
Trivium	80	1	1314	1	327.9	2580	3.823	175.1
Trivium×2	80	2	660	2	574.7	2627	3.954	182.8
Trivium×4	80	4	332	4	473.9	2705	4.149	184.6
Trivium×8	80	8	168	8	471.7	2952	5.071	203.4
Trivium×16	80	16	86	16	467.3	3166	5.339	214.4
Trivium×32	80	32	45	32	350.9	3787	7.501	282.5
Trivium×64	80	64	24	64	348.4	4921	10.677	374.2
F-FCSR-H	80	8	225	8	392.2	4760	7.973	269.3
F-FCSR-16	128	16	308	16	317.5	8072	13.731	470.1
Grain128	128	1	513	1	925.9	1857	2.698	167.7
Grain128×4	128	4	129	4	584.8	2129	3.806	183.4
Grain128×8	128	8	65	8	581.3	2489	4.898	205.1
Grain128×16	128	16	33	16	540.5	3189	6.882	254.6
Grain128×32	128	32	17	32	452.5	4617	11.442	344.7
Mickey128	128	1	417	1	413.2	5039	8.144	310.7
Mickey2(80)	80	1	261	1	454.5	3188	5.195	196.5
Pomaranch80	80	1	472	1	124.5	5357	10.547	569.3
Pomaranch128	128	1	594	1	104.9	8039	16.185	878.4
Moustique	96	1	202	1	476.2	9607	16.078	464.0
Decim80	80	1	1012	0.25	427.3	2603	3.894	157.7
Decim128	128	1	1617	0.25	309.6	3819	6.052	242.2
Edon80×4	80	8	1869	0.0473	207.9	4969	7.775	280.1
Edon80pl	80	1	392	1	243.3	13010	20.467	478.9
AES [4]	128	32	50	2.37	131.2[a]	5398	-	-
AES [5]	128	8	1016	0.124	80.0[a]	3400	-	-

[a] Results are for different CMOS processes (Satoh 0.11, Feldhofer 0.35). Power cannot be scaled reliably between different processes and libraries. The area can be scaled to $0.13\mu m$ for comparison.

Table 3. Derived metrics for maximum clock frequency

Design	Max Throughput, $Mbps$	Estimated Power, μW	Energy/bit, pJ/bit	Area-Time, $\mu m^2 - \mu s$	Tput/Area, $kbps/\mu m^2$	Power-Area-Time $nJ - \mu m^2$
Grain80	724.6	7772	10.72	9.26	107.99	72.0
Grain80×4	2777.7	8569	3.08	3.13	319.33	26.8
Grain80×8	5063.2	9247	1.82	2.24	445.78	20.7
Grain80×16	9876.5	11929	1.20	1.70	588.26	20.3
Trivium	327.9	5618	17.14	40.79	24.51	229.2
Trivium×2	1149.4	10283	8.95	11.85	84.40	121.8
Trivium×4	1895.7	8559	4.51	7.40	135.17	63.3
Trivium×8	3773.6	9360	2.48	4.06	246.62	38.0
Trivium×16	7476.6	9777	1.31	2.20	455.50	21.5
Trivium×32	11228.0	9658	0.86	1.74	571.88	16.9
Trivium×64	22299.6	12677	0.56	1.14	874.13	14.5
F-FCSR-H	3137.2	10255	3.26	7.86	127.13	80.7
F-FCSR-16	5079.3	14503	2.85	8.23	121.38	119.5
Grain128	925.9	15283	16.50	10.39	96.20	158.9
Grain128×4	2339.1	10505	4.49	4.71	211.97	49.6
Grain128×8	4651.1	11646	2.50	2.77	360.52	32.3
Grain128×16	8648.6	13399	1.54	1.91	523.09	25.6
Grain128×32	14479.6	15093	1.04	1.65	604.92	24.9
Mickey128	413.2	12512	30.27	63.21	15.82	790.9
Mickey2(80)	454.5	8701	19.14	36.35	27.50	316.3
Pomaranch80	124.5	6969	55.96	223.01	4.48	1554.3
Pomaranch128	104.9	9063	86.37	397.15	2.51	3599.6
Moustique	476.2	21347	44.83	104.59	9.56	2232.7
Decim80	106.8	6577	61.55	126.28	7.91	830.6
Decim128	77.3	7316	94.52	255.80	3.90	1871.6
Edon80×4	9.8	5670	576.13	2617.43	0.38	14840.8
Edon80pl	243.3	11174	45.92	277.18	3.60	3097.3
AES [4]	311	-	-	90.12	11.10	-
AES [5]	10	-	-	1776.33	0.56	-
Better is:	higher	lower	lower	lower	higher	lower

Table 4. Derived metrics for an output rate of 10 Mbps (estimated typical future wireless LAN)

Design	Clock Frequency, MHz	Estimated Power, μW	Energy/bit, pJ/bit	Area-Time, $\mu m^2 - \mu s$	Tput/Area, $kbps/\mu m^2$	Power-Area-Time $nJ - \mu m^2$
Grain80	10.00	109.45	10.94	671	1.490	73.4
Grain80×4	2.50	34.07	3.40	870	1.150	29.6
Grain80×8	1.25	22.88	2.28	1136	0.880	26.0
Grain80×16	0.63	19.47	1.94	1679	0.596	32.7
Trivium	10.00	175.06	17.51	1337	0.748	234.1
Trivium×2	5.00	93.38	9.34	1362	0.734	127.2
Trivium×4	2.50	49.27	4.93	1402	0.713	69.1
Trivium×8	1.25	29.86	2.99	1530	0.654	45.7
Trivium×16	0.63	18.41	1.84	1641	0.609	30.2
Trivium×32	0.31	16.09	1.61	1963	0.509	31.6
Trivium×64	0.16	16.35	1.63	2551	0.392	41.7
F-FCSR-H	1.25	40.63	4.06	2468	0.405	100.3
F-FCSR-16	0.63	42.25	4.22	4185	0.239	176.8
Grain128	10.00	167.72	16.77	962	1.039	161.4
Grain128×4	2.50	48.69	4.87	1104	0.906	53.7
Grain128×8	1.25	29.92	2.99	1290	0.775	38.6
Grain128×16	0.63	22.36	2.23	1653	0.605	37.0
Grain128×32	0.31	21.85	2.18	2394	0.418	52.3
Mickey128	10.00	310.72	31.07	2612	0.383	811.6
Mickey2(80)	10.00	196.49	19.65	1652	0.605	324.7
Pomaranch80	10.00	569.34	56.93	2777	0.360	1581.2
Pomaranch128	10.00	878.38	87.83	4167	0.240	3660.6
Moustique	10.00	464.02	46.40	4980	0.201	2311.0
Decim80	40.00	619.10	61.91	1349	0.741	835.3
Decim128	40.00	950.52	95.05	1980	0.505	1882.0
Edon80×4	211.25	5761.22	576.12	2576	0.388	14840.5
Edon80pl	10.00	478.88	47.88	6744	0.148	3229.7
AES [4]	4.22	-	-	2798	0.357	-
AES [5]	80.63	-	-	1763	0.567	-
Better is:	lower	lower	lower	lower	higher	lower

Table 5. Derived metrics operating at 100kHz clock (low-end RFID/WSN applications)

Design	Throughput, Mbps	Estimated Power, μW	Energy/Bit, pJ/bit	Area-Time, μm² – μs	Tput/Area, kbps/μm²	Power-Area-Time, nJ – μm²	Latency, μs	Power-Area-Latency, μJ – μm²	Power-Latency, nJ
Grain80	0.100	3.29	32.96	67,098	0.0149	221	3,210	70.99	10.58
Grain80×4	0.400	4.47	11.19	21,747	0.0460	97	810	31.54	3.62
Grain80×8	0.800	6.09	7.61	14,198	0.0704	86	410	28.38	2.49
Grain80×16	1.600	9.33	5.83	10,493	0.0953	97	210	32.89	1.95
Trivium	0.100	5.54	55.36	133,747	0.0075	740	13,140	972.87	72.74
Trivium×2	0.200	5.74	28.71	68,092	0.0147	391	6,600	516.14	37.90
Trivium×4	0.400	5.95	14.89	35,061	0.0285	209	3,320	277.22	19.77
Trivium×8	0.800	7.05	8.82	19,127	0.0523	135	1,680	181.35	11.85
Trivium×16	1.600	7.43	4.64	10,259	0.0975	76	860	104.88	6.39
Trivium×32	3.200	10.25	3.20	6,135	0.1630	62	450	90.56	4.61
Trivium×64	6.400	14.31	2.23	3,986	0.2509	57	240	87.62	3.43
F-FCSR-H	0.800	10.58	13.23	30,847	0.0324	326	2,250	587.78	23.81
F-FCSR-16	1.600	18.29	11.43	26,153	0.0382	478	3,080	2357.93	56.34
Grain128	0.100	4.34	43.48	96,250	0.0104	418	5,130	214.70	22.30
Grain128×4	0.400	5.60	14.00	27,588	0.0362	154	1,290	79.74	7.22
Grain128×8	0.800	6.90	8.62	16,127	0.0620	111	650	57.86	4.48
Grain128×16	1.600	9.36	5.85	10,333	0.0968	96	330	51.06	3.08
Grain128×32	3.200	14.77	4.61	7,480	0.1337	110	170	60.12	2.51
Mickey128	0.100	11.17	111.69	261,204	0.0038	2,917	4,170	1216.64	46.57
Mickey2(80)	0.100	7.10	71.08	165,249	0.0061	1,174	2,610	306.58	18.55
Pomaranch80	0.100	16.13	161.35	277,724	0.0036	4,481	4,720	2115.12	76.15
Pomaranch128	0.100	24.80	248.07	416,742	0.0024	10,338	5,940	6140.88	147.35
Moustique	0.100	20.56	205.58	498,044	0.0020	10,239	2020	2068.22	41.53
Decim80	0.025	5.43	217.28	539,689	0.0019	2,931	10,120	741.69	54.97
Decim128	0.025	8.41	336.54	791,977	0.0013	6,663	16,170	2693.63	136.04
Edon80×4	0.005	10.49	2217.91	5,441,651	0.0002	57,132	18,690	5054.66	196.22
Edon80pl	0.100	25.05	250.51	674,421	0.0015	16895	3,920	6622.82	98.20
AES [4]	0.237	-	-	118,054	0.0085	-	500	-	-
AES [5]	0.001	-	-	1,421,064	0.0007	-	10,160	-	-
Better is:	higher	lower	lower	lower	higher	lower	lower	lower	lower

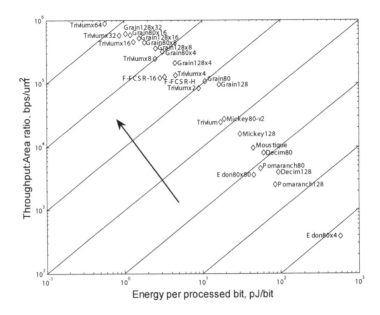

Fig. 17. $0.13\mu m$ Standard Cell CMOS design performance metrics at maximum throughput, arrow shows improving performance

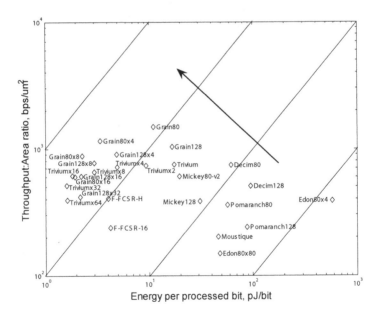

Fig. 18. Performance metrics for notional Wireless-LAN at 10Mbps throughput, arrow shows improving performance

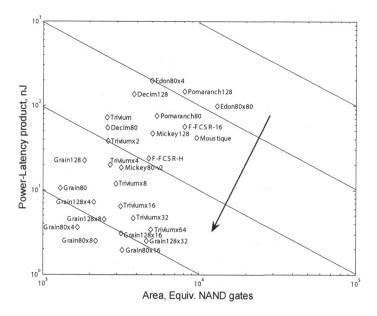

Fig. 19. Performance for low-end RFID/WSN application at 100kHz clock, arrow shows improving performance

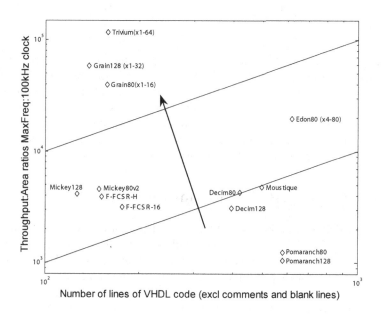

Fig. 20. Flexibility as Throughput: Area for MaxFreq:100kHz clock versus Simplicity as lines of VHDL

5   Require Even Lower Power?

For the primary set of results presented in this paper a typical general purpose standard cell library was used on a $0.13\mu m$ process with standard process options for all the designs. The previous section provides a set of readily comparable results between all of the Phase 3 hardware candidates. This section is only included to demonstrate the advantage to any hardware design by moving to a specialist low power library, selecting low-leakage process options and moving to a more advanced design flow significant power savings can be achieved at the expense of considerable additional design effort. At relatively low clock rates relative to the critical path the core voltage may be reduced accepting longer propagation delays thus further reducing the power consumption. As an example, Table 6 shows the results for Grain and Trivium.

Table 6. Results using a specialist low power library

Design	Grain80×8	Grain128×16	Trivium×8
Interface bits	8	16	8
Core voltage, V	0.8	0.8	0.8
Area, NAND GE	2796	4057	3244
Clock for 10Mbps, MHz	1.25	0.625	1.25
Power (10Mbps), μW	10.710	8.761	15.108
Energy/Bit (10 Mbps), pJ/bit	1.071	0.876	1.511
Power-Area-Time, $nJ - \mu m^2$	11.5	13.6	18.8
Power (100 kHz clk), μW	0.857	1.403	1.209
Power-Latency (100kHz clk), pJ	352	463	2056

At 100kHz Grain80×8 shows approximately a factor of 7 improvement in power-latency product (for the same VHDL source) by changing the library, process options and flow. These results have been included as a reminder that comparison in absolute units between different designs must be made using the same technology, libraries and process options and to demonstrate the low resource nature of stream ciphers using an advanced flow and process options for those who wish to make absolute comparisons with other designs.

6   Evaluation ASIC for Stream Ciphers

At time of writing there has been little published work on the side-channel attacks such as differential power analysis, differential EM-analysis and fault injection techniques. To assist this effort, prototype quantities of an ASIC containing all the Phase 3 hardware candidates have been designed and submitted for fabrication on $0.18\mu m$ CMOS (Fig. 21). All the designs share a common synchronous serial interface (including handshaking) with multiplexers and clock-gating to select the cipher for testing. A total of 15-designs are included as tabulated in Table 7.

Table 7. Cipher implementations

1 Moustique	6 F-FCSR-H	11 Mickey128
2 Edon80	7 F-FCSR-16	12 Pomaranch80
3 Trivium	8 Grain80	13 Pomaranch128
4 Decim80	9 Grain128	14 Grain80 (×8 internally)
5 Decim128	10 Mickey2(80)	15 Trivium (×8 internally)

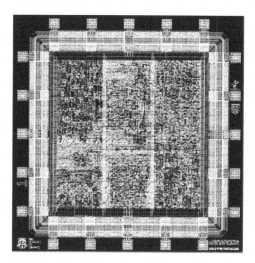
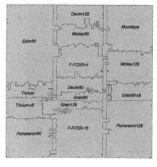

Fig. 21. Layout for eSCARGOt (European Stream Ciphers Are Ready (to) GO)

7 Conclusions

This treatment has considered the entire set of Phase 3 candidates in the hardware profile. Using the two sample applications of a notional future wireless network (WLAN) and low-end radio frequency identification tags / wireless sensor network nodes (RFID/WSN). The table below provides the *first documented attempt to summarise quantifiable results* for all the performance dimensions specified in [2] for each of the candidate ciphers. The authors' overall view relative to the AES is summarised by the left hand column.

And finally, from the results obtained, it is clear that the overall area is dominated by the flip-flops used to store the internal state; this leads to the following general guidance for the development of low-resource hardware stream ciphers:

- the internal state should be composed from key/IV with minimum padding to prevent constant keystream cases,
- the internal state should be stored using a shift register composed of simple D-type flip-flops (without reset/preset, etc),
- there should be a non-linear (filter) function which is trivial in terms of area,

Table 8. Summary of comparative results

Power-Area-Time Max. clock	Power-Area-Time WLAN	Power-Area-Time RFID/WSN	Flexibility (design space)	Simplicity (code lines)
★ Trivium($\times 64$)	Grain80($\times 8$)	Grain80($\times 8$)	Trivium	Mickey128
Grain80($\times 16$)	Grain128($\times 16$)	Grain128($\times 16$)	Grain128	Grain128
Grain128($\times 32$)	Trivium($\times 8-32$)	Trivium($\times 8-32$)	Grain80	Mickey2(80)
⌣ F-FCSR-H	F-FCSR-H			Grain80
F-FCSR-16				Trivium
				F-FCSR-H
				F-FCSR-16
Mickey2(80)	F-FCSR-16	F-FCSR-H	Edon80	Decim128
·· Mickey128	Mickey2(80)	Mickey2(80)	Decim80	Decim80
‾ Moustique^a		Decim80	Decim128	Moustique^a
			Moustique^a	
Decim80	Mickey128	Mickey128	F-FCSR-H	Pomaranch80
Edon80	Decim80	Pomaranch80	F-FCSR-16	Pomaranch128
Pomaranch80	Pomaranch80	F-FCSR-16	Mickey2(80)	Edon80
⌢ Decim128	Decim128	Moustique^a	Mickey128	
Pomaranch128	Pomaranch128	Decim128	Pomaranch80	
	Moustique^a	Edon80	Pomaranch128	
	Edon80	Pomaranch128		

^{a}Moustique is the only self synchronising stream cipher so should be considered of significant merit irrespective of other performance metrics.

- feedback tap selection for the SR should allow for replication of the filter function(s) to permit a more parallel state update and output thus increasing the available P-A-T tradeoffs,
- the trade-off between filter function complexity and mixing phase cycles should be evaluated at an early stage of development, and
- *any* N-bit word *S-boxes* should be avoided as they are a significant consumer of area and power.

Acknowledgement

The authors wish to thank the developers of the candidate ciphers for all their commitment and effort in continuing to refine their submission and further for their assistance in understanding and resolving minor discrepancies between the descriptions and reference designs.

References

1. ECRYPT, Call for Stream Cipher Primitives (April 12, 2005), http://www.ecrypt.eu.org/stream/call/
2. Batina, L., Kumar, S., Lano, J., Lemke, K., Mentens, N., Paar, C., Preneel, B., Sakiyama, K., Verbauwhede, I.: Testing Framework for eSTREAM Profile II Candidates. In: SASC (2006), www.ecrypt.eu.org/stream

3. Good, T., Chelton, W., Benaissa, M.: Review of stream cipher candidates from a low resource hardware perspective. In: SASC (2006), www.ecrypt.eu.org/stream
4. Good, T., Benaissa, M.: Hardware results for selected stream cipher candidates. In: SASC (2007), www.ecrypt.eu.org/stream
5. Good, T., Benaissa, M.: Hardware performance of phase-III stream cipher candidates. In: SASC (2008), www.ecrypt.eu.org/stream
6. Satoh, A., Morioka, S., Takano, K., Munetoh, S.: A Compact Rijndael Hardware Architecture with S-Box Optimization. In: Nagi, K. (ed.) Transactional Agents. LNCS, vol. 2249, pp. 230–254. Springer, Heidelberg (2001)
7. Feldhofer, M., Wolkerstorfer, J., Rijmen, V.: AES Implementation on a Grain of Sand. IEE Proceedings on Information Security 152, 13–20 (2005)

Author Index

Lecture Notes in Computer Science

Sublibrary 4: Security and Cryptology

For information about Vols. 1– 3876
please contact your bookseller or Springer

Vol. 4499: Y.Q. Shi (Ed.), Transactions on Data Hiding and Multimedia Security II. IX, 117 pages. 2007.

Vol. 4464: E. Dawson, D.S. Wong (Eds.), Information Security Practice and Experience. XIII, 361 pages. 2007.

Vol. 4462: D. Sauveron, K. Markantonakis, A. Bilas, J.-J. Quisquater (Eds.), Information Security Theory and Practices. XII, 255 pages. 2007.

Vol. 4450: T. Okamoto, X. Wang (Eds.), Public Key Cryptography – PKC 2007. XIII, 491 pages. 2007.

Vol. 4437: J.L. Camenisch, C.S. Collberg, N.F. Johnson, P. Sallee (Eds.), Information Hiding. VIII, 389 pages. 2007.

Vol. 4392: S.P. Vadhan (Ed.), Theory of Cryptography. XI, 595 pages. 2007.

Vol. 4377: M. Abe (Ed.), Topics in Cryptology – CT-RSA 2007. XI, 403 pages. 2006.

Vol. 4356: E. Biham, A.M. Youssef (Eds.), Selected Areas in Cryptography. XI, 395 pages. 2007.

Vol. 4341: P.Q. Nguyên (Ed.), Progress in Cryptology - VIETCRYPT 2006. XI, 385 pages. 2006.

Vol. 4332: A. Bagchi, V. Atluri (Eds.), Information Systems Security. XV, 382 pages. 2006.

Vol. 4329: R. Barua, T. Lange (Eds.), Progress in Cryptology - INDOCRYPT 2006. X, 454 pages. 2006.

Vol. 4318: H. Lipmaa, M. Yung, D. Lin (Eds.), Information Security and Cryptology. XI, 305 pages. 2006.

Vol. 4307: P. Ning, S. Qing, N. Li (Eds.), Information and Communications Security. XIV, 558 pages. 2006.

Vol. 4301: D. Pointcheval, Y. Mu, K. Chen (Eds.), Cryptology and Network Security. XIII, 381 pages. 2006.

Vol. 4300: Y.Q. Shi (Ed.), Transactions on Data Hiding and Multimedia Security I. IX, 139 pages. 2006.

Vol. 4298: J.K. Lee, O. Yi, M. Yung (Eds.), Information Security Applications. XIV, 406 pages. 2007.

Vol. 4296: M.S. Rhee, B. Lee (Eds.), Information Security and Cryptology – ICISC 2006. XIII, 358 pages. 2006.

Vol. 4284: X. Lai, K. Chen (Eds.), Advances in Cryptology – ASIACRYPT 2006. XIV, 468 pages. 2006.

Vol. 4283: Y.Q. Shi, B. Jeon (Eds.), Digital Watermarking. XII, 474 pages. 2006.

Vol. 4266: H. Yoshiura, K. Sakurai, K. Rannenberg, Y. Murayama, S.-i. Kawamura (Eds.), Advances in Information and Computer Security. XIII, 438 pages. 2006.

Vol. 4258: G. Danezis, P. Golle (Eds.), Privacy Enhancing Technologies. VIII, 431 pages. 2006.

Vol. 4249: L. Goubin, M. Matsui (Eds.), Cryptographic Hardware and Embedded Systems - CHES 2006. XII, 462 pages. 2006.

Vol. 4237: H. Leitold, E.P. Markatos (Eds.), Communications and Multimedia Security. XII, 253 pages. 2006.

Vol. 4236: L. Breveglieri, I. Koren, D. Naccache, J.-P. Seifert (Eds.), Fault Diagnosis and Tolerance in Cryptography. XIII, 253 pages. 2006.

Vol. 4219: D. Zamboni, C. Krügel (Eds.), Recent Advances in Intrusion Detection. XII, 331 pages. 2006.

Vol. 4189: D. Gollmann, J. Meier, A. Sabelfeld (Eds.), Computer Security – ESORICS 2006. XI, 548 pages. 2006.

Vol. 4176: S.K. Katsikas, J. López, M. Backes, S. Gritzalis, B. Preneel (Eds.), Information Security. XIV, 548 pages. 2006.

Vol. 4117: C. Dwork (Ed.), Advances in Cryptology - CRYPTO 2006. XIII, 621 pages. 2006.

Vol. 4116: R. De Prisco, M. Yung (Eds.), Security and Cryptography for Networks. XI, 366 pages. 2006.

Vol. 4107: G. Di Crescenzo, A. Rubin (Eds.), Financial Cryptography and Data Security. XI, 327 pages. 2006.

Vol. 4083: S. Fischer-Hübner, S. Furnell, C. Lambrinoudakis (Eds.), Trust and Privacy in Digital Business. XIII, 243 pages. 2006.

Vol. 4064: R. Büschkes, P. Laskov (Eds.), Detection of Intrusions and Malware & Vulnerability Assessment. X, 195 pages. 2006.

Vol. 4058: L.M. Batten, R. Safavi-Naini (Eds.), Information Security and Privacy. XII, 446 pages. 2006.

Vol. 4047: M. Robshaw (Ed.), Fast Software Encryption. XI, 434 pages. 2006.

Vol. 4043: A.S. Atzeni, A. Lioy (Eds.), Public Key Infrastructure. XI, 261 pages. 2006.

Vol. 4004: S. Vaudenay (Ed.), Advances in Cryptology - EUROCRYPT 2006. XIV, 613 pages. 2006.

Vol. 3995: G. Müller (Ed.), Emerging Trends in Information and Communication Security. XX, 524 pages. 2006.

Vol. 3989: J. Zhou, M. Yung, F. Bao (Eds.), Applied Cryptography and Network Security. XIV, 488 pages. 2006.

Vol. 3969: Ø. Ytrehus (Ed.), Coding and Cryptography. XI, 443 pages. 2006.

Vol. 3958: M. Yung, Y. Dodis, A. Kiayias, T. Malkin (Eds.), Public Key Cryptography - PKC 2006. XIV, 543 pages. 2006.

Vol. 3957: B. Christianson, B. Crispo, J.A. Malcolm, M. Roe (Eds.), Security Protocols. IX, 325 pages. 2006.

Vol. 3956: G. Barthe, B. Grégoire, M. Huisman, J.-L. Lanet (Eds.), Construction and Analysis of Safe, Secure, and Interoperable Smart Devices. IX, 175 pages. 2006.

Vol. 3935: D.H. Won, S. Kim (Eds.), Information Security and Cryptology - ICISC 2005. XIV, 458 pages. 2006.

Vol. 3934: J.A. Clark, R.F. Paige, F.A.C. Polack, P.J. Brooke (Eds.), Security in Pervasive Computing. X, 243 pages. 2006.

Vol. 3928: J. Domingo-Ferrer, J. Posegga, D. Schreckling (Eds.), Smart Card Research and Advanced Applications. XI, 359 pages. 2006.

Vol. 3919: R. Safavi-Naini, M. Yung (Eds.), Digital Rights Management. XI, 357 pages. 2006.

Vol. 3903: K. Chen, R. Deng, X. Lai, J. Zhou (Eds.), Information Security Practice and Experience. XIV, 392 pages. 2006.

Vol. 3897: B. Preneel, S. Tavares (Eds.), Selected Areas in Cryptography. XI, 371 pages. 2006.